CHALLENGES FOR SOUTH ASIAN RESOURCES AND INFORMATION SERVICES

Essays in Honour of Dr. Ravindra N. Sharma

About the Editor

Dr. Rajwant Singh Chilana is an Associate Professor of Library Administration at the University of Illinois, Urbana-Champaign, USA since February 2003. He holds MSc (Zoology), MLS, and PhD degrees from the University of Rajasthan, Jaipur, India. Earlier he served as Librarian at the University of British Columbia, Vancouver, Canada, and University of Delhi, India as well as Library Manager at the Fraser Valley Regional Library, British Columbia (Canada). Dr. Chilana also worked as Chief Librarian at the Guru Nanak Institute of Comparative Study of Religions, New Delhi. In December 2005 he was presented with the Best Librarian award by SATKAL Trust for his outstanding contributions in promoting librarianship in India, Canada and United States. In 2004, Dr. Chilana also received Fellowship by the Society for the Information Science (India) for his significant contribution to librarianship. He has published six books and over thirty five research papers, and twenty book reviews on various aspects for South Asian librarianship. His latest book "*International Bibliography of Sikh Studies*" was published by Springer in 2005, and is also available as online searchable database. He has received many scholarships and fellowships from the University of Illinois as well as Indo-Canadian Sastri Institute (Canada) for various research projects relating to India. Dr. Chilana is actively involved in various professional organizations, and has been Member at Large, Executive member and Vice-Chair Elect of the Asian, African and the Middle Eastern Section (AAMES) of the Association of College and Research Libraries (ACRL), an organ of the American Library Association. He is founding editor of the *AAMES Newsletter*.
Email: rchilana@uiuc.edu, rchilana@gmail.com

Challenges for South Asian Resources and Information Services

Essays in Honour of Dr. Ravindra N. Sharma

Edited by

Rajwant Singh Chilana

CONCEPT PUBLISHING COMPANY, NEW DELHI-110059

Cataloging in Publication Data—DK
Courtesy: D.K. Agencies (P) Ltd. <docinfo@dkagencies.com>

Challenges for South Asian resources and information services : essays in honour of Dr. Ravindra N. Sharma / edited by Rajwant Singh Chilana.

p. cm.

Ravindra Nath Sharma, b. 1941, Indian library and information scientist; contributed articles.

Includes bibliographical references.

Includes index.

ISBN 13: 9788180695278

ISBN 10: 8180695271

1. Library education—India. 2. Library education—South Asia. 3. Libraries—Information technology—India. 4. Libraries—Information technology—South Asia. 5. Library information networks—India. 6. Library information networks—South Asia. 7. Information services—India. 8. Information services—South Asia. I. Sharma, Ravindra N. (Ravindra Nath), 1941- II. Chilana, Rajwant Singh, 1952-

DDC 020.710 54 22

ISBN-13: 978-81-8069-527-8
ISBN-10: 81-8069-527-1

First Published 2008

Published and Printed by
Ashok Kumar Mittal
Concept Publishing Company
A/15-16, Commercial Block, Mohan Garden
New Delhi-110059 (INDIA)
Phone : 25351460, 25351794
Fax : 091-11-25357103
Email : publishing@conceptpub.com

Dr. Ravindra N. Sharma

Foreword

I am indeed glad to know that Dr.R.N. Sharma, a well known Library and Information Scientist is being honoured by his co-professionals and admirers with the presentation of a Festschrift. Dr. Sharma undoubtedly deserves such an honour for his wide-ranging contributions to the profession in different capacities such as an administrator, an author, a researcher and, of course, a great friend of library users. His range of professional activities has not been confined to the United States where he has finally got settled. He has been actively busy at the international levels as well in several ways such as consultancy work in different countries and with his involvement in several international organizations such as IFLA and UNESCO.

I have known Dr. Sharma for more than 25 years and have always been much impressed by his inquisitive outlook and pro-active approach in various professional matters and challenges. Frankly speaking, he certainly deserves many more honours for his contributions and am quite sure that they would follow during the years to come.

The vital role libraries, information centers and knowledge centers play in education; spread of literacy, research and overall socio-economic development of a country or society is well recognized in the present day world. Information, whether in the form of empirical data, or, in the developed form called knowledge is, therefore, being rightly regarded to day as a vital national resource , as essential to the nation's well being as any natural resource such as water and minerals. In addition, beyond the frontiers of a country it provides an important basis for international relations, peace, prosperity and overall development of the world. The wealth of popular, intellectual, scholarly and research resources in libraries, information centers and information systems of a country is, therefore, one of the greatest strengths of a nation. But like several natural resources information or knowledge resources as well, if kept unexploited or untapped as also unsupported and uncoordinated in growth and usage, would certainly be in a danger of being wasted. They need to be not only used aggressively but also efficiently and effectively. Also, it needs to be mentioned that Information is different from several other resources in the sense that it is greatly dynamic in growth and certainly infinite in quantum. It has to be not only collected and organized in a proper manner but also to be disseminated among the people simply because the quality of people in a country is known primarily by the fact that how well informed its citizenry is. It has been rightly said that 'a country that reads, actually leads'.

Historically speaking, a substantial part of human culture has been handed down to the generations in the form of recorded knowledge. This resource consists of documents such as clay tablets, books, journals, and other categories of texts: of audio and visual materials, and of other units of information and data that can be processed and organized by a computer. In recent years these records have become increasingly varied through technological extensions of written words, pictures and sounds. For example, a significant part of a country's information resources is today on films, magnetic tapes, video-cassettes, CD-ROMs, DVDs and in computer files. As the nation's knowledge grows and the number of these records increases our dependence upon them also increases proportionately and the need to gain access to them becomes more essential and even crucial. Libraries, information centers, information systems and other information facilitators are, therefore, among the most important custodians of this rich cultural heritage which gets recorded. They must therefore be adequately equipped, organized, financed and interconnected so as to make these resources accessible to all the people in a country, and even in the world at large. This undoubtedly requires active support from the governments, and the public and private agencies and institutions.

It is because of these and such like other developments that the present society is being rightly designated as 'information society' and even as 'knowledge society'. Since the 1970s, fast developments in Information Communication Technology (ICT) have already brought vast changes in the economic, industrial, cultural and sociological spheres and ushered in an era which can be even described as 'information revolution'. Daniel Bell even calls it as 'post-industrial society' which in a way is being used as synonymous with the term 'information society' (*The Coming of Post-industrial Society*, 1986, New York, Basic Books). Such an 'information society' may, in general terms, be defined as one in which the quality of life as also the prospects for social change and economic development depend increasingly on information and its exploitation. In such a society, the living standards, pattern of work and leisure, the education systems, R&D activities and marketing activities are all influenced markedly by information. This is evidenced today by an increasing array of information-intensive products and services, produced and communicated through a wide range of media, many of them electronic in nature. The emergence of Internet and its allied facilities,have really changed the whole concept of information intensive society of today.

In such a society, library and information professionals, knowledge workers and others dealing with information related matters really face a great challenge so as to provide the right information at the right time and, in the right format.

Dr. R.N. Sharma with his strong academic and professional qualifications obtained from the University of Delhi and in the American Universities, is undoubtedly well equipped to appreciate the changing scenario and function as a LIS specialist in an effective and efficient manner. His close and active association with organizations such as the American Library Association (ALA), the Association of College and Research Libraries (ACRL), the International Federation of Library Associations and Institutions (IFLA) and other associations genuinely reflects his professionalism and a keen desire to work for the upgradation and development of LIS profession in the developed and developing countries. While his achievements and activities have been duly highlighted in the Festschrift itself, I may like to mention two specific occasions when I was also very much involved: firstly, he was the organizer of a session on 'Research and Academic Librarian: A Global View' at the 6th ACRL National Conference held at Salt Lake City in 1992 where I was one of the six speakers invited from countries such as Australia, Brazil, Russia, Kenya, United Kingdom and India; and, secondly, he took the initiative to get the First South Asian-American Librarians Conference as a Pre-IFLA Conference held in New Delhi in 1992 where he acted as Chairman of the US Organizing Committee and I functioned as Chairman of the Indian Organizing Committee. Recently in August 2007, he had the honour to be invited to address the Pre-IFLA Conference in Dakar, Senegal (Africa) and thus became the third Indian to be so honoured. Earlier, Prof. A. Neelameghan addressed the IFLA General Conference in 1980 at Manila and I did that at Chicago in 1985.

In conclusion I may add that Dr. Sharma is among the very few migrants in the USA who have earned a really high name in the Library & Information Science profession nationally and internationally. We in India certainly feel proud of him and I am sure that he would continue bringing more laurels during the years to come.

Professor P.B. Mangla
(Ex) Head, Department of Library
& Information Science
Dean, Faculty of Arts
University of Delhi
(Former) President, Indian Library Association
Vice-President, IFLA (The Hague)

New Delhi
January 26, 2008

Acknowledgements

On behalf of my professional colleagues, well wishers and friends, I sincerely thank Dr. Ravindra N. Sharma for kindly giving his consent for bringing out a felicitation volume in his honor. I wish to place my gratitude to Professor P.B. Mangla for having agreed to write a foreword for this publication. Thanks are also due to all contributors for sending research papers, and their suggestions, support and cooperation in our endeavour for brining out this volume. I would like to place on record my grateful thanks to Concept Publishing Company, New Delhi for accepting this book for publication.

Contents

PART III
NATIONAL AND PUBLIC LIBRARIES

PART IV
SPECIAL LIBRARIES

Introduction

RAJWANT SINGH CHILANA

Dr. Ravindra N. Sharma, Dean of the Library at Monmouth University, West Long Branch, New Jersey (USA), is an outstanding Asian American library professional. Since last 30 years, he has worked in various capacities in a number of academic libraries in United States, and has been a popular professional with high scholarship and intellect. Dr. Sharma is highly regarded for his communication and analytical skills. His personality symbolises conviction, perseverance, courage, integration, leadership and inspiration laced with simplicity, maturity and worldly wisdom. He received his Masters in Arts (History) from the University of Delhi, India, and earned Master of Library and Information Science from the North Texas State University, and was conferred Ph.D. in Information and Library Studies from the State University of New York at Buffalo. Since 1982, he has presented over 30 research papers at various conferences and seminars, and has served on more than 30 committees of Association of College and Research Libraries (ACRL), and American Library Association (ALA). Dr. Sharma has sustained a distinguished record of writing books and journal articles as well as presentations which have made Americans and others more aware of global issues in librarianship. He has authored and edited ten books, and has published more than 250 research papers, editorials, interviews, conference reports, and book reviews in various professional journals of Asia, Europe, and North America. Since 1984 Dr. Sharma has been the Editor of *Library Times International*, and has also served on the editorial committees of books and reputed journals.

Dr. Sharma has served ALA, ACRL, and the International Federation of Library Associations (IFLA) admirably by chairing and serving on many committees dealing with international issues. During the year 2003-04, Dr. Sharma chaired the Asian, African and Middle Eastern Section (AAMES) of ACRL, and was instrumental in bringing out the first issue of the *AAMES Newsletter* as well as *AAMES brochure*. During 1993-94, he was president of the Asian/Pacific American Librarians Association (APALA). He was involved in the ACRL International

Relations Committee (1998-2002) and served as chair of the Near East and South Asia Committee, a sub-committee of the International Relations Committee (1996-98). Dr. Sharma was also a member of the ACRL Research Committee (1989-93), and the Racial and Ethnic Diversity Committee (1997-98). Most recently he served his term on the ACRL Standards & Accreditation Committee (2001-05).

In 2005, the Association of College & Research Libraries recognized Dr. Sharma for the Academic/Research Librarian Award for his outstanding national and international contributions to academic and research librarianship and library development. The award, sponsored by YBP Library Services, carries $3,000 cash and a plaque. It was a great honour for the Asian American librarians in North America that for the first time in the history of ACRL/ALA the award was given to an Asian professional. Dr. Sharma is the only librarian of Asian origin to achieve this distinction so far. He is a professional of high repute and is an active librarian who has won many others awards, grants and honors. Earlier, in 1997, Dr. Sharma received the Humphrey/OCLC/Forest Press Award for his "significant achievements and contributions to International Librarianship."

As a tribute to this dedicated and outstanding professional, his friends, colleagues and well wishers, around the globe, have suggested to bring out a felicitation volume in his honour on the topic: "Challenges for South Asian Resources and Information Services". Many leading professionals and teachers of library and information science from various countries were invited to write papers for this volume. A total of 35 research papers were received from United States, India, Bangladesh, Sri Lanka and Pakistan on different aspects of South Asian librarianship. These papers have been grouped under eight sections.

The first part on "Library and Information Science Education" contains six papers from the teaching faculty in South Asia. Krishan Kumar and Jaideep Sharma discuss growth, development and challenges in their paper "Library and Information Science Education in India", while A. Amudhavalli suggests the need to recruit the next and new generation of professionals in her interesting paper on "Library and Information Science Professionals: New Faces and New Phases." In her paper on "Library and Information Science Education in South Asia" Paramjeet Kaur Walia traces the emergence of library and information science (LIS) education and describes the current status of LIS education as well as different patterns and levels of LIS education being followed in South Asia. She also examines some of the problems being faced by LIS education in South Asian countries because of the changing scenario. Kanwal Ameen, a professor from Pakistan, in her paper provides an overview of library education in Pakistan with information about various courses taught in the universities. She also presents the role of foreign library experts in the development of library education in Pakistan.

Neena Talwar-Kanungo in her research paper "Library and Information Science Education in India through Distance Mode with a Case Study of Curriculum Development at Indira Gandhi National Open University, New Delhi, India" analyses the ways wherein the LIS curriculum is conceptualized, developed and carried out at the second largest Open University in the world.

In their paper Kshema Prakash and K. Santi Swarup emphasizes the need based library and information science curriculum in view of the emerging global trends and opportunities with special reference to challenges faced by professionals in India. They suggest that a strong foundation level professional education is a must for service excellence, especially in a vibrant, dynamic and ever changing wonderful field of library and information science.

Part II on "University Libraries" is comprised of five papers from senior academic professionals. S.D. Vyas discusses some problems and prospect in the Indian University libraries in information technology era. He suggests that university libraries in India are now under tremendous influence of information technology, and this will force them to organize the collection as well as improve their services.

In his paper, Inder Vir Malhan stresses the importance of strategic planning for developing Indian university libraries into knowledge resource and service centers. He examines that the knowledge based work environment demands problem solving information at greater speed and as per user convenience, and discusses what changes are taking place in the emerging knowledge society and what way the university libraries should respond to these changes. Prabha Sharma, in her paper, 'Library and Information Services in Higher Education for Visually Challenged Students—Case Study of the Rajasthan University Library, Jaipur', has done a good job in providing services offered to blind students in her library. Lokesh Sharma and Rajesh Singh have done an extensive survey for their study to provide information that librarians can use to make important decisions about collection development (print and electronic), training to staff and library services by collecting data from the users and also making provision of library resources orientation programs at the Ratan Tata Library of Delhi University Library System. In her paper on "From Raga to Remixes: Is There Accessibility in Academic Libraries?" Deepa Banerjee provides a good account of collections and services available on South Asian music in some academic libraries in the United States. She also discusses the growing interest of music among the South Asian Diaspora, and thus need for more resources in all formats.

Part III deals with organization and services in National & Public Libraries, and has four papers. "Founding of the National Library of Bangladesh—A Post Colonial Experience" by Abulfazal M. Fazle Kabir provides historical account of the development of the National Library. In his paper on "New Choices for

Bibliographical Services in a Wired Planet: Reflections on the National Library of India", R.K. Sharma presents the state of public and national libraries and an overview of the bibliographic information services available with them. He also mentions several of the challenges facing libraries in determining their present and future roles in the nation's as well as in a global information infrastructure. Web based bibliographic services provided in the British Library and Library of Congress have been discussed. Sharma stresses the need for availability of national bibliographic databases in machine-readable form on the Web that provide better bibliographic organization and control of material.

In his paper "Bangladesh's Frustrated Librarians: Formidable barriers to information exist in one of the world's most densely populated countries", Ron Chepesiuk discusses some problems faced by the librarians of Bangladesh.

In their paper on "Public Library System and Services in Andaman & Nicobar Islands of India: The State of the Art Report", Sunil Kumar Satpathy and Y. Ganesh recommend that library legislation should be enacted in the Islands for the planned development of public libraries and information centers. They suggest that development of public libraries should be in a phased manner and there should be a separate directorate for its proper administration and management, as well as a nominal library cess should be imposed on public so that they realize the value of libraries and information centers and the services.

The fourth part contains seven papers dealing with various aspects of information services in special libraries. The contribution by B.M. Gupta, Usha Mujoo Munshi and P.K. Mishra on "Regional Collaboration in Science & Technology among South Asian Countries" presents a study on the outputs of science and technology collaborations among South Asian countries through the analysis of co-authored research papers published during the period 1994-2004 in the journals covered by the *Web of Science.* This study analyses these collaborations from various angles like nature, science and technology areas, institutions involved and their impact on individual fields. Ramesh Kundra and Divya Srivastava discuss the pattern of publication of SAARC countries in area of medicine and collaboration among SAARC countries in their paper "Collaboration Patterns among SAARC countries in the area of Medicine: Status and Issues". The purpose of the paper is to show that studies reported from these countries are focused more towards the issues being discussed in developed countries. The ABIA project is a global network of scholars co-operating on an annotated bibliographic database for publications covering South and Southeast Asian Art and Archaeology. The paper by Ramesh C. Gaur presents an overview of ABIA South and Southeast Asian Art and Archaeology Index, its structure, programme, publications and contributions of Indira Gandhi National Centre for the Arts (IGNCA), New Delhi to this project. The paper "Libraries and Information Centers on Women's

Studies in India: An Overview" by Parul Zaveri examines the role of various libraries and information centers for women's issues in India. She also made some useful suggestions to coordinate activities of these libraries and information centers. The paper by P. R. Goswami "Organization and Dissemination of Social Science Research Information: Indian Scenario" provides a background of social science research in India and discusses an overview of present state of organization and dissemination of different types of information sources that are used by Indian social scientists. He also discusses the activities of the proposed social science libraries network in India. I. Mudannayake in his paper "Working together with AGRINET—Agriculture Information Network of Sri Lanka" describes the development of the Agriculture Information Network in Sri Lanka for improving access to agriculture information in the country. This paper also mentions bibliographic utilities, user seminars for agricultural scientists, training of AGRINET member librarians, and some other relevant issues.

The part fifth on 'Information Systems & Networks' has six papers. In his scholarly article 'Information Technology Enlivens: Chaos and Creation of Life Needs', M.A. Gopinath presents interesting guidelines and pathfinders, and discusses secrets of chaos and creation along with other topics. The paper 'Impact of Information Technology on Indian Library Sources and Services' by H.S. Chopra mentions the importance of new communication and information technologies in the improvement of library services in India.

Binh P. Le in his paper 'Multipurpose Community Telecenters: Transforming South Asian Societies into Information Societies' traces the proliferation of many telecenters, and examines the need of necessary development conditions, community participation, community's demand-driven information services, and financial self-sustainability.

H.K. Kaul traces the development of the first network in New Delhi (India) in his paper "DELNET—Developing Library Network: The Operational Network in South Asia". He also discusses objectives, organizational set up, membership, standards, and online databases available through this Network in South Asia.

"Access to E-Resources and Scholarship: The Role of Library Consortia in India" by R.K. Bhatt states the proliferation of various electronic resources and their accessibility in many libraries through the Indian consortia. Tella Ramadevi presents an overview of various types of resources available in her paper 'Information Resources on South Asia—Printed, Online and Digital'.

The sixth part on Bibliographical Control is comprised of six papers. A paper by T. A.V. Murthy and M. Kanakachary entitled "Bibliographic Control of Indian Language Publications" mentions the tremendous growth of publications in Indian languages, and suggests a need for the bibliographical control. They also present a proposal to establish a national, regional and local information centers for languages. S.P. Singh and Tariq Ashraf discuss many problems and suggest some solutions in developing good collections in Indian libraries in their paper "Building Print Collection—Issues and Problems: An Indian Perspective".

Liladhar R. Pendse's paper on "Explaining the Dawn of Colonial Portuguese Periodicals in Estado da India" highlights the importance of print media as a vehicle for the expression of popular culture in India, and discusses development of Portuguese language periodicals. The essay "South Asia Publishing and American Academic Libraries: A Personal Account, 1965-2006" by N. Gerald Barrier presents a more personal account based on four decades of interaction of the author with American library programs and Indian publishers. He examines that over the years the book trade has changed dramatically, as have U.S. library programs, and widening access to India through new programs and especially the internet.

The seventh section of this volume on "Technical Services" contains two papers. In the paper "Authority Control of Romanized Arabic Names in OPAC" by Veerankutty Chelatayakkot and V. Jalaja, authors try to analyze and implement authority control mechanism in Romanised Arabic names as displayed in OPAC. The paper "Classification and Cataloguing Services: Skill requirements of a large academic library in digital environment: A case study of JRD Tata Memorial Library" by K.S. Chudamani and H.C. Nagarathna explores developments in the technical services at the JRD Tata Memorial Library of the Indian Institute of Science, Bangalore. Authors suggest the need to acquire new skills by the Library and information science professionals in view of changing technologies.

The last section contains two miscellaneous papers. "Future of reference service and reference librarians" by B. Mini Devi who examines the changing dimensions of reference service in view of new information technologies, and suggests that the modern reference librarians should be flexible and creative, possess excellent communication skills, and should have ability to market library information products and services. And the coverage of the paper "Research methodology and problems in South Asian Studies" by Sunita Vaze is limited to humanities that encompass philosophy, religion, languages, literature and art. She discusses the needs of a general researcher, and ideas and information in this article are based on the necessity of the work performed by the reader in the research library's atmosphere.

Part I
Library and Information Science Education

1

Library and Information Science Education in India

KRISHAN KUMAR and JAIDEEP SHARMA

Introduction

With a population of 1.1 billion, India is the world's largest democracy. Large majority of its population is young, ambitious and dynamic with great aspirations. Its economy is growing by leaps and bounds, at an average rate of 8 per cent annually. The world is watching its growth and development with admiration and awe.

Alongside old India, becalmed in a bygone age, there is a new India that is emerging. "This is the India of booming IT services, outsourcing, Bollywood, state-of-the-art communications, and the legion of service industries that support these fast-growing areas of income generation. With its huge, aspirational middle class—highly skilled, self-confident and determined to succeed—this is an India which seems to have more in common with the first world economies of America and Europe than its own subcontinent... The past three days of insights, observations and initiatives on modern India has this year attracted a record number of foreign participants, all drawn by the palpable sense of excitement that surrounds India's vast market potential and its accompanying legion of business opportunities. The international zeitgeist which once centred on China has moved unmistakenly over the past years to India, which with its youthful and fast growing population, its robust legal system, rule of contract, respect for intellectual property rights, and above all its proud democratic tradition, is thought by many business people to be a greater opportunity for profitable growth than its bigger and now more-developed Asian rival."(Warner, November 29, 2006)

India is a land full of opportunities for future. The country has entered the era of information age and is preparing to become knowledge-based society. The library schools should take advantage of the changing environment and the opportunities that are becoming available, to build strong library schools with innovative curriculum and high quality research output that are able to turn out excellent library and information professionals with requisite skills, knowledge and necessary attitude required to serve the emerging information society with distinction. They should not be only employable but able to compete globally. Let these library schools create a strong presence in the library profession through excellence in research and training.

The environment in which a library professional has to work is changing fast. The emergence of information resources in electronic format in the late 1980s and, especially, the advent and dominance of the Internet in the 1990s has led to new and welcome emphasis on giving prominence to the wants of library users. Some professionals consider the development of global electronic access to information as a threat to the very future of the physical library, but others regard it as an opportunity to rethink, redefine and to reshape, library services based on needs of their users, in a fast-changing information environment. The digital libraries are beginning to predominate the scene. Traditional library professionals are feeling lost in the new world of digital libraries. They are also feeling a sense of identity crisis. In this changing information environment, the library schools are required to develop a kind of education to equip the graduates with skills needed to help customers to use not only libraries but also information sources in different forms and formats. They must be educated as 'information empowerment specialist' rather than mere experts in 'bibliographic instruction'. Indian library schools must accept these challenges to train professionals who can compete with professionals at the international level.

It may be relevant here to mention about the changing situation in library schools. In 1972, curriculum was revised at Delhi library school. In master of Library and Information Science (L&IS), one course entitled computer application in libraries was introduced. There was no teacher on the faculty, who could handle it. Therefore, in-charge of the computer centre was requested to teach this course. The teacher did not know much about library science. The emphasis was on programming. For practical work, they had to go to the computer centre, where they got a slot for one or two hours per week. The amount of time they got for practical was inadequate. The school was totally dependent on outside help. Even in 1990s, very few teachers of L&IS were available, who could handle this area. Today, teachers within library schools are available, who can handle courses related to computer application. Many teachers in L&IS are there, who have obtained qualifications and enough experience to teach such courses. In addition, information technology has advanced and library science students are not expected to learn about programming. User friendly library application packages are available, that are not too difficult to use. Library schools have build up their own computer laboratories, so that students can get hands on experience for long hours, under the supervision of their teachers. Handling desktop computer, designing and searching databases is exciting and enriching experience unlike 1960s, when learning computer application was tedious, time consuming and a back-breaking. Today, the situation has completely changed, cost of hardware has come down, open source library application software are becoming available free on the internet, UGC and other authorities are giving funds generously for setting up computer laboratories. In 1996, after great deal of efforts, Delhi Library School (University of Delhi) was provided funds by the university. The school was given grant for the purchase of three PCs. No money was provided for site preparation, furniture, printer, internet, voltage stabilizer etc. No staff for training the students or supervision of the laboratory was sanctioned. The students and teachers contributed money from their pocket for site preparation, printer and internet. Furniture and voltage stabilizer were borrowed from the Delhi University Library. Now, the situation has completely changed, there are two computer laboratories, each teacher has been given a PC and the department's library has three terminals. State-of-the art equipment is available for classroom teaching and for exposure of the students for learning application of information technology.

Library and Information Science (L&IS) education here means education for library and information professionals. It is a process of creating library scientists and information scientists. L&IS is a life-long process. After initial formal education, it continues in the form of continuing education and staff development.

History

Phases

History of library education in India can be divided into four phases as given below:

(i) *Early period*: It starts from the year 1911, when William Alanson Borden started a training programme in 1911, in the princely state of Baroda. It was the first library school to be established in India. Thus, the history of library education in India began in the year 1911.

(ii) *Period of Acceptance*: This period starts with 1938, when a post-graduate diploma course was initiated at the University of Madras mainly due to the efforts of Dr. S.R. Ranganathan. The Department of Library Science at University of Delhi initiated a post-graduate course in 1947 and awarded its first diplomas in library science in 1948. In 1948, University of Delhi became the first university in India to institute a degree course in Library Science (a post-graduate course). In 1949, the first batch completed the study programme of two years. They received their B.Lib.Sc. degrees in 1949. In 1949, a two-year course leading to the award of M.Lib.Sc. degree was introduced to replace the previous programme of B.Lib.Sc. The first batch received their M.Lib.Sc degree in 1951. It was the first university in (the British) the Commonwealth to introduce this course at master's level. In1951, University of Delhi became the first university in the country as well as in (the British) Commonwealth to introduce doctoral studies in library science by framing regulations for doctoral programme in library science. D.B. Krishna Rao was the first person to register as a Ph.D. candidate at University of Delhi in the 1952-53 academic sessions. The first Ph.D. in library science was awarded in 1957 to D.B. Krishna Rao by University of Delhi under the guidance of Dr. S.R. Ranganathan. Initiation of Ph.D. programme at University of Delhi was his crowning glory.

(iii) *Period of Growth*: This period starts in early sixties, when there was sudden growth of library education. The main reason was the allocation of funds for libraries in Third Five-Year Plan of Government of India. Another major factor was the support extended by UGC to libraries and library education. Many new library schools were started in sixties.

(iv) *Period of Modernization*: This period started in early 1990s, when modernization of libraries started taking place. Government of India gave a thrust to application of information technology, through various incentives and UGC also gave liberal funding for establishing of computer laboratories. Library schools started revising their curriculum introducing courses on computer application in libraries and also included chunk of information science. It is also during this period that the library schools established computer laboratories for giving hands on experience to their students. This is also a period of consolidation.

Some Landmarks

Some of the landmarks in the history of library education are described in the next few paragraphs.

William Alanson Borden (1853-1931), an American-trained librarian, was invited by His Highness the Maharaja Sayajirao III, Gaekwar of Baroda (1862-1939), to establish libraries in the princely state of Baroda. Borden started a training programme in 1911, in the state. It was the first library school established in India. This short training programme was initiated to create a cadre of persons to man the newly created libraries in the state. Thus, the history of library education in India began in the year 1911. However, a more systematic training programme was initiated by Asa Don Dickinson (1876-1960), another American librarian, at Punjab University, Lahore (now in Pakistan). This was the first University level course in India. In 1928, the Madras Library Association started a 'summer school' for college librarians and lecturers-in-charge of college libraries. This was the first summer school organized in India.

In 1929, a regular certificate course in Library Science (short-term part-time course) of three months duration was initiated by Madras Library Association. Later on, it was extended to six months. S.R. Ranganathan was instrumental in instituting this course. In 1931, the University of Madras took over the School of Library Science instituted by Madras Library Association. The University continued to run the certificate course in librarianship through a summer vacation course of three months. In 1937, the University of Madras introduced with effect from July 1937, one year post-graduate diploma course. This was the first full-time course conducted in India, another landmark in the history of library education. This was also the first diploma course conducted by a university.

Since, the history of library education in India begins with the year 1911, therefore, it shall complete, hundred years in 2011, we are just four years away. The year 2011, will be a centenary year. We are sure that it shall be celebrated in a big way. That would be an occasion for introspection. We have travelled a long way. During this period of 96 years, we have made significant progress.

Today, library and information science is a full-fledged discipline in its own right. It is recognized as a university subject of study and research, worthy of study at the university level at par with other disciplines due to its intellectual content.

S.R. Ranganathan

We can certainly claim that library and information science education in India is well established. The major credit for this must go to Dr. S.R. Ranganathan. He was the architect of library education in India, and also a master educationist. He stands tall and gave shape to library education in the country and dominated the scene like a colossal from late twenties till his death in 1972. Any history of library education would be incomplete without mention of the part played by him. He is considered as the architect of professional education in India. He was a master educationist and a teacher of teachers. He is basically responsible for establishing three leading library schools in the country, namely, Madras Library School (University of Madras), Delhi Library School (University of Delhi) and Documentation Research and Training Centre, Bangalore. He was a teacher of Library Science from 1929 to 1972, except for a short period, 1955-57, when he lived in Zurich. He was head of the library school at University of Madras from 1938 to 1944, head of the library school at Banaras Hindu University, Varanasi, 1945-47. He held the position of Honorary Professor in library science at University of Delhi (1947-55), Vikram University (1957-59), Ujjain, Documentation Research and Training Centre (1962-72), Bangalore.

In 1947, Ranganathan was appointed a Honorary Professor in the Department of Library Science at University of Delhi. Prof. S. Das Gupta happened to be the head of the Department. Due to the efforts of both, the library school initiated a post-graduate course in 1947 and awarded its first diplomas in library science in 1948. In 1948, University of Delhi became the first university in India to institute a degree course in Library Science (a post-graduate course). In 1949, the first batch completed the study programme of two years. They received their B.Lib.Sc. degrees in 1949.

In 1949, a two-year course leading to the award of M.Lib.Sc. degree was introduced to replace the previous programme of B.Lib.Sc. The first batch received their M.Lib.Sc. degree in 1951. It was the first university in (the British) Commonwealth to introduce this course at master's level.

In 1951, University of Delhi became the first university in the country as well as in (the British) Commonwealth to introduce doctoral studies in library science by framing regulations for doctoral programme in library science. In 1952, D B Krishna Rao was the first person to register as a Ph.D candidate at University of Delhi in the 1952-53 academic session.

In 1956, S.R. Ranganathan, donated a sum of rupees one lakh to the University of Madras, on the occasion of its centenary to be held in 1957, for establishing Sarada Ranganathan Chair in Library Science. This was the first chair to be established in the country.

The first Ph.D. in library science was awarded in 1957 to D.B. Krishna Rao by University of Delhi under the guidance of Dr. S.R. Ranganathan. Initiation of Ph.D. programme at University Delhi was his crowning glory. During the period of his stay at University of Delhi, from 1947 to 1955, he along with Prof. S. Das Gupta, the then Head of the Department, initiated, post-graduate Diploma, Bachelor of Library Science (it was later on replaced by two-year Master of Library Science), Master of Library Science and doctoral programmes. Both Ranganathan and Das Gupta (his disciple and a great scholar) worked as a team. In the process they created history.

Looking back, one can say, the programmes started at Delhi Library School were signficant landmarks in the history of library education in India. Without a great man like Ranganathan, higher education leading to master's degree and doctoral levels would have got delayed by a few decades.

In 1962, Documentation Research and Training Centre (DRTC) were established by Indian Statistical Institute at Bangalore with S.R. Ranganathan as an Honorary Professor. DTRC has earned high reputation both at national and international levels. This centre came into being due to the efforts of Ranganathan and the support provided by Prof. P.C. Mahalonobis, who then happened to be the founder and Honorary Director of Indian Statistical Institute.

He was a great teacher, who used discussion method of teaching, with great success, involving participation of each student. He adopted the Indian tradition of great *gurus*, involving question and answer approach, between disciples and their *guru*.

Dr. Ranganathan did not have smooth sailing. Jealousy and hatred followed him. He had to face hostile attitude of his contemporaries, who were not willing to recognize library science as a discipline for study and research at the university level. Prof. L.R. Sivasubramaniam, the then Dean of Faculty of Law, University of Delhi, said, "I know the so-called great developments made by SRR in Library Science. He has moved from a 'single dot' (decimal) to 'double dot' (colon). Does it need research and getting a Ph.D." (P.N. Kaula *in* Ranganathan, 1992, p. 394). Further, "out of jealousy he put hurdles in starting the Master's degree programme and also to the Ph.D. programme at the university. But due to the support of Sir Maurice Gwyer, the Vice-Chancellor, besides SRR's advocacy, both the masters of M.Lib.Sc. and Ph.D. programme went through the Academic Council. Even then the Dean, Faculty of Law did not lie low and would pass sarcastically sharp comments with reference to the need for research in library science." (P.N. Kaula *in* Ranganathan, 1992, p. 393). It must be said to the credit of Ranganathan that he was highly regarded by leading academics of his time, who gave him full support in his initiatives. Otherwise, he would not have succeeded in leaving a blazing trail. These eminent men included, Dr. S. Radhakrishnan, the then Vice-Chancellor of Banaras Hindu University (later he became President of India), Sir Maurice Gwyer, the then Vice-Chancellor of University of Delhi, Prof P. C. Mahalonobis founder and Honorary Director of Indian Statistical Institute, and Dr. C.D. Deshmukh, Chairman, UGC. They all gave full support to him in taking library education forward.

He initiated a pattern of library education at the University of Madras, in 1938 by initiating a university level course. This course drafted by him was adopted by other library schools in India in due course of time. He developed it further at Delhi. During his stay there from 1947 to 1955, he developed a syllabi for post-graduate diploma and Master of Library Science. The pattern of education implemented at Delhi Library School served as a trend setter in the country. Later, he gave a new curriculum through UGC report published in 1966, that was adopted by library schools all over the country. That sustained up to early seventies. Present programmes have been built on the foundations that were laid by him. He wrote extensively on all aspects of library science, bringing out books, reports, research papers etc. Many of the books are used even today as a basic text by students of library and information science. He worked constantly to professionalize library education in the country. He started from a scratch. He dared to venture into initiatives that others did not dare to. He had to face hurdles in his initiatives but ultimately he succeeded. By 1972, when he died, library education as a discipline of study and research had become well established. There is no doubt that he was a genius of twentieth century. We shall not see another man of his caliber in our life time.

Growth of Library Schools

In 1947, at the time of independence, there were just five library schools at the university level. By the end of 1950s, there were 13 such schools. According to the *Directory of Library and Information Schools in India* published in 1988, covers information about 93 schools and other institutions in India, offering training in library and information science at different levels. According to it, there are sixty-six university departments that offer a bachelor's degree in library and information science, thirty-eight of which offer master's degree in library and information science, and four of which offer master of philosophy degree in library and information science. There are nineteen schools that offer a doctoral programme in library and information science. There are also three schools offering correspondence courses for a bachelor's in library and information science. There are two documentation schools. (Chopra *et al.*, 1988, preface)

Today, there are 146 library schools [85 university level library schools, 27 universities offering library and information science courses through correspondence or distance education and 32 colleges and institutes conducting library and information science programmes, 2 organizations, namely, NISCAIR (formerly INSDOC) and DRTC, offer two-year associateship in Information Science. 120 universities are offering bachelor's degree; 99 offer master's degree including 21 library schools that conduct two-year integrated master's programme; 18 offer M.Phil degree (based on data gathered by the present authors); 63 offer Ph.D. degree.(Singh, 2004, p. 1)

Thus, library science education has done a great deal. It is quite impressive. The growth in quantitative terms is quite impressive. However, this growth is unplanned. There is proliferation of library schools and library courses because there is no national policy and no accreditation of library schools or programmes.

Leading Library Schools

The following are considered as the leading library schools:

- Aligarh Muslim University, Aligarh
- Andhra Pradesh, Waltair
- Banaras Hindu University, Varanasi
- Documentation, Research and Training Centre, Bangalore
- NISCAIR (formerly INSDOC), New Delhi
- Guru Nanak Dev University, Amritsar
- Jadavpur University
- Karnataka University, Department of Library and Information Science, Dharwar
- MS University of Baroda, Vadodara
- NEHU, Department of Library and Information Science, Shillong
- Pune Uiversity, Pune
- SNDT, Mumbai
- University of Delhi, Department of Library and Information Science
- University of Calcutta, Calcutta
- University of Madras, Department of Information Science
- University of Mysore, Department of Information Science
- IGNOU (among distance and open education schools), New Delhi

The criteria used to identify the leading library schools are given below:

(i) *Status*: Full-fledged department, with a full-time professor (preferably) or a reader as the head,

(ii) Courses conducted: At least M.LISc and Ph.D.,

(iii) *Faculty*: (a) At least five full-time teachers with Ph.D. in library and information science,

(b) Teacher-student ratio being one to eight,

(c) Average number of papers contributed to learned periodicals per year per teacher being two. Instead of papers, it may be research monograph or report of a survey.

Students: Minimum qualification for admission being 50 per cent or higher to first year programme, except for reserved category. It would be desirable to have admission test for the purpose.

(iv) *Infrastructure*: (a) Computer laboratory with at least twenty computers (one computer for two students),

(b) Library facilities with at least five thousand volumes and twenty current periodicals in library and information science,

(c) Two classrooms, room for teachers, one big room for the computer laboratory, big hall for the library to accommodate the collection as well as seats at least for twenty students and five teachers, office for the department with at least three staff members,

(v) *Curriculum*: Recently revised curriculum (within last five years) with at least four courses (25%) out of sixteen courses devoted to computer application in libraries and information science, covering both B.Lib.Sc. and M.Lib.Sc.

(vi) *Teaching methods and Tools*: Use of discussion method and information technology,

(vii) *Reputation*: High reputation among teachers of library science and library professionals,

Delhi Library School at University of Delhi has been a pioneer in library education.

Due to the efforts of two great librarians, Dr. S.R. Ranganathan and Prof S. Das Gupta, the Department of Library Science was instituted in 1946 under the Faculty of Arts. It was established as a properly constituted academic department in the university. It was the first independent department of its kind at the university level. Thus, University of Delhi became the first university in the country to establish a department like other discipline. The Department started one-year post-graduate Diploma in Library Science in 1947. Four students were admitted and the first batch received Diploma in Library Science in 1948. In 1948, B.Lib.Sc. (Bachelor of Library Science) was started. This was one academic year course after one year Diploma in Library Science. University of Delhi became the first university in India to institute a degree course in library science (a post-graduate course).Thus, in 1949, two graduates received the degree of B.Lib.Sc. However, in 1949, Master of Library Science (M.Lib.Sc.) course was introduced and the first three graduates received the degree in 1951. Thus, B.Lib.Sc. course was renamed M.Lib.Sc. It was the first university in (the British) Commonwealth to introduce this course at Master's level.

Dr. S. Ranganathan served as Honorary Professor from 1947 to 1955. After his retirement in 1955, the Department was unable to offer M.Lib.Sc. course during 1956-58. However, one candidate was admitted in 1958 under special circumstances. This course was revived in 1959. Till 1968, this was the only department in the country to provide facilities for a degree programme at Master's level and research leading to a Ph.D. degree in Library Science. In 1951, this university became the first university in the country as well in (the British) Commonwealth to introduce doctoral studies in library science by framing regulations for doctoral programme in library science.

Ph.D. programme was initiated in 1952. Two Ph.D. candidates were accepted during 1952-53 academic session. Only one of them completed the course and was awarded a Ph.D. degree in 1957. D.B. Krishna Rao was the first person to receive a Ph.D. from an Indian library school under Dr. S.R. Ranganathan. His topic was Facet Analysis and depth classification of agriculture.

In 1978, University of Delhi introduced M.Phil in library and information science. It became the first university in the country to start M.Phil in this discipline. Contribution of Madras Library School have been described as landmarks under the section dealing with "History".

Turnout

Since the mid-1970s, there has been sudden increase in the number of library schools.

About fifteen hundred B.Lib.Sc./B.L.I.Sc. degree holders, two hundred master's degree holders, and twenty-five associateships are now awarded each year. (Mangla, 1984-85, p. 247)

Uptil 1967, the number of graduates who were awarded degrees in India were 5651. (Anis Khurshid, 1970, p. 74)

In a paper read in 1987, it was estimated that "average turnout every year is about 2,450 at graduate level (70 departments admitting an average of 35 students) and 380 at master's level (38 department admitting an average of 10 students). (Aggarwal and Manohar Lal, 1992, p. 34)

Today, the average turnout would be 5308 (120 library schools may turnout 120 × 35 bachelor's degree holders, 99 library schools may turn out 99 × 10 master's degree holders and 18 schools may produce 18 × 3 M.Phil. degree holders and 64 schools may produce about 64 Ph.Ds. To this we may add 35 students with associateship in information science. Thus, the total turnout being more than five thousand. The number would certainly be more because a large number of professionals are being produced by distance and correspondence courses. If we assume that another three thousand graduates are being turned out by these, then the total number can go up to more than eight thousand.

Role of UGC

UGC has played a significant role in the growth and development of library education in the country. It has laid down, qualifications for teachers of library and information science. It has issued through its various committees, standards for library education including curriculum. Given special grants for establishing computer laboratories. Department of Information Science at University of Madras has been given special assistance. This has been a great impetus in the growth and development of the department. The suggestion for changing the nomenclature from diploma in library science to bachelor of library science originally came from a UGC committee. In 2006, UGC stipulated that those who have passed M.Phil in L&IS are not required to pass UGC Net. According to a UGC circular dated September 22, 2006, the Commission "approved exemption from NET to M.Phil. and Ph.D. degree holders from appointment to the post of Assistant Librarian". As a consequence there was unprecedented rush for admission to M.Phil. At University of Delhi, there are five seats. In some years, a few seats used to lie vacant due to lack of qualified candidates. All along, this course was not popular. Not many candidates applied. But in the admission for the academic session, 2006-07, there was unusually heavy rush for seats. At Delhi School, 93 candidates applied for admission to 5 seats. Fifty-three were called for the interview and 10 were finally admitted. They all continue to be on the rolls as on October 28, 2006. The situation has changed completely due to change in the qualifications for library jobs. This also shows the importance of UGC in L&IS education. As a result, there is increasing rush for admission to M.Phil. in L&IS. Often, it has played the role as an agent of change. UGC sent a circular in 2003 to universities receiving financial support that their grants will be stopped unless their curriculum was revised. As a result, curriculum was revised in early twenty-first century by library schools, even by those that had not revised them for a long time.

UGC has been encouraging continuing education and staff development. In this connection, with grants from UGC, universities have established Academic Staff colleges. Continuing education in L&IS is made available to librarians and teachers of library and information science in the form of refresher courses and orientation programmes. (Krishan Kumar, 2007, p. 155)

During the last ten years or so there has been reduction in funds provided to universities by UGC, as a consequence, to save funds, universities are not filling up posts falling vacant, or filling junior level positions on temporary or *ad hoc* basis against senior posts (a lecturer may be employed against the post of a professor). It has also been encouraging the employment of retired teachers, paying on the basis of number of lectures delivered.

Levels of Courses

Basically, Indian library schools are providing library education at four levels:

(i) B.L.I.Sc. (Bachelor of Library and Information Science)/B.Lib.Sc. (Bachelor of Library Science)
(ii) M.L.I.Sc. (Master of Library and Information Science)
(iii) M.Phil (Master of Philosophy)
(iv) Ph.D.

Bachelor of Library and Information Science/Bachelor of Library Science

Universities previously awarded post-graduate diploma but later on renamed it as Bachelor of Library Science. Now all universities running one year post-graduate course award a Bachelor of Library Science (B.Lib.Sc.) or Bachelor of Library Science and Information Science (B.L.I.Sc.). Aligarh Muslim University was the first university to switch from Dip.Lib.Sc. to B.Lib.Sc. in 1958-59. At present, 120 library schools offer bachelor's degree (Singh, 2004, p. 2)

Master of Library and Information Science/Master of Library Science

In 1949, at University of Delhi, a two-year course for M.Lib.Sc. degree was introduced to replace the previous programme of B.Lib.Sc. The first batch rerceived their M.Lib.Sc. degree in 1951.

In 1965, Banaras Hindu University, Varanasi, was the second university to start M.Lib.Sc. but it was discontinued during 1968-69. The Department of Library Science, University of Bombay, also started M.Lib.Sc. course in 1967. Panjab University followed in 1970 and in 1971, Aligarh Muslim University, Karnataka University, Mysore University and Vikram University also started M.Lib.Sc. At present, there are 99 library schools that are offering master's degree. Out of these 21 are offering a two-year integrated programme. (Singh, 2004, p. 2)

M.Phil.

M.Phil. in L&IS is conducted at 18 library schools. It was a guideline from UGC, as a result of which some library schools introduced M.Phil. programme. All along, M.Phil. was not popular. Many candidates did not apply for admission. However, from the academic session 2006-07, the demand for this course has suddenly increased. At the Department of Library Science, University of Delhi, in the academic session, 2006-07, 93 candidates applied for admission to five seats. Fifty-three candidates, who fulfilled minimum qualification for admission, were called for the interview and ten of them were finally admitted. They all continued as students as on October 28, 2006. In the past, usually, it was difficult to fill the five seats. The situation has completely changed due to change in qualifications by UGC.

Ph.D.

In 1951, University of Delhi instituted a doctoral programme in Library Science. This was the first such programme in the whole of the British Commonwealth. The credit for the same goes to S.R. Ranganathan and S. Dasgupta. The first Ph.D. in library science was awarded to D.B. Krishna Rao. He was awarded Ph.D. in 1957. The topic of his research was 'Facet analysis and depth classification of agriculture'. S.R. Ranganathan was the supervisor. He retired from University of Delhi in 1955. After he left, the Ph.D programme became defunct. Dr. J.S. Sharma initiated Ph.D research at Panjab University. S.K. Sharma, Pandey was awarded Ph.D. in 1977, under the supervision of Dr. Sharma. This was the second Ph.D. to be awarded in library science. Thus, there was a gap of 20 years between the two Ph.Ds. It may be added that during this period, a few librarians and teachers of library science did receive Ph.Ds. in library science from non-library science departments.

In a paper read at a National Seminar held in 1987, the author mentioned that "there are 69 departments at university and college levels imparting B.Lib.I.Sc./B.Lib.Sc. course. Out of these, 39 departments are offering M.L.I.Sc. course. There are 30 universities offering doctoral programme" (Krishan Kumar, 1992, pp. 135-36). This shows that Ph.D. programme was well established by late 1980s. It must be admitted that many of the departments had yet to produce any Ph.D. According to P.S.G. Kumar, 31 universties including IIT Delhi have awarded Ph.Ds., many of these 31 institutions have no department of library science (Kumar, 1987, pp. 302-303). Around this period, Universities of Andhra, BHU, Calcutta, Delhi, Karnataka, Panjab, Poona and Rajasthan were active centres of doctoral research in library and information science. "Up to late 1970s there were not many library science Ph.D theses in India. ...Now, we have about 60 Ph.D. theses. The rate of Ph.D turnout is about ten annually" (Satija, 1992, p. 103). Ph.D. programme is now well established. Two candidates were registered in 1952-53 at Delhi Library School, for the first time in the country. Thus, Ph.D. programme has been in existence for more than five decades. There are around 50 Ph.Ds. being produced annually. There are 63 library schools offering Ph.D. programme.

It may be added that two candidates have been awarded D.Litt. degree in library and information science. They were Dr. D.B. Shukla by Utkal University and Dr. M. Taher from Agra University.

Admission Requirements

For admission to bachelor's degree course, usually minimum qualification is BA/B.Sc., but in recent years, those who are being admitted often have a good master's degree in an academic discipline. The trend is that candidates with higher academic qualifications are applying for admission.

In some library schools, they conduct an admission test and/or interviews for admission, in addition to minimum academic qualifications prescribed for the purpose.

For admission to master's degree course, a good bachelor's degree in library science is prescribed. Many library schools conduct an admission test. Some schools have also prescribed professional experience as an essential requirement as well.

Qualifications for admission to M.Phil. and Ph.D. vary from school to school. In Ph.D., two to three years of residence is essential in many universities. In some universities, only a short period of residence is required.

As regards associateship in information science, candidates having a bachelor's degree in engineering, technology, medicine or library and information science are given preference.

Course Content: A Proposal

Course content for a two-year integrated programme leading to a degree of Master of Library and Informtion Science is given below:

Core Courses

These are compulsory courses:

First Year

- Information, communication and society
- Information processing and organization (theory)
- Information processing and organization (practice)
- Information sources and communication media
- Information services
- Information and communication technology: Basics (this will also cover

elementary knowledge of programming languages such as PASCAL, C, C^{++}, java etc.)

- Information and communication technology: Application
- Project: documentation list and literature survey

Second Year

- Information systems (national and international systems—NISSAT, NASSDOC, DESIDOC, INIS, AGRIS, MEDLARS, MEDLINE, INSPEC etc)
- Information technology and systems design
- Storage and retrieval of recorded knowledge
- Planning and management of library and information centres
- Planning and management of information systems
- Library automation (planning, criteria for choosing applications software, criteria for choosing hardware, implementation, after implementation; overview of available applications softwares)

Networking and internet technology (networking-concepts, topologies, types-LAN, MAN, WAN; hypertext, hypermedia, multimedia; Integrated Services Digital Networks (ISDN), open systems, interconnection (OSI); networks such as ERNET, NICNET, DELNET, JANET, BLAISE, OCLC, INFLIBNET; Internet—components, services, web browsers and search engines).

Research Methods Including Statistical Methods

Electives

A student may choose any two of the following courses:

- Industrial library system
- Health science library system
- Public library system
- Academic library system
- Business library system
- Research and technical library system
- Law library system
- Archival records librarianship
- Preservation and conservation of library materials
- Informatics, bibliometrics and scientometrics

- Information system and services for R&D
- Management information systems
- Information systems and services for planning
- Environmental information systems and services
- Application of artificial intelligence to library and information science
- Technical report writing
- Dissertation/project report

Note: The dissertation/project work, must include directed fieldwork.

It will enable students to apply the theoretical knowledge of concepts and practices learned in the course work. They will carry out professional-level work under the formal guidance from a qualified supervisor/mentor. Students typically will get involved into tasks and projects that constitute professional-level (beginning professional level) work. In addition, fieldwork will provide learning opportunity for students. He will gain practical experience. He will be able to achieve networking in the profession, by interacting and through communication with library professionals. This way, he will also develop a professional identity and self-awareness. Directed fieldwork tasks usually involve skills and knowledge that the student has already begun to learn in the teaching programme but has not enough mastery over these. One project of this nature, for example, may be online services provided under "ask librarian" site of a university library.

Workshops

There should be a series of workshops for students. Some are compulsory and he can choose any four of the optional workshops. Each workshop may be of one day or two days, depending upon amount of information to be imparted to the students. The number of students to be admitted to a workshop is restricted to 25. Every two students, should get one computer. The workshop should be conducted in a computer laboratory. One LCD should be made available to the instructor. The teacher from the library school may conduct the workshop. In case, no teacher has expertise on the topic, then an outsider may be invited and paid for the purpose. He can be a working librarian or a teacher of library and information science or any other expert. At the end of workshop, the student will be assessed on the basis of assignments/project/ multiple choice questions etc.

Cumpulsory or Core Workshops

- Citation using a particular style accepted by the library school,

- Designing of databases using MS Access,
- Designing of spreadsheet using MS Excel,
- Statistical analysis using SPSS,
- Flow charts and diagrams based on MS Visio Pro,
- Presentation of a research paper using MS Word,
- Presentation of a research paper using Power point,
- How and where to find information on L&IS, with special reference to Internet resources,
- Use of open source softwares:
  (a) Linux,
  (b) My SQL data base, KOHA, D-Space, GDLS (Digital Library Software),
- How to build a digital library,
- Designing of web sites,
- Blogging (online communication phenomenon),
- Optional Workshops.

A student *can choose any four of the above workshops.*

Records management (inventory, classification, retention scheduling, storing and protecting; managing electronic records, records management software, imaging systems etc.).

Advanced Web Searches

Copyright

- Designing information products and services.
- Content management (creation, capture, delivery, customization and management of content) (the scope being to cover web publishing and also publishing to multichannel outputs, such as paper, web and wireless).
- Information architecture (it is the process of organizing online information so that it is clear, meaningful, meeting the needs of its website users).
- Information audit and mapping.
- Managing electronic records.

Course Delivery

Now the time has arrived, when Indian library schools should start using e-Learning on a large scale for achieving excellence in library education. Library schools belonging to open and distance education are already using some of the interactive tools to some extent.

E-Learning is any learning that utilizes a network (LAN, WAN or Internet) for delivery, interaction, or facilitation. This would include distributed learning, distance learning (other than pure correspondence _), CBT delivered over a network, and WBT can be synchronous, asynchronous, instructor-led or computer-based or a combination.

The following interactive tools are used to deliver content to learners:

- Asynchronous (E-mail, Listservs, Web Forums, Newsgroups, BBS).
- Synchronous (Chat, shared whiteboards, teleconferencing, videoconferencing, MOOs & MUD).

Asynchronous tools:

- *E-mail*—Used for questions and discussion.
- *Listservers*—Basically e-mail to everyone in the class or section at once.
- *Web Forums*—Also called discussion forums or bulletin boards. They are probably the most common form of interaction in online courses.
- *Newsgroups*—Public forums that use the Usenet system.
- BBS—A computer bulletin board that you dial, and use like a web forum + email + file transfer.

Synchronous tools:

- *Chat rooms*—Can be either moderated by an instructor or un-moderated for class.
- *Shared Whitebords*—Allow class members to write on the same digital whiteboard Application sharing. The same program and file can be shared for demonstration or collaboration.
- *Teleconferencing*—Could be used to deliver instructor audio, or for collaboration—Videoconferencing—Either from expensive, high quality, dedicated systems, or from less reliable desktop versions.
- MOOs &MUDs—Virtual worlds where users take on avatars and interact in various ways (http://www.elearners.com/resources/elearning-faq.asp) (Accessed on November 2, 2006).

  Classroom lectures, digitally taped and are made available after the class.

Supplementary materials and links to the state-of-the-art research materials for each paper are available on the web site of the library school. Bulletin board for students to post queries on the subject related to each paper are also created.

Faculty

In the 1950s, the teaching was generally conducted by part-time teachers. Mostly, they were the librarians working in their university libraries. The university librarian used to be the head of the department of library science. The situation began to change substantially in 1960s. In 1970s, there were still many library schools that either solely or mostly depended on part-time teachers. Today, the situation has changed completely. Very few library schools have part-time teachers. Invariably, a full-time teacher is the head of the library school. There may be exceptions.

Prof. S.R. Ranganathan became a full-time honorary professor in 1947 at Delhi library school. He held this position from 1947 to 1955. The Aligarh library school appointed a full-time lecturer in library science in 1956. In early 1960s, ten library schools were able to appoint one or more full-time teachers. These schools included Aligarh, Banaras, Calcutta, Delhi, Kerala, Madras, Nagpur, Panjab, Rajasthan and Vikram. (Kaula, 1962, pp. 225-226)

Though originally the library schools were initiated and headed by the university librarians, gradually full-time teachers were made the heads in many universities over a period of time. In a paper read at a national seminar in 1987, Kumar mentioned that 48 schools were headed by full-time teachers, 18 by university librarians and 6 were temporarily kept under the headship of librarians. (Kumar, 1992, p. 23)

Even in 1980s, most of the heads were part-time teachers. In 1980s, based on the recommendations of UGC, developments in librarianship in India and other countries, and the efforts of library science teachers in the state of Punjab and union territory of Chandigarh, the three library schools, namely, Punjabi University at Patiala, Guru Nanak Dev at Amritsar and Panjab University at Chandigarh received independent status after a "prolonged struggle". The three schools also appointed full-time heads of their independent schools. (Bansal and Tikku, 1988, p. 400)

In 1990s, the situation improved a great deal. For instance, Delhi Library School had in 1947, one full-time honorary professor and three part-time teachers. University librarian was the head. During 1992-93, it had nine full-time teachers consisting of four professors, two readers, two lecturers, one librarian-*cum*-lecturer and one part-time teacher. One of the professors was the head.

The situation has greatly changed. Library schools are normally headed by a full-time teacher, who get the same pay scales and various facilities given to other teachers. There are some library schools that have still majority of faculty manned by part-time teachers with a university librarian as the head. Even such schools are increasing full-time faculty over a period of time.

The teachers who initiated early courses were pioneers; they had to fight against odds. They were less qualified. They had done some kind of certificate or diploma. Some of these names include William Alanson Borden (1853-1931), Asa Don Dickinson, S.R. Ranganathan (1892-1972), S. Bashruddin, S. Das Gupta, etc. they were all dedicated people who had to struggle to get recognition for library science as discipline of study and teaching.

Up to early sixties, it was difficult to get qualified faculty. No Ph.Ds. were available for faculty positions. Today the position is that majority of the faculty have a Ph.D. in library and information science. Those who do not have a Ph.D. would be registered for Ph.D. Many of them would have done courses in IT or may even possess diplomas or degrees in IT.

Students

Library schools are now able to attract students who are well qualified. Large percentage of them may have already a master's in some other discipline. Many them have some exposure to IT. Most of them are ambitious and dynamic young men.

National Policy for L&IS Education

There is a need to have a national policy for library and information science education.

The national policy should make provision for National Commission on L&IS Education; Indian Council of Library and Information Science; and National Institute for L&IS and also indicate objectives, functions, order of priorities, ways of mobilization of resources, utilization of education and technology, goals, etc.

A National Commission on L&IS Education should be appointed. It should be directly responsible to a national committee headed by the Minister of Human Resource Development (Government of India).

There is need to set up an Indian Council of Library and Information Science (ICLIS). It should be representative body representing library schools, professional organizations, Ministry of Education and Culture (Government of India), UGC, etc. it should be an autonomous body and be provided funds on continuous basis.

It should perform the following functions:

"(i) Accreditation of library schools;
(ii) Laying down of standards for L&IS education covering syllabi, financial

status, faculty, library facilities, physical facilities, admissions, administration, etc.;

(iii) Funding of research programmes, fellowships, scholarships, etc.;

(iv) Funding of continuing education programmes for teachers and librarians; and

(v) Coordination." (Krishan Kumar, 1992, p. 138)

A criteria should be laid down for a library school to be granted accreditation, taking into consideration different factors such as collection on L&IS, facilities, etc.

Standards for L&IS should be laid down covering aspects. These would serve as criteria to be used for accreditation of a library school. In addition, ICLIS should prepare a model syllabus for different levels. This should be developed keeping in view the present and future requirements.

Funds should be made available to strengthen library schools. These may be provided so as to encourage specialization in different areas such application of computer, techniques (classification, cataloguing and indexing), management, services (such as bibliographical and documentation service), etc.

A National Institute for L&IS (NILI) should be set up. Its aim should be to achieve educational excellence. It should carry out the functions of training, research and advisory services. We are living in an age of information and communication technology. Therefore, teaching and research pogrammes must reflect this. NILI should experiment with new techniques and provide guidance in this matter to various library schools and libraries in the country.

Guidelines

Guidelines are given below for developing an excellent library school that can compete at the global level:

Administrators

Build up a library school that can deliver first rate quality professionals who are always innovating and are committed to provide top-notch customer service.

Adopt modern principles and practices used in managing great academic institutions.

Constantly make a quest for excellence in whatever is done, may be, it is administration, teaching, learning or research.

Must develop a culture through work ethics and an intensive drive to excel within the institution where teaching and learning can be sustained retaining high quality even under intense competitive pressure to excel. Keep in mind that people excel, when they are provided free, fair and a political environment for, teaching, learning and research.

Believe in zero-politics. Back stabbing or *chamchagiri* should not be permitted. Encourage open debate on issues of concern and create an environment conducive for this. However, open and honest disagreement on administrative and academic matters should not only be tolerated but must be expected from the faculty.

Faculty

Attract first rate faculty by offering work culture conducive for high quality research and teaching, excellent infrastructure and prospects for future growth. Indeed, the reputation of the school matters a great deal.

The faculty should be consist of the people with a mission and passion in their eyes to succeed, come what may against all odds. They should be relentlessly engaged in improving their teaching and learning process on continuous basis.

At the end of a semester, the students should be asked to fill up a questionnaire assessing each course conducted by a teacher, giving their opinion and suggestions to bring improvements. This is a normal practice in western countries. The assessment by students is kept confidential but brought to the attention of the teacher concerned.

Students

In terms of her demographic composition, India is the youngest in the world. This advantage is also going to be there during the next few decades. The available pool contains many young, bright, vibrant and talented people. It is a challenge for library schools in India to identify from this pool, bright young people who can be trained to acquire necessary skills that can enable them to become first rate library and information scientists who can compete in the global workplace, holding their own. Let them choose the best and offer them high quality training, turning out first rate talented library and information professionals. The library schools need to develop admission procedures to tap into this vast pool of young graduates, who are bright, having potential to develop into first rate librarians, who are super-efficient human resources, who are deeply committed to provide top-notch customer services and capable of bringing out first rate quality products based on increasing quality innovation. Admission should be based on qualifications, aptitude, general awareness, and communication skills. There should be an admission test followed by an interview. In case a library school has a big reputation, bright people would get attracted to such a school.

Issues, Developments and Trends, and Suggestions

Some of these issues have been identified in literature (e.g., Singh, 2004, pp. 4-6).

Quality of Graduates

Are the graduates turned out by our library schools employable? According to a recent study that appeared as NASSCOM report, that only 10 per cent college graduates (and 25 per cent of engineering graduates) are employable. Even some of the century-old universities are in a bad shape . Thus, urgent reforms are needed in the higher education in India. A library science graduate may be asked, are you employable? Is your library school an elite one, whose students are snatched by companies, research organizations, national level bodies etc.? Our library schools are a part of the total system. Therefore, there should be no doubt that similar situation also exists in case of our products. We should produce library professionals with necessary skills, knowledge and attitudes, for the twenty-first century, who are employable. There is a need to produce library professionals, who have great communication skills, who are confident, who are able to present their views effectively and boldly. Above all they should cultivate critical thinking that should make them employable. If they are not employable, then we should figure out as to what needs to be done to improve the situation?

Let us hope the Knowledge Commission set up by Government of India will come up with some meaningful and implementable recommendations to improve quality of education in our institutions of higher learning including library schools.

Prolification of Library Schools

There has been prolification of library schools. As there is no accreditation of library education programmes, therefore, there is no control on the emergence of library schools that do not even have the basic facilities. Emergence of such a large number of library schools has led to oversupply of library professionals. This has resulted in a mismatch between demand and supply. Besides, the quality of professionals turned out is not up to the mark. This is something unfortunate. There is an increasing problem of unemployment leading to frustration among young graduates. This is giving a bad name to some library education programmes. This is a matter of great concern.

Distance education was initially started basically to help in-service librarians to improve their professional qualifications. That phase has been over long back. The output through distance education is several times more than through formal system of education. There is nothing against distance education, though it has certain weaknesses. Distance education has some limitations due to its very nature. It is not easy to ensure in-depth instruction and learning. The emerging technologies do help a great deal in overcoming its limitations. The fact of the matter is that some of the distance correspondence education programmes have been initiated without adequate infrastructure. There may not be adequate number of tools like catalogue codes, classification schemes, lists of subject headings, textbooks and recommended books and information and reference sources made available at the study centre. Due to the short duration of contact programme and counselling, it becomes difficult to provide for adequate practical training. The students basically depend on printed material supplied by the library school. The notes on reference sources given in the printed material may be short but from examination point of view, it may be good enough. He may totally depend on these notes and may be able to score high marks without personally handling the sources and acquiring personal knowledge. In case, the study centre does not provide adequate access to these. This can also happen under formal education as well. In some universities, there are not adequate number of teaching centres, computer laboratories and lack of active involvement of the students in teaching-learning process.

Faculty Strength

Reputation of a programme depends, a great deal, upon the academic record, knowledge of the subject, teaching experience, output and professional involvement of the faculty. The faculty strength must be adequate. It must follow the norms laid down by the Curriculum Development Committee of UGC (University Grants Committee, Curriculum Development Committee, 1992).

Lack of Library Facilities

Lack of Library Facilities is a matter of great concern. There are many schools that do not have access to adequate library collection of basic text-books, reference books, tools (classification schemes, cataloguing codes, thesauri and lists of subject headings, etc). No library school should be established without having a well equipped library.

Information Technology

In twenty-first century, no library school can exist without having adequate access to information and communication technology. There are many library schools without well-equipped computer laboratory. A library school must have a modern IT laboratory with networking facilities. At least two students should be provided one terminal. It should have at least four to five library application software.

Curriculum

In some library schools, curriculum has not been revised for a long time. It must be revised every five years. It must revised keeping view, the changing environment in libraries, information centre and documentation centres and also the future needs. Large chunk of information science and computer application in libraries must be covered. This area should at least constitute 25 per cent of the whole syllabus at all levels of courses. A model curriculum has been proposed for two-year integrated Master of Library and Information Science programmed.

Admission Criteria and Number of Seats

The admission criteria should be based on kinds of professionals required by libraries. It is desirable that performance in the admission test and interview, along with academic qualifications should form the basis of admission. The number of seats should take into consideration the job positions likely to be available in the market place.

Mentorship

A student who is admitted to a library school must be attached to a teacher, who should serve as a mentor. His role will be to help him take decisions about the choice of courses, area of specialization, internship, field experience and in his professional development.

Internship

It is desirable that a student must have good exposure to library practices, services and issues. For duration of one month at the end of first semester, two months at the end of second year and again for one month after the end of third semester and one month after the final examination, he must undergo internship in a library supervised by a mentor. There will be overall control and direction provided by his mentor from the library school. We can call the teacher, an advisor or mentor or supervisor. The whole programme must focus on training the student in a particular specialization and making him suitable so that when he joins any library, he should be able to use IT with confidence and should be well equipped to serve as an excellent library professional. He will have constant dialogue with his assigned teacher and submit a report at the end of each period of internship. The mentor at the library should be asked to submit a report on the performance of the student. The student must be evaluated on the basis these reports as well as the interview. It as is desirable that the library, where he is doing internship should pay a fixed amount per month or based on number of hours.

Dual Responsibility

In twenty-first century, it is expected that a library school should be a full-fledged one under a full-time head. All along there was criticism of university librarians also being the head of the library school but in some of the states like Maharashtra and Karnataka, a professor of L&IS is also designated as in-charge of university library, thus, holding dual responsibility. This is not a desirable practice.

Barriers to Research

Faculty

(a) Inadequate strength of the faculty: Faculty strength being inadequate, they are often overburdened with classroom teaching, research and administration.
(b) Non-availability of faculty with research experience to serve as research supervisors. The situation has improved over the years.

Research Scholars

(a) Lack of aptitude for research: A person who is disinterested and indifferent to research cannot become a good researcher. Often, people join research without the necessary aptitude for it.
(b) Lack of scholarship: Due to lack of scholarship, the candidate for research may not prove to be good material to serve as a bright researcher.
(c) Lack of commitment to research: A good researcher is interested in research for its own sake.
(d) Lack of good academic background that could serve as a good preparation for research: many of facilities.

Those who come from the humanities often do not have proper understanding of scientific approach that is usually required in library research.

(a) Lack of incentives after getting a doctoral degree: Most of those, who come to this field, possess a master's degree. It is a long journey before one is able to successfully attain a Ph.D. One is not sure about getting a job consummate with the qualifications, after getting his Ph.D.

(b) Inadequate financial support.

(c) Lack of good library facilities and services: In case the library school is situated in a small town, then there may not be suitable library facilities and services available locally. He may have to visit a metropolitan town like Delhi, Mumbai or Hyderabad that have better facilities.

(d) Lack of environment conducive to research within library school and the profession.

(e) Lack of long research tradition in the library and information profession.

(f) Lack of recognition to research contribution made by the researchers.

(g) Research results merely remain on paper: Often librarians consider them as a theoretical exercise. Their findings are often not accepted by professionals by and large.

Discipline of L&IS

(a) Inadequate growth of the subject.

(b) Lack of Essential Data: Either essential data has not been gathered or has not been organized properly or is not easily accessible. Sometimes, the data may be available with the library but the library may refuse access based on confidentiality or due to fear of being exposed.

Trends

There are certain trends that are emerging:

- Library schools are emerging as full-fledged departments with full-time head and full-time teachers, with computer laboratories having state-of-the-art equipment along with networking. Individual teachers are being provided computer terminals in their rooms.
- Two-year integrated master of Library and Information Science is being offered by increasing number of library schools. There are atleast 21 such library schools. There are a number of advantages, if such a programme is introduced along with a semester system.
- Some library schools have introduced M.Sc. in information science instead of Master of Library and Information Science.
- Post-graduate diploma courses are being introduced in some specialized fields of study, such as library automation, archives and documentation, networking and information technology etc.

- Faculty is increasingly getting involved in taking courses in IT and attending seminars, conferences, etc. on IT. They are also writing more and more on IT, contributing to journals, conference proceedings.
- There is a flood of seminars, conferences, workshops on newer technologies, thanks due to UGC, INFLIBNET and National and state governments. This is due to the change of attitude towards IT at all levels.
- Library schools have increasingly set up their own websites. However, in many cases, these are not being updated regularly. Often, these are not easily accessible.
- Faculty is beginning to use technology for teaching in the classroom. Distance education library schools are doing a good job in applying technology for teaching-learning process.

The curriculum is being revised increasingly including aspects of information science and computer application. Newer topics like digital library, virtual library, electronic library, creation of websites, internet searching, meta documents, open source softwares, library automation, networking, etc. are finding a place. There is now less emphasis being given to teaching of library classification and library cataloguing.

Students are getting greater exposure to IT. Some of the students coming to library schools have good expertise in computer application. This is a great advantage to library schools. There are some leading library schools, which are turning out students, who are quite skilful in handling IT. The day is not far off, when each student will have his lap top as an essential tool for his learning. There are many library schools in the West, where a student is expected to have his lap top, when he comes to the class or goes to the library.

Conclusion

Library and information science education in India has completed a long period of 96 years. We have succeeded in building a strong foundation. Library schools at University of Delhi, University of Madras, DRTC, INSDOC, IGNOU, Aligarh Muslim University, NEHU etc. are the trail blazers. Of course, library schools initiated by Borden and Dickinson lead the pack. In the history of library education, the name of Dr. S.R. Ranganathan will be written in golden letters, as he was a pioneer associated with many of the leading library schools, and gave a lead. He ventured into the unknown territory, in spite of opposition to forward looking initiatives taken by him.

The first five decades was a period of slow growth. Beginning with 1960s, there was fast growth. Since 1990s began a period of consolidation. It is also a period of modernization, involving the application of information and communication technology in teaching and learning process. It is also a period, when many aspects of computer application in libraries and information science were also incorporated.

Now, university library schools constitute full-fledged departments like any other university department, usually headed by a full-time teacher, quite often a professor. Large majority of the faculty consists of full-time teachers, with a doctoral degree in library and information science; some of them also have expertise in computer application in libraries.

Now, most of the university library schools have their own computer laboratories. Many of the schools have library science, libraries attached to the department.

India has a large population of bright young people. They are growing technologically savvy. Many of the library schools get flood of applications for admission, especially those with high reputation.

A library school can, if it chooses carefully, get good candidates but reservation policy is a drag. You cannot do anything about it. It would desirable, if reservation of seats were not applicable to professional courses like library and information science. Many neighbouring countries send their students for pursuing library science courses to Indian universities. Due to increasing globalization, lot of young people go abroad for higher studies. It would be desirable that Indian library schools redesign their programmes to achieve international standards, so that they can attract more international students. This will make our school earn foreign exchange as well as create diverse environment conducive for teaching and learning of high order. This can enable them to survive as well as thrive.

If we look back, then we can recall the situation in the late 1950s, say 1958, there was no degree programme (diploma in library science at post-graduate level was prevalent), university librarian used to be the head of the department, the faculty used to be part-time with a few exceptions, the faculty had done diploma courses, in some cases they had a certificate in library science. There was limited amount of literature accessible to students.

From above it should be clear that the situation has improved tremendously. There was very little in terms of infrastructure. The teachers were part-time, who were practical librarians, who had expertise in practical librarianship, who concentrated on teaching the practices and routines prevalent in their library. Obviously, there was less emphasis on theory. Lectures were the only method used for teaching, followed by the examination at the end of the year. Of course, there were exceptions.

We would like to end on an optimistic note. Let twenty-first century in L&IS education be Indian century in this field. Let library schools in India lead the next wave of innovation. Let them reinvent themselves. Let us harness the large talent that is available today. The library schools need to work with a big bold goal. Indians by nature are intelligent people, hardworking, with powerful imagination and innovative ideas. Given the will to succeed, nothing can stop us from succeeding. What is very important is to build up an environment where innovative ideas can be experimented and implemented. Today, India is a leader in computer education. Indian IT experts are regarded as world class and are in great demand globally. The question arises if Indians are leaders in IT, why not in library education. Let us have a national vision that should synchronize with twenty-first century reality and turnout library professionals who can compete globally and not only survive but thrive in the emerging smart economy. We are sure that our dream will be fulfilled during the next two decades or may be earlier.

Indian library schools should introduce international programmes to attract international students. They can develop online courses for Indian as well as international students. Whatever is done, total quality and quality in everything must be the focus. It must be kept in mind that India has the necessary technology, expertise and experience. Believe in yourself and believe that you can do it. It just is matter of faith. Faith can move mountains. We will certainly succeed. Let us dedicate ourselves to achieve excellence in all aspects of library education.

References

Aggarwal, S.P. and Manohar Lal (1992), Library and information science education in India in Kumar, P.S.G. and Vashishth, C.V., *Library and information science in India*, New Delhi, Sterling.

Anis Khurshid (1970), Library Education in South Asia, *Libri*, 20, no. 1-2, 1970, pp. 59-60.

Bansal, G.C., and Tikku, U.K., Library science education in Punjab, *International Library Review*, 20, 1988, pp. 395-403.

Chopra, H.R. *et al.* (1988), *Directory of Library and Information Schools in India*, Chandigarh, Arun Publishing House.

Kaula, P.N. (1962), Education for librarians in India, *Library World*, 63, pp. 225-26.

Kaula, P.N. (1992), An evaluation of his life and work *in* Ranganathan, S.R. (1992), *A librarian looks back: An autobiography of Dr. of S.R. Ranganathan*, appended with an evaluation of his life and work by Prof P.N. Kaula, New Delhi, ABC Publishing House.

Krishan Kumar (1992), A proposal for national policy for library and information science education, *in* Kumar, P.S.G and Vashishth, C.V., *Library and Information Science in India*, New Delhi.

Krishan Kumar (2007), *Library Management in Electronic Environment*, New Delhi, Har-Anand Publications.

Kumar, P.S.G. (1987), Research in Library and Information Science in India; a Bibliography of Ph.D., M.Phil. and M.L.I.S. Dissertations, New Delhi, Concept Publishing Company.

Kumar, P.S.G. (1992), Education for librarianship in India, in Kumar, P.S.G. and Vashishth, C.V., *Library and Information Science in India, New Delhi*, Sterling.

Mangla, P.B., Library and Information Science Education in India in Gupta, B.M., *et al.*, ed, *Handbook of Libraries, Archives and Information Centres in India*, New Delhi, 1984-85, p. 247.

Ranganathan, S.R. (1992), *A librarian looks back: An autobiography of Dr. of S.R. Ranganathan*, Appended with an Evaluation of his Life and Work by Prof P.N. Kaula, New Delhi, ABC Publishing House.

Satija, M.P. (1992), Garnering the Fruits of Research: Sources on Indian LIS dissertations, in Kumar, P.S.G. and Vashishth, C.V., *Library and Information Science in India, New Delhi*, Sterling.

Singh, S.P. (2003), Library and Information Science Education in India: Issues and trends, *Malaysian Journal of Library & Information Science*, Vol. 8, no. 2, December 2003: pp. 1-17.

University Grants Commission (India), *Library and Information Science* (Curriculum Development Committee on-) (Chairman: P.N. Kaula) (1992), Report, New Delhi, UGC.

Warner, Jeremy (Nov. 29, 2006), *India looks set for lift-off as Western eyes start to roam away from China* (http://news.independent.co.uk/business/analysis and features/article 2023861.ece) (accessed on Nov 29, 2006)

2

Library and Information Science Professionals: New Faces and New Phases

A. AMUDHAVALLI

By 2020, some 80 per cent of today's librarians will have retired. It is vital that enthusiastic, energetic, educated information professionals replace them. Hence the need to recruit the next and new generation of professionals. Since the Schools of Library and Information Science (LIS) traditionally attract second or third level entrants, the status of the information profession is a cause for concern. In addition, many new information-related jobs from diverse sectors outside the boundary of conventional libraries now attract LIS graduates and compete with conventional libraries as employers. It is a great time to enter the information profession, but poses several key challenges for LIS schools and employers in India and elsewhere, as a new generation of information professionals are expected to tackle jobs in a changing scene and settings.

The common concern is about the challenges of recruitment and of keeping curricula relevant for new jobs in new settings and new responsibilities in old settings. Hence, the LIS schools must keep curricula vital and attract enough young entrants to leave successfully to match and fill the vacancies caused by retirements and to fill new types of jobs, and provide choices and flexibility in scheduling that appeal to full and part-time students, both those pursuing a first career and those changing careers. Since 1990s, library professional associations and the LIS schools have studied the future need for information professionals, the current curricula of LIS, and how curricula should change in the future to meet new needs. Schools have been constantly making changes. Recruitment of right personnel and revitalizing relevant academic programs have been a recurrent theme. What role information professionals will play in the field in the future warrants an attempt to identify essential competencies expected of the young entrants.

The competencies expected of professional entrants which can be translated into broadly recommended coursework, are knowledge and skill of:

- Information resources,
- Information management,
- Information access,
- Information systems and technology,
- Research,
- Information policy.

Schools have built core curricula around these competencies, but coursework by and large focuses mostly on the first three topic areas. However, slowly and subsequently strive hard to add and change required courses or content that provided knowledge in the last three areas. Unlike the past, it is found that a few LIS schools are vibrant, dynamic, changing field that is undertaking an array of initiatives. But the changes in course content are inadequate and the LIS Schools have to change and provide more flexibility and choice.

There is also a considerable confusion in the profession of librarianship as a whole on two crucial issues. The first is the inability to distinguish between education and training in librarianship. Education is the realm of the library schools, but training is the duty of the employing institution. Everything cannot be accomplished at the schools itself. Only a basic awareness and education are furnished to the school candidates and the real time training and skills have to be obtained at the work points. Work culture, adaptability, orientation and inclination to the job are gained over a period of time at the field work. A great way for employers to recruit information professionals is to pick somebody with potential and support them through their education. This works now because there are so many distance-education or evening and weekend LIS programs.

The second is a lack of consensus and clarity regarding the levels and nature of LIS course contents. It is in transformation in Indian LIS schools towards adaptation.

The six trends that are featuring current curricular changes are:

(1) LIS curricula are addressing broad-based information environments and information problems. Though jobs in libraries remain important in

designing LIS education, most schools now also offer education that prepare students for jobs in other environments and situations.

(2) A distinct core of skills and commitment has taken shape that is predominantly user-centered. Faculty and approach may come from multidisciplinary areas, but a focus on understanding users and meeting their needs distinguishes LIS curricula.

(3) LIS schools and programs are increasing the investment and infusion of information technology into curricula. LIS schools integrate the use of information technology into all aspects of the LIS curricula.

(4) LIS schools are experimenting with specialization within the curriculum. Since students can't learn everything in a master's degree program, schools offer specializations in areas such as archives, school media, medical librarianship, or records management.

(5) Instruction is offered in different formats, providing students with flexibility, including distance education, variant scheduling, and collaborative courses with other departments or other universities.

(6) Curricula are expanding into related degrees at the undergraduate, post graduate and doctoral levels. New undergraduate programs are growing especially rapidly.

This provides a blueprint towards success for those schools that may not be keeping up, a picture of education in a vital profession, and as an important tool of intake policy.

We are moving towards the top of the cycle in desirability of placement of our graduates in both library and non-library environments. Schools of LIS must work to help fill the demand because there is 'a danger we are in such demand that employers (particularly in corporate settings) will start waiving the requirement for a degree'. This could have negative effects on both schools of LIS and the profession.

Students have become much more "technologically astute than in the past," particularly in the areas of networking, internet issues, design of information products and services, and electronic publishing. LIS graduates bring skills in technology and searching along with knowledge of personal liberty and privacy issues. Multiple language abilities will be very useful in these jobs and in our global information economy. LIS fresher is in such a demand that many are employed as they graduate and stay in those organizations with an upgrade or a raise.

With the many openings in corporate sectors, it is not surprising that a majority of current LIS students hope to work in academic, special and even public libraries. But their career goals, even within library settings, are quite varied. Today's LIS students are also quite diverse in their background. A majority of students in LIS programs are now part-time. Distance education students in particular are usually part-time students, many working while they pursue their master's degree and who bring a wealth of experience to their education. Part-time and distance students often pursue their degrees to upgrade their skills and knowledge for advancement in their current workplace or area of employment. In the long years of part-time study, not all hold to their initial jobs or plans.

Variety and a world of choices are the two common themes with current students. LIS students today can pick from many different types of jobs and work environments. LIS schools are working on keeping up with technology, planning recruitment, and revising curricula, but I wonder how LIS programs can continue to be all things for all people. How can programs provide sufficient courses and educational opportunities for those who want to become competitive intelligence specialists, children's librarians, electronic publishers, and academic reference librarians? In particular, how can they do all this while maintaining or growing doctoral and undergraduate programs and bringing in new recruits for master's degree programs?

Cooperative initiatives with other academic departments and with the work places through practical and other programs help. In the old on-campus environment, each LIS program stood on its own. In a distance-education environment, many opportunities emerge for sharing specialties, faculty, and coursework between LIS programs in different schools. Discussions on how this might work have to be thought of. Opportunities for graduates have expanded and the Internet boom was creating a new market for information skills.

All these propose changes in curricula, faculty, and diversity in library education and calls for a restructuring of library education for the 21st century. This is the real challenge for LIS educators. When new recruits come to school they need to find a continually revitalized and diverse curriculum that will prepare them for a vast variety of jobs. The solution to the library education crisis must have many elements. I suggest here a number of areas in which change, in many cases radical change, is needed and wrap them up in an overall proposal in conclusion.

- *Curricula*—The hub of the question of library education, as it is with any level of education in any subject, is what is taught. It is instructive to look at what goes on in conventional libraries and the non-conventional new sectors and spheres lying beyond library walls and the areas in which a would-be information professional should be knowledgeable. And we are to devise a core curriculum that would apply to all schools across the country and feature employability feature.

- *Faculty*—The most important part of the resolution of the LIS education lies in the quantum and quality of the faculty members in Schools. Most of the teaching positions are vacant and LIS schools are often under staffed. Many contemporary LIS faculty members lack aptitude, commitment, abreast of current trends and developments in the field, ethics, little or no experience of working in libraries, research mind, communication and focus in teaching. It is not without significance that Schools depend largely upon adjunct faculty, either the practicing librarians or experts in related fields of interests. This needs to be revamped to ensure and enhance the regular faculty's strength and capabilities.
- *Information Professionals*—Many of the working professionals still spend much of their time providing reference services, with an increased time spent evaluating and selecting content, bringing information resources to the desktop, and organizing information on intranets. But information skills, no matter how up-to-date, are not enough in today's competitive information environment. The need for these information professionals to keep a user-focused attitude, establish a strong information services brand within their organization, and build customer loyalty through quality services that meet users' expectations and field orientation and adaptability are to be emphasized.
- *Pedagogy*—Information skills are easily and frequently taught in school. Positive attitudes about selling yourself, recognizing the needs of the organization, and building customer loyalty are not as common in LIS schools or as easily taught. Business schools have traditionally been more successful in instilling these types of attitudes, but not just because of a course or two. Instead, such attitudes fit with a deep-seated philosophical base of business curricula and the psychology of students attracted to business schools. Such attitudes appear less often in LIS entrants. Specialization in coursework can help solve some of this conflict. Electives that cover topics like the non-profit information industry, information entrepreneurship, and business intelligence with values and viewpoints in these courses are to be taught.
- *Accreditation*—There are two basic models by which a profession can seek to control education for its would-be members. The first is based on a consensus on the core requirements for a person to be educated in that profession leading to agreements on the basic curriculum to be taught in the schools that are certified to educate future members of that profession. The second approach is to accredit each school based not on national standards but on that school's own vision and mission and to judge them on the latter.

This provides a blueprint for success for those schools that may not be keeping up, a picture of education in a vital profession, and as an important tool of intake policy.

Put simply, I would like library schools in India and elsewhere to:

- deliver a nationally agreed core curriculum to national and international standard levels,
- have a core faculty (not including adjuncts) capable of teaching and doing research in all areas addressed by the core curriculum,
- concentrate on teaching and research of current relevance,
- teach and do research in other areas only when they have a satisfactory coverage of the core areas,
- be accredited in terms of national standards for function, structure, and performance, and
- cooperate with library practitioners in all kinds of library to ensure coordination of library education in the schools and library training in the libraries and a smooth flow of new librarians from library schools to libraries.

Can we get there from here? Can LIS education and training coexist in harmony? Can the LIS schools and the employers work together to produce a requisite/need based core curriculum? Can we revamp the educational system towards nationally agreed standards? Can we reconceptualize LIS to make it attractive to future generations of librarians?

References

Corcoran, Mary (2000). Dagar, Lynn; and Stratigos, Anthea, "The Changing Roles of Information Professionals: Excerpts from an Outsell, Inc. Study," *Online*, vol. 24, no. 2, March/April 2000, pp. 28-34.

Cronin, Blaise and La Barre, Kathryn (2004). Mickey Mouse and Milton: Book Publishing in the Humanities. *Learned Publishing* 17, pp. 85-98.

"Educating Library and Information Science Professionals for a New Century: The KALIPER Report," Executive Summary, July 2000. KALIPER Advisory Committee, ALISE, Reston, Virginia.

Lynch, Mary Jo, "Reaching 65: Lots of Librarians Will Be There Soon," *American Libraries*, March 2002, pp. 55-56.

Pollicino, Elizabeth B. *Challenges Facing Higher Education for the New Century: The Impact on Promotion and Tenure in LIS Education*. Juried paper presented at the National Conference of the Association for Library and Information Science Education, San Antonio, TX, January 2000.

Tenopir, Carol, "I Never Learned about That in Library School," *Online*, vol. 24, no. 2, March/April 2000, pp. 42-46.

Terrell, Tom and Gregory, Vicki L., "Plenty of Jobs, Salaries Are Flat," *Library Journal*, vol. 126, October 15, 2001, pp. 34-40.

Yarmonlinsky, Adam. *Tenure: permanence and change-academic* tenure. http://www.findarticles.com/p/articles/mi_m1254/is_n3_v28/ai_18371667. Accessed September 5, 2005.

3

Library and Information Science Education in South Asia

PARAMJEET KAUR WALIA

Introduction

Today information is regarded as a vital resource and plays a significant role in the socio-economic, scientific and technological development of the world level. There is a vast reserve of information in the world available in various forms. Developments in Information and Communication Technology (ICT) make generation, organization, storage and dissemination of information processes easy and also provide access to information irrespective geographic limitations. The dynamics of information handling has changed due to the use of IT.

As a result of the increased application of information and communication technologies (ICT) in libraries, the job of a librarian information scientist is more than likely to involve activities of a highly technical nature, requiring knowledge and understanding not just of traditional practices in library and information services, but also of the latest technological developments.

The term librarianship changed its nomenclature to library science then to library and information science adding new dimension to its field at every stage. It has also changed its philosophy and focuses from 'preservation for posterity' to 'books are for use' and then 'global access to information'. It has the attributes of being a discipline of disciplines. The subject commenced its advent with a clinical approach and gradually attained the status of a scientific field, emerged subsequently as one of the subjects of highly disciplinary approach, with a blend of theories, philosophies and practices incorporated from various other subjects. This changed scenario has effected the LIS education all over the world. Application of ICTs in libraries information centers have posed many challenges to the LIS professional as well as LIS education.

South Asian Association for Regional Cooperation (SAARC) came into existence in 1985 for various programmes of cooperation and development in the region. Out of the seven countries who are members of SAARC, provision of LIS education is available only in India, Pakistan, Bangladesh and Sri Lanka, whereas, no such facilities at present exist in other three countries in the region, viz. Bhutan, Maldives and Nepal.

India, Pakistan, Bangladesh and Sri Lanka have similar systems and traditions in administration, education, research, and library development including LIS education. Major factors affecting the library schools in the South Asian region are globalization, lack of reliance of education programmes to the needs of the country, financial constraints and increasing social accountability. In addition to these factors, the evolving status of LIS profession and the professional education has become a challenge to the library schools. Library schools in South Asia need to play a positive proactive role by adopting diverse strategies to survive the challenges posed by their social, political, economic and technological environment.

LIS Education in India

India has already developed a vast infrastructure of education and research facilities consisting of schools, polytechnics, colleges, universities/institutions of higher learning, national laboratories and research institutions/organizations. At present, there are 342 universities/institutions including 18 central universities, 211 State universities, 95 deemed universities and 5 institutes established under state legislation and 13 institutes of national importance. There are 17,625 colleges, out of which 5386 have been recognized by the UGC.

In India there are as many as 69 institutions offering, certificate courses in library and information science. These includes 40 associations, 15 degree colleges/ private institutions, 5 distance education institutions/universities, 3 regular universities, 3 government departments, and 3 other agencies.

There are 33 institutions offering diploma in library and information science course of which 11 are degree colleges and polytechnics, 7 regular universities, 2 are open universities and other institutions. In additions to these there are 20 junior colleges offering DLISc under JOC (job oriented course) scheme which is considered equivalent to 10+2 programme.

Maximum numbers of institutions are offering BLISc courses. These are 104 in number. Out of these 48 are Library and Information Science departments in regular universities, 27 are degree colleges, 12 are distance education universities/ institutions, 6 are self-finance courses run by various institution/universities, 2 are deemed universities, 2 are evening colleges. There are 7 other institutions including library association which offer Bachelor of Library and Information Science (BLISc) course. Further more are 8 institution offering library and information science as an optional subject in BA degree course. These include 7 degree colleges and 1 regular university. In addition, one college is offering B.A. (Hons) and B.A. (Pass) course in library and information science.

There are as many as 92 universities institution imparting Master Degree programme in library and information Science and related fields of which 70 are offering one year MLISc programme, 15 offer two year MLISc, 2 universities offer two year MSc in library and information Science, I regular university imparts 2 year MSc in information Science programme, and one deemed university offers two year Master of Information Science (MISc) and 2 deemed universities offer Associate ship in Information Science (AISc) and 1 university is offering two year MIM (Master of Information Management) programme under fully self finance scheme.

Of the 70 universities of offering one year MLISc programme 44 are regular universities, 6 distance education institution/universities, 8 self finance courses for a period of 2 years, and 4 are self finance courses of year duration, 7 are degree colleges and 1 is deemed university. Out of 15 universities offering two year MLISc programme, 12 are regular universities, 2 are Degree College and 1 is run under self finance course by one university.

There are 4 PG Diploma courses offered by 4 institutions, viz. PGDADM and Post MLISc course are offered by one regular university each and while PGDIT is under self-finance by one university, the PGDLAN is imparted through distance education.

There are 52 Universities/Institutions providing Ph.D. Degree and 15 are providing M.Phil. degree. Of the 52 universities offering Ph.D. 51 are regular universities and one is an open university. Out of 15 institutions offering M. Phil. degree 13 regular universities, 1 each is offered under self-finance scheme and 1 through distance mode. NISCAIR, New Delhi and DRTC, Bangalore are offering two years Associateship in Information Science which is recognized by some universities equivalent to Master's degree.

The above analysis clearly indicates that there is large number of institutions imparting LIS education under regular scheme, awarding variety of library and information science degrees/certificates. Other include degree colleges, associations distance education institutions/universities, deemed universities, colleges and Government departments.

As it is evident that there are adequate facilities available in India for the development of manpower in LIS but the rapid growth of the schools of LIS has brought in some serious problems also. There is wide variation in the resources available to each of these schools and the educational standards maintained by them. In spite of shortcomings in Indian LIS educational system, the professional competency of our working personnel is quite good. The teaching institutions here not only provide educational facilities to their own nationals but also to the students coming from several other developing countries in Asia and Africa. The professionals trained here occupy prestigious positions in regional and international organizations. The need is to improve and strengthen the existing infrastructure.

LIS Education in Pakistan

Pakistan has made progress in several areas such as education, industry, agriculture, health, scientific and technological research. There are at present 22 universities, 691 colleges and a fairly large number of research institutes and laboratories in the country. The laboratories and research institutes function under the umbrella of several bodies such as the Pakistan Atomic Energy Council, Pakistan Council of Scientific and Industrial Research, Pakistan Agricultural Research Council, and Pakistan Medical Research Council. Research and Development (R&D) activities are carried out in several industrial organizations as well.

At the time of its emergence as an independent sovereign state in August 1947, Pakistan inherited four libraries of significance. Three of them, viz. Punjab University Library (founded in 1882), Punjab Public Library (founded in 1884) and Punjab Civil Secretariat Library (founded in 1885) were located at Lahore and the fourth was Dacca University (1921), now in Bangladesh.

This position gradually improved from the late 1950s and significant progress has been made in different types of libraries and information services, particularly in university and special libraries, during the past three decades or so. The National Library of Pakistan today occupies a new building completed in the late 1980s with a total collection of about 90,000 volumes. Other libraries in 1989 included: 22 universities with a total of 142 constituent libraries, 435 college libraries, 331 special libraries, 281 main public libraries and 464 school libraries. The Pakistan Scientific and Technology Information Centre (PASTIC) was established in 1974 with its headquarter at Islamabad. The Pakistan National Scientific and Technical Documentation Centre (PANSDOC) was established earlier in 1957. These libraries and documentation centers are managed on modern lines by qualified personnel. Library systems and networks are being developed at national provincial levels.

The first library school at Punjab University Library, Lahore was started by an American Asa Don Dickinson in 1915. Until 1956, courses at the undergraduate level leading to a certificate in library science were conducted by library associations as well as at Punjab, Dacca and Peshawar Universities.

The first post-graduate diploma course in library science was started in 1956 at Karachi University. The universities of Punjab and Dacca (Now in Bangladesh) started courses at the diploma level in 1959, followed by the University of Peshawar in 1962, Sindh University in 1970, Islamia University, Bahawalpur in 1981 and Baluchistan University in 1983. The Universities of Karachi and Dacca added the master's degree programmes in 1962, Punjab University and Sindh University in 1974, Peshawar University in 1983, Islamia University in 1984 and Baluchistan University in 1985. In addition, Allama Iqbal Open University at Islamabad a few years ago started a 2-year M.A. programme in L&IS through distance education. Therefore, there are now 7 universities conducting master's degree programmes, and 6 of them (excluding the Allama Open University) call their first year programme a diploma/bachelor degree in Library and Information Science.

While several new areas have already been included in the course content, particularly at the master's level as in several Indian Library Schools, emphasis continues to be mostly on the traditional subjects. The establishment of computer laboratories in some library schools for use by the students and teachers is certainly an innovative step in the direction of modernizing the curricula.

Although Karachi Library School has provision for a Ph.D. degree and Sindh University for M.Phil., the research component in library schools, as in several other countries in the region, needs to be further developed.

LIS Education in Bangladesh

Bangladesh emerged as an independent state in December 1991, Prior to it, the geographic area of Bangladesh was the eastern wing of Pakistan, the infrastructure for education and research comprised of school, polytechnics, colleges, universities and research institutions. At present, it has 12 universities, including 1 open, 2 private universities, the University of Dhaka (founded in 1921) being the oldest and a number of research institutes. It has about 114 public libraries, 6 university libraries, approximately 285 college libraries a few libraries in schools and about 100 special libraries attached to government departments, research institutes and organization.

It also has Bangladesh National Scientific and Technical Documentation Centre (BANSDOC), Bangladesh National Library and National Medical Library of Documentation Centre. In addition to these, libraries of foreign countries such as the British Council and the United States Information Services are playing significant role in disseminating information to the community.

The Library Association of Bangladesh (LAB) conducts two courses in library science, viz. one year post-graduate diploma course in library and information science and certificate course at undergraduate level of 6 month duration.

The University of Dhaka is the only university conducting post graduate courses leading to the award of Master's degree in L&IS. It started a one year diploma course in 1959, which was modelled on the course offered by the University of London. In 1962, the university launched a one-year Master's degree course in library science. In 1976, a two-year Master's degree programme was introduced. The diploma course was abolished in 1988 and a three-year degree honours course was launched in 1988. The university of Rajshahi started a one-year post graduate diploma course in 1991. The university introduced two-year M.Phil. degree programme in 1976, a doctoral programme was added in 1979.

The course contents at various levels, i.e diploma, bachelors and master's and M.Phil. have been revised but they still remained traditional in real sense. Certain new components such as information and communication technology, system analysis, library networks etc. have been incorporated but due to lack of infrastructure facilities practical demonstrations are not included in the teaching programmes.

LIS Education in Sri Lanka

Sri Lanka has made significant progress in the field of education, agriculture, health, science and technology. There are at present 10 universities and several institutes of higher learning and research. In addition to National Library of Sri Lanka, there are several public, school, college, university and special libraries.

Formal Library Education in Sri Lanka commenced in the year 1963, with the introduction of a part-time course run by the then Ceylon Library Association. Subsequently there had been two attempts to introduce full-time course in this field of study. The University of Ceylon, Peradeniya started a full time Post-graduate Diploma course in Librarianship in 1961. This course was terminated in 1965. The second attempt was in 1969 by the two Junior University Colleges, Dehiwala and Palalai. This was a two-year full time Diploma course. With the abolition of Junior University Colleges this course was terminated in 1970. The Sri Lanka Scientific and Technical Information Center offered short service courses from time to time.

Currently, there are only two institutions that run library education programmes at para-professional and professional level. They are the Sri Lanka Library Association and the University of Kelaniya. Sri Lanka (Ceylon) Library

Association was formed in 1960, and incorporated by Act of parliament in 1974. The association began its library education programme in 1961. At the inception its courses were influenced by the British system of library education. The association runs the following courses: (a) First Year Course, (b) Intermediate Course, and (c) Final Year Course.

The number of contact hours for each course varies from 120 to 140 hours. Although the duration of the three-tier time programme is scheduled to be three years most of the students who embark on this study obtained their qualification within a range of four to six year. This reveals a very high wastage. The obvious reasons being the part time nature of the course, the dependence on visiting staff and the lack of other facilities.

The library science courses, that are run by the Department of Library Science, University of Kelaniya, were started in 1973 and the following full-time and part-time courses are offered:

(a) Undergraduate Programme
- ➢ B.A. General Degree with Library Science as one of the three subjects.
- ➢ B.A. Special Degree in Library and Information Science and Archival Science.

(b) Post Graduate Programme
- ➢ Post Graduate Academic Diploma in Library and Information Studies.
- ➢ Master's Degree in Library Science (1987)
  (Duration one year after completing the Post-Graduate Diploma)

(c) Part-time Certificate Course
- ➢ Certificate Course in Library and Information Science part-one (1997)
- ➢ Certificate Course in Library and Information Science part-Two (1997)
- ➢ Professional Advanced Certificate in Library and Documentation (1997)

  Duration of each course is one year.

In 1984 the name of the Certificate Course was changed to Diploma in Library and Information Science.

Courses content of the B.A. Degree (Library Science as one of the three subjects):

(i) Libraries, librarianship and historical bibliography.
(ii) Library materials—Acquisition, processing and care.
(iii) Library materials—Bibliographic organization.
(iv) Library materials—Uses and services.

Curricula of the Special Degree course in library science and information science is as follows:

Part I

- LIS 301 Libraries, librarianship and library science.
- LIS 302 Organization and administration of libraries.
- LIS 303 Bibliography, reference, and information services.
- LIS 304 Archival Science I.
- LIS 305 Archival Science II.

Part II

- LIS 401 Classification theory.
- LIS 402 Cataloguing theory.
- LIS 403 Practical classification and cataloguing.
- LIS 404 Information science and documentation services.
- LIS 405 Literature survey and bibliography.
- LIS 406 Technical English.

Post Graduate Diploma

The Post-Graduate Diploma syllabus was revised in 1986. Accordingly the duration of the course was one year full-time and two years part-time. The curriculum consists of core subjects and optional subjects. All students are required to take the core subjects and six optional subjects.

Core Subjects

(a) Management and organization of libraries.
(b) Information services and organization.
(c) Information retrieval.

Optional Subjects

(a) History of libraries
(b) Public library services
(c) Special library services
(d) School library services
(e) Health libraries and information services

(f) Communication and mass media
(g) Audio-visual studies for librarians
(h) Publishing, book trade and libraries
(i) Library automation
(j) Serial publications
(k) Literature and libraries for children and young people
(l) Archival administration and record management

Master of Library Science

The duration of the course is one year full-time or two years part-time. The course contents are:

(a) Research project,
(b) Management of libraries,
(c) Media librarianship, and
(d) Research Project (Dissertation).

Research is essential to the development of the profession. Concerted efforts are made to meet this demand. The Library Association commenced its Fellowship programme in 1990. The Fellowship is granted to Associates after completion of a research project.

Library and Information Science has yet to emerge as a well recognized discipline of study and research at the post-graduate level in Sri Lanka. The emphasis until recently was on undergraduate level courses excepting that the Kelaniya Library School had been conducting post-graduate diploma course and a master's degree course for several years. The introduction of the M.L.I.Sc. programme at Colombo University is certainly an important development in the direction of expanding training facilities at a higher level in the country.

Education for librarianship in Sri Lanka has shown very show and uneven progress due to non-availability of qualified teachers of library science, lack of infrastructure facilities and absence of a national information policy.

Conclusions

The overall pattern of the library and information science and their levels, content and durations share many features in all the four countries. Also, all these countries have (a) limited research activity in the library schools; (b) no system of accreditation at the national level; (c) no comprehensive manpower surveys and manpower planning for librarianship; and (d) a shortage of suitable faculty for the different levels in the library schools. Training courses were started with part-time teachers, usually drawn from university libraries and with university librarians as heads of the library schools, but now the trend in most of these countries is to have full-time faculty of the same caliber and having the same status, facilities, and privileges as in other departments of the universities.

Librarianship as a profession has largely emerged from the adolescent state in India, Pakistan, and Bangladesh and to some extent even in Sri Lanka, and library schools have certainly made vital contribution in this process. Because of their close geographic proximity and similarities in their systems as well as in their problems, the library schools in these countries can certainly gain a great deal, if various ways and means can be explored and used to develop a system of mutual co-operation among them. Some ideas in this respect might be regional seminars on topics of common interest, exchanges of teachers, and exchange of course materials. With such a system of co-operation the library school can play more effective roles not only in their respective countries, but also possibly in the South Asia region, and even throughout the developing countries of the world.

References

Khurshid, A. (1997). Library education in Pakistan. In: *Encyclopedia of Library and Information Science.* New York, Dekker, Vol. 21, pp. 282-299.

Mangla, P.B. and Vashistha, C.P. (1976). Library and information science education in India. *Journal of Library & Information Science. 1,* pp. 127-160.

Mangla, P.B. (1978). Levels of training in Library and Information Science: Admission Requirements and Duration. *Library Science with a Slant to Documentation.* 15, pp. 125-131.

Mangla, P.B., (1994). Library and information science education in South Asia: India, Pakistan, Bangladesh and Sri Lanka. *Education for Information,* 12 (4), pp. 423-425.

Neelameghan, A. (1974). Education of librarians and documentation in India. In: *Encyclopaedia of Library and Information Science.* New York, Dekker, Vol. 11. pp. 312-349.

Ranganathan, S.R. (1973). Productivity in library education. *Herald of Library Science.* 12, pp. 1-8.

Talawar, V.G. (2005). Library and information science education in India. Some issues In: Eds Quality education in library and information in science. 22nd IATLIS national conference 24-24 November 2005 Tiruchirapalli edited by N. Laxman Rao, and S. Sundarshan Rao: Hyderabad, IATLIS, pp. 1-3.

Wijetunge, (2006). Pradeepa conceptual model of Adaptive Evolution for the survival of Sri Lanka library schools: a prototype for South Asian library schools In: B.D., Eds. Building curriculum with a difference: A visions for LIS education in the 21st century. 23rd IATLIS National Conference, 23-25 November, 2006, Patiala, edited by C.R. Karisiddappa and B.D. Kumbhar: Dharwad IATLIS, p. 183.

4

Library Education in Pakistan: An Overview

KANWAL AMEEN

Introduction

Library Education (LE) started in Pakistan as early as 1915 at the University of the Punjab. Since then a number of developments have taken place. Presently, eight universities have been offering regular programs in LE. This paper aims to demonstrate the major developments in LE from past through present. It also aims to highlight its overall state since the beginning of the 21st century.

Beginning of LE: from Certificate Course in 1915 to DLS in 1959

The certificate program in 1915 was started at the University of the Punjab in Lahore by Asa Don Dickinson. It was the second regular university library education program after Columbia University program of Melville Dewey. Dickinson was a missionary and disciple of Dewey. Credit for earning this landmark honour goes to Professor James C.R. Ewing, an American national and the then Vice-Chancellor of University of the Punjab, who submitted a proposal to the University Syndicate to recruit "A trained librarian to thoroughly arrange the library and to train a class of young men for such work" (Qarshi, 1992). Anwar (1990-91) has thrown light on various contributions of Dickinson during his one year stay in Lahore. An important one was the writing of the first ever textbook on library education entitled *Punjab Library Primer.* It was published by the Punjab University in 1916 and is considered a classic piece of library literature.

The first batch of Dickinson's program had 30 students, who were all male—unlike the feminine image of library profession in America and Europe. Most of the students were staff members of the Punjab University (PU) Library and its affiliated colleges, having varied levels of academic qualification. Dickinson and his wife delivered lectures for a month and after that there was practical training of library work for three months. The courses they taught were as follows:

- Decimal Classification
- Cataloguing and Library Handwriting
- Book Selection and Acquisition Routines
- Library Administration

The course remained suspended for about one year after Dickinson's departure and was later revived by Mukand Lal. It was again discontinued during 1946-49 due to the independence movement in the Subcontinent and its aftermaths. Later, it was revived in 1950 and was upgraded into 'Diploma in Library Science' (DLS) in 1959 with addition of a course on "Reference Service". The duration was also extended to one year. The detail of its commencement in various universities of the country is as follows:

- University of Karachi, 1956
- University of the Punjab, Lahore, 1959
- University of Peshawar, 1962
- University of Sindh, Jamshoro, 1970
- University of Balochistan, Quetta, 1981
- Islamia University, Bahawalpur, 1983

Core Subjects with Varied Titles in DLS

Each university has had developed its own set of core and optional courses. Following are given the core courses only, which have been taught under different phases and coverage level: Classification, Cataloguing, Administration of Specific Type of Libraries, Foundation of Librarianship, Library Management and Reference Services.

DLS was a terminal course and diploma holder would get job as a librarian. After some years' practical experience, interested persons would get admitted for master's degree. Master's program would focus mainly on academic and theoretical learning of the subject rather than professional skills.

Master in Library Science (MLS)

MLS program was first started in the University of Karachi in 1962. This was a milestone step in the development of LE in the country as it enabled the introduction of MLS programs in other universities of Pakistan. Dr. Abdul Moid played instrumental role in introducing post diploma LE. He himself obtained a master's degree in library science from the University of Michigan (USA) in 1955 and Ph.D. in 1964 from the University of Illinois; he was the first Pakistani to receive the degree of Ph.D. in Library Science. Following universities started MLS programs:

- University of the Punjab, Lahore, 1974
- University of Sindh, Jamshoro, 1974
- University of Peshawar, 1982
- Islamia University, Bahawalpur, 1984
- University of Balochistan, Quetta, 1985
- Bahauddin Zakariya University, 2004

Core Subjects with Varied Names

The schools have been offering commonly following core subjects, however, with varying names and content coverage: Comparative Classification and Comparative Cataloguing; Theory of Information Science or its component; Research Methods in Librarianship; Literature or Sources of Humanities, Social Sciences, etc.; Management of Specific types of Libraries; Thesis (Optional). With the dawn of the 21st century the courses on Marketing of LIS and IT got specific attention. From 2006 all the universities have introduced the course on Marketing of LIS as an optional course, except PU where it is compulsory. The MLIS is a two-year consecutive degree program and not with termination after first year. All schools got changed their name from "Library Science" to "Library and Information Science" (MLIS) during the 1990s.

Ph.D., M. Phil in Library Science/M. Phil Leading to Ph.D.

Ph.D. in Library Science

University of Karachi again took lead in introducing Ph.D. program in 1967 following British pattern, based on dissertation writing only, without any course work. Seven students got registered but the degree was conferred upon only one candidate in 1981. After that, next degree was awarded in 1995 from the University of Karachi. Other universities also followed British system up till now. Under this method Islamia University in Bahawalpur produced 1 Ph.D., Punjab University in Lahore produced 2 and most recently Sindh University has also awarded 1 doctoral degree; all candidates were faculty members of these universities. Nonetheless, HEC is now forcing to introduce American pattern requiring course work before dissertation writing. The universities have been proceeding on this pattern to comply with HEC requirements except Karachi University. Presently, seven candidates are engaged in conducting their doctoral research at the Karachi University following the old system (Malahat, 2006) and two in Quetta (Ilyas, 2006).

M.Phil. in Library Science/M.Phil. Leading to Ph.D.

University of Sindh started M.Phil Leading to Ph.D. program in Library Science in 1981, for which no course work was required. Six students were got registered but none of them completed. University of Karachi started M.Phil. in 1985, a two-year program one year course work and thesis writing but no one applied for the admission (Ajmal, 2006). Nonetheless, three faculty members got M.Phil. degree on successful completion of their theses from the University of Balochistan in Quetta.

University of the Punjab took lead in offering first of its kind M.Phil. leading to Ph.D. program in 2005 following the HEC study plan. It comprises 2 semester course work, and on its successful completion writing of research theses. It is a terminal program and the successful candidates would be eligible for admission in Ph.D program after fulfilling its admission requirements, if they wish so. University of Sindh has also started the same program commencing from 2007.

Output of the Schools

It is estimated that more or less 450 students are produced annually through regular program by eight LIS schools in the country. There is a significant increase in the enrollment in the new century due to the commencement of evening programs in the Universities of the Punjab and Peshawar. Presently, the admissions are on merit, i.e. based on their previous academic record. However, it is observed that the students joining LIS field have a low social and academic profile. So far, in sum 855 research theses at MLIS and Ph.D. levels have been produced by all schools.

Foreign Ph.Ds.

There are faculty members and professionals who got the opportunity to get higher studies abroad, but not all of them returned. Anyway, in total 12 Pakistanis got doctoral degrees from America or England.

Role of HEC (formerly UGC) in Promoting LE in the Country

Curriculum Revisions

Library schools would revise their curriculum suiting to their indigenous conditions after years. At the same time, University Grants Commission (UGC) of Pakistan setup Curriculum Revision Committee for Library Science to formulate a uniform curriculum for all library schools. The first draft appeared in 1991. Three revisions have been produced so far by inviting experts from all schools (UGC, 1991, 1995, 2002). But, the schools have altered these courses according to their local requirements. Information science component was introduced in 1981 in UGC courses and got adopted by schools shortly. The UGC played significant role in devising these courses by coordinating meetings of experts in this regard. However, facilitating the provision of needed human and material resources to LIS schools have been a seriously neglected aspect.

Continuing Education: Workshops and Seminars for Librarians

HEC has organized several special seminars and workshops to update the knowledge of librarians. Furthermore, a number of formal meetings, workshops and seminars have been conducted under National Digital Library program for librarians throughout the country (Arif, 2006).

Role of Foreign Library Experts in Library Education

Following section briefly highlights the coming of foreign experts in the country and their role in the development of LE.

- L.C. Key, Consultant to Government of Pakistan, proposed establishment of Post Graduate Diploma Program at Universities of the Punjab and Dacca in 1956.
- Gerald M. Coble conducted a 2-month Refresher Course for working Library Staff University of Peshawar in 1956.
- Robert P. Lang, Fulbright Professor, suggested Master in Library Science at University of the Punjab in 1961.
- IDRC/UNDP mission proposed a one year Information Science Course at Qauid-e-Azam University, Islamabad in collaboration with PASTIC in 1976.
- C. Fosket, UNESCO expert, proposed PASTIC as focal point for workshop on subject such as Computer-based Information System, Resource Sharing, Computer-based Cataloguing and Audio-visual Material in 1986.
- Sarah K. Vann, Professor of emeritus, proposed Seven Courses for DLS and MLS instead of Six Courses and Practical in 1987. (Khurshid, 2000)

Conclusion

By and large, library education in the country has been based on the traditional librarianship. Curriculum revisions would aim to introduce ever emerging developments in the international librarianship, but at very slow pace. The revisions could not be implemented in letter and spirits due to lack of needed faculty and material resources. Recently, again all schools have revised their curriculum and the problems of needed human and material resources still persist. However, there is much more awareness regarding producing research by faculty and research students. Then, there is far better communication and sharing of knowledge among the faculty and professionals due to the availability of modern affordable information and communication technologies. The present Government has been paying specific attention to the promotion of higher education and digital technologies. Hence, there are opportunities for library schools and faculty members to grow by availing these opportunities offered by HEC.

References

Ajmal Khan. (2006). *Status of Library Education in Pakistan Till 1990.* An unpublished assignment presented by M.Phil. student.

Arif, Mohammad. *Library Education in Pakistan after 1990.* An unpublished assignment presented by M.Phil. student.

Anwar, Mumtaz Ali. (1990-91). The Pioneers: Asa Don Dickinson. *World Libraries,* 1(2). Retrieved December 20, 2005, from http://www.worlib.org/vol01no2/anwar_v01n2.shtml

HEC. (2002). Curriculum of Library Science for B.A/BLIS/MLIS. HEC: Islamabad.

HEC. *National Digital Library.* http://www.digitallibrary.edu.pk/

Ilyas, M. (Assistant Professor, Dept. of LIS, Quetta University). Personal Communication, July 30, 2006.

Khurshid, Anis. (2000). *Planning and management of library and information services in Pakistan.* Karachi: Library and Information Services Group.

Malahat Kaleem Sherwani (Professor and Chairperson, Dept. of LIS., Karachi University). Personal Communication, June 20, 2006.

Qarshi, Afzal Haq. (1992). *Development of Curriculum at University of the Punjab: Dickninson's contributions and afterwards.* In Sajjad ur Rehman, Abdus Sattar & Afzal Haq Qarshi (Eds.), *Library Education in Pakistan* (pp. 77-94). Lahore: PULSAA.

UGC. (1991). Curriculum in Library and Information Science for B.A/B.Sc. & B.COM. and Master of Library and Information Science. Islamabad.

UGC. (1995). *Revised Curriculum of Library and Information Science for MLIS.* Islamabad.

5

Library and Information Science Education in India through Distance Mode: Curriculum Development at Indira Gandhi National Open University

NEENA TALWAR-KANUNGO

Introduction

Terms like open distance learning, distance education, continuing professional education, correspondence courses, remote learning, and life long learning, etc. relate to a situation where the learner and the teacher interact at a distance. This mode of learning is getting momentum worldwide, especially in the developing countries. India is no exception to this trend. India with a population of more than one billion, with high level of diversity in every field, has groomed its learners to the distance mode of learning at the secondary as well as higher education levels. Indira Gandhi National Open University (IGNOU), New Delhi became the first university in imparting quality Library and Information Science (LIS) education through the open mode. This was a major step in making LIS courses available in the areas where the professional and technology-oriented education had not reached.

Brief History of LIS Education in Open Distance Learning

According to the Association of Indian Universities Handbook[1] , in total 167 universities, affiliated colleges/institutions, directorates of distance education are offering variety of LIS courses at various levels (certificate, diploma, bachelor's, master's and even doctoral). In India, out of 13 open universities 9 are offering LIS education through open mode. Open Distance Learning (ODL) system in India has emerged as a vehicle to provide LIS education to the fresh entrants as well as to the working professionals without the boundaries of age, gender, caste, location, etc. The advent of Information Communication Technology (ICT) has facilitated the learning process bridging the gap between the teacher and the taught.

LIS education through distance mode has been there for more than two decades now. Directorates of Distance Education, Institutes and Open Universities started providing the LIS education to not only the fresh entrants but also to the working professionals to enhance their qualifications, skill and professionalism. Different Open Universities, especially IGNOU, made a significant contribution by offering LIS courses at all levels to those who could not get the opportunity in the formal system to study at their own pace. Thus, the LIS education has also reached the unreached effectively. In the year 2005 IGNOU enrolled 3500 students in Bachelors in Library and Information Science (BLIS), 873 in Masters in Library and Information Science (MLIS) and 122 in Post Graduate Diploma in Library Automation and Networking (PGDLAN).[2] The data suggests that IGNOU, through the ODL mode, has made LIS education accessible to far more people than could have been envisaged by any university within the conventional system. Moreover, it just not the number, but more importantly, the quality and relevance of LIS courses and curriculum which differs from the conventional pattern quite considerably. Along with the traditional LIS courses IGNOU has incorporated a number Information Communication Technology (ICT) oriented courses. With the growing introduction of technology in the Indian libraries, demand for IGNOU courses is on the rise and this trend is likely to continue in future.

IGNOU offered the first LIS course at bachelor level (BLIS) in the year 1989, revised it in 2000, and subsequently translated the course from English to Hindi (national language) in 2003. Then the next initiative was the launching of Master's in LIS in 1994, which was revised in 2005. Taking a step further the university offered the Ph.D. programme in LIS during 2000. As Indian Libraries started undergoing the process of automation, the university introduced two courses in order to meet the challenge of training human resources in this area. Thus, it offered Post Graduate Diploma in Library Automation and Networking (PGDLAN) in 2004 and CICTAL (Certificate in ICT Application in Libraries) in 2006.[3] All these programmes were introduced following a systematic and carefully laid-out procedure. To understand this procedure, it would be worthwhile to examine the different stages, which comprise conceptual planning, designing, developing and launching of these programmes. (See the Flow Chart)

Fig. 5.1 Flow Chart of LIS Curriculum Design and Course Development Process in IGNOU

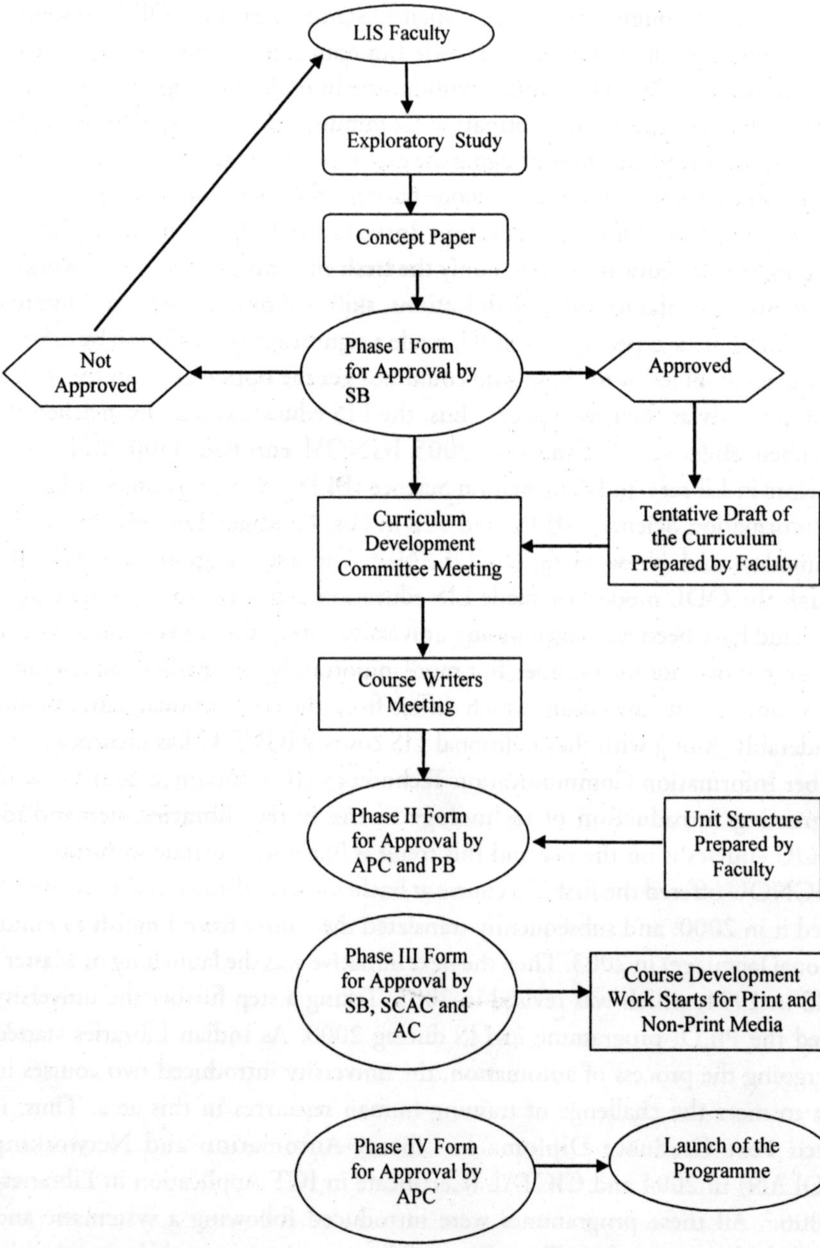

[*Note*: SB—School Board; APC—Academic Programme Committee;
PB—Planning Board; SCAC—Standing Committee of the Academic Council.]

Curriculum Design Process

Though there exists enough literature covering studies on the processes, methods and models used in the course material development, very little has been said about the designing process. Inglis (2003)[4] describes the conceptual mapping process in course designing citing two studies by Rowland (1992)[5] and Keppell (2000)[6]. Both Rowland and Keppell examine the course designing in an instructional design context. Whereas Rowland takes into consideration the role of both experts and novices in course designing, Keppell emphasizes on the interactions amongst the design committee members during the designing process. Hence, Inglis observes, that there is currently no widely accepted form of design representation for use in designing learning packages used in distance education.[7]

The STRIDE Manual[8] of IGNOU discusses many models of course development process by categorizing them into three broad areas, namely, course team models, existing material models and fast track models. The IGNOU by and large follows the course team model in the development of various courses. Course Team Model, based on the concept of teamwork, was originally developed by the United Kingdom Open University (UKOU). The course team for the IGNOU's LIS programmes included members from the faculty, external subject experts, editors, special invitees, and faculty members from distance education of IGNOU, producers, and scriptwriters. The experience of LIS faculty has shown that the course team model has helped in producing quality course materials in stipulated time frames.

The curriculum design and development is an extremely laborious and time-consuming process. In curriculum development conceptual planning and operational aspects go hand in hand. While the conceptual planning is the sphere of the concerned faculty and subject experts, the operational procedures involves seeking approvals as well as guidance from a number of university's statutory bodies, like School Board, Planning Board, Academic Programme Committee, Academic Council, Standing Committee of Academic Council. Various divisions of the university like, Planning and Development Division, Academic Coordination Division, Regional Services Division, Finance Division, and Students Registration and Evaluation Division are simultaneously consulted to determine the nature and scope of student support services necessary for the programmes.

In distance learning the curriculum design and development must adhere to the philosophy of creation of powerful and efficient learning environment that motivates the students to self-learning. Based on this the LIS faculty has adopted the following steps in the designing of curriculum for its various courses.

Steps in Curriculum Design

Course outline prepared by the teacher in conventional system can be considered as one of the forms of curriculum designing. Inglis also considers it as a "design document". On the one hand course outline gives information to the students about what is to be studied on the other it tells the teacher about the ideas and concepts to be covered in the course. Similar approach has been followed in IGNOU in designing curriculum for LIS courses. In this paper the term "programme" has been used to refer to any degree course like BLIS, MLIS or doctoral degree whereas the term "course" refers to the parts within the programme; for example, course BLIS-01: Library and Society or course MLIS-04: Information Institutions, Products and Services are parts of BLIS and MLIS programmes respectively. Any programme in this university comprises number of courses and each course has blocks on the sub-themes of the course. The block comprises the units (lessons) concerning the particular theme of the block. For instance, the revised MLIS programme consists of 13 courses (6 core courses plus one course on dissertation work and 6 elective courses. The student has an option to choose any two out of the 6 elective courses). Each course has been further subdivided into an average of 4 blocks and blocks contain an average of 4 to 5 units. The programme curriculum designing included the following steps:

Step 1

Exploratory Study: The proposer of the programme (faculty member) is responsible for the proper planning, designing and execution of the programme. Before initiating this process the faculty assesses the need, the potential learner group, the availability of infrastructure, i.e. equipment, hardware, software and resource persons for counselling, practical work and finally, the market value of the programme. Let us take the example of PGDLAN programme; the proposer of the programme before launching the said programme did the survey assessing the need for such a specialized course. Then the faculty invited the LIS experts from universities, professionals from information industry, and practicing librarians/directors from information/documentation centers in order to receive their input before starting such a specialized course. This exercise was also done to assess the job potential for PGDLAN students in the existing networked environment. The exploratory study can also be carried out by directly talking to the students or through survey method. There is another possibility that the subject expertise of an internal faculty in a particular field may prompt him/her to develop the course. Besides, sometimes the government or the industry approaches the university to start a particular course.

The LIS faculty has conducted exploratory studies[9] for almost all of its programmes to assess the following:

- User's needs, their educational and economic background;
- Employment opportunities available after completion of this programme;
- Economic viability of the programme; the number of students who will opt for this programme;
- Academic relevance of the programme.

After completing this study the Phase 1: Programme Proposal Form is filled by the proposer of the programme and submitted to the School Board for approval after the discussion in the faculty.

Step 2

Preparation of Concept Note: Once the need to launch the programme has been established the next stage is to prepare the concept note. Concept note is the foundation of the course design and development. According to the STRIDE Manual, it should contain: "the need, market demand, academic relevance, social relevance, programme objectives, target group, programme level and type, medium of study, outline of the contents, strategies to develop and deliver the programme, and meeting the objectives of the university."[10] Preparation of concept note is a responsibility of the proposer of the programme but at the same time this process is the first step in the teamwork embedded in sharing of ideas.

Once the concept note is finalized and Phase II: Programme Concept Form is filled and placed before the Academic Programme Committee (a Standing Committee of the Planning Board) for approval and subsequently to the Planning Board for ratification. On getting the confirmation from these statutory bodies, the faculty starts preparing the curriculum design of the programme. In this stage the concerned faculty works out the cost of delivery of the programme in consultation with the Planning and Development Division of the university. Approval of Phase Form--II is the indication of the approval of the programme concept in principle.

Step 3

Curriculum Design: On the basis of concept paper the faculty prepares a tentative draft of the contents for the curriculum. The draft is prepared keeping in view the existing literature on the proposed theme as well as the comparative study of the curriculums offered by different universities on this field and the latest trends. To illustrate this point, the LIS faculty of IGNOU has studied the syllabus or course structure of PGDLAN of University of Hyderabad, PGDIT (Post Graduate Diploma in Information Technology) of University of Kerala, etc.

Attending workshops or seminars on the similar field also helps in this process. Informal discussion with renowned scholars on the theme is another method of generating ideas for designing. The faculty deliberates at length on the draft syllabus pointing the weaknesses and highlighting the strengths. The proposer of the programme incorporates the suggestions and finalizes the draft document to give it a structured shape. While designing and developing the courses the faculty considers the following:

Composition of the Curriculum Design Committee

Detailed Outline of the Programme

Total credits of the programme (One credit is equivalent to 30 hours of study work by the student and for a four credit course a student has to devote 120 hours which includes reading the unit, doing self-check exercises, writing of assignments, completion of practical hours, watching and listening to A/V programmes and preparation for examinations.):

- Number and Names of the Courses,
- Number and Names of Blocks and Units,
- Practical Component,
- Identification of Course Writers,
- Themes for Audio and Video Programmes,
- Teleconference and Interactive Radio Counselling Schedule,
- Counselling,
- Budgeting,
- Evaluation Methodology,
- Delivery Mechanisms,
- Launch date of the Programme.

The Curriculum Design Committee (CDC) also known as Expert Committee has the ultimate responsibility of designing the curriculum. It consists of Director of the concerned school of studies, faculty members,[11] and external experts with the programme coordinator the convener of the committee. External are renowned professors/academics/professionals who are chosen on the basis of their expertise. This committee gives a final shape to the course design-after in depth brainstorming sessions and deliberations. The faculty works out on the recommendations of the

CDC a detailed structure of the curriculum indicating the courses, blocks, and units. It also decides the modalities of the course writers meetings, course production and delivery mechanism, A/V programmes, selects the study centers and programme work centers, and sets the deadline for the launching of the programme, etc. After this exercise Phase III: Programme Design and Detailed Programme Report Form is filled for getting approval for the programme structure and curriculum from School Board and Academic Council.

Step 4

Course Writers Meetings: Once the curriculum and other details are finalized and approved, the faculty, on the basis of detailed programme report, starts working to convene the Course Writers Meetings (CWM). Before the CWM the faculty works out on the following aspects:

- Distribution of courses to the course coordinators,
- Identification of the course writers and course editors,
- Classification of Blocks and Units,
- Designing the structure of each of the Units,
- Selection of A/V Programmes and identification of the contributors.

Deciding the Time Frame

Before the commencement of the CWM the concerned course coordinator prepares a detailed paper on the course, which comprises the introduction to the course and the contents of each of the unit along with practical component as well as the A/V media production details. For print media, the contents of every unit, according to their sequence, are discussed during the CWM. Take the example of one of the revised courses of MLIS programme, namely "MLIL-101: Information Sources, Systems and Services," which consists of four blocks covering 19 units. Each and every unit of the course in sequence was discussed at length in the CWM. For instance, discussion on the structure of one unit named "Intelligent Agents"; being a new theme, was very informative and a learning experience for the team members. As it has been already mentioned, the unit writers are subject experts and the units are allocated to them on the basis of their specialization. In the CWM these experts or unit writers come prepared on their respective units. Before finalization, the contents of each unit of a course are scrutinized at length. A time frame is given to the writers to send the unit to the course coordinator. The other details like format of the unit, remuneration, etc. are also provided to them.

Orientation: Orientation of the unit writers to write for the distance learners is very important. These print materials are not simple written documents but are meant for distance learners who are away from face to face learning. The student has to make an effort to learn herself/himself. Therefore, these materials are called Self Learning Materials (SLM) during the CWM the unit writers are oriented to write units in the interactive mode putting self-check exercises in between the sections of the unit, etc. These self-check exercises are meant to ascertain how much the learner has grasped from a particular section. The SLM helps the learners to learn without the help of the teacher. The difficult areas in a particular course are tackled during the counselling sessions organized by the Study Centers of the university for the students.

Practical Component: The advent and growth of information and communication technology (ICT) has necessitated the inclusion of this emerging area in the teaching and learning of library and information science. This will cater to meet the growing demands of the users and also train the professionals to cope with the growing demands of the users. Keeping this in view, the LIS faculty of IGNOU has incorporated IT component in all of its certificate, diploma and degree courses. The number of hours of IT exposure, hands on computers, etc., are decided at the curriculum designing stage, depending on the nature of the course and availability of infrastructure and resource persons. The LIS faculty has made compulsory 15 hours of practical in one of the courses of BLIS Degree, namely, "BLIS-07: Information Technology: Basics" and for MLIS programme approximately 100 hours for four courses.[12] As PGDLAN is a programme with a strong IT component, the learners of this programme are required to do more than 380 hours of practical work. For CICTAL the students are required to do 144 hours of practical work to successfully complete the programme.

Regional Centers, Study Centers, Tele Learning Centers and Work Centers or Specific Programme Centers of the university play a very crucial role in imparting the required practical learning to the students. The LIS faculty has made it mandatory to complete the practical component to pass any particular programme. The skills imparted through the practical component help the learners to work in a technology-oriented environment. According to Computer Industry Almanac Press Release, the PC penetration in India is close to 2 per cent and Internet usage is approximately 5 per cent and also indicated that PC and Internet penetration and usage will be on the higher side in the case of populous and developing countries.[13] The data suggests that in future there is a growing need for technology-oriented courses in LIS discipline, which will cater to the growing demand for such category of jobs. Not many traditional universities in India are offering courses suitable for professionals working in the networked environment. IGNOU has taken the initiative and has recognized the demand of learners by offering courses like PGDLAN and CICTAL, thereby bridging the gap between demand and supply of manpower in network society.

Course Development Process

Course development process includes both the print and the non-print media.

(a) Print Media

Self-learning material is the base of open distance learning system. Though the arrival of multi media in the ODL system has greatly facilitated the learning process, it has not yet replaced the print media.

Writing and Editing Work: In Course Writers Meeting the contents and the contributors are decided, and accordingly, the units along with the instructions are sent to the unit writer by the course coordinator. After the receipt of the units the course coordinator goes through them to ensure that the contents confirm to the ones approved by the CWM. Then the units are formatted according to distance mode format. The missing points like incomplete references, placements of tables and graphics, illustrations at the right places, elaboration of key words are taken care of by the course coordinator. The faculty sometimes receives a unit in the shape of an academic note from the writer, not written according to the format of distance mode. In such a situation the faculty transforms the academic note into a full unit. The faculty also ensures that units do not contain factual errors and nothing is lifted from any source without proper acknowledgment.

Once the faculty is satisfied with a unit in its totality, then it is sent for subject editing. The editor edits the unit from the angle of academic content. There are cases when the editor transforms a unit entirely and in some cases even rewrites the unit. At times, the editor requests the unit writer to elaborate certain points and cite more examples to make the learning for the students easy. To illustrate this, a number of examples were added during editing stage in some practical oriented courses in LIS, like Library Classification Practice and Library Cataloguing Practice. The editor's job is very responsible and accountable. If some error (factual and otherwise) goes unchecked, it is the combined responsibility of the author, editor, writer and the course coordinator.

The edited copies of the units come back to the faculty. The faculty reads them thoroughly and again contact the editor or even the author to clarify any such thing, which may seems unclear or unintelligible for the students. Till the units are finalized for printing the faculty remains in constant touch with the author and the editor. The emergence of the Internet and the facility of e-mail and chatting have facilitated the instant communication.

Language Editing Work: The corrections and suggestions are incorporated in the units of the course and the final edited copy becomes ready for the language editing. The university has its own language-editing cell. During the language editing the editor calls for one or two sessions with the respective course coordinator for clarifications. As we know that the language editor is not the LIS subject expert, s/he may require certain clarifications for proper editing. Corrections after the language editing are incorporated by the concerned faculty. The course coordinator reads all the units once again from the point of view of academic content, formatting, language editing, etc. At this time any correction, suggestion could be taken care of; but once it is printed nothing can be done till the printed copies are exhausted.[14] That's why the faculty ensures that the units are complete and error-free in all respects. The faculty also reads the final proofs and gives order for printing. At this stage the Phase IV: Programme Launch Approval Form is filled and placed before Academic Programme Committee for getting approval to launch the programme. The content of this form indicate that the faculty is ready with the course materials along with A/V programmes for launch of the programme. And various divisions of the university are also ready for providing necessary support services for the implementation of the programme.

Once the programme is launched the various divisions of the university take over their tasks. The advertisement of the programme, admission, and material distribution, conduct of examination and declaration of results are some of the activities of the respective divisions of the university.

Translation Work: The faculty of LIS translated the entire BLIS courses into Hindi language and launched it in 2003. The great demand from the north and central India and the university's policy were the chief driving forces to produce the Hindi version of this very popular programme[15] of the university. The faculty called it as transcreation work. It means that the translator, who is a subject expert in the case of BLIS translation, can expand any given concept with the help of examples, etc. in Hindi language as against in the translation work where the translator is bound by the boundaries of the text given to her/him for translation. Before transcreation work was actually assigned to the subject experts, who have command in national language, the LIS faculty prepared the "Glossary of Terms in Library and Information Science (English-Hindi)" in the year 1999. Preparation of Glossary was the first step in transcreation. The terms in the English version of BLIS courses were chosen for translation and these English terms were given appropriate Hindi equivalent in the Terminology Preparation Committee meeting. This committee was comprised LIS subject experts with command in national language. This glossary is the compilation of finalized Hindi translation of English

LIS related terms. At the time of transcreation this Glossary was given to the transcreator to maintain uniformity in the use of Hindi terms in the print material. All the other processes in relation to course development, from unit writing to printing, are adhered to in the transcreation process.

Revision Work: As the policy every course or programme of the university is supposed to be revised after five years of its launch. The need for revision is determined by the faculty and sometimes feedback from learners and experts also plays a role in it. The faculty, from time to time, reviews its courses as well as A/V programmes for the purpose of revision. The faculty of LIS has the experience of revision of its two major programmes BLIS and MLIS. The concerned course coordinators took the responsibility for revision of their respective courses. Each course in both the programmes was taken individually to see the areas for revision. Each course coordinator prepared the concept paper of their courses explaining the need for the revision; suggestions with regard to additions and deletions of units were also placed before the faculty meeting. After discussing all the courses of BLIS programme, the faculty decided to introduce a major revision for the course BLIS-07: Information Technology: Basics. The remaining courses of the said programme were revised wherever needed. Accordingly, a draft paper was prepared by the programme coordinator stating the purpose of revision, level of revision of various courses and the budget required for it. In the case of MLIS revision the faculty merged the two originally offered courses (MLIS-02: Information Systems and Programmes and MLIS-04: Information Institutions, Products and Services) into a new course, entitled MLII-101: Information Sources, Systems and Services and split an existing course MLIS-06: Information Technology into two courses, namely MLII-103: Fundamentals of Information Communication Technologies and MLII-104: Information Communication Technologies-Applications.

The faculty also introduced a new core course on dissertation writing. Through this course students will learn how to initiate research work and it will also expose students to writing skills. The revision of both the programmes was considered to be a major revision. Phase Zero Form for revision is to be filled and placed before the School Board and Academic Council for approval. After getting the approval from these bodies the revision work starts by the respective course coordinators. The same course development process has been followed in the revision of courses. As in any new course, the course coordinator receives the freshly written units, but in the case of revision the revised as well as freshly written units are received. The revised units are those units, which are based on the earlier written units of the course(s). In this case the concerned course coordinator has to read the revised units along with the original unit. Rest of the procedures is the same.

(b) Non-Print Media

Within the framework of the curriculum, the CDC members suggest the topics for A/V programmes. The committee members along with the faculty finalize the areas to be covered in non-print media. According to IGNOU norm a four-credit course should have at least one video and two audio programmes. The number can be more or less depending on the nature of the course. The SRIDE Manual[16] has identified four approaches to integrate the A/V media with the print media. The approaches are complementary, integrated, supplementary and independent media approaches. For the LIS courses the faculty has followed supplementary media approach and produced such programmes, which perform supplementary role in instructional pattern of the ODL system. For example, in the BLIS programme the faculty has produced series of videos on classification systems and cataloguing practices. These videos supplement the print material covering the courses BLIS-03P: Library Classification Practice and BLIS-04P: Library Cataloguing Practice. The contents of the videos overlap the print material; hence, the students who cannot access the A/V programmes are not at a loss. These programmes have enhanced the practical skills of the distance learners.

Development Procedure

Production of A/V programme is a teamwork. Once the team members (course and content coordinator, producer, script writer) finalize the theme to be produced the actual work starts. Planning work for A/V is the same; difference comes at the stage of production and presentation.

Initial Stage: *Content Note*: Producer and content coordinator discuss the theme and the way to it would be presented. The content note is prepared first providing the outline of the contents to be included in the programme, programme name, course code and name, block number and name and information regarding the team members. This note is a guiding tool and is referred to at various stages of production.

Once the theme is decided the next step is to decide the format of the programme. The programme can be studio-based, or documentary-type, or interview-based. The LIS faculty has used all these methods. For example, the video on the "Delhi Public Library (DPL)" is a documentary-based programme where the functioning, collection and services of the DPL has been shown with a background commentary explaining the visuals. Series of video programmes on classification and cataloguing practices are studio-based demonstrating the actual classification and cataloguing of documents step by step. These programmes are very much in demand as they teach students the fundamental skills of classification and cataloguing.

Detailed Academic Note is prepared on the basis of the content note. In this note the details with proper references for graphics, pictures or clips are given. It indicates the exact places to show graphics, etc. in the video programme.

Script Writing: Script can be written by the producer or by the faculty member or by some external expert. The ultimate responsibility lies with the producer, but in the case of some of the LIS video programmes the faculty took the initiative of not only writing but also presenting the programmes. Apart from the contents the script demands the details like shots, camera angels, and lighting. Once the script is finalized for production the content coordinator reviews it.

Production Stage: Apart from the academics, the technicians, cameraman and equipments are required in the production stage. According to the STRIDE Manual the producer ensures the booking of the studio, budget, experts, permission to shoot outdoor location, recording details, set design, graphics, editing, etc.

Editing: After the shooting process is over the producer and the content coordinator sit at the editing table to see the logical flow of the contents, placements of the graphics, references, and places, and the names of the contributors.

Preview: Next comes the stage of previewing. The rough cut of the programme is shown to the faculty and the concerned audiences for approval. They can suggest, criticize the programme and point out factual mistakes, if any. At this stage some of the corrections can be carried out and some can be noted down for future references and revision. But in the case of factual errors they must be taken care of by the producer as well as the content coordinator.

When it gets approval after the incorporation of suggestions the video programme is ready for duplication and distribution for use at study centers or for telecasting. Radio counselling and interactive (two-way video and audio) teaching through the EDUSAT[17] is the other methods used for enhancing and supplementing the knowledge needs of the learners.

Conclusion

This paper demonstrated that the designing and development of LIS programmes for the distance learners are a tedious task wherein various steps and processes are to be meticulously followed. Adoption of such processes has helped in developing quality teaching and learning materials in IGNOU which are not only being used in the Open Distance Mode but are found also to be in great demand in the conventional LIS education system.

IGNOU has proved that the absence of the teacher in imparting LIS education is not a hindrance. The university has rather innovatively and meticulously used multimedia and ICT along with the satellite communication in providing LIS education to distance learners even to the remotest and underdeveloped regions. However, there is a critical observation that the open universities in India are producing more number of LIS professionals than the requirement of the job market.[18] Such a fear may not be baseless, but one would hardly disagree that the Open Distance Learning in India has democratized the professional education in which the IGNOU plays a stellar role. The types of courses it has introduced in LIS discipline and the number of students it has attracted shows the success of the university in revolutionizing the LIS education in ODL environment.

Notes

1. Association of Indian Universities, (2004). *Handbook on Library and Information Science* 2004. AIU: New Delhi.
2. Indira Gandhi National Open University, (2005). Vice-Chancellor's Report. IGNOU: New Delhi.
3. For details about the curriculum of all the LIS courses visit the website at: http://www.ignou.ac.in
4. Inglis, Alistair, (2003). Facilitating team-based course designing with conceptual mapping. *Distance Education*. 24, 2; 247-263.
5. Rowland, G., (1992). What do instructional designers actually do? An initial investigation of expert practice. *Performance Development Quarterly*.5,2; 65-86.
6. Keppell, G., Principles at the heart of an instructional designer: subject matter expert interaction. In: R. Sims and others, (Eds). Learning to choose—choosing to learn. Proceedings of 17th Annual Conference of Australasian Society for Computers in Learning in Tertiary Education.Coffs Harbour: NSW. pp. 317-326.
7. Inglis, Alistair. Facilitating team-based course designing with conceptual mapping. *Distance Education, op cit.*
8. Indira Gandhi National Open University, (2006). STRIDE. Manual for Programme and Course Coordinators. IGNOU: New Delhi. pp. 34-37.
9. *Ibid.*, p. 12.
10. *Ibid.*, p. 14.
11. Sometimes, the invitation is extended to the members of other faculties of IGNOU; for instance, in case of PGDLAN the faculty members of the School of Computer and Information Science were invited to give their input for this course.
12. Courses on Information Sources, Systems and Services, Information Processing and Retrieval. Fundamentals of Information Communication Technologies and Information Communication Technologies-Applications.
13. Computer Industry Almanac Press Release. (May 26, 2006) Available at http://www.c-i-a.com/pro506.htm and Computer Industry Almanac Press Release, (January 4, 2006), Available at http://www.c-i-a.com/pro106.htm
14. However, in case of errors in the printed units, corrigendum can be added.
15. An average of 3000 students per year take admission in this programme.
16. Indira Gandhi National Open University (2006). STRIDE. Manual. *op.cit.*, p. 55.

17. It is India's first satellite dedicated to education.
18. Jeeven, V.K.J., Education for library and information science on distance mode in India: A critique. *Librarian Career Development.* 7,2; 1999; 7.

References

Association of Indian Universities (AIU), (2004). *Handbook on library and information science.* AIU: New Delhi.

Bravo, Blanca Rodriguez, (2005). Audiovisual and multimedia content in the curriculum for librarianship studies at the University of Leon in Spain. *IFLA Journal.* 31, 3; pp. 234-40.

Clyde, Laurel A., (1991). Steps in the design and development of distance learning courses. In: Woolls (Blanche), Ed. *Continuing professional education: An IFLA guidebook.* (IFLA publications no.55). Saur: London. pp. 23-34.

Gupta, D.K., and Ghosh, S.B., (2002). Opportunities and strategies for continuing professional education in India through distance mode. In: Ward, Patricia Layzell, Ed. *Continuing professional education for information society.* (IFLA Publications no.100). Saur: Mnuchen. pp. 49-60.

Indira Gandhi National Open University, Staff Training and Research Institute of Distance Education (STRIDE), (2006). *Manual for programme and course coordinators.* IGNOU: New Delhi.

Indira Gandhi National Open University, (2005). *IGNOU profile.* IGNOU: New Delhi.

Indira Gandhi National Open University, (2006). *BLIS programme guide.* IGNOU: New Delhi.

Indira Gandhi National Open University, (2006). *MLIS programme guide.* IGNOU: New Delhi.

Indira Gandhi National Open University, (2006). *PGDLAN programme guide.* IGNOU: New Delhi.

Indira Gandhi National Open University, (2005). *Vice–Chancellor's Report.* IGNOU: New Delhi.

Inglis, Alistair. *Facilitating team-based course designing with conceptual mapping.* Distance Education. 24, 2: 2003: 247-263.

Jeeven, V.K.J., *Education for library and information science on distance mode in India: A critique.* Librarian Career Development. 7, 2; 1999; 7.

Karisidappa, C.R., Library and information science curriculum for the developing countries. World Library and Information Congress: 70th IFLA General Conference and Council. 22-27 August 2004, Buenos Airs, Argentina. See http://www.ifla.org/ivifla70/prog04.htm

Mynott, Glen and others. A distance learning course in research skills for public librarians—An evaluation. *New Library World.* 101, 1159: 2000: 315-324.

Tam, Maureen. Constructivism, instructional design, and technology: Implications for transforming distance learning. *Educational Technology and Society.* 3, 22; 2000. See http://ifets.ieee.org/periodical/vol_2_2000/tam.htm

Wang, Xuemi and others. Design issues in a cross-institutional collaboration on a distance education course. *Distance Education.* 26, 3: 2005: 405-423.

6

Development of Need Based Library and Information Science Curriculum: Emerging Global Trends, Opportunities and Challenges

KSHEMA PRAKASH and K. SANTI SWARUP

Introduction

It is said that change is the only phenomenon that is constant. This irony however has more implications to it as one of the greatest challenges faced by mankind is how to cope with the change. The probable solution to it is to evolve and develop oneself to adapt to such a change.

As knowledge becomes more valuable, there is a growing need to manage it effectively to capture its full benefit. In order to be a part of successful knowledge society, the available knowledge should be effectively distributed and managed. This is possible only by means of proper infrastructure which allows transferring or sharing of best practices across the entities leading to sound knowledge management. Without this process, the existing critical knowledge cannot be found in time. Lessons are learned individually by each entity instead of sharing others' experiences and benefiting from them. Knowledge is of little value if it cannot be found when required. At the same time, 're-inventing the wheel' whenever a new project starts does not make sense. Unless the existing knowledge is managed in an organized manner, one cannot keep up with the cutthroat competition.

IT in a Knowledge Era has a strong impact on library and information professionals. Technology being the driving factor for transformation, it has altered how services are provided, research is conducted, and learning occurs. With pin-pointed emphasis to libraries, digital technology has dramatically changed print-on-paper library model that has been mainstay of higher education and research. Computer based services have gained momentum in India after the year 1992. Today, users depend less on traditional libraries and information services to meet their needs. The new technologies include, Digital Libraries and Institutional Repositories which are a spin off from the e-publishing and open access concepts, on-line databases, knowledge bases, subject portals which are the resultants of high speed Internet and World Wide Web, e-learning tools, viz., blogs, vlogs, podcasts, vidcasts, and online courses through content management systems like Blackboard, Desire, Learn, Moodle, Angel etc. Hence, it is time that libraries must learn to adopt by appropriately modifying, supplementing, and inventing services while maintaining the core values so important to their role at the centre of the institution. This requires certain core competencies that have to be possessed by the library and information professional, suitable to the modern day needs. In a nutshell, the mission of a library and information professional—providing excellent information service to patrons—with special emphasis on right information at the right time—has added several new dimensions to this task. It also indicates that with the changing times, employer expectations have also soared high. The examples discussed below give a broad overview of changing employer expectations.

As the call for Next Generation Librarian at Wayne State University System (2006) states in their position purpose "...currently seeking a dynamic, creative, and self-directed individual to join our talented team of librarians, web developers, multimedia specialists, instructional designers, and systems administrators. As the "Next Gen Librarian" you will play a leading role in exploring, implementing and supporting transformative technologies that will enhance access to our electronic resources and services."

According to them, the newly created position's essential duties will be to provide leadership and vision for "transformative technologies" in the provision of library resources and services. The incumbent is expected to create communication venues and distribute content *via* digital tools such as blogs and wikis for the library system website; Develop and deliver library instruction through podcasts and multimedia webcasts; promote community *via* new technologies within the library and virtually via IM and other emerging communication mechanisms; enhance their Library System web presence with current content and methods for distribution such as RSS; investigate and implement new technologies that may enhance the Library System's web presence; provide training and support for other librarians on new technologies; maintain currency in information technology, librarianship, and instructional design; collaborate with other librarians to develop shared resources in support of the libraries' mission and strategic directions; collaborate with other librarians to perform outreach and communicate information about the Libraries' online resources and services to clients; participate positively as a member of working groups and teams to develop/implement policies and procedures, facilitate decision-making, resolve problems, implement assigned projects, improve customer service and ensure smooth delivery of services; communicate effectively and positively with unit management, with colleagues in other units and with colleagues within the unit to provide effective and efficient services that meet customer needs and promote a positive team environment; generate funding through grant and foundation proposals; and perform other duties typically assigned to librarians in Public Services (virtual reference, instruction, etc.).

In such a multi tasking environment a library and information professional has to have a strong IT base coupled with sound management and leadership skills. This is the case of global level. To substantiate the fact that India is also in a position to leap-frog into a knowledge society, taking a look at the requirements identified by the British Council, India for the position of Head, Library Network (India and Sri Lanka) called for (2006).

"...will be responsible for leadership of the British Council's network of 13 libraries in India and Sri Lanka,.... As a part of the senior management team, this post will have an exciting and challenging role in developing the libraries for the future—continuously updating their services to make them relevant and valuable to their members and deploying new technologies where appropriate."

Consequent upon the development and use of new technology several changes have been brought in the library and information services. The information professional is now expected to possess an all new set of skills to handle the digitized environment. The challenge is how a library and information professional can adapt to digital environment in order to effectively and efficiently deliver services and enhance performance. Many of the changes are acceptable to the library and information professionals, however, there may be some opposition against its use due to lack of perception regarding its advantages, frustration caused in using software, lack of proper infrastructural facilities, lack of interest in some professionals, etc. Thus, a study on the challenges faced by the present library and information professionals and identification of suitable measures to overcome such issues becomes paramount at this juncture.

Significance and Need of the Study

Kathleen McGown's research work "Knowledge Management in the Twenty First Century: The Role of the Academic Librarian" (2000) examined the book paradigm in the libraries and the shift towards digital paradigm within the academic library.

She used the paradigm model developed by Thomas Kuhn, the science historian, in his book: *The Structure of Scientific Revolutions*, where he observed that a paradigm shift occurs whenever a new analytic framework changes the understanding of how a system operates. Kuhn's hypothesis of paradigm shift has become influential beyond the worlds of pure science and academia. McGown states that in librarianship, the parameters and rules are changing due to this paradigm shift and the basic assumptions of service-oriented profession are being revised. So, in order to survive and sustain, be it an individual or an organization, there is every need to understand and adapt to the new paradigms. The truth of we being in the midst of unparalleled change still holds. We—means society in a generic sense and—We—means library and information professionals in a more specific sense. Many aspects of the knowledge era are transforming the role of librarians and other library staff. The most compelling of these includes the information explosion and new tools for information access. In this age of great change in information formats, delivery models, and technologies, an important new role emerges for the library and information professional. Collaborating broadly with other information professionals and the faculty, the librarian is evolving from an information organizer and provider seated at a desk, to an active participant in the instructional and research processes. Today's educational milieu enables librarian and the user to work together, wherever each may be located; physical proximity is no longer essential. As librarians concentrate their efforts on designing and implementing services, paraprofessionals and staff specializing in particular functions will assume the responsibility for the delivery of these services.

Due to the transformations in the working environment, the traditional librarian has slowly slipped into a new role with an enhanced attitude. Technology has become the driving change across the entire range of library responsibilities also. In any library setup we have an acquisitions librarian, serials librarian, reference librarian, librarian-technical services and systems support professional. In a large setup depending upon the parent organization and the library collection the number of information professionals may vary. Sometimes it might be one man show also. But the tasks are the same. Earlier acquisitions and serials librarians used to procure material in traditional fashion, today still select and purchase material but through comparatively new methods, viz. online ordering and virtual purchasing through e-commerce procedures. Not only that but they also deal with many "access without ownership" issues involving leased electronic databases, fulltext journal articles and other services that are acquired only virtually. Cataloguers are moving into new roles, they now process not only books but also poly media/multi format documents. Cataloguers today create records that accommodate multiple means of accessing a particular resource. Now to supplement MARC, Meta data and Meta tag system has evolved and cataloguing the Internet itself is a task that has fallen to librarians. Reference librarians have recently been experiencing a double jeopardy. While continuing to serve patrons in the library, many reference librarians are now supporting a growing clientele of remote access patrons. Also the services, viz. Inter Library Loan and Document Delivery have transformed to Electronic Document Delivery and Resource Sharing through networks *via* e-mail and Internet.

With literature growing in polymorphic formats, blogs, wikis, podcasts of lectures etc. are gearing importance. Blogs are one of the emerging e-learning tools today. Blogs have empowered people to share important information over the Internet very easily. Instructional blogging operates as a knowledge-centered instructional tool. In this model the instructor involves students in research activities, engages them in discussions with practitioners, and leads them through developmental concepts of the discipline's knowledge domain. Stuart Glogoff's course content (2005), in-fact his entire instructional modules are available through his blog and lectures are podcasted according to specific schedules. Students are encouraged to maintain their own blogs for online discussions and submission of assignments. Because of their public nature, blogs can be used as a directive learning tool to provide students with equal access to important information, to expand students' understanding of specific issues, and to direct students to explore additional material, opines Glogoff.

Since information is a key resource for the economic, socio-cultural and political development of a nation, the onus is on—Right Information to the Right Customer at Right Time and Right Cost. This can be achieved successfully through sound strategic management of information services.

It means the Library and Information Professional is expected to possess management, business and marketing skills, along with the advanced technological skills surpassing the traditional skills. Marigold Cleeve (1994) is of opinion that a librarian of the future will require Interpersonal Skills, Marketing Skills, Negotiating Skills, Business Skills, Networking Skills, Flexibility, need to be inventive, combining if possible linear and lateral thinking methods with an easy transfer from one to the other, being both reactive to changing alignments in team formations, and proactive in leading them, constantly updating and upgrading knowledge and possess better language skills.

Apart from this, technology also plays an important role in the above context. According to Suliman Al-Hawamdeh (2002), technology facilitates the process of transmitting and exchanging information. Computer mediated communication such as email, tele-conferencing etc., help to maintain continuity and connection between conversations, especially for those in different locations. Collaborative tools enable the professionals of an organization to work together and work virtually regardless of the geographical location. Technology can also be used to catalogue expertise of organizational members and as a result facilitating access to the right people and enhancing knowledge sharing. Especially, in context of library and information centres, technological advancement forms an integral part of developmental programmes in this new era. Web technology allows organizations to build Web and knowledge portals that can handle substantial amount of information and make it accessible to users anywhere anytime.

Thus this situation justifies the purpose of the study as to how an information professional succeeds with his skills in the new dawn and plans meticulously for rendering excellent service. The main purpose of this research is to study what new set of skills is required by a library and information professional in this transformed environment. Further it also aims to examine how well the information professionals are able to adapt and articulate their knowledge so as to contribute their chunk towards the interests of the parent organization.

Existing Literature Survey

A study of the subject interests of LIS students in Singapore was carried out by Khoo, C. *et al.* (2004) via a questionnaire survey of students and graduates of the Master of Science (M.Sc.) information studies program at the Nanyang Technological University, Singapore, as well as survey of applications to the program. Cluster analysis was performed on the questionnaire data. The respondents were clustered based on the elective subjects that they selected in the questionnaires. For both sets of data, two distinct clusters were found—a library-oriented cluster and an information technology (IT)/information management-oriented cluster. In each cluster, further sub-clusters were found that correspond to known specializations in the field. An analysis of the relationship between the clusters and the areas of specialization selected by respondents indicated some ways of improving the areas of specialization defined in the M.Sc. program. The cluster analyses were found to yield useful results and provided a better understanding of the students' interests and how the interests were structured.

Amin, S. (2003) has examined the library and information education in three countries, viz. the US, the UK and India. He made a comparative study of existing education and training facilities for library professionals by considering different attributes such as, the history and development of LIS education in the three countries, their structure, curriculum, teaching techniques and evaluation and accreditation. He observes that all the three countries have different approaches to various courses of LIS. However, the curriculum is influenced by a number of factors including the academic level of the programme and its length, requirements of the accrediting professional association, and the ethos of the parent educational institution etc. He also notes that the teaching and evaluation techniques are more or less similar in all the three countries. After examining all these factors, meeting local needs is paramount, says Amin.

Singh, S.P. (2003) studied the problems of library ana information science education in India. As per her data, in India, as many as 85 universities and 32 colleges and institutions affiliated to universities are offering regular courses, whereas 27 universities are conducting LIS courses through distance education. Different levels of LIS programmes in India are:

(a) Certificate course in LIS
(b) Under-graduate diploma in LIS
(c) Bachelors in LIS
(d) Post Graduate Diploma in Library Automation and Networking
(e) Masters in LIS
(f) Associateship in LIS
(g) M.Phil. in LIS
(h) Ph.D. in LIS, and
(j) D.Litt. in LIS
(h) *Other programmes*—Advanced Training Course in Information Systems Management and Technology.

However, lack of proper accreditation, mushrooming library schools and falling standards, inadequate faculty strength in terms of quantity as well as quality, lack of library facilities, IT laboratories and ICT facilities in order to provide hands-on experience to students are the present day problems of LIS courses in India. Upon her detailed study she concludes that there is a strong need for a national accreditation body which will apply rigorous parameters to help establish quality control in LIS courses.

Karisiddappa (2004) discusses the pros and cons of LIS education scenario in the developing countries and stresses on the need for a model curriculum. He suggests a modular approach in formulation of the Model Syllabi. He was one of the main contributors to the UGC model curriculum developed for LIS education in India which was released in the year 2001 by UCG, India. After going through a process of deliberation, on the subject and on observing the needs of the departments, the task of structuring the curriculum was so suited, the adoption by different departments of LIS with varying levels of infrastructure facilities prevailing in the country.

Jestin and Parameshwari (2002) suggest resource sharing, networking, developing soft skills and active initiatives from professional associations as probable solutions to overcome the challenges faced by the library and information professionals in India in the new millennium. They also opine that good technical;

IT skills coupled with managerial skills are a must for the future library and information professionals to sustain in their field.

Objectives of the Study

The study is expected to achieve the following objectives:

- To study the challenges faced by Library and Information Professionals in academic and research libraries in India.
- To identify measures for overcoming the challenges.

Collection of Data and Methodology

Brody, F.E. (2001) employed a two-fold web survey method to study the status and practices of the top quartile of Association of Research Libraries while investigating the transitional situation from print collections to electronic formats.

A Delphi study was undertaken by Harer, J.B. (2001) that identified the critical processes and performance measures of quality that can serve as a framework for academic libraries that intend to implement continuous quality improvement programmes.

Sharma, J. (2001) had employed survey method by administering self-rating questionnaires at four point Likert Scale in his research work which speaks about the professional competencies, employer expectations and the curriculum for library and information science education in India.

Generally library and information centres are broadly classified into three categories, viz. Academic Libraries, Research/Special Libraries and Public Libraries. Academic Libraries are those which are attached to academic institutions such as schools, colleges, universities etc. Research/Special Libraries are those which are attached to research organizations, industries, corporate offices or centres of specializations. Public libraries are those libraries that have been established for general public use. They may be city level, district level, state level or national libraries established by government or by any other libraries meant for general public use.

Target of the study were research libraries and academic libraries at university level because these are the libraries which have experienced the techno-sweep due to the nature and organizational objectives of their parent organizations, in India. The transition from books to bytes, i.e. form print to digitized formats is evident in these libraries. With an assumption that the professionals working presently must have been facing certain challenges due to the transition in terms of knowledge and skills, the respondents were targeted from these sectors.

In this study, the primary data was collected from a randomly selected heterogeneous sample of LIS professionals working in academic and research sectors in India, with the help of Directory of Selected Libraries in India (2003). A total of about 300 questionnaires were sent to these professionals by post and e-mail, and other contacts. A response of 47 valid questionnaires was received. The questionnaire has two parts. In the first part, the challenges faced by library and information professionals were graded using Likert scale. The data collected form the questionnaires in this part are analyzed using factor analysis. Factor analysis is used to identify the important combination of challenges faced by the library and information professionals in their jobs.

The second part consisted of an open-ended question relating to measures for a smooth transition, i.e. towards accepting change and transformation from traditional approach to a modern approach of LIS profession. Content analysis was carried out to find out significant measures.

Data Charateristics

The sample data is collected from 47 respondents across India. The actual and proposed sample size is 100 respondents. Out of proposed 100 sample size, only 47 valid responses were received.

Librarywise distribution: The libraries were categorized into two groups viz., academic and research libraries.

Table 6.1

Library type	Size	Frequency %
Academic—A	29	61.7
Research—R	18	38.3
Total	47	100.0

Responses of 29 (61.7%) were from academic libraries and 18 (38.3%) were from research libraries.

Agewise distribution: The age of respondents was categorized into two classes. 25-40 years category is for young professionals, whereas 41-60 is for senior professionals. The agewise distribution is given below.

Table 6.2

Age group	Size	Frequency %
25-40	36	76.6
41-60	11	23.4
Total	47	100.0

The statistics show that 76.6 per cent respondents are in the age group of 25-40 and 23.4 per cent respondents are in the age group of 41-60 years.

Qualification wisedistribution: The qualifications are classified into four levels as follows:

(1) B.LIS—Bachelors in library and information science with a master's degree in any other subject.
(2) M.LIS—Masters in library and information science with or without any other master's degree.
(3) M.Phil.—Master of philosophy in library and information science.
(4) Ph.D.—Doctorate in library and information science.

The distribution table is given below:

Table 6.3

Qualification	Size	Frequency (%)
B.LIS	1	2.1
M.LIS	23	48.9
M. Phil	2	4.5
Ph.D.	21	44.6
Total	47	100.0

According to the above results, 2.1 per cent of respondents carry a bachelor's degree in Library and Information Science with a master's degree in some other subject. 48.9 per cent of respondents possess a master's degree in Library and Information Science with or without another masters degree. 4.5 per cent respondents are master of Philosophy in Library and Information Science. Whereas 44.6 per cent of respondents hold doctorate in library and information science.

Sexwise Distribution

Table 6.4

Sex	Size	Frequency %
Female (F)	7	14.9
Male (M)	40	85.1
Total	47	100.0

Out of 47 respondents 7 were women and 40 were men. That corresponds to 14.9 per cent of female respondents whereas male respondents were as much as 85.1 per cent.

Challenges faced by Library and Information Professionals in the present day situation

The responses given by the library and information professionals in the first part of the questionnaire designed for the survey, challenges faced by the professionals, are summarized below. For convenience, the questions have been coded as C1, C2, C3....C10.

The challenge based on information technology being a key driver for transformation of library and information centers.

C1

	Weight Given	Frequency	Per cent	Valid Per cent	Cumulative Per cent
Valid	Strongly Agree-1	36	76.6	76.6	76.6
	Agree-2	10	21.3	21.3	97.9
	Cannot Say-3	1	2.1	2.1	100.0
	Disagree-4	0	0.0	0.0	0.0
	Strongly Disagree-5	0	0.0	0.0	0.0
	Total	47	100.0	100.0	

From 46 (97.9%) responses generated, for weights 1and 2, indicate that the professionals agree that information technology has been a key driver for transformation in library and information centers.

The challenge of information explosion to libraries

C2

	Weights Given	Frequency	Per cent	Valid Per cent	Cumulative Per cent
Valid	Strongly Agree-1	23	48.9	48.9	48.9
	Agree-2	22	46.8	46.8	95.7
	Cannot Say-3	0	0.0	0.0	0.0
	Disagree-4	2	4.3	4.3	100.0
	Strongly Disagree-5	0	0.0	0.0	0.0
	Total	47	100.0	100.0	

From 45 (95.7%) responses generated, for weights 1 and 2, indicate that the librarians consider information explosion as a serious problem.

The challenge of internet revolution.

C3

	Weight Given	Frequency	Per cent	Valid Per cent	Cumulative Per cent
Valid	Strongly Agree-1	13	27.7	27.7	27.7
	Agree-2	19	40.4	40.4	68.1
	Cannot Say-3	2	4.3	4.3	72.3
	Disagree-4	9	19.1	19.1	91.5
	Strongly Disagree-5	4	8.5	8.5	100.0
	Total	47	100.0	100.0	

From 32 (68.1%) responses generated for weights 1 and 2, indicate that the professionals feel internet revolution is challenging their profession.

Flexibility, Openness and Creativity

C4

	Weight Given	Frequency	Per cent	Valid Per cent	Cumulative Per cent
Valid	Strongly Agree-1	31	66.0	66.0	66.0
	Agree-2	14	29.8	29.8	95.7
	Cannot Say-3	2	4.3	4.3	100.0
	Disagree-4	0	0.0	0.0	0.0
	Strongly Disagree-5	0	0.0	0.0	0.0
	Total	47	100.0	100.0	

Forty-five (95.7%) responses generated for weights 1 and 2, indicate that the library and information professionals need to be flexible, open to changes and also become inventive and creative in order to have a smooth transition from traditional to modern.

Personal Attributes

C5

	Weight Given	Frequency	Per cent	Valid Per cent	Cumulative Per cent
Valid	Strongly Agree-1	29	61.7	61.7	61.7
	Agree-2	17	36.2	36.2	97.9
	Cannot Say-3	0	0.0	0.0	0.0
	Disagree-4	1	2.1	2.1	100.0
	Strongly Disagree-5	0	0.0	0.0	0.0
	Total	47	100.0	100.0	

Forty-six (97.9%) responses generated for weights 1 and 2, indicate that the respondents agree that team spirit, proactive nature and self-motivation are equally important skills now in their trade.

Information Technology (IT) and Networking Skills

C6

	Weight Given	Frequency	Per cent	Valid Per cent	Cumulative Per cent
Valid	Strongly Agree-1	27	57.4	57.4	57.4
	Agree-2	17	36.2	36.2	93.6
	Cannot Say-3	1	2.1	2.1	95.7
	Disagree-4	2	4.3	4.3	100.0
	Strongly Disagree-5	0	0.0	0.0	0.0
	Total	47	100.0	100.0	

Forty-four (93.6%) responses generated for the weights 1 and 2, indicate that IT and networking skills, i.e. sound knowledge of Information and Communication Technology tools and techniques are in demand today even in library and information field.

Presentation and Communication Skills

C7

	Weight Given	Frequency	Per cent	Valid Per cent	Cumulative Per cent
Valid	Strongly Agree-1	23	48.9	48.9	48.9
	Agree-2	23	48.9	48.9	97.9
	Cannot Say-3	1	2.1	2.1	100.0
	Disagree-4	0	0.0	0.0	0.0
	Strongly Disagree-5	0	0.0	0.0	0.0
	Total	47	100.0	100.0	

Forty-six (97.9%) respondents think that presentation and communication skills are also essential besides possessing subject knowledge.

Interpersonal Relationships

C8

	Weight Given	Frequency	Per cent	Valid Per cent	Cumulative Per cent
Valid	Strongly Agree-1	11	23.4	23.4	23.4
	Agree-2	31	66.0	66.0	89.4
	Cannot Say-3	2	4.3	4.3	93.6
	Disagree-4	3	6.4	6.4	100.0
	Strongly Disagree-5	0	0.0	0.0	0.0
	Total	47	100.0	100.0	

Forty-one (89.4%) respondents feel that the library and information professional should maintain good interpersonal relationships also.

Management Skills

C9

	Weight Given	Frequency	Per cent	Valid Per cent	Cumulative Percent
Valid	Strongly Agree-1	11	23.4	23.4	23.4
	Agree-2	28	59.6	59.6	83.0
	Cannot Say-3	4	8.5	8.5	91.5
	Disagree-4	4	8.5	8.5	100.0
	Strongly Disagree-5	0	0.0	0.0	0.0
	Total	47	100.0	100.0	

As many as 28 (59.6%) respondents agree that management skills, viz. marketing, negotiating, business etc. skills are a must for the modern library professional and 11 (23.4%) strongly vouch for it. This accounts for 39 (83.0%) positive response.

Readiness to upgrade knowledge

C10

	Weight Given	Frequency	Per cent	Valid Per cent	Cumulative Per cent
Valid	Strongly Agree-1	30	63.8	63.8	63.8
	Agree-2	15	31.9	31.9	95.7
	Cannot Say-3	2	4.3	4.3	100.0
	Disagree-4	0	0.0	0.0	0.0
	Strongly Disagree-5	0	0.0	0.0	0.0
	Total	47	100.0	100.0	

As many as 45 (95.7%) respondents agree that they should always be ready to upgrade their skills and knowledge.

Semantic Differential Profile

Semantic differential profile is a graphical representation of the mean weights of the responses given by the respondents in the part 1, challenges in the questionnaire.

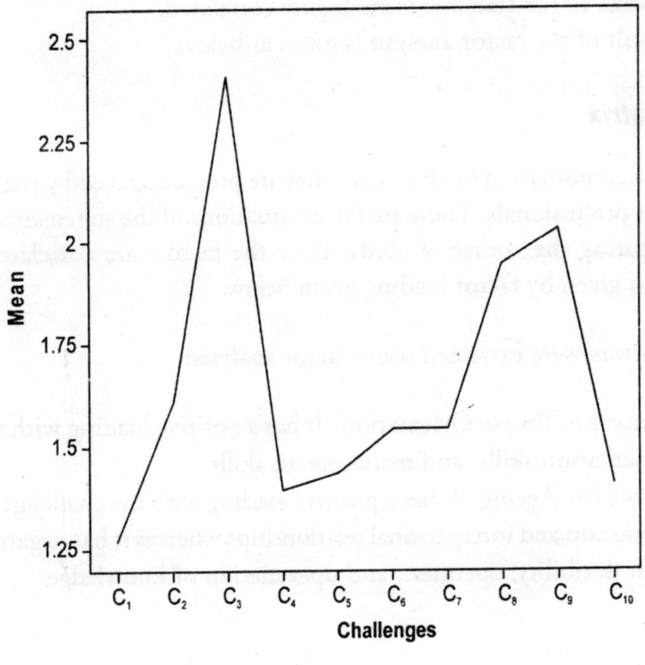

A semantic profile of the challenges faced by the library and information professionals indicates that, on the following aspects, the respondents agree to a large extent as:

- Information technology has been a key driver for transformation in library and information centres.
- A modern library and information professional has to be flexible, open to changes, inventive and creative.
- Team spirit, proactiveness and self-motivation are equally important skills for library and information professionals.
- IT and Networking skills are a must for today's Library and Information Professional.
- Presentation and Communication skills are a must for Library Professionals.
- Library and Information Professionals must always be ready to upgrade their skills and knowledge.

Factor Analysis

Factor analysis was carried out to find out the significant factors affecting the library and information professionals in the industry today. Using data from a large sample, factor analysis applies an advanced form of correlation analysis to the responses to a number of statements. The purpose of this analysis is to determine if the responses to the statements are highly correlated.

The result of the factor analysis is given as below.

Factor Matrix

Factors are a combination of challenges that are presently faced by the library and information professionals. These are linear equations of the statements (variables) measured during the course of study. How the factors are correlated with the statements is given by factor loading given below.

Four factors were extracted using factor analysis:

— Factor 1 is 'People Orientation'. It has a positive loading with team spirit, presentation skills, and management skills.

— Factor 2 is 'Ageing'. It has a positive loading with the challenge of internet revolution and interpersonal relationships whereas it has negative loadings with flexibility, openness, and upgradation of knowledge.

Component Matrix (a)

	Component			
	1	2	3	4
C1	.339	-.400	-.076	.444
C2	.383	.372	.573	-.194
C3	-.045	.508	.455	.498
C4	.422	-.635	.261	.243
C5	.696	.031	.020	-.423
C6	.367	-.082	-.555	.420
C7	.767	.383	-.055	-.038
C8	.481	.584	-.136	.311
C9	.552	-.235	-.321	-.286
C10	.296	-.515	.642	.070

Extraction Method: Principal Component Analysis.
a 4 components extracted.

— Factor 3 is 'Information Processing'. It has a positive loading with the challenge of information explosion and readiness to upgrade the skills whereas it has a negative loading with IT and networking skills.
— Factor 4 cannot be considered as it is representing only one attribute which is internet being a challenge.

Communality and Eigen Values

Communalities indicate the proportion of variance in the responses to statements, which are explained by the three factors. Eigen values are used to indicate how well any given factor fits the data from all the respondents on all of the statements. Eigen values of above 1 or close to 1 are considered best.

Communalities

	Initial	Extraction
C1	1.000	.478
C2	1.000	.651
C3	1.000	.716
C4	1.000	.708
C5	1.000	.665
C6	1.000	.626
C7	1.000	.740
C8	1.000	.687
C9	1.000	.544
C10	1.000	.770

Extraction Method: Principal Component Analysis.

Total Variance Explained

Component	Initial Eigen values			Extraction Sums of Squared Loadings		
	Total	% of Variance	Cumulative %	Total	% of Variance	Cumulative %
1.	2.274	22.740	22.740	2.274	22.740	22.740
2.	1.774	17.745	40.485	1.774	17.745	40.485
3.	1.454	14.538	55.023	1.454	14.538	55.023
4.	1.082	10.816	65.840	1.082	10.816	65.840
5.	.825	8.253	74.093			
6.	.752	7.518	81.611			
7.	.578	5.782	87.393			
8.	.499	4.994	92.387			
9.	.402	4.024	96.410			
10.	.359	3.590	100.000			

Extraction Method: Principal Component Analysis

The four factors have Eigen value equal to or greater than 1.0 indicating that they best fit the data obtained from the responses to the challenges in part 1 of the questionnaire. Also, the four factors together explain almost 65.84 per cent of the total variance in the responses to the statements.

Comparison of Mean Scores of Respondents based of type of Libraries

The mean scores of the challenges as rated by the respondents from two type of libraries, i.e. academic libraries and research libraries were compared for identifying if there were any major differences between their responses. The graph plotted below explains that there is no major difference between the responses filled in by the library professionals belonging to academic and research libraries.

	Libcode	N	Mean	Std. Deviation	Std. Error Mean
C1	Academic	29	1.31	.541	.101
	Research	18	1.17	.383	.090
C2	Academic	29	1.62	.677	.126
	Research	18	1.56	.784	.185
C3	Academic	29	2.59	1.296	.241
	Research	18	2.11	1.323	.312
C4	Academic	29	1.41	.628	.117
	Research	18	1.33	.485	.114
C5	Academic	29	1.45	.686	.127
	Research	18	1.39	.502	.118
C6	Academic	29	1.34	.484	.090
	Research	18	1.83	.985	.232
C7	Academic	29	1.38	.494	.092
	Research	18	1.78	.548	.129

(Contd.)

	Libcode	N	Mean	Std. Deviation	Std. Error Mean
C8	Academic	29	1.83	.658	.122
	Research	18	2.11	.832	.196
C9	Academic	29	1.86	.743	.138
	Research	18	2.28	.895	.211
C10	Academic	29	1.48	.634	.118
	Research	18	1.28	.461	.109

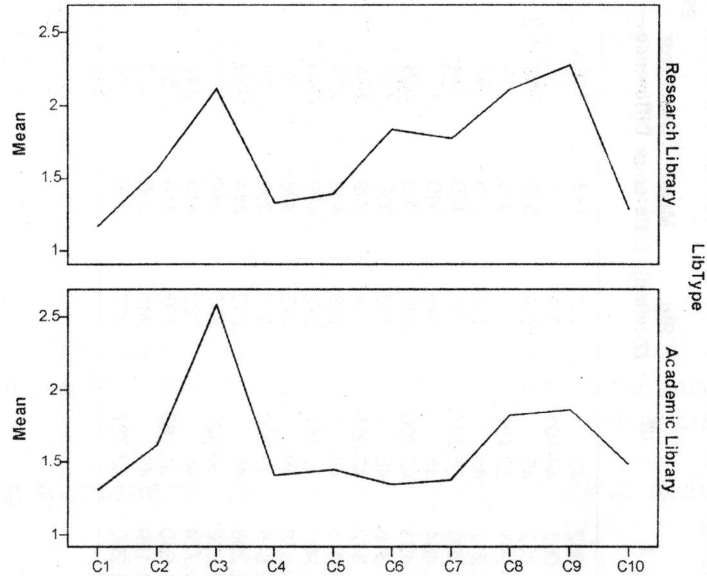

The challenges enumerated in C3, C6, C7 and C9 relate to the Internet, IT and networking skills, presentation, communication skills and management skills. The statistics show that the respondents from academic libraries and research libraries differ in their opinions to some extent, though not much, and do not consider Internet to be a very serious challenge to their professions. As for the IT and networking skills are concerned, the research library professionals agree to a less extent when compared to the academic library professionals. The probable reason being their working environments, in India, the research library professionals are more adept at IT and networking tasks as a routine. This might be a reason that they may not feel it as a challenge. Similar is the case with other challenges, viz., presentation, communication skills and management skills. In India, the kind of exposure research library professionals receive is assumed to be more encouraging when compared to academic library professionals due to different reasons. So also, the professionals in research library sector may have to imbibe the above skills as a part of their routine. This explains the variation. Detailed statistical values confirming the mean score comparison are given in the table of independent samples test below.

Independent Samples Test

		Levene's Test for Equality of Variances		t-test for Equality of Means						
		F	Sig.	t	df	Sig. (2-tailed)	Mean Difference	Std. Error Difference	95% Confidence Interval of the Difference	
									Lower	Upper
C1	Equal variances assumed	4.258	.045	.982	45	.332	.144	.146	-.151	.438
	Equal variances not assumed			1.063	44.101	.294	.144	.135	-.129	.416
C2	Equal variances assumed	.249	.620	.302	45	.764	.065	.216	-.369	.500
	Equal variances not assumed			.291	32.191	.773	.065	.223	-.390	.520
C3	Equal variances assumed	.800	.376	1.212	45	.232	.475	.392	-.314	1.265
	Equal variances not assumed			1.206	35.603	.236	.475	.394	-.324	1.274
C4	Equal variances assumed	1.618	.210	.464	45	.645	.080	.173	-.269	.430
	Equal variances not assumed			.493	42.700	.625	.080	.163	-.249	.410
C5	Equal variances assumed	.748	.392	.318	45	.752	.059	.187	-.317	.436
	Equal variances not assumed			.342	43.655	.734	.059	.174	-.291	.410
C6	Equal variances assumed	5.750	.021	-2.275	45	.028	-.489	.215	-.921	-.056
	Equal variances not assumed			-1.962	22.167	.062	-.489	.249	-1.005	.028
C7	Equal variances assumed	.350	.557	-2.578	45	.013	-.398	.155	-.710	-.087
	Equal variances not assumed			-2.515	33.300	.017	-.398	.158	-.721	-.076
C8	Equal variances assumed	.147	.703	-1.296	45	.202	-.284	.219	-.724	.157
	Equal variances not assumed			-1.226	30.020	.230	-.284	.231	-.756	.189
C9	Equal variances assumed	.545	.464	-1.724	45	.092	-.416	.241	-.901	.070
	Equal variances not assumed			-1.650	31.188	.109	-.416	.252	-.930	.098
C10	Equal variances assumed	5.092	.029	1.189	45	.241	.205	.172	-.142	.552
	Equal variances not assumed			1.280	43.737	.207	.205	.160	-.118	.528

Suggestive Measures

The sample professionals were asked to give their suggestions for improvement of present situation and they gave the following measures.

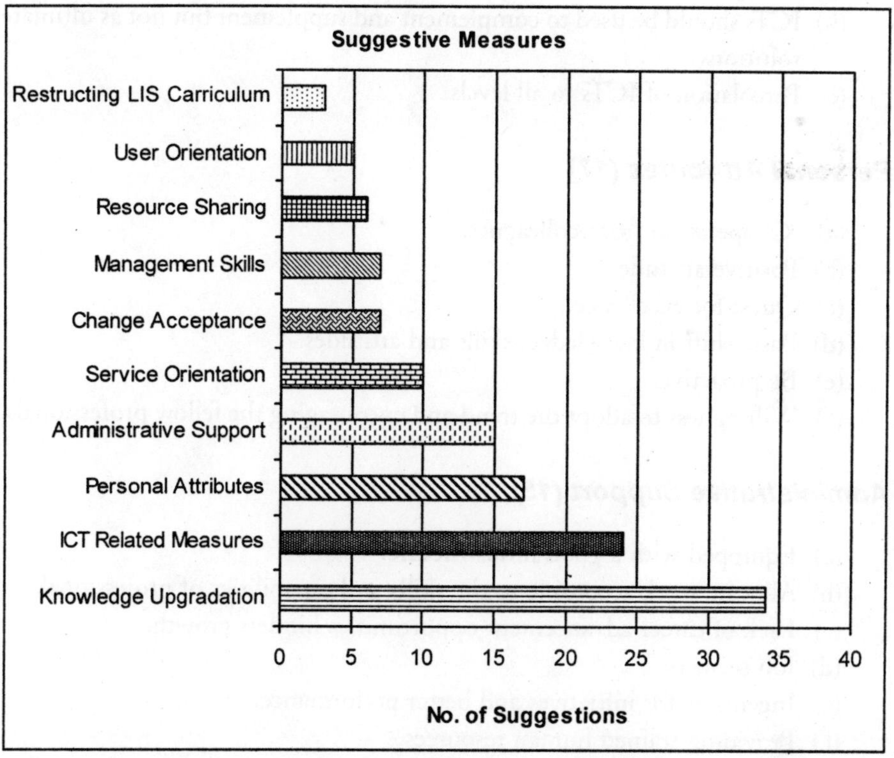

Knowledge Upgradation Related Measures (34)

(a) Staff Training.
(b) Skills and knowledge upgradation.
(c) Continuing Professional Development activities.
(d) Attending training, conferences and workshops.
(e) Keep abreast with new technology.
(f) Adequate training facilities.

ICT related Measures (24)

(a) Keep up with the technological developments.
(b) Librarians should upgrade their soft skills.
(c) Adopt to new technology.

(d) IT and networking skills compulsory for LIS professionals.
(e) Switching over to e-media.
(f) Transition from traditional to modern should be in phases.
(g) Computer and internet literacy a must.
(h) ICTs should be used to complement and supplement but not as ultimate solutions.
(i) Percolation of ICTs to all levels.

Personal Attributes (17)

(a) Cooperation from colleagues.
(b) Positive attitude.
(c) Quest for excellence.
(d) Basic shift in knowledge, skills and attitudes.
(e) Be proactive.
(f) Willingness to adopt the trend and encouraging the fellow professionals.

Administrative Support (15)

(a) Equipped with a good infrastructure.
(b) Allocate work according to the skills and capabilities of professionals.
(c) Lack of career advancement opportunities hinders growth.
(d) Job security.
(e) Incentives for initiatives and better performance.
(f) Providing trained human resources.
(g) Support from parent organization.
(h) Management should be taken into confidence in every endeavour.
(i) Encouragement and motivation from management.

Service Orientation (10)

(a) Technology should serve the purpose of a service factor.
(b) Selfless service to the community.
(c) Dedication to profession.
(d) Quality control.
(e) Innovative methods to restructure services.

Change Acceptance (7)

(a) Should adapt to the changing environment.

(b) Change the mindset of the staff.
(c) Motivation is necessary for effective change over.
(d) Proper attitude towards change needs to be cultivated.
(e) Learning from changing environment.

Management Skills (7 suggestions)

(a) Managerial skill coupled with communication skills.
(b) Management skills with respect to changing scenario.
(c) Marketing skills are necessary.

Resource Sharing (6)

(a) Resource sharing between libraries.
(b) Knowledge sharing.
(c) Libraries networking.
(d) Inter-library interaction and cooperation.
(e) Consortia approach.

User Orientation (5)

(a) Training end users.
(b) Regular user orientation.
(c) Creating user awareness regarding new services.
(d) Face to face interaction.
(e) Inclination to provide new services to the user groups.
(f) Knowledge of end users' requirements.

Restructuring of LIS curriculum (3)

(a) More of ICT in syllabus.
(b) Topics based on change management, modern tools and techniques, management skills, leadership skills, should form a part of LIS curriculum.
(c) Emphasis on practical training and updation of curriculum according to latest trends.
(d) LIS schools and associations should plan proper teaching programmes.
(e) Restructuring of LIS curriculum in Indian universities with respect to global standards.

Upon analyzing the 47 valid responses, it has been observed that the largely recommended measure for overcoming the challenges presently faced by the library and information professionals is knowledge upgradation. It implies that the professionals must continuously be in the conquest of knowledge acquisition through various opportunities available.

The next suggested effective measure is regarding the developments in the field of ICTs. The analysis also reveals that personal attributes of the library and information professionals, like positive attitude, proactive nature, open mindedness etc., contribute to overcome the challenges to a great extent. Administrative support, dedication towards service, managing change effectively and possessing management skills further contribute towards a smooth transition.

However, the analysis rates restructuring of LIS curriculum as a relatively insignificant measure for overcoming the challenges faced by the library and information professionals.

Recommendations and Conclusion

The above analysis clearly shows that the present professionals have positively agreed upon majority of the challenges and have also come up with some suitable measures to overcome these challenges. Nevertheless, the very fact that the respondents have not identified the effective restructuring of the present LIS curriculum as a linchpin in the process of smooth transition proves that this aspect to be addressed. More so, because, this forms the core of imparting information and further producing capable and competent library and information professionals.

The LIS curriculum forms the base of not only the present changing scenario of the trade but, more importantly the future of the field. Once the curriculum is restructured and upgraded to amalgamate various skills like managerial capability, managing change and other important attributes along with sound ICT and Networking concepts, the library and information professionals would no more have to struggle to imbibe important and essential skills externally. Thus it would help the future professionals to emerge to be more confident, resourceful and adept at addressing the needs of the users effectively in a naturally acquired manner. Thus development of need based LIS curriculum keeping in view the challenges faced by the professionals today and the requirements of the profession, will help produce potentially sound future professionals. Such a step at grass roots level, will not only raise the confidence level and potentiality of the emerging professionals but will certainly help improve social stratification in India.

This recommendation can be substantiated by considering the following case based evidence. KALIPER was ALISE's (Association for Library and Information

Science Education, Virginia) two-year project, conducted between 1998 and 2000 by a team of twenty scholars from thirteen programs in the U.S., Canada, and England. Educating library and information science professionals for a new century—KALIPER (the Kellogg-ALISE Information Profession and Education Renewal) report (2000) states that their project intended to analyze the nature and extent of major curricular change in LIS education in the U.S., Canada and England. It reports that six trends are shaping the curricular change in the library and information science programmes, viz.,

"(1) In addition to libraries as institutions and library-specific operations, Library and Information Science (LIS) curricula are addressing broadbased information environments and information problems.

(2) While LIS curricula continue to incorporate perspectives from other disciplines, a distinct core has taken shape that is predominantly user-centered.

(3) LIS schools and programs are increasing the investment and infusion of information technology into their curricula.

(4) LIS schools and programs are experimenting with the structure of specialization within the curriculum.

(5) LIS schools and programs are offering instruction in different formats to provide students with more flexibility.

(6) LIS schools and programs are expanding their curricula by offering related degrees at the undergraduate, master's, and doctoral levels."

The report enumerates the factors affecting change by identifying the forces that motivated curricular change and affect its direction. It says "There is evidence that the factors that promote change may, in some situations, be the same ones that inhibit it. Some of these factors are demands of students, employers, graduates, and professional associations for graduate competencies; growth and expense of supporting emerging technology; internal campus relationships and positioning; availability and/or presence of faculty with new subject expertise; competition from other LIS programs; and availability of financial support for innovation."

KALIPER Report also suggests some measures for overcoming these challenges such as—faculty at all levels must be supported in their research into changing information environments, societal access to information, and the uses of information. Also, "Library and information science's commitment to ethics and values, user-centeredness, and focus on access must be sustained. The challenges of the next decade are apparent. The consensus is that the trends identified in this report in curriculum content and delivery will continue. Infrastructure investments must stay abreast of changing technology. Recruiting doctoral students and developing new faculty who share the vision for the changes identified in LIS curricula is essential."

The professionals around the globe and across various nations in general are embedded with same values and ethos and they are more or less facing similar challenges in their professions. Hence, it is time that even developing nations like India address these issues, starting from grassroots. A sound foundation is a pre-requisite for a strong construction. So also a strong foundation level professional education is a must for service excellence, especially in a vibrant, dynamic and ever changing wonderful field of Library and Information Science.

References

Al-Hawamdeh, S. (2002). Knowledge Management: Re-thinking information management and facing the challenge of managing tacit knowledge. *Information Research*. 8 (1).

Amin, S. (2003). *The Comparative Study of LIS Education in India, UK and USA*. http://drtc.isibang.ac.in/~saiful/colloq/lis_edu.htm

Brody, F.E. (2001). Planning for the balance between print and electronic journals in the hybrid digital library: Lessons learned from large ARL Libraries, Dissertation Abstracts International website http://wwwlib.umi.com/dissertations/ (DA 3013240).

Cleeve, M. (1994). *Capturing Utopia. Librarian Career Development.* Vol 2(1), pp. 30-32.

Directory of Selected Libraries in India (2003). Student Aid Publications, Delhi.

Glogoff, S. (2005). Instructional blogging: Promoting interactivity, student-centered learning, and peer input. *Innovate* 1 (5).

Harer, J.B. (2001). Performance Measures of Quality for Academic Libraries Implementing Continuous Quality Improvement Programs: A Delphi Study. Dissertation Abstracts International website http://wwwlib.umi.com/dissertations/ (DA 3011718).

Jestin, J.K.J. and Parameswari, B. (2002). Challenges for Library Professionals in India in the New Millennium. *Library Philosophy and Practice*. 4(2).

KALIPER Advisory Committee, ALISE (2000). Educating Library and Information Science Professionals for a New Century. The KALIPER Report (Executive Summary). Association for Library and Information Science Education, Virginia.

Karisiddappa, C.R. (2004). Library and information science curriculum for the developing countries. Proceedings of World Library and Information Congress: 70th IFLA General Conference and Council, 22-27 Aug, Buenos Aires, Argentina. http://www.ifla.org/IV/ifla70/prog04.htm

Khoo, C. *et al.* (2004). A Cluster Analysis of LIS Students in Singapore and Implications for Defining Areas of Specialization. *Journal of Education for Library and Information Science.* 45 (1). pp. 36-57.

Kuhn, T. (1996). *The Structure of Scientific Revolutions.* University of Chicago Press, Chicago.

McGown, K. (2000). *Knowledge Management in the Twenty-First Century: The Role of the Academic Librarian.* Dissertation Abstracts International. 61(7).

Singh, S.P. (2003). Library and Information Science Education in India: Issues and Trends. *Malaysian Journal of Library & Information Science*. 8(2). pp. 1-17.

Sharma, J. (2001). *Professional Competencies in Modern Libraries*. Author's Press, Delhi.

Times of India, 26 March 2006, p. 12.

Wayne State University System. 2006. http://www.lib.wayne.edu/

Part II
University Libraries

7

Indian University Libraries in Information Technology Era: Problems and Prospects

S.D. VYAS

Introduction

Dr. S. Radhakrishnan, Chairman of University Education Commission (1948-49) said that a library is heart of an academic institution. Dr. D.S. Kothari, Chairman of Second Education Commission (1964-66) also reemphasized the key role of the libraries in the life of universities. However, within span of past few decades the role of the libraries has become marginal which means that whether there is a library in the university or not the life of the university goes on. Dr. Shankar Dayal Sharma, Former President of India says "a library is more important than a university because a library can function without a university, whereas a university cannot do without a library."

In the last five decades the following developments have taken place in higher education system of India.

Every state has opened atleast one Open University during last two decades. Universities have suffered on account of budget cut particularly it affected journal subscription of libraries.

Establishing a national information library network (INFLIBNET) in the late eighties.

Library automation is gaining momentum in higher education libraries.

Our progress is satisfactory so far number of universities is concerned. The following table indicates the growth of university libraries along with student population.

S.No.	Year	Number of Universities	Number of Students
1.	1927	15	91,000
2.	1947	17	1,50,000 (app.)
3.	1951	28	1,86,650
4.	1991	180	44,25,247
5.	2000	200	80,00,000
6.	2006	280	1,00,00,000 (app.)

The above table shows great expansion of higher education. There is rise of more than fifty times in student population since 1951. At present one per cent population have gone for higher education whereas if we look at 1951 census *vis-à-vis* student population it was around half per cent. Although there is nothing appreciable rise yet there is a positive sign of development of higher education.

It is to be noted that most of the students are there in the universities not because of the interest in higher education, but they have nothing to do elsewhere. If there is guarantee of an employment perhaps student population going in for higher education shall dwindle. Only those who are really serious to study higher education shall be there in universities and colleges.

Ideally speaking, libraries are delivery rooms for the birth of new ideas as said by Prof. K. Venkata Reddy. Modern education is its call it intellectual workshops. Our higher education commissions have termed the role of library in higher education is like heart in human body. Prof. K. Venkata Reddy says further "the quantitative expansion of libraries resulting in the increased number of users is heartening, but the qualitative aspect has not been given proper attention, leading to a decline in the standard of library services."[1]

Comparative Situation of University Libraries (1985-2005)

Two decades back the situation of Indian university libraries was as follows as depicted by A.R. Sethi and Shyamala Moorthy with a comment on the current situation.

Thirty three per cent of the university libraries in India are functioning without university libraries (In Rajasthan all the Universities are without librarian except two deemed universities. Overall situation in India has not improved yet). According to INFLIBNET Annual Directory forty seven universities now have librarians. It means situation has improved over a period of two decades.

Fifty per cent of the university libraries have less than Rs. ten lakh budget. (It is to be noted that budget allocation of universities should be calculated at six per cent of the total university budget as suggested by Higher Education Commission).

Seventy per cent of the libraries have a book collection less than two lakhs and subscribe to not more than 1000 journals. (We are far behind average American and British library collections of university libraries.) Subscribing to 1000 journals is a dream now-a-days because of escalation of prices of foreign journals. Another development is of UGC-INFONET consortia for e-journals. Now above 4000 journals are made available online to the universities through UGC-INFONET consortia.

Till 1985 only two per cent of the university libraries have some of their library operations computerized. Now INFLIBNET during last one decade has funded more than 150 university libraries for library automation. Hence fifty per cent of the university libraries have gone for computerization. Had they provided the funds for libraries automation a decade earlier the situation would have been different?

In twenty five per cent of university libraries, the staff strength ranges between 3 to 20. Now it is hoped that with application and introduction of computers, the pressure of the library staff shall be less. This is heartening to know that seventy five per cent of the libraries have more than twenty staff members in the libraries. It was estimated than on an average 39 persons are working in the university libraries. It is a good number.

A little more than twenty five per cent libraries have an annual budget of Rs. five lakhs. (Now situation is different as universities are trying to give more funds to libraries because universities think that giving funds to libraries is like self-funding as the library belongs to all.)

Most of the libraries are providing traditional services like circulation, inter-library loan and reference services only. Reprographic services are provided by eighty per cent and microfilming facility in thirteen per cent only. (At present there is hardly any university library without reprographic facility. Microfilming facility did not increase as it is in the beginning of digital information era. This digital development proved fatal to micrographic technology).[2]

In 1967 the British UGC Committee on Libraries rightly said "books and journals are expensive, and with great increase both in the number of universities and in the total university population, it is important that library services should be organized in the most effective and economical way possible."[3]

The above Committee Report's recommendations are useful to us to provide better library services because our higher education system reflects British pattern of education. The British UGC Committee on Libraries feel that more funds for libraries is a kind of self-funding to the universities because libraries fight on behalf of the university. This committee also commented on the role of the university library:

"If one of the main purposes of a university education is to teach students to work on their own reading by students must be preferable to attendance at a lecture unless the lecture is superior in presentation or content to the available literature."[4]

Library Co-operation

Indian universities have not been fortunate in practicing library co-operation as at national level inter-library loan is missing. If librarians know each other at personal level then things are different. Indian Library Association (ILA) and Indian Association of Special Libraries and Information Centres (IASLIC) have discussed the issue of library co-operation in their annual conferences, and have passed resolutions also, yet in practice inter-library loan is not followed. To some extent library co-operation is dictated by geographical considerations. India is geographically at least ten times larger than United Kingdom (UK). Moreover there is hardly networking of public libraries in India as we find in UK. UK academic libraries get support from the public libraries. In India managers, engineers, doctors, public figures etc. in the absence of public library system depend upon academic libraries for their reading. However, at local level library co-operation is working well as we find Developing Library Network (DELNET) is successfully meeting the needs of Delhi researchers, scientists, managers and others. H.R. Chopra comments on resource sharing among university libraries "India being a vast country, it is very difficult to establish such a system at national level. But efforts can be made in this respect. This is possible only in phases and not at stretch. Inter-library loan is always possible at this level."[5]

A.C. Tikekar narrates an incident during the time when D.N. Marshall was the librarian. Long ago T.N. Chaturvedi, present Governor of Karnataka asked in for a book which was available in Bombay University Library. D.N. Marshall without wasting much time and fuss posted the book to him. T.N. Chaturvedi later said that he wrote to several university libraries, but he received negative reply from them saying that they have the book in the library, but their library rules do not permit them to send the book to outsiders. Few university libraries did not care to respond to him. This incident reflects D.N. Marshall's personality who advocated and implemented inter-library loan in real practice. [6]

K.P. Sinha Committee (1959) also emphasized the need for library co-operation of university libraries with public libraries for the simple reason that the university libraries are the most developed libraries in the country. Sinha Committee Report recommended for the preparation of union catalogues of various types of reading material.[7]

Problems of University Libraries

Prof. K. Venkata Reddy says "the quantitative expansion of libraries have resulted in the increased number of users is heartening but the qualitative aspect has not been given proper attention, leading to decline in the standard of library services. He highlights the following problems:

- Shortage of space since most of the buildings came up many years ago and extension proposals did not materialize expeditiously,
- Despite the fact that the annual intake of books has tripled, the staff strength in most universities continues to be the same as during 60s,
- There is unprecedented financial crisis in universities,
- There is increase in enrollment and explosion of knowledge on an unprecedented scale,
- There is tremendous rise in prices of books and periodicals,
- The number of periodicals is being reduced to the detriment of research activity.[8]

Prof. Krishan Kumar rightly says about the condition of Indian university libraries. He says "Due to various factors, libraries are faced with tremendous problems. There are increasing demands made upon the university libraries, which it is not in position to meet." He lists the following problems of university libraries:

- Scattering of resources,
- Scarcity of resources,
- Increasingly complex organization,
- Tools developed by librarians are too complex to use,
- Underutilization and misuse of existing resources,
- Time consuming procedures and processes,
- Too many internal conflicts,
- Lack of data for decision making,
- Lack of professionalization,
- Lack of full support from the authorities,
- Lack of proper appreciation on the part of users, and
- Lack of academic status and facilities for professional development.[9]

Besides the above problems, there are few more problems which are listed below:

- Lack of proper staffing several universities are without librarians for years.
- Relevant recommendations of the committees, commissions and annual conferences of Indian Library Association and Indian Association of Special Libraries and Information Centres have not been implemented.
- Funds for information technology applications were given late.
- Libraries are not user oriented.
- Lack of proper book selection and book reviewing tools for Indian publications as well as for Indian languages.

Despite a good number of university libraries as well as college libraries available in each state, library services are not adequate. Public libraries are still a weak link and can hardly support academic libraries.

Undergraduate and postgraduate students need reading rooms. This is becoming increasingly necessary owing to overcrowding in the hostels and distractions of radio, television and tape recorders. Students bring their personal books in the reading hall. There should be a provision for consulting library books along with personal books.

University libraries should have a good stock of frequently used books with sufficient number of seats. At least any university library despite even being a new university should have 200 to 300 seats. University libraries should get good number of journals with photocopying facility. In this respect INFLIBNET made good efforts to provide access to online journals under UGC-INFONET consortia. Although the service was launched three years back it is yet to become popular. It has made tremendous hope for research scholars to get access at their universities. Full text journal articles can be down loaded. According to INFLIBNET so far not less than 1 million pages from online journals have been taken. This shows the use of UGC-INFONET journals is increasing. It is disappointing to note that an average university library subscribes to 250 journals. Hence facility of e-journals through UGC-INFONET consortia is a boon to research scholars and faculty members of the university. UGC shall review the model licensing of this consortia after three years. Availability of UGC-INFONET journals has enhanced the quality as well as quantity of journals. Still the facility of UGC-INFONET journals available through consortia model has to be publicized. These journals are still under used. The use of the e-journals is increasing in the field of computer science, electronics, biotechnology, bioinformatics microbiology, pharmaceutical chemistry, chemoinformatics, chemistry and physics, but this e-journal facility is yet to become popular among humanities and social science scholars. Usually the social science and humanities faculties do not have physical facilities as their counterparts in sciences in the universities.

Role of American Centres and British Libraries

The American centres and British libraries have their libraries in all the metropolitan cities of the country. They are providing excellent library services to the people. Anyone can become member of the library and books are sent to outstation scholars. American Studies Research Centre, Hyderabad has played a significant role in providing library facilities to American literature, government and politics, history, communication and sociology scholars of the country. Books and Xeroxed articles were sent to outstation scholars who are members of the Centre. Even the Central Institute of English and Foreign Languages Hyderabad also provided library service to outstation scholars in the field of linguistics and literature.

Indian University Librarians and their Contribution

Dr. S.R. Ranganathan became the first university librarian of Madras University who underwent library science education and training in London University. He also became president of ILA. Dr. S.R. Ranganathan's overall contributions to the library science profession are visible in every sphere. He was an internationalist in his thinking. S.R. Ranganathan influenced Indian library scientists in general and academic librarians in particular. These are S. Das Gupta, S. Bashiruddin, P.N. Kaula, B.V.R. Rao, Girja Kumar, A.P. Srivastava, P.S.G. Kumar, C.D. Sharma, K.S. Deshpande, D.N. Marshall, N.N. Gidwani, J.S. Sharma etc. Those who have become Presidents of Indian Library Association in post-independent India, many of them have come from university library system. They are B.V.R. Rao, Girja Kumar, P.N. Kaula, and P.S.G. Kumar. A few who have become Presidents of the Indian Library Association were basically teachers of library science. They are P.B. Mangla, Krishan Kumar, C.P. Vashishth and J.L. Sardana (all from University of Delhi). During last one decade P.S.G. Kumar, C.R. Karisiddappa, Muttayya Koganuramath have also occupied the position of President of the Association. They also headed university libraries.

Those who did not become the President of Indian Library Association yet they left indelible imprint on academic librarianship are D.N. Marshall, K.S. Deshpande, N.N. Gidwani, C.P. Shukla, A.P. Srivastava. D.N. Marshall passed ICS examination in early 30s, but later he dedicated his life for Bombay University Library. K.S. Deshpande is known for his leadership and was a librarian and Head of the Department of Library Science, Dharwar University. He also brought out Timeless Fellowship. N.N. Gidwani is known for his documentation list Index India which made him an international librarian. C.D. Sharma followed N.N. Gidwani in late 80s when he became Editor of Index India and then librarian of the University of Rajasthan. C.D. Sharma had almost three decades of teaching experience and then joined as a librarian. P.S.G. Kumar had his career in teaching and during last few years of his academic career he became librarian of Nagpur University. In Maharastra the State Government passed an act that Head of the Department of Library Science and librarian should be same. A Reader of the Library Science Department can become in charge of the university library. It is strange rule because it is contradictory to UGC policy. UGC says that the posts of librarian and head of the department are two independent positions and each have full time jobs.

Application of Information Technology in University Libraries

University libraries have received financial support from UGC-INFLIBNET centre for library automation. The centre provided training in the use of information technology and later they provided money for data entry, telephone and buying hardware items needed for library automation and library networking. The centre provided a good support to begin library automation. This facility was provided to the universities for first five years. The period should have been extended for few more years. INFLIBNET also prepared library management software called Software for University Libraries (SOUL) and made available to academic institutions at reasonable cost with installation facility through their technical staff. SOUL software has helped the university libraries to prepare their bibliographical database. However, SOUL modules of acquisition, circulation and periodicals control do not work smoothly. Future of INFLIBNET will be decided by the libraries who could sustain the problems, pressures and onslaught of information technology. The success story of university libraries going for library automation shall decide the performance of INFLIBNET. INFLIBNET also developed Document Delivery Centres for which the Centre provided the funds to large university libraries of India. But the Document Delivery Centres have failed to provide service as no university would like to send journal articles to other libraries happily.

Krishan Kumar has given the following suggestions to solve the problem of university libraries:

- ➢ Improved access to resources. It means co-ordination between different units. Information sources be made accessible to ever used. Machine readable catalogue with networking facility be made available. Library hours should be convenient to users. User orientation should be given so that they know about the resources available at different locations. Accessibility should be increased. One way is to digitize important documents.

- *Innovative Practices*: New ways and new practices be followed. The library staff should be encouraged to put forward their ideas.
- Exchange of university publications is a useful device to build up a library collection.
- Through resource sharing only maximum use can be made of limited resources.
- User education programmes should be encouraged.
- University libraries be built up a user friendly library to increase the use of library resources.
- Signage (science of signs) should be used to make a library convenient to use. A library guide be given to the users so that they know about library and its divisions.
- Some kinds of bibliographical reading lists be made available to users to begin with.
- *Management of Resources*. A librarian need to know about modern management science to run the library management effectively.
- Librarian should use management tools to solve the problems. These tools include system analysis and operations research.
- *Contingency Approach*. Indian libraries are faced with serious conflict situations within libraries. A manager must study the conflict situation and solve the problems keeping in view his style of functioning. He should read the books on management of libraries. A librarian should set up a good example and should create a healthy climate conducive for healthy growth of individuals. There can be different styles of management which depends upon the librarian.
- *Professionalization*. Library professionals should accept professional ethics and follow them in practice.
- *Education of Authorities*. The librarians have not been given due recognition by the society. Authorities need to be educated about the significance of the role a university library plays in the fulfilment of university objectives.
- *Friends of the Library*. Friends play an important role in the growth and development of a library.
- *Strengthening of Professional Organizations*. Professional associations should be strengthened so that they can fight for the cause of the profession. Unfortunately our professional associations are weak because less than 10 per cent are the members of professional associations.
- *Modernization*. It offers solutions to the problems.
- *Application of Information Technology*. Use of computers and telecommunication, reprography etc. has a special place in modernization.

Libraries are successfully applying information technology to achieve better results. The tools of information technology have become cheaper but with more speed, more powerful and greater versatility. Old and rare books collection can be now put on digital format.

- *Research.* Research can lead to certain findings. These findings should be examined carefully for their fruitful application. The libraries should involve in preparing plans, budgets, and annual reports, maintenance of data etc.[10]

A.A.N. Raju gives the following advantages of research—

- Extension of boundaries of knowledge, thereby creating new knowledge.
- Makes it possible for new application of existing knowledge.
- Helps in finding solutions to the problems.
- Leads to continuing advancement of scholarship.
- Brings recognition and prestige to the individual as well as to the department.
- Teachers become better teachers.
- Attracts better faculty.[11]

Conclusion

University libraries in India are now under tremendous influence of information technology. This will force them to organize the collection as well as improve their services. Universities should fill up the vacant posts of librarians. Since technological change is occurring fast, library professionals' education has to be kept up-to-date. Therefore university libraries shall have to start staff development programmes as one time received education is not enough. University libraries in India have old and rare collection also which has to be preserved for the posterity for which digitization projects should be under taken. UGC should initiate digitization programme for academic libraries so that universal accessibility of documents is ensured through networking and Internet. Academic institutions are under transition. Library services, in the absence of public library system in the country should be extended to other professionals also who otherwise cannot become members of the university libraries.

References

1. K. Venkata, Reddy (1994). Libraries as Intellectual Workshop. In *New Horizons in Library and Information Science.* Editors: C.P. Vashishth [and others]. Madras, T.R. Publications, p. 71.

2. A.R. Sethi and Shyamala, Moorthy (April-September 1985). University Libraries in India: Some Facts, Some Figures. *ILA Bulletin*, 21, 1-2, p. 71.
3. Great Britain (1967). University Grants Committee. *Report of the Committee on Libraries.* London, HMSO, Foreword. p. iii.
4. Great Britain. University Grants Committee p. 11.
5. H.R., Chopra (1991). Resource Sharing in University Libraries in India. In *Outstanding Studies in University Librarianship.* Edited by S.P. Sood and C.L. Sharma, Jaipur, RBSA Publishers, p. 149.
6. Arvind, Tikekar (2006). *Remembering Professor D.N. Marshall on the Eve of his Birth Centenary*, Mumbai, Published by Arvind Tikekar, pp. 6-7.
7. India, Ministry of Education (1959). Report of Advisory Committee for Libraries, 1959. New Delhi. Manager of Publications, (Chairman: K.P. Sinha) pp. 61-62.
8. K. Venkata Reddy. p. 73.
9. Krishan, Kumar (1993). University Libraries: Problems and Solutions. In *Academic Libraries: Role in the National Development.* Editors: Dorothy Issac, A.A.N. Raju and L.S. Ramaiah. Madras, T.R. Publications, p. 4.
10. Krishan Kumar. pp. 4-11.
11. A.A.N. Raju (1993). Library and Information Science Researchers in India. In *Academic Libraries: Role in the National Development.* Editors: Dorothy Issac. N.A.A. Raju and L.S. Ramaiah, Madras, T.R. Publications, pp. 14-15.

Bibliography

Deshpande, K.S., *University Library System in India*, New Delhi, Sterling, 1985.

Gelfand, M.A., *University Libraries for Developing Countries.* Paris, Unesco, 1971.

India, Ministry of Education, *Report of the Education Commission 1948-49*, Delhi, 950 (Chairman : S. Radhakrishnan).

India, Minstry of Education. *Report of the Education Commission 1964-66.* Education and National Development. Delhi, 1966 (Chairman : D.S. Kothari).

8

Strategic Planning for Developing Indian University Libraries into Knowledge Resource and Service Centres

INDER VIR MALHAN

Introduction

In the present turbulent times and increasingly uncertain, complex and competitive world, the accumulation, processing and strategic use of cutting edge knowledge is playing predominate role for propelling growth and advancement in almost every sector of economy. In the last two centuries 'industrial production' determined the economic advancement of a nation. In the present century, generation of new knowledge, management and use of knowledge resources is becoming crucial in the creation of wealth. Knowledge and idea based companies such a Microsoft, Google, Amazon. Com, Tata-Consultancy are thriving on their knowledge assets and making the life and work easier for human beings around the world. Effective management of knowledge resources is now playing a key role in wealth creation and world's most strong economies are no more emphasising on industrial production but rather becoming powerhouses of knowledge. In knowledge based society what one own is not as important as what one knows. A single patent embodying important ideas and potential applications may considerably enhance the economic power of the inventor or innovator.

An awareness of what is happening and what is important in a developing knowledge based society, can help information professionals to restructure their institutions, redesign their systems, ameliorate their operations, manage change and reorient their services to needs and conveniences of contemporary and anticipated future customers. Knowledge based societies have mainly been created by the information technology revolution and are fueled by the Internet. Because of globalization, growing competition and speedy access to vast global information resources, one can witness a spurt in knowledge activities and an enormously accelerating speed in work and action, "A generation ago, the average person had a 100,000 hours working life (40 hours × 50 weeks × 50 years). To day, we can do everything that person did in a tenth of time, a mere 10,000 hours. According to Peter Cochrane, Head of Research for British Telecom Labs, in the next generation people will be able to do that in 1000 hours."[1] In the knowledge based societies slow and steady loses the race and only fast and steady wins the race. It is because of speed of information accessibility, information users now prefer to go for Google instead of browsing through the books and riffling through the microfilm reels.

In the agricultural societies power centered around the sword. In the industrial societies pen became mightier than the sword. In the knowledge societies the keyboard and mouse are more powerful than the pen because they lead to saving of time. Because everyone is trying to do and accomplish more and still more in a given time, life in knowledge society is guided by the calendar and run by the cloak. Time management is like life management. Saving of time means finding opportunities to do something more. Thus people are spending a lot of money to save time and several products and services are being developed which find quick market acceptability because they save time. "In 2003, electronic journals linked through SFX saved Yale researchers, faculty and students 17,365 hours."[2] Some organizations are even allowing flextime and work performance from homes in the interest of improved work performance.

An individual simply cannot cope up with the fast pace of knowledge society. The concept that one person can do everything is no longer valid. In the coglomerate of institutions and the Internet, strategic alliances, cooperation, collaboration on mutually beneficial areas and agreeable terms will help to achieve quick success. However, relationships will work on the principle of 'symbiosis' and not on the functionality of osmosis. Relationships will continue as long as interests and purposes are common, ethics are observed, transparency is maintained and benefits of work effort percolate to every human participant in the collaborative work venture. The young people particularly are now more strategic and setting up their own life missions, goals, objective and purposes. In the process of seeking their purposes, in everything, they are even getting alienated from their own families and their communities and getting connected to cyber communities. Collaborative learning, participative decision making, shared accountability, mitigating drawbacks and eliminating problems through knowledge sharing is getting greater attention in the knowledge society. "A three and a half page paper written by 371 authors affiliated to 44 institutions in 12 countries across the world indicates the growing extent of collaboration and coordination in the scientific and technical work in the world."[3]

Information is recognized as important resource in the emerging knowledge societies and hence there is enormous growth of information. In ocean of information float abundance of ideas, which encapsulate essential knowledge. However, an idea is like a fish, if one do not hook it, it may be hooked by someone else. Abundance of ideas have produced a variety of goods and services. The challenge now is to make right choices. To have quick access to facts and product information, quality, specifications and values before making choices is now also a part of work.

In the knowledge society, the hierarchical and bureaucratic management structures are getting dismantled and are being replaced by spatial management, because knowledge and expertise resides in every perceptible human mind and not a prerogative of high fliers. The knowledge seeker in fact is trying to find a connection between what already exists in his/her mind and what exists in his external environment. Continuing education and capacity building is therefore very important in knowledge societies. Industrial society recognized learned men and women; the knowledge society places high value on learning men and women because human beings become obsolete as quickly as machines and require to be continuously equipped with new skills and competencies. However, it is not the machines but human beings who ultimately decide what information is critical for the organization and can give any context or meaning to the information received or communicated. Because of high competition, constant hunt for talent is the focus of knowledge societies. Organizations are trying very hard to employ the best possible persons with the belief that innovations will automatically follow once the best brains are hired.

India and the Knowledge Society

India is not yet a knowledge society but there are very strong islands of it. Indian polity has recognized the need for developing India into a knowledge based society as country's top economist is its Prime Minister and the best scientist is its President. A large number of Indian engineers and scientists have made their mark in India and abroad. A strong talent pool in science and technology exists in India and country is becoming a hub for R & D work of many multinational companies. About 200 MNCs have already set up their R&D facilities in India.

A strong base of artisans and semi-skilled workers and abundance of traditional knowledge resources exist which can lead to innovations if properly exploited and utilized. For instance, scientists from Indian Institute of Technology (IIT), Delhi invented Mangal turbine to produce electricity between two to ten kw. This device costs hardly Rs. 12,000 and design can be replicated by rural artisans. "The IIT team however owes a thank to a farmer, namely Mangal from Uttar Pradesh for this device. While conducting a routine survey in Uttar Pradesh in 1998 scientists met... Mangal, who showed them a water wheel he had designed of wooden blades to lift water from a river in his village Bhailoni Lodh."[4] A vegetable seller from Ratool village in Bagpat, Uttar Pradesh, has developed a helicopter with the help of other vegetable sellers and friends. "This two seater, home made helicopter which if approved will be made available for just Rs. 100,000, claims an association of innovators."[5] Such artisans, other semi-skilled workers and progressive farmers if given little training and access to information can do wonders in product innovation and better contribute to the economic development of the country. "For 42 year old A.V. Narayanaswami, a coffee planter in Wayanad, it has been a labour of love to his vocation as a farmer and as a Keralite concerned about the woes of the state's farm sector. His huge data collection currently runs into over 1.5 lakh web pages in more than 300 modules. The database covers the state's farm potential, new norms of production, packaging and marketing."[6]

A lot of traditional knowledge is not in recorded form and remains confined to families and communities who are using this knowledge. Traces of traditional knowledge also exist in tribal communities, which never came out of their boundaries of their action. There is a fear of lot of traditional knowledge becoming obsolete because of lack of communication. "For example, in medieval India the art of making fine and film thin muslin was well known. The art died because the weavers were reluctant to share this art with others."[7] This happened because transfer of work skills and traditional knowledge remained the individual privilege and was guarded by communities for centuries. On the contrary in the western world most part of knowledge was recorded and preserved. Nicholas Copernicus was born on February 1473, yet his great work *Revolutions* was only published in March 1543, two months before he died."[8] Another example concerns Evariste Galois. "In 1830, Evariste Galois, a student in his first year at Ecole Normale, was killed in a duel at the age of 21. The night before he wrote letter explaining his theory of the solution of algebraic equations. This was the foundation of entirely new branch of pure mathematics, the theory of groups, which has completely transformed our thinking about the nature of algebra and geometry."[9] However there is a new hope of communication of knowledge recorded in some important manuscripts because such works are being digitized.

Government, learned societies and even corporate sector have started contributing towards the improvement of information sector and development of human resources. Government of India has set up NICNET which is largest government owned information network in the world. "The Indian Society of

Agricultural Professionals aims to reach out to at least 100,000 agri-business professionals during the next five years and provide answers to questions like can olive be grown in India? Or is there a market for grafts from Maharashtra to remote Assam? [10] Tata Consultancy has offered a plan to help the country alleviate illiteracy and another company, namely WIPRO is making contribution in computer literacy.

"In the telecommunication sector fierce price competition has resulted in Indian mobile telephony becoming one of the cheapest in the world; more than 47 million people had mobile phones at the end of 2004."[11] By the end of this year, one in every 13 Indians will have a mobile phone, which will create an adequate environment for information sharing. India is though among the ten countries having maximum number of the Internet users, but when we compare it with its demographic statistics the usage of the Internet and penetration of computers is very low. A large majority of population still cannot afford to buy computers. "For instance a PC in India costs around 24 months of average percapita income as compared to China's 4 months and the USA's 12 days."[12]

"India's knowledge management problems are diverse because the country has a unique mixture of the best and the worst kind of situations. It has the fastest jet planes and also 6 million bullock carts. It still has steam engines but also super fast air-conditioned trains. It has pigeon post and speed post. The country has tribesmen who never made a phone call and never travelled in a train but also business executives moving in and out of aircrafts. The country has premier educational and research institutions but also primary schools without blackboards. The country trains world-class engineers in various fields but 45 per cent of the population is illiterate."[13]

There is thus other side of the picture too. The use of information in India by a large majority of population is tardy and in several cases bureaucracy helps only to delay access to information. In some cases even blocking and clogging of information has remained a characteristic of work for finding means of out performing others. At some places conservative attitude of handling and holding information do not let the information reach upto their prospective users. There is a greater emphasis on generation and accumulation of information and lesser emphasis on dissemination and use. "According to latest National Sample Survey Organization report, 60 per cent of farmers in India have no access to agriculture technology. Disturbed by this report the Union Agriculture Ministry is now considering a proposal to revamp Indian Council of Agriculture Research (ICAR)... in a bid to bridge the gap between technology generation and technology dissemination."[14] Wherever public sector fails to make the mark, the private sector steps in. ITC one of India's largest exporters of agricultural commodities has launched e-choupal in June 2000. "ITC's e-choupal has already reached 3.1 million farmers and is expanding into 30 new villages a day-making it Corporate India's most ambitious rural initiative ever."[15] Choupal means a village square where elderly villagers meet for discussion of topics of importance. E-choupal is infact Internet based agricultural information service through which villagers can access agricultural information of their concern, buy seeds, fertilizers etc. and sell their agriculture produce.

Making available the need based information right into rural areas is essential. However, people's capacity building to facilitate most effective use of information is equally important. The execution of mental abilities of an information user to grasp relationships directly depends upon the availability of relevant information. However, information users can perceive, interpret and draw relationships of information within limits of their own knowledge and level of education. In India, we are not able to make most effective use of potentialities of our manpower because a little less than half of the people are illiterate. We are also not able to make use of full potentialities of our literate manpower because of problems such as unemployment, underemployment in some cases and lack of information literacy. Lack of information literacy hampers access to right information may leads to inappropriate action and hence underutilization of people's potential. To solve all such problems the Government of India constituted a National Knowledge Commission to the Prime Minister on June 13, 2005. This Commission is functioning under the chairmanship of Sam Pitroda and has following terms of reference.

(a) Build excellence in the educational system to meet the knowledge challenges of the 21st century and increase India's competitive advantage in the fields of knowledge.
(b) Promote creation of knowledge in S&T laboratories.
(c) Improve the management of institutions engaged in intellectual property rights.
(d) Promote knowledge applications in agriculture and industry.
(e) Promote the use of knowledge capabilities in making government an effective, transparent and accountable service provider to the citizen and promote widespread sharing of knowledge to maximize public benefit.

Converting Indian University Libraries into Knowledge Resource and Service Centres

Most Indian University Libraries are presently based on the model of providing access to organized collections, assist the users in information search and circulate documents within the stipulated period of time. Some have automated their operations for greater efficiency and provide additional facilities for use of the Internet and e-journals. These services are not enough to meet the information service requirements of emerging knowledge society. Moreover, university libraries now have no monopoly for providing academic information, as alternatives are available for accessing academic information. University libraries are thus also facing fierce competition from alternative information services. In such a situation what strategies we should have in place for converting them into knowledge resource and service centers?

Though every university library functions and undergoes changes according to its own mission, objectives, environmental scanning, funding, leadership and staff, there are some common developmental strategies which can be adopted for metamorphosis of these libraries into knowledge resource and service centers.

(1) University library is often referred as the heart of institution or nerve centre for various activities. "However, when viewed from a senior management perspective from an industrial age corporate mentality—they often have been classified as overheads unable to demonstrate visible contributions to the productivity and profitability of the enterprise."[16] University library system thus should not be considered a peripheral service but one of the core unit of the institution central to the knowledge activities of the university.

(2) University libraries should develop quality control methods and criteria to strictly evaluate and acquire print and e-information resources which the academic community may use. In addition to this, these libraries must jointly evaluate the open access Internet information resources and create virtual libraries for rendering just in time information. Libraries even must go beyond these efforts to collect information and index useful blogs and thus create expert databases for providing referral service to establish person to person contacts and link information with information in the interest of generation of new knowledge. They should also encourage cross disciplinary communication of information among related fields.

(3) Under the INFLIBNET programme, the UGC must set up a monitoring and review committee to speed up the process of retro conversion of catalogue records in Indian Universities and set time targets for this so that online union catalogue of Indian university libraries is made available for the identification and location of collections. Libraries not having adequate staff for this purpose must get this work done through out sourcing. UGC may stop funding such libraries that are not making a steady progress in this direction.

(4) There is no place for stand alone libraries, university libraries must get connected to various library networks. In addition to this, they must integrate and establish synergetic relationships to other information institutions to provide outreach services and make still greater contribution for dissemination of knowledge. For instance, agricultural university libraries may collaborate with rural public libraries for dissemination of agricultural information and transfer of agricultural technology in rural areas. Similar arrangement can also be made with association of agro based industries, for mutual sharing of information. The NML, USA has sponsored projects for public libraries for health literacy.

(5) There is a gap between users' knowledge of information resources and services and ongoing developments in the information world. Because of this gap even the existing services such as journals made available under the Infonet are not adequately used. University libraries, therefore, must organize information literacy classes to convert human beings into human resources. At the national level, the UGC must develop a policy document to integrate information literacy with the courses of study. This will also help to bridge the digital divide.

(6) There is also a gap between the existing knowledge of library personnel and skills and competencies required to handle newly emerging information tools and technologies. A continuing education program for library personnel should be in place for greater contribution of library personnel. When the staff is trained new technologies and methods of handling information automatically get integrated in their work culture. As library professional role is no more limited to merely classification and circulation of documents, they should also take initiatives to continuously learn to improve their skills and competencies to stay competitive and stay ahead.

(7) University library personnel should share ideas to develop innovative library and information services. They should continuously find ways to counter delays in information access, lower costs, increase service. "The common knowledge database projects at Rutger's University allows reference librarians to share resources and strategies for serving academic library patrons."[17]

(8) University libraries should also introduce large scale administrative reforms and do away with rigid rules in favour of flexible provisions which helps everyone. They should metamorphose into performance oriented libraries and not procedure oriented libraries. If some procedures are inevitable, they must save users time and should not be inconvenient for users.

(9) University libraries should devise services, which may help in work processes and work flow of the institution. For this, the university library may even collaborate with other units of the institution. For instance, the library may collaborate with faculty to develop e-content guides for various courses of study, develop a online database of ongoing research projects, develop information products and tools urgently required by the institution, etc.

(10) University libraries should have strategies in place to deal with new technological advances and developments. Universities must have strategies to use every development in IT to their advantage. An IT cell be set up which constantly keep watch on the developments in the IT and see what is relevant, cost effective and latest hardware and software for the university library system. Latest knowledge management tools and techniques and useful databases should also be evaluated for their usefulness for the university.

(11) Users are hard pressed of time and no more visiting the university library to spend their leisure or read any document. They are mostly visiting the library with a purpose and when they are looking for information, they are trying to solve their problems. Professionals must help them in a sympathetic way, guide them through wit and skill and ultimately seek reflection of satisfaction and smile on their faces. Every university library must have its website to keep them informed. Users are now facing the challenges of info stress and hence they should not be loaded with information but provided most relevant and pinpointed information.

(12) The ultimate emerging in-house operation in the university libraries is quality filtering and trafficking of information so that the right information reaches the right person at the right place. The ultimate role of university library professionals is to act as consultant to solve users problems at hand through information prescriptions and provide referral services and thus build their capacities to make them more effective, productive and successful in their work.

(13) An average user is facing the double challenge of fast pace of knowledge society on one hand and an ocean of information on the other hand. Users generally have no time to find what is best for them in a given situation. Here lies a great opportunity for university libraries to become knowledge resource and service centers. University libraries, however, should constantly research what more they can do to serve the user communities, add value to library services and add convenience to the lives of user communities and save their time. A knowledge resource and

service center will succeed in its mission only when its users start succeeding in achieving their objectives. As the information is getting unbundled, these centers must provide information-packaging service and facilitate on demand customization of information packages. They should constantly improve quality of their service and achieve zero defects between information asked and information supplied.

(14) While facilitating metamorphosis of university libraries into knowledge resource and service centers, every care should be taken that these centers do not largely commercialize their services. Their services should be free and fast because for millions of poor Indians they will be oasis for knowledge. Their services infact should be rendered in a humanistic way.

Case Study of the University of Jammu Library

Up to the year 1997, the University of Jammu Library system was almost in an anarchic state. The library had no properly counter, the staff stopped classifying and cataloguing documents, collections were not organized and some users placed them in cabinets and almirahs and locked them for their exclusive use. Because of this situation, faculty members never returned books that they got issued from the library. University's efforts to negotiate and appoint a full time professional librarian always failed as no one ever wanted to take over in such a library situation. Library and vendor conflicts, user staff conflicts, conflicts even among users were often witnessed and conflict management was almost the full time job of its manager. The library had no money even to replace a window pane broken due to users' violence. The Inflibnet grant provided by the UGC to set up Inflibnet Lab was not utilized for years. The workforce was highly demoralized and had not enough motivation for work except to perform the assigned duties. No meeting of library committee was held for more than ten years. No training programme was ever organized for library staff. As there was no property counter, users starting taking their own belongings and books inside the library. Under such a background the authorities resolved to modernize the University of Jammu Library systems and skeptics doubted whether a library that is not even rendering the traditional services ever be modernized.

A library monitoring committee was constituted in 1998 and environmental scanning started to identify the problem areas. The major problem areas identified were senior library staff members stagnation, lack of funds, age old statutes, lack of concern, resistance to change, etc. It was noted that in past few years some senior staff members including the Deputy Librarian in charge were concerned for their promotions, as they have been stagnating at the same position for more than a period of quarter century. The Deputy Librarian in charge retired but for rest of the senior staff members revision of grades and promotions were recommended. At the same time process of promotions of rest of the staff was also initiated. This led to a turn around situation in the library. A substantial change was noticed in staff's attitude towards development of the library and staff's positive participation in this process. The Inflibnet Lab was set up and the technical processing work began again in 1998. A property counter was established and collections were arranged with the help of concerned staff. Two more floors were added to the library building and age old rules and statutes were revised as a part of the process of administrative reforms. A new reference facility was set up. By the time the National Accreditation and Assessment Committee (NAAC) team visited the library, all the sections of the library were functional and a new service entitled 'Documentation on the J&K' was also started. An Internet lab was set up in 2003 and work for the complete automation of the library was started. Initially a decision was taken for bar coding of documents and later on it was decided to take the library ahead of present times and hence decisions were taken in favour of RFID technology. The process of internal restructuring of the Library was also started to improve work flows and make the library most inviting and peaceful place for study and information search.

In the next phase of development, the process of library development was integrated with organizational development as the university applied for ISO certification. As a part of this effort the library developed its mission statement, i.e. 'To provide need based library and information services which facilitate convenience to users and exceed expectations of users'. Objective statements were quantified and targets were set for retro-conversion and complete automation of the library. A library development fund and a local fund were instituted to meet the additional financial requirements of the library.

The staff was trained in handling machines and in the use of Lybsys software. University of Jammu Library is now a most peaceful place for study and information search and no conflicts are now noticed. The university authority helped to remove all hurdles for the all-round development of the library. While the university got ISO certification, the in-built mechanism of ISO certification helped the University of Jammu Library to develop into the most modern library in Northern India and it is now moving ahead towards its mission of developing a knowledge resource and service center.

The development model of the University of Jammu Library can be helpful for the development of other university libraries in India. From this model conclusions can be drawn that development of organizations and employees go hand in hand. To ensure optimum performance and development, organizations must care for their employees. In-built mechanisms and procedures of NAAC and ISO not only help the organizations to achieve quality but also set the pace for their further development. A turn around in the university fortunes is often attributed to a hero at the top. Leaders bring about change through strategic use of institutional resources and by winning the hearts and minds of the workforce.

Notes and References

1. Menon, Paddy, "New work speed, new terms." *The Tribune*, December 2, 2002, p. 3.
2. Kathleen, Bauer, "Trends in electronic content at the Crushing Whitney Medical Library: 1999-2003." *Journal of Electronic Resources in Medical Libraries*. 1(4) 2004, pp. 31-43.
3. "Cross sections and Transverse Single-Spin Asymmetries in Forward Neutral-Pion Production from Proton Collisons at vs=200GeV. *Physical Review letters* 92(17) 30 April 2004, pp. 1-6.
4. Meenal Dubey, "Let there be light, the IIT Way," *The Hindustan Times*, August 14, 2005, p. 6.
5. Sayeed Khan, Home-made chopper for Rs. 1 Lakh. *The Sunday Tribune*, Jalandhar, May 14, 2006, p. 24.
6. M. Suchitra, "Farmer who grows data", *The Tribune*, December 2, 2002, p. 3.
7. Namrata Khairah & K.P. Singh, "Knowledge Management in Corporate Organisations". Unpublished document, p. 7.
8. Rosen, Edward, "Copernicus published as he perished". *Nature* 241 (5384) February 16, 1973, p. 433.
9. John, Ziman, *The Force of Knowledge. The Scientific Dimension of Society*, Cambridge: Cambridge University Press, 1976, p. 120.
10. Hrederick, Noronha, "Farming questions, web based solutions," *The Tribune*, October 7, 2002, p. 2.
11. India and the Knowledge Economy, Leveraging Strengths and Opportunities; a World Bank Report launched at Washington D.C. on June 28, 2005 p. 2.
12. http://www.i4 donline.net/dec 04/rural India.pdf
13. I.V. Malhan and Anjali Gulati, Knowledge Management problems of developing countries with special reference to India", *Information Development*, 19(3), p. 211.
14. R. Suryamurthy, "ICAR revamp to benefit farmers". *The Tribune*, September 27, 2005, p. 2.
15. Rohit Saran, "To boldly go where". *India-Today*, December 13, 2004, pp. 48-54.
16. I.V. Malhan and Shivarama Rao, "From Library Management to Knowledge Management: A Conceptual Change", *Journal of Information & Knowledge Management*, 4(4) December 2005, p. 1.
17. Ronald C. Jantz, "Knowledge Management in Academic Libraries: Special Tools and Processes to Support Information Professionals". *Reference Services Review*, 29(1), 2001, pp. 33-39.

9

Library and Information Services in Higher Education for Visually Challenged Students: Study of the Rajasthan University Library, Jaipur

PRABHA SHARMA

Introduction

There is a growing consensus that human development must be at the core of any development. Education—the empowerment of individuals through the provision of learning is truly a human right and is a social responsibility. Education leads to individual creativity, improved participation in the social, economical, cultural and political life of society and hence to more effective contribution to human development.

In 1994 WHO, ILO and UNESCO issued their Joint Position Paper with the following definition of Community Based Rehabilitation. Community Based Rehabilitation (CBR) is a strategy within community development for the rehabilitation, equalization of opportunities and social integration of all people with disabilities. CBR also include thinking about issues of visually challenged people's lives at all times, and not exclusively about rehabilitation. Visually challenged disabled people should also have access to all services which are available to other people in the community, such as community health services, child health programmes, social welfare and especially Higher education.

Higher education plays an important role in the life and welfare of a nation. The institution of higher education, namely, universities and colleges—transmit, interpret and advance knowledge, thereby widening the horizons of intellectual attainment. Moreover, they are the main instruments for providing professional skills to the society, which are vitally important to the economic growth and stability of the society. The University library is a part and parcel of a university system. The success of academic programmes depends on the library facilities and services. The establishment of well-equipped libraries and closer integration with the teaching programme, thus, has become the matter of paramount significance. The University library is an important link between the theoretical teaching of the teacher and practical implementation of the student. A properly equipped library and its intelligent management and usage, form an integral and essential part of modern university education. The prime objective of University libraries is to provide reading and research materials and information to all readers including visually challenged students.

Visually challenged students have the same information needs as sighted readers. They also want access to relevant information in their chosen accessible format. The technological advances can make it possible. Therefore, library facilities may be provided to them in all fields and subjects at higher education level also so that they also develop to their full potential, ensuring equal opportunities and social integration. Such library services have been available for decades in most developed countries and are provided free or at nominal cost.

Background and Goals

Globally, in 2002 more than 161 million people were visually impaired, of whom 124 million people had low vision and 37 million were blind. More than 90 per cent of the world's visually impaired live in developing countries. But there is no country in the world today, where the affliction of blindness is as widespread as in India, nor where the ratio of blindness to population (350 millions) is so high. The totally blind are estimated at one and a half millions, the partially blind at three millions. The earliest school for the blind was founded rather more than fifty years ago at Amritsar by English missionaries, while schools at Calcutta and Ranchi followed some ten years later. Even today there are only about twenty organizations for the blind in the whole of India and out of these; few have adequate library and information resources to provide the services to the blind persons. In regard to higher education the situation is not very satisfactory.

The guidelines framed by the Government called "The Persons With Disabilities" (Equal opportunities, protection of rights and full participation) Act

(1995) ensures that the appropriate Governments and Local authorities implement the Act which says:

(1) ensure that every child with a disability has access to free education in an appropriate environment till he attains the age of 18 years.
(2) endeavour to promote the integration of students with disabilities in the normal school.
(3) promote setting up special schools in government and private sector for those in need of special education in such a manner that children with disabilities living in any part of the country have access to such schools.
(4) endeavour to equip the special schools for children with disabilities with vocational training facilities. Although this Act has introduced reservations in educational institutions, yet it makes little provision for the development of support services which can enable the visually challenged to enter the mainstream.

Rajasthan, with an area of 3,42,239 sq. km. is the biggest state of India in area. Climatically, Rajasthan is the driest state in the country. The largest desert (Thar-desert) is situated in the northern part of this state. The state is divided in to 32 districts, 15 sub-divisions, 241 tehsils, 9188 gram panchyats and a total of 39810 revenue villages. There are thirteen universities at present in the state. The University of Rajasthan is the oldest institution of higher learning in the state of Rajasthan. The University aims to impart higher education with quality and social relevance. It has 6 constituent colleges, 11 recognized research centers, 37 postgraduate departments and 305 affiliated colleges. University of Rajasthan has a vision of itself as a disabled friendly institution for the pursuit of higher education. It is committed to have reservation for physically handicapped students.

Rajasthan University library came into existence in Jaipur in the year 1949. It was created in corner of the office of the first Vice-Chancellor in Kesargarh Palace, which was later shifted to the present building in October 1958. Pt. Jawaharlal Nehru, the then Prime Minister of India inaugurated the building on 2nd October 1959. Over the years, to achieve the aims and objectives of the higher education, Rajasthan University Library has been playing a vital role. The first Librarian of this University was Late Prof. M.V. Mathur who joined in 1953. University Library caters for the needs of postgraduate students, research scholars, teacher fellows, M.Phil. students, faculty members and permanent non-teaching staff. Besides members of Senate, Syndicate, Academic Council, permanent teachers of the colleges affiliated to the university also can become members of the library. Special membership is given to retired faculty members and gazetted officers of Government of Rajasthan and local departments of Government of India. The library collection is well organized in order to render services to the users. The books are grouped in many sequences like general books, textbooks, reference books, theses, reports, and set collections etc.

The library owns a very rich collection of documents. It has a total collection of around 4,02,428 books, 63,823 back volumes of periodicals, 15,231 theses, 3,701 microfilms/micro-fiches, 17,580 reports, 186 manuscripts and 129 video-CDs. Currently 202 journals are being subscribed by the library. Various services rendered by the library are—General guidance and orientation to users, reference services, reprographic services, inter-library loan services, circulation services, and users consultation. The CD-NET and CD-ROM database services have been created and provided to the users and the users have direct access to the computers. The library has quite a number of CD ROMS for full text articles, multimedia and CDs which come along with books. The library has started providing Internet search service since 1997. E-Mail Service is also available for the users. Users are allowed to create their e-mails and collect the incoming emails. The database of theses and books, which has been entered into the computer, is also available for online access within the library to the users. Very recently, in March 2006, the connectivity of Internet for online access through university campus wide area network (WAN) has been provided in the library, which has been activated on some computer points by the INFONET centre of the UGC. With the active efforts of the library about 4078 e-journals of various publishers are available through UGC INFONET E-journals Consortium to the library.

Unfortunately, the library does not have any special library facilities for visually challenged students, whereas the present situation demands immediate remedies to fulfil the need. The fact may well be portrayed by the fact that recently the Department of Higher Education, State Government of Rajasthan has instructed to its Universities to cater for the needs of the blind/visually handicapped students.

In fact, the University has a vision for itself as a disabled friendly institution for the pursuit of higher education. It is committed to have reservation for physically handicapped students as per Government of Rajasthan policy. Merely giving admission to them is not enough to ensure that they will successfully be able to pursue their chosen courses of study. There are not yet any good library facilities for visually challenged students in the state at the higher education level. Furthermore, after personally interviewing visually challenged persons it has been observed that these students hesitate to take admission in higher education courses in the state of Rajasthan because the library and information services in the state are not fully equipped to fulfil the educational pursuits of the visually challenged students. It is felt that the time has come for the University libraries to move into another aspect of library service that is totally new in line with the 'caring society concept'. To provide equal information and education amenities seems to be necessity and quite feasible at present. Information technology has given more opportunities to provide equal library services to all including visually challenged users. Library facilities may be provided to visually challenged students in all fields and subjects so that they also develop to their full potential, ensuring equal opportunities and social integration.

Planning Library and Information Services for Visually Challenged Students in Rajasthan University Library—Jaipur

In order to plan efficient and effective library and information services—the following aspects are essential.

Objective

To provide library and information services to the users who are unable to read traditional printed material due to visual disability for higher education. Therefore, bridge the gap between desired basic resources and services and actual present conditions and open new horizons for effective library and information services for the visually challenged students in the State of Rajasthan.

Membership

Membership to the service will be given to the postgraduate students, research scholars and M.Phil. students and users who so ever register with the library as per rules of the library. Once they become member, they can enjoy all the services provided in the library during library working hours.

Visually Challenged Accessible Building

University Library building may be reviewed to incorporate ramps at the entrance and interiors of the building to allow free and easy mobility so that the building of the university library becomes accessible to visually challenged students so that they could use and move without difficulty and assistance.

Collection Development

There are four types of format that can be accessed by the visually challenged students: Braille (a tactile script based on raised dots), audio books, large-print books, and electronic text which can be heard as synthesized speech on a computer with appropriate software. Users tend to have their personal preferences in respect of this range of formats and University library service should offer access to all of them.

These collections are not easily available. There are significantly fewer books available commercially in accessible formats compared to what is published in print for the general public. The need to build collections in alternative formats and make them available for readers makes it necessary to develop special services. Therefore libraries have to arrange the following:

- ➤ Production and library facilities for Braille books.
- ➤ Production and collection of Audio books.
- ➤ Collection of unabridged electronic texts.

For such a library service to take off, University library require, the following as prerequisites.

Legislative

(1) Copyright Exemption: To free the translation of print media into formats such as audio recording, Braille, large-print and digital text from the current requirement of prior copyright permission.

(2) Mandatory requirement that every publisher in India using computerized composition of books used for higher education provide soft copies of every title using a prescribed disability electronic file format such as that of the DAISY standard. This will permit any text book required by a print-handicapped student to be converted into Braille, large-print or synthesized speech.

(DAISY is an international standard for accessible multimedia which is available for all including people with disabilities and indigenous and illiterate people to share information and knowledge. When the computer is connected with Braille display, the text is shown both on the screen and on the Braille display at the same time.)

The users of higher education libraries are mission oriented people and accordingly library professionals should develop the collection. There are some international libraries which have been developed in the advance countries. Before planning to develop library and information services for the blind users, the existing international libraries must be consulted and based on their collections, services and experience, libraries move towards designing the library and information services for the visually challenged users.

Equipments Needed

To facilitate the services to the visually challenged persons the equipments such as Braille printers, Braille embosser*, Braille display*, Duxbury Braille translator software*, Trackballs*, Arkinstone Reading Machine*, Screen enlarger*(The detailed description of each equipment mentioned are given below) and tape duplicators, reader (a text—to speed reading machine with synthesized speech output), closed circuit TVs for magnifying regular text, PCs with CD-ROMS, Power Macs with CD-ROMS, large print tape writers, special track tape recorders, computers that are having adaptable equipments such as voice eyes are needed.

(i) A Braille Embosser, hooked to a computer, produces high-speed Braille prints.

(ii) Braille display used by the blind people that is placed under the normal keyboard. When the user mark text on the screen the Braille display shows, in Braille (tactile signs, point script). When the person types something on the keyboard it also shows what is being written.

(iii) Duxbury Braille translator software—This software is needed to reformat electronic texts for Braille production.

(iv) Trackballs can assist those who have difficulty in controlling a mouse.

(v) Arkinstone Reading Machine can scan printed materials and read in a human-like robotic voice. This equipment is truly a breakthrough as those who come to use this equipment could "read" whatever documents or books without involving a third party.

(vi) Screen enlarger help the low vision users to see what is written on the screen. To be able to read well it is important that the web pages are so that text and background have a good contrast. To read printed information people with a low vision use a read-TV that can enlarge the text up to 25 times. There are so many softwares available to facilitate these users, i.e. enlarge text, listen to their e-mail messages, guide the users to new places, HTML reading, English to Braille converters and speech reading progmme etc.

Services

Visually challenged however students have many more needs than just access to the print media. The libraries are supposed to provide—

- Production of reading material in Braille.
- A recording studio.

- Computer lab equipped with computers for vision-impaired.

The potential and possibilities are endless. The library needs to bring its collection and services closer to the blind. By setting up a separate section for visually challenged students. The Libraries will be supposed to provide following services:

(1) Reading and consulting facilities for Braille books and large-print books.
(2) Listening facilities with head phones (talking books and other documents).
(3) Reference Service.
(4) Computers with online search and e-text preparation. The library will provide the Computer with Internet facility. The possibility of accessing the Internet by the blind will be a real information and technological break through.
(5) Circulation service.
(6) Recording facility.
(7) Mail bag service—This service will enable registered users on request to receive audio cassettes through the mail. Return of materials is also through the mail. This service could be available statewide. Libraries may plan to update mail bag service users profile to keep up-dated on their latest interests so the libraries could meet their changing needs.

Training of Staff

In order to create efficient and effective library and information services for the visually challenged students, training of library staff on a regular basis is essential to familiarize with important aspects of disability and visually challenged users in the library. The professional staff must be prepared to give individual attention so as to understand their strongest communication mode. Training programs for University library staff dealing with special equipments and collections for visually challenged students may be arranged. This can be done by professionals of special education. Thereby libraries and library professionals can play a significant role in promoting efficient library services to the visually challenged students.

Training of Users

Training of visually challenged users should be provided on a regular basis. Training may be arranged in using the special facilities and access to equipments available for them in the University library. Auto speaking guides for users should be designed in such a manner which cover all related aspects and can help them to use the services easily. Orientation programmes may be arranged for visually challenged users at regular intervals.

Financial Support and Assistance

Adequate financial support in order to sustain the above mentioned library services and subsequently expand them to suit the latest technological advancement are needed. With the financial support of State Government and University Grants Commission, services for visually challenged may be developed. Many international organizations such as UNESCO and IFLA encourage the training and continuing education of professionals in the field service to visually handicapped readers. They promote international inter-library loan materials for visually handicapped readers. They are also providing guidelines for the establishment of library service to visually handicapped persons in countries where it does not exist or is inadequate, thus bridging the information gap.

Conclusion

Therefore, to sum up, it may be concluded that with implementation of above proposed plan, visually challenged users will come in the mainstream, build self-reliance and independence, special integration with dignity, satisfy emotional needs and improve their quality of life by achieving higher education. The task includes the great and urgent work of helping the blinds to overcome their handicap by higher education that they may take their place as normal citizens. The close integration of the library and information services for visually challenged students/ blinds may not apply only to University interests within the community, but to state, region and country and to a certain degree, to research and scholarly pursuits, all over the world. Adhering to the proverb 'charity starts at home', and with an aim to develop and provide library and information services for visually challenged students/blinds in our own state and move forward to an advanced level in the country, region and ultimately the world.

References

Global estimate of visual impairment, by World Health Organization (WHO) region (millions), 2002.

http:\\www.ifla.org

http:\\www.unesco.org/webworld/libraries/manifestos/librarian.html

http:\\www.niso.org/about

Kishore, Rangashri. Voice of India's Disabled: Demanding Equality in Library Services in Proceedings of 65th IFLA Council and General Conference Bangkok, Thailand, August 20—August 28, 1999.

Kuffalikar, Chitra Rekha and others. Reaching the Unreached through Information Literacy Progrrames: An Overview in Proceedings of Fifty-second All India Library Conference, 26-29 December, 2006.

Kuffalikar, C.K. Libraries as Rehabilitation Centres. Proceedings of the IASLIC National seminar on Library Profession at Crossroad, November, 2000, Bhopal.

Mukherji, Anahita. Learning disabled students wins battle against school. *Times of India* 17 September, 2006, P5, C2-5.

Rajasthan University Library at a glance, University of Rajasthan—a brochure.

Rosemary, Kavangh and Beatrice, Christensen Skold. Eds. Libraries for the Blind in the information age guidelines for development. IFLA Report No. 86.

Vui Yin Wong. Sabah State Library: reaching out to the print handicapped in Proceedings of 65th IFLA Council and General Conference, Bangkok, Thailand, August 20—August 28, 1999.

www.uniraj.ernet.in

10

Information and Communication Technology: Library Resources Orientation Programmes at Ratan Tata Library of Delhi University Library System

LOKESH SHARMA and RAJESH SINGH

Introduction

The present study deals with library resources orientation programmes at Ratan Tata Library (RTL) of Delhi University Library System (DULS) for the P.G. students at Delhi School of Economics (DSE) of Delhi University. During presentations 198 questionnaires were distributed among the P.G. students of the four departments at Delhi School of Economics (DBBSE). 198 Responses on purpose of presentation, the use of various electronic resources, views about RTL were analysed using percentage method. The goal of this study is to provide information that librarians can use to make important decisions about collection development (print and electronic), training to staff and library services by collecting data from the users and also making provision of library resources orientation programmes. Resources could be best utilized and exploited once their contents are known and how to make use of them is explained to the library users.

1. Library Resources Orientation Programme: What

In the beginning of each academic session, there has been a practice of providing

Library Resource Orientation Programme to its newly enrolled library users by the Ratan Tata Library (RTL), one of the major library units of Delhi University Library System (DULS) at Delhi School of Economics (DSE), University of Delhi.

Till yester years lecture method was being used for the Library Resources Orientation Programme (LROP). This was basically to acquaint the users in the areas like privileges of library users, different collections and their placement in the library and services. From the current academic session, i.e., 2006-07, an attempt has been made by the University Librarian to acquaint the library users in exploring and using electronic resources of all kinds in their field of study and research, in addition to the traditional print and other resources of the library.

Therefore, just after the start of the present academic session the University Librarian, Delhi University Library System organized four separate LROPs at Delhi School of Economics for the departments of Commerce, Economics, Geography and Sociology in consultation with the respective departments. Each LROP was of two hours duration. The method was lecture-*cum*-presentation using electronic and multimedia. The theme was covering the following using resources of Delhi University Library System and the Ratan Tata Library:

- Introduction: Need of Information in teaching and learning
- Information Resources
- How to get relevant information
- Search Formulation
- Practical Exposure
- Electronic Resources

All electronic presentations were designed by the Deputy Librarian, Coordinator, Electronic Resources in consultation with the respective departments and the University Librarian. All presentations, using electronic and multimedia, were given in the respective departments by the University Librarian. Using lecture method, the Deputy Librarian, Incharge of the Ratan Tata Library acquainted all the participants about privileges of library users, different collections and their placement in the library and services at RTL.

Electronic Resources: Why

Libraries of all sizes and types are embracing digital collections, although most libraries will continue to offer both print and digital collections for many years to come. New purchases and purchases of journals, magazines, and abstracting and indexing services are heavily weighted towards digital, while digital books (e-books) are only beginning to become a presence in library collections.

Libraries prefer digital collections for many reasons, including, but not limited to, the following: digital journals can be linked from and to indexing and abstracting databases; access can be from the user's home, office, or dormitory whether or not the physical library is open; the library can get usage statistics that are not available for print collections; and digital collections save space and are relatively easy to maintain. When total processing and space costs are taken into account, electronic collections may also result in some overall reductions in library costs.

Such a dramatic switch from print collections to digital collections has an impact on library users and users' perceptions of the library. Many researchers have attempted to predict or measure that impact through surveys, transaction log analysis, and other research techniques. Librarians would like to be able to use the information and conclusions generated by the many research studies, especially because it is time consuming to conduct good research on their own and because the best measures of impact come after decisions are already made and collections are converted. Unfortunately, the conclusions of various studies sometimes seem contradictory, and it may be difficult to judge which research studies offer valid and reliable findings. The opinion literature outnumbers the research literature, and it may be a challenge to distinguish fact from opinion.

The goal of this study is to provide information that users can be well informed by using LROPs focusing their areas of interest and feedback from the participants can be best used to make important decisions about collection development, betterment in library services, and overall improvement of the library.

Although this introduction refers to the resources as digital resources or digital libraries, the less precice, but more commonly used terms electronic resources or electronic libraries have been used throughout as synonyms.

DULS/RTL-Website

The members of the Ratan Tata Library can access DULS/RTL-Website by clicking on Libraries on the webpage of Delhi University accessing http://www.du.ac.in for any of the following information:

Delhi School of Economics and Ratan Tata Library	Books, Journals and Other Electronic Resources
History Information for Members and Borrowing Facility Departments Staff	Collections Electronic Resources e-Journals Subscription—2006 List of Serials Holding List of Theses and Dissertations Online Journals and Databases UGC-InfoNet UGC-InfoNet (Subjectwise E-Journals)

Library Services
Current Contents Document Reservation Facility Inter-Library Loan New Additions to the Collection OPAC Photocopying Services

Presentation Focused on Databases Accessible Through Delhi University Campus Network

The presentation was basically focused on using databases accessible through Delhi University Campus Network listed below:

Xreferplus has an access to the full text of the best reference books, along with images, customizable data, visual concept maps of results, sound, maps, and more	To access database click here: http://www.xreferplus.com/
Item 13 ABI-INFORM Complete includes, ABI/INFORM Dateline, ABI/INFORM Global, and ABI/INFORM Trade and Industry	To access database click here: http://proquest.umi.com/login/ipauto
Item 11 Academic Search Premier	To access database click here: Academic Search Premier
Item 2 *ACM Portal*: Portal of the Association for Computing Machinery: access the digital library and guide to computing literature in full text.	To access database click here: http://portal.acm.org
American Chemical Society Publications: Online access to the 31 full-text journals and magazines of the ACS from volume—1 from way back to 1879.	To access database click here: http://pubs.acs.org/about.html
American Institute of Physics: Online access to 11 full-text Journals and magazines published by the AIP from 1997 onwards.	To access database click here: http://www.aip.org

(*Contd.*)

American Institute of Physics: Online access to 11 full-text journals and magazines published by the AIP from 1997 onwards.	To access database click here: http://www.aip.org
American Physical Society: Online access to 8 full-text journals published by the American Physical Society from 1997 onwards.	To access database click here: http://publish.aps.org
Blackwell Synergy: Blackwell Synergy holds the full-text content for most of Blackwell's journals, the majority of which are published on behalf of international scholarly and professional societies.	To access database click here: http://www.blackwellsynergy.com/servlet/useragent?func=showHome&type=journals&action=1
Business Source Premier Item 3	To access database click here: Business Source Premier
Cambridge University Press Journals: Full-text Journals published by the Cambridge University Press in Humanities, Social Sciences and Science covering 1400 new publications annually since 1997 onwards.	To access database click here: http://journals.cambridge.org
Cell Press: Nine cell biology full-text journals: cell, immunity, neuron, molecular cell, structure, etc.	To access database click here: http://www.cellpress.com
Current Abstracts Item 7	To access database click here: Current Abstracts
Elsevier Science Direct (Full-text Collection of 1500 Journals on trial till 10th June, 2006) Science Direct is the world\'s largest electronic collection of science, technology and medical full-text and bibliographic information	To access database click here: http://www.sciencedirect.com/
Emerald Journals (Library Science Journals Only): Emerald publishes the world's widest range of management and library and information services journals, as well as a strong specialist range of engineering, applied science and technology journals.	To access database click here: http://www.emeraldinsight.com/
For comprehensive search to all the EBSCO Databases use the search engine Item 10	To access database click here: http://search.epnet.com
Humanities International Complete Item 5	To access database click here: Humanities International Complete
Lexis-Nexis Academic Universe Item 12	To access database click here: http://web.lexis-nexis.com/universe
Library, Information Science and Technology Abstracts Item 9	To access database click here: Library, Information Science and Technology Abstracts
Regional Business News Item 8	To access database click here: Regional Business News
Scopus: Abstract and Citation Database Item 1	To access database click here: http: //www.scopus.com/scopus/home.url
SocINDEX with Full Text Item 4	To access database click here: SocINDEX with Full Text
TOC Premier	To access database click here: TOC Premier

(*Contd.*)

Item 6	
Encyclopaedia Britannica: Encyclopedia Britannica, Inc. is one of the world's most trusted sources of information on every topic imaginable—from the origins of the universe to current events and everything in between. This Encyclopedia Britannica reference tool can be used by Faculty and research scholars including colleges across the university as the national site licensing is taken	To access database click here: http://search.eb.com
Euclid: Project Euclid is a user-centered initiative to create an environment for the effective and affordable distribution of serial literature in mathematics and statistics. Euclid provide 18 Journals.	To access database click here: http://projecteuclid.org
Ingenta Gateway: Provides access to more than 14 million citations from over 27,000 journals in all subject areas from 1988 to the present. It provides access to more than 6000 full text online publications. It covers around 260 academic and professional publishers worldwide.	To access database click here: http://deihi.library.ingentaconnect.com
JSTOR: JSTOR is a fully searchable database containing various online journals in full-text from different subjects including Social Science and Humanities.	To access database click here: http://www.jstor.org/browse
Kluwer Online Journals: Access to Kluwer journals in subjects including science, technology, humanities and law from 1997 onwards. It provides access to 2,65000 articles and over 50,000 articles published annually from 1997 onwards. It has received acclaim for having highest number of citations per paper.	To access database click here: http://journals.kluweronline.com/
MathSciNet: MathSciNet is a fully searchable database. The MathsSciNet entry for each Annals paper from 1884 to 1997 is linked to the original on JSTOR.	To access database click here: http://web5s.silverplatter.com/webspirs/start.ws?customer=c180484
Nature: Full-text access to the journal from the nature publishing group.	To access database click here: http://www.nature.com/nature
Oxford University Press—Online Journals: OUP is the world's largest University press. It provides full-text access to articles in Social Sciences, Science and Humanities.	To access database click here: http://www3.oup.co.uk/jnls/online/
PapersInvited database (Conference Alert database): PapersINVITED was conceived and developed to assist researchers at all levels—scientists, professors, post-docs and students who are seeking publishing opportunities for their research papers in all disciplines.	To access database click here: http://www.papersinvited.com
Project MUSE (John Hopkins University): Online access for 222 scholarly journals in arts & humanities, social sciences and Mathematics at the Johns Hopkins University from 1999 onwards. It is a bibliographic databases namely Analytical abstract, Catalysts chemical hazard, Laboratory hazard, Methods in organic synthesis and Natural Product reports are accessible.	To access database click here: http://muse.jhu.edu/journals
Portland Press: Full-text access to four journals, namely: Biochemical Journal, Biochemical Society Transactions, Biotechnology and Applied Biochemistry and Clinical Science is being made available with the archival access from 1996 onwards.	To access database click here: http://www.portlandpress.com
Royal Society of Chemistry: Royal Society of Chemistry, the largest organization in Europe for advancing the chemical sciences provides access to full-text articles from 23 journals from 1997 onwards. It also includes	To access database click here: http://www.rsc.org

(*Contd.*)

access to Bibliographic Databases namely: Analytical Abstracts, Catalysts and Catalysed Reactions, Chemical Hazards in Industry, Laboratory Hazards Bulletin, Methods in Organic Synthesis, Natural Product Updates.	
Science Magazine (A.A.A.S.): Online access to the Science magazine published by the American Association for the Advancement of Science. It provides access to the full-text contents from October 1996 through latest issue.	To access database click here: http://www.sciencemag.org/
SCOPUS : Scopus is a revolutionary new navigational product for all sciences from Elsevier. Apart from being the world's biggest abstract database covering 25 million abstracts from over 13,450 titles across.	To access database click here: http://www.scopus.com/
SpringerLink: SpringerLink offers electronic and printed literature from Springer-Verlag. A full-text access is made available for around 550 journals from 1997 onwards.	To access database click here: http://www.springerlink.com
Taylor & Francis Online Journals: Taylor & Francis Journals including the imprints of Taylor & Francis, Carfax, Routledge, and Spon Press, together with 63 journals from the former Scandinavian University Press. Full-text access is available for 1030 journals from 1998 onwards in most cases.	To access database click here: http://journalsonline.tandf.co.uk
UN and other international agencies publications: This link provides the list of UN and other International Agencies Publications. Like Asian Development Bank (ADB), Demographic and Health Surveys, Human Development Resource Centre, International Monetary Fund (IMF), International Organizations of the world, International Statistical yearbooks, United Nations, UNESCO: Communication and Information, UNESCO Natural Sciences Portal, UNESCO Social & Human Sciences, UN databases, UN-HABITAT, UNDP, UN Statistics Division (United Nations), United Nations Educational, Scientific & Cultural Organization, UNESCO Institute for Statistics, UNICEF Statistical Data, WHO Statistical Information System (WHOSIS), World Trade Organization (WTO).	To access database click here: http://csl.du.ac.in/online/un-international.htm

Users' Responses

To obtain responses of the participants of all the four presentations, 198 questionnaires were distributed among them. Questions asked are given in the appended questionnaire and have been marked 1-9 for responses to be given in ticked form on a 4 point scale ranging from Strongly Agree, Agree, Disagree, to Unsure. The last question no.10 is for getting their suggestions on the overall presentation and the working of RTL.

The responses and percentage on various questions have been presented subject wise in Tables 1-4.

Following Abbreviations have been used:

TNR : Total Number of Respondents

Table 1 : Department of Commerce

Questions	Student Participants 56									
	1	2	3	4	5	6	7	8	9	10
1. TNR	56/100%	56/100%	56/100%	76/100%	56/100 %	69.4/100 %	56/100 %	96.4/100 %	56/100%	Program be supported by printed material (10%)
2. SA	39%	33%	41%	12%	34%	57%	30%	44%	27% Excellent	Presentation be brief (15%)
3. A	61%	66%	57%	74%	59%	29%	68%	52%	68% Good	Password be provided for Electronic Resources (25%)
4. DA	—	—	2%	14%	7%	4%	—	2%	5% Fair	Staff be trained for public dealing (20%)
5. NS	—	—	—	—	—	10%	2%	2%		Multiple copies of textbooks be made available (30%)

Table 2 : Department of Economics

Questions	Student Participants 67									
	1	2	3	4	5	6	7	8	9	10
1. TNR	67/100%	92%/100 %	95%/100 %	98%/100 %	98%/100 %	98%/100 %	98%/100 %	67/100%	67/100%	Presentation be brief (20%)
2. SA	19%	26%	61%	50%	41%	54%	23%	28%	11% Excellent	Passwords for all Electronic Databases be made available (25%)
3. A	75%	68%	38%	49%	56%	41%	66%	53%	66% Good	More computers be made available (20%)
4. DA	—	6%	—		3%	5%	6%	5%	23% Fair	Staff should be courteous (20%)
5. NS	6%	—	1%	1%	—	—	5%	4%		

Table 3 : Department of Geography

Questions	Student Participants 37									
	1	2	3	4	5	6	7	8	9	10
1. TNR	100% of 37	100% of 37	100% of 37	100% of 37	100% of 37	100% of 37	100% of 37	100% of 37	100% of 37	One suggested it should be repeated
2. SA	21%	30%	30%	19%	16%	38%	30%	40%	22% Excellent	One suggested for enhancement of more Electronic Resources
3. A	66%	65%	59%	78%	65%	59%	65%	54%	75% Good	For subscribed databases password be made available so that at home it can be used (25%)
4. DA	13%	5%	11%	3%	—	3%	3%	3%	3% Fair	Increase more Reference Books in Geography (20%)
5. NS	—	—	—	—	19%	—	3%	3%		Increase more Journals in Geography (10%)

Table 4 : Department of Sociology

Questions	Student Participants 38									
	1	2	3	4	5	6	7	8	9	10
1. TNR	100% of 38	100% of 38	100% of 38	97% of 38	97% of 38	100% of 38	100% of 38	100% of 38	100% of 38	One suggested for More stacks guides
2. SA	29%	16%	47%	26%	26%	53%	37%	42%	26% Excellent	Two (06%) suggested staff be asked to be courteous
3. A	68%	54%	53%	66%	66%	37%	60%	52%	66% Good	15 (39%) suggested it was Excellent and Eye-Opener
4. DA	03%	—	—	05%	05%	03%	03%	03%	08% Fair	One (3%) suggested it be made Online
5. NS	—	—	—	—	—	08%	—	03%		

SA : Strongly Agree
A : Agree
DA : Disagree
NS : Not Sure

Analysis

The analysis of the responses received on the basis of various presentations reveals the following:

- response was overwhelming,
- the effort was appreciated by one and all,
- the presentation should have been more specific and concise,
- it has provided a direction to all the new entrants for proper utilization of library resources,
- staff must be polite and courteous,
- more computers and Electronic Database be provided,
- password for subscribed databases be made available to the users,
- copies of Textbooks be multiplied, and
- number of Journals in some subjects been increased.

Conclusion

The goal of this study is to provide information that users can be well informed by using LROPs focusing their areas of interest and feed back from the participants can be best used to make important decisions about collection development, betterment in library services, and overall improvement of the library.

References

Bailey, Charles W. *Scholarly Electronic Publishing Bibliography*. Available at http://info.lib.uh.edu/sepb/sepb.html.

Boykin, Joseph F. (2002). LibQUAL+™ As a Confirming Resource. *Performance Measurement and Metrics* 3(2): 74-77.

Eason, K., S. Richardson, and L. Yu. (2000). Patterns of Use of Electronic Journals. *Journal of Documentation* 56(5): 477-504.

Friedlander, Amy (2002). *Dimensions and Use of the Scholarly Information Environment: Introduction to a Data Set.* Washington, DC: Council on Library and Information Resources. Available at http://www.clir.org/pubs/reports/pub110/contents.html

Guthrie, Kevin M. (2002). Lessons from JSTOR: User Behavior and Faculty Attitudes. *Journal of Library Administration* 36(3): 109-120.

Institute for the Future, (2002). *E-Journal User Study. Report of First Survey*. Available at http://ejust.stanford.edu/findings/survey1.pdf.

Kidd, Tony (2002). Electronic Journal Usage Statistics in Practice. *Serials* 15(1): 11-17.

King, Donald W. and Carol Tenopir. 2000. The Cost and Price Dilemma of Scholarly Journals. Proceedings of the 63rd Annual Meeting of the American Society for Information Science, Chicago, November 2000. Volume 37: 63-66.

OCLC, (2002). How Academic Librarians Can Influence Students' Web-Based Information Choices. OCLC White Paper on the Information Habits of College Students. Available at http://www2.oclc.org/oclc/pdf/printondemand/informationhabits.pdf.

Palmer, Janet P. and Mark, Sandler (2003). What Do Faculty Want? Netconnect (Winter): pp. 26-28.

Seeds, Robert S. (2002). Impact of a Digital Archive (JSTOR) on Print Collection Use. *Collection Building* 21(3): 120-122.

Tenopir, Carol and Donald W. King (2002). A Glimpse of the Future Use of Scholarly Journals with Data from the Past and Present. Proceedings of the 22nd Annual Charleston Conference.

11

From Raga to Remixes: Is there Accessibility in Academic Libraries?

DEEPA BANERJEE

With the increasing South Asian population in North America since the 1970s, a South Asian Diaspora has formed in the West. The trends in the diaspora culture are evolving continually and music is a significant part of this culture. Music manifests in it, the social and cultural changes of the community. Although this evolution is evident, first generation immigrants still enjoy the traditional elements of South Asian music that they brought with them as well as the modern music of their host countries.

The youth from the South Asian Diaspora have invented new musical styles, which represent a combination of Eastern and Western music. These musical forms have evolved within the South Asian expatriates away from the subcontinent.

In fact, the impact of South Asian music is so profound that the non-South Asian communities in the West are also trying to learn and understand the traditional as well as modern musical elements of South Asia. Everyone interested in this music must have access to these musical resources that reflect the traditional and modern trends. Where do they turn to access such resources? Often, many turn to academic libraries. Then a pertinent question arises whether the academic libraries of North America are making printed and recorded South Asian musical resources accessible to this growing clientele.

This article envisages a portrayal of the changing forms of South Asian music in the East as well as in the West. The intent of this article is not only to present the changes in musical styles but also to identify whether these musical resources (printed and recorded) that reflect the traditional and changing forms of music are easily accessible to the interested groups. What are the academic libraries doing to locate, acquire, maintain and disseminate the printed and recorded musical resources of South Asia? This brings us to the beginning of this exciting journey through the musical world of South Asia.

South Asian music encompasses music from India, Pakistan, Bangladesh, Sri Lanka, Nepal and Tibet. Music is linked to their social and religious cultures. Each South Asian country has its unique musical style, e.g. classical, folk and film music in India, Sufi music, Qawwalis and Ghazals in Pakistan, Buddhist ritual chants, Singhalese folk music and drumming in Sri Lanka and music by Damai and Gaine musicians in Nepal.

This article will concentrate on Indian music with its many forms and styles, its impact on the West and the evolution of new trends in the South Asian Diaspora. This is because Indian music embraces classical, popular, folk as well as Sufi music, Qawwali and Ghazals from the neighbouring countries.

A Brief History of Indian Music

The history of Indian music has its roots in the Vedas (4000-1000 BC), the scriptures which contain hymns. Music was expressed in the form of hymns till 12th century. The Muslim rulers from Persia invaded India from northwest in the 13th century. The period, 1300-1800 AD observed remarkable changes in the music style as the Muslim rulers blended their music styles with the prevalent style and made it more melodious and flexible (Jairazbhoy, 1971). However, the South Indian music remained free from exogenous influence. This period also saw the evolution of two distinct styles of Indian music, namely, *Carnatic* (South Indian) and *Hindustani* (North Indian).

Carnatic tradition is still prevalent in four Southern states of India (Karnataka, Tamil Nadu, Kerala and Andhra Pradesh) but Hindustani music stretches itself to all of the other parts of India.

During the time of Muslim rule, Hindustani music changed many shapes and forms ranging from *Dhrupad* (which originated in 13th century as temple music and brought to court by Raja Mansingh Tomar) to *Khayal* which was invented in 18th century by Adarang and Sadarang in the courts of Mohammed Shah Rangile.

Some other musical creations of that era are Sufi music (music by Sufi saints who came to India from Persia), Qawwali (Muslim devotional music invented by Amir Khusro), and devotional literature and songs called "bhajans" by Surdas, Tulsidas and Kabir.

Dhrupad, a serious style of singing with fixed compositions and rhythmic variations has declined in popularity since 18th century. Very few contemporary musicians (with the exception of Dagar brothers and few others) practice *Dhrupad* style. *Khayal*, on the other hand, is still a very melodious and popular style of music. It is a blend of Indian and Persian music and is characterized by improvisation and ornamentation (Jairazbhoy, 1971). *Khayal*, in Persian, literally means "imagination". The *Khayal* compositions are sung in different ragas.

Both Carnatic and Hindustani music use "*Raga*" and "*Tala*" as a basis for their singing.

"Indian music has given the world raga and *tala*—*raga* as the melodic microcosm and tala embracing the rhythmic aspect" (Gautam, 1980, p. 18). Another definition is that "a combination of *swaras* (notes) in certain order of ascent (called *arohana*) and descent (called *avarohana*) produces a *raga*"(Iyengar, 2003, p. 36).

Carnatic music belonged more to the temples and religious schools than to royal courts. Modern "*Kritis*" (formats of Carnatic composition) were originally derived from *Sankeertanas* composed by Tallapaka Annamacharya. "The term *kriti* refers to the composition, where claim to permanence lies principally in its music and not in its lyric". (Iyengar, 2003, p. 23).

Modern Kritis are a combination of *Bhava* (expression), *raga* and *tala*. Three musicians, Thyagaraja (1767-1847), Muthuswami Dikshitar (1776-1835) and Syama Shastri (1762-1827), who were contemporary composers during the rule of Maratha kings, contributed to the standardization of *kriti* format as the most important form of Carnatic music (Iyengar, 2003).

During the period of British Raj (1857-1947 AD), famous Hindustani musical *gharanas* (schools) in the North were established. *Khayal* style branched out in various gharanas with each gharana having its own distinct style. These *gharanas* were named primarily after princely states like Gwalior, Agra, Kirana, Patiala and Mewati (Karnani, 2005).

The following other Hindustani semi-classical musical styles developed during this period:

(i) *Tappa*: The compositions are in Punjabi and rendered in a fast tempo.
(ii) *Thumri*: The compositions are in Braj language and the text revolves around description of Lord Krishna. These are rendered in lighter *ragas* such as *Kafi, Piloo* and *Jhinjhoti*.
(iii) *Bhajans*: These are devotional songs and not necessarily confined to a particular *raga*.
(iv) *Ghazals*: These are love poems in Urdu language and do not strictly follow the classical rules of raga. *Ghazals* are very popular in India today.

This period was also the era of recorded music and film music. European instruments such as violin and harmonium became indispensable instruments while performing classical music.

Another wave of changes came to Independent India in 1947 after the British Raj with the advent of new technologies and recording companies. Film music, facilitated by the recording companies, became very popular. Classical Indian music also started reaching the West.

Classical Music in the West

Ferrel (1997) rightly points out that "Indian Music has passed through the musical and cultural filter of the West in a number of ways." This is because music is an aspect of a social and cultural system and it must respond to social and cultural conditions and changes (Neuman, 1976).

As Indian classical musicians (who were mainly instrumentalists) started travelling to the West in the 1950s, Indian music became a part of Western popular culture. Ravi Shankar, Ali Akbar Khan and Ustad All Rakha became very popular in the West with the sitar, the sarod and the tabla (Ferell, 1997).

Ravi Shankar changed the Western perception of Indian music with his magical sitar performances and collaboration with pop, jazz and rock musicians such as George Harrison, Pete Townshend, Peter Gabriel, John Mclaughlin and Frank Zappa. The adoption of sitar in popular music is a unique example of how elements of music from one culture can be used in another culture in a different context. The term "raga" was effortlessly combined with "rock" (Ferrell, 1997, p. 13).

Ravi Shankar's collaboration with Yehudi Menuin brought out two albums: "East meets West" and "In Celebration". The Beatles used Indian music in their album, and Ravi Shankar appeared on their album.

By the 1970s a few Indian music schools were also established in the USA, such as, Ali Akbar Khan College of music in California. In 1969, Ravi Shankar became Billboard Magazine's "Musician of the Year". Some talented musicians from India also settled in the USA which also helped in spreading Indian music in the USA.

Later on, L. Subramaniam, a talented violin player joined Pandit Ravi Shankar and George Harrison in 1974 for a tour in Bangladesh. *Garland*, *Spanish Wave* and *Indian Express* are examples of his fusion albums. In the eighties and nineties, Zakir Hussain and Vishwa Mohan Bhatt were involved in fusion experiments. Zakir Hussain, the *tabla* maestro, fused his percussion ensemble with sounds from the East and West. Similarly, Vishwa Mohan Bhatt, a Mohan Veena player, collaborated with Ry Cooder, to produce fusion music (Ferrell, 1997).

Popular Music In India

While the West was experimenting with classical Indian music since the 1960s, a new taste for popular music was developing in India. The popularity continues even now and the bulk of Indian popular music is produced, marketed and distributed commercially on a mass scale (Manuel, 1988).

Film music is the largest category of popular music in India. In the early period, film music was based on classical and semi-classical music styles and folk music. Regional film music was mainly based on folk songs. Film music from the 1940s to the 1970s was composed and sung by very limited but very talented musicians, for example, music composers such as Hemant Kumar, Shankar Jaikishan, Naushad and singers such as Lata Mangeshkar, Mohd. Rafi, Kishore Kumar etc. There was domination of one vocal style created by film studios and super imposed upon a diverse listening audience (Manuel, 1988).

The modern Indian film music incorporates western musical elements (Pop and Rock) and Western instruments, for example, piano, violin, keyboard, synthesizer, etc., along with *tabla* and *dholak.* Film music combined with latest technology has the power to attract audiences beyond language barriers. The catchy popular tunes from the films like *Chalte Chalte, Devdas,* and *Parineeta* attract broader audiences including the ones who cannot understand Hindi.

In India, film music is a part of everyday life and can be heard in shops, homes, restaurants, and buses. Film music is heard through cassettes, DVDs, Internet sites and MP3 players. Television is another major source of film music, and it has spread the music to South Asian Diaspora community in the West through Zee, Sony and other TV channels. Reality television shows including *Sa Re Ga Ma Pa*, Indian Idol and Fame Gurukul (where young singers compete to be selected as India's playback singers) engage audiences all over the world to participate in the show by giving them an opportunity to vote for their favourite participants. These reality TV shows have offered extremely talented singers such as Shreya Ghoshal and Kunal Ganjawala to the Indian film music industry. These promising shows (that are gateways to a bright future for so many participants) encourage younger generations to take popular music seriously.

Folk Music

The popularity of a wide variety of folk music from different regions of India has lessened due to film music, pop music, private albums, and reality TV shows. However, folk music is still being incorporated in film music and remixes. Bhangra music has regained its popularity in the West. Some regional festivals and celebrations still give prominence to folk styles. A few examples include *Dandiya* from Gujarat, *Lavani* from Maharashtra, *Bhangra* from Punjab and *Bauls* from Bengal.

South Asian Music in Diaspora

In 1970, the changes in immigration laws resulted in a lot of South Asians migrating to North America. Therefore, since the early 1970s, it was the South Asian Diaspora which brought and developed Indian music in North America.

They formed a number of organizations to promote Indian classical music, mainly by getting artists from India and organizing their concerts in North America. SPICMACAY and Ragamala are a few examples of such organizations. These organizations are now hosting concerts by talented musicians that have nurtured their Indian musical training in the USA through established Indian music schools.

Because of the South Asian Diaspora's growing interest in Bollywood (Bombay film industry) music, top playback singers and directors, e.g. A.R. Rahman, Sonu Nigam, Himesh Reshamiya and many others, tour North America and perform in all the major cities. These concerts attract thousands, who dance to the catchy and fast musical numbers.

Also, South Asian university students form musical groups. At the University of Pennsylvania, a small a cappella men's ensemble named "Penn Masala" was formed approximately ten years ago. The group has produced five CDs including songs that are featured in movies. This group, along with other university groups, promotes Indian music to the university community through stage shows.

Indian Music took new forms and shapes due to continuous musical experiments by young South Asians in the West who naturally combine the traditional and the modern as well as the Eastern and Western. Some of these musical forms include Desi music, Bhangra music and India pop.

Desi Music

Desi (indigenous) music, a recent phenomenon, is a musical invention by young South Asians in the diaspora community. Desi music mainly refers to Hindi remixes (combination of Hindi film songs and Western beats) and Bhangra (Punjabi) music. This music is a tool for young South Asians to express their unique cultural identity and to integrate and unite all the young South Asians. "Desi music scene arising only in recent years has become an epicenter for the creation and mediation of Indian American youth consciousness. From the extremely heterogeneous, regional, religious, social and cultural Indian heritages of these youth, desi music has been vital in the formation of an integrated Indian American youth community" (Diethrich, 2000, p. 64).

He further comments "It also helps maintain diasporic relationship with the homeland through the use of current Hindi film songs, which along with websites, magazines and satellite media including a 24 hour satellite broadcast. MTV India allow Indian Americans to be continually informed about what is hot in Indian popular culture. This emphasizes the great impact of global capitalism and technology for strengthening diasporic links" (Diethrich, 2000, p. 55).

Bhangra Music

Bhangra music has its roots in Punjab. The new form of Bhangra by South Asian youth has the traditional music and the Western beat. This combination makes bhangra music appealing to Non-South Asians as well. This music has more exposure to people through Satellite television, B4U Music TV channel.

The New York Bhangra Scene, described as follows reflects the popularity of Bhangra music. "Today, the growing New York Bhangra scene presents a remarkably diverse South Asian Community ranging from working class urban kids to middle class professionals. Hip hop is one unifying influence. Local clubs have monthly Bhangra parties. Spots like Metronome, Chinaclub, The Bank and Tunnel have also joined the Bhangra scene" (Samantha and Bhatnagar, 1998, p. 45).

Some other Musical Trends

The young Indian Americans have also been experimenting with the musical trends that have their roots in Britain.

"Indipop" as the name itself suggests, is a combination of Indian and Pop music. The song track "Ever So Lonely" sung by Sheila Chandra in 1982 with sitar and tabla is one such example of early Indipop in Britain (Ferrell, 1997).

Another musical form is a fusion of jazz and ghazals. Nazma Akhtar's album "Qareeb" by Triple Earth Record in Britain is an example of yet another fusion of jazz and ghazal styles (Ferrell, 1997).

There are further fusion experiments of rap and Indian music by "Apache Indian" and "Fun-Da-Mental" music group in Britain.

The recent Broadway musical "Bombay Dreams" a joint venture of A.R. Rahman (Indian film music director) and Andrew Lloyd Webber has further popularized Indian film music. It has presented Indian film music in a very novel form to the West.

"World Music" is yet another new term that is gaining prominence. "Modern society is demonstrating an increased consciousness of world community and a growing awareness of ethnic identity. Education for this kind of society makes ethnic music, not only a desirable component in the curriculum but also an urgently needed one" (Trimillos, 1972, p. 90).

Music as a cultural object has great significance for the growing sense of ethnic identity in America. Indian and Pakistani music style "Qawwali" has currently regained its popularity as one of the components of "World Music." Nusrat Fateh Ali Khan from Pakistan brought Qawwali to the Western audiences in the eighties (Ferrell, 1997).

The beginning of the 21st century is experimenting with different manifestations of the South Asian music. It would be interesting to watch the continuous evolution and social outcome of these new musical trends and experiments.

The modern society is very conscious of the rich presence of South Asian music and there is a constant effort to gain a deeper understanding of this music.

Are the Academic Libraries Making South Asian Musical Resources Accessible?

To offer a more extensive knowledge of South Asian music, music departments or ethnomusicology departments in academic institutions in North America are offering South Asian musical courses. Consequently, a huge responsibility lies on the shoulders of the academic libraries to make the existing printed and recorded South Asian music resources available to support the courses and the needs of the faculty and students.

What are the academic libraries doing to locate, acquire, maintain and disseminate the printed and recorded musical resources of South Asia?

A wide range of issues regarding acquisitions, maintenance and dissemination of these collections need to be addressed to answer the above questions.

In the process of finding some answers to the above questions, I have surveyed six academic libraries to identify the depth of their South Asian music collections and their methods of acquisitions, cataloging and the circulation of these materials. This survey is also an attempt to identify the future goals of these libraries in this area as far as technology; digitization and other related issues are concerned. These libraries are Harvard University's Eda Kuhn Loeb music library, Wesleyan University library, University of Chicago's (UC) music library, University of California-Berkeley's (UCB) Jean Gray Hargrave music library, University of California-Los Angeles (UCLA) music library and University of Washington music library (UW).

I selected the music libraries of the above mentioned universities because these are the leading Universities with an emphasis on ethnomusicology or world music programs.

The survey questions included queries about the size of the collection, collection strategies (ownership *vs.* access), acquisition methods, levels of cataloging, subject specialization of the librarians, technologies that make these resources available, and other related issues.

The data collected through these surveys from the above mentioned libraries reveal some interesting facts and cover a range of issues revolving around South Asian music collection. These surveys reveal the following facts:

Summary of Survey Results

Collection

Majority of the institutions surveyed have separate ethnomusicology archives, musical collections, with the exception of the UCB.

Majority of these libraries collect books, CDs, DVDs, videos, sound recordings and notated music resources. Some libraries such as UCB also collect serial publications that deal with music. These collections primarily serve the diverse teaching and research needs of the music department or ethnomusicology division that offers undergraduate major and graduate programs in South Asian music.

UCLA mainly collects books and music scores

UC's South Asian music collections consist of approximately 4,000 sound recordings. It also collects books, scores and videos (VHS and DVDS).

Harvard collects music research material in vernacular and English languages, despite its preference for English language. It does not collect children's music literature, music education, therapy literature, or recorded compilations. Instead, Harvard attempts to comprehensively collect material with depth and cultural/historical resonance.

Wesleyan collects books, CDs, videos, and occasionally printed music. A great deal of importance is given to the faculty requests. The library exercises a slight preference for South Indian music collection, as it is the focus of their music department. In addition to the material that the library purchases, there is also a world music archive that contains over 2000 field and concert recordings of Indian music. The library does not actively collect recordings for the archives but a lot of recordings come as a donation by the students, faculty and the visiting artists who are associated with Ethnomusicology program.

UW mostly collects books, CDs, cassettes and LPs. It also buys materials that are published and recorded in US.

Acquisitions

The bulk of all these acquisitions are based on the research needs of the faculty and students from ethnomusicology or music departments. Most of the libraries surveyed participate in South Asia Cooperative Acquisitions Program (SACAP in New Delhi and Islamabad) except Wesleyan. However, Wesleyan cooperates with two other consortium members, Trinity College and Connecticut College. For ethnomusicology or world music material, the partner schools depend on Wesleyan.

UCB's bulk of standard acquisitions are from SACAP (South Asia Cooperative Acquisitions Program) or European Academic Press supplemented by faculty and student requests. Their acquisitions of recordings are solely based on teaching needs and faculty requests. Occasionally, local vendors are contacted to fulfil faculty requests such as CD recordings from materials originating in the 1940s and 1950s.

UCLA's acquisitions consist of all the South Asian music publications by major western publishers and the resources that come to their attention through reviews, faculty requests and South Asian publishers' catalogs. The library also receives material through a US exchange program.

UC also Receives Materials through SACAP

Harvard's archive of world music specializes in the area of South Asian Music. The library takes great care to routinely include a large quantity of sound recordings and visual materials from this area. The library relies on a variety of resources to maintain a high level of academic musical collection. These resources include reviews of sound recording and media found in scholarly, ethnomusicology and popular music journals, citations found in articles and newspapers, professional society newsletter announcements of media publications, and websites of university ethnomusicology departments with media publication general websites of music, film and cultural societies. It also acquires materials through SACAP program and relies on vendors; for example, CD Roots, Smithsonian Folkways and South Asia Books.

Wesleyan primarily depends on the catalogs from South Asian publishers such as Bagchee for the acquisition of books. It orders audio and video recordings through vendors, including Rhinebech Records, Amazon.com, and many more.

University of Washington's (UW's) acquisitions are based on research needs of the faculty and students. Most of the South Asian music materials are acquired through SACAP. Western publications are acquired through major book distributors such as YBP, and music recordings are acquired through the regular dealers such as Silver Platter.

Please refer to the tables below for the rest of the survey results.

Genre

The table below shows different genres that are collected by the different libraries that were surveyed.

University of California-Berkeley	University of California-Los Angeles	University of Chicago
Northern and Southern Indian classical music and faculty requests.	All genres that are studied including classical, popular, and traditional.	All genres that are studied including classical, popular, and traditional.
Harvard	Wesleyan	University of Washington
North and South Indian classical music, folk, tribal, contemporary, and film music.	Carnatic music and less frequently Hindustani music. It also collects Bollywood and South Indian films.	Mostly traditional music that is not of the popular genre. Does not collect pop music.

Budget Allocation

All the libraries surveyed have no separate budget allocation for South Asian music materials. Budgets are allocated either for all the South Asian acquisitions (not just music) or all the music material (not just South Asia).

University of California-Berkeley	University of California-Los Angeles	University of Chicago
UCB has a total base funding divided into three categories: monographs, continuations and serials. Sound recordings are part of monograph funds. No specific amounts are put aside with any type, genre, or area in mind.	UCLA's funds are allocated by media i.e. monographs, serials, sound recordings, scores etc rather than subjects.	No separate budget for South Asian music.
Harvard	Wesleyan	University of Washington
No separate budget for South Asian music.	No separate budget for South Asian music.	No separate budget for South Asian music.

Access: Please see the table below for comparative analysis of circulation policies.

University of California-Berkeley	University of California-Los Angeles	University of Chicago
Books and scores circulate but sound and video recordings are for in-house only.	Circulation of sound recordings is restricted to faculty and students only. Ethnomusicology collections do not circulate.	All the collections, including books, scores, sound and video recordings circulate.
Harvard	Wesleyan	University of Washington
All the collections circulate. For the most fragile and rare recordings-dubbed copies are provided on I-pod or burned CDs.	Books, scores and CDs from the general collections circulate. LPs and some scores have certain restrictions. "World Music" collections are for in-house only.	Books circulate but recordings don't circulate.

Access vs. Ownership

University of California-Berkeley	University of California-Los Angeles	University of Chicago
Access is more important than ownership.	Access is more important than ownership.	Prefers ownership but increasingly, access remains the only option due to cost and space considerations. Electronic access to resources is gaining more importance.
Harvard Prefers ownership until or unless the issues of long-term archiving and preservation of the digital files are addressed.	Wesleyan Prefers ownership but increasingly, access remains the only option due to cost and space considerations. Ownership is more important for ethnomusicology rchives collections as they reflect the reputation of the institution.	University of Washington It depends on the importance and relevance of the material to UWs curriculum and research interests.

Technology used to Provide Access

All these libraries provide access to online catalogs/e-resources/Internet use, CD players, cassette players, VHS and DVD players and microform readers.

University of California-Berkeley	University of California-Los Angeles	University of Chicago
Provides DAT player, reel to reel player and MIDI player.	Streams via I-tunes. Produces CD for items on cassette tapes or LPs.	Transmits sound recordings electronically through password protected, streamed websites. Provides electronic access to South Asian music through Smithsonian Global Sound.
Harvard Provides on-line sound files linked to finding aids.	Wesleyan Streams audio recordings for some course reserves.	University of Washington Has a fully equipped music listening center.

Digitization

University of California-Berkeley	University of California-Los Angeles	University of Chicago
Collections have not been digitized yet.	Collections on demand have been digitized.	Some recordings have been digitized which are available on password through protected streamed websites.
Harvard South Asian music collections have been digitized partially, such as, James A. Rubin collection of South Asian music.	Wesleyan There is a future plan to digitize the "World Music" archives.	University of Washington Collections have been partially digitized.

Cataloging

University of California-Berkeley	University of California-Los Angeles	University of Chicago
Catalogs SACAP music materials based on the cataloging information provided by SACAP.	Provides full cataloging as they have a cataloger proficient in South Asian languages.	Provides full cataloging as they have a cataloger proficient in South Asian languages.
Harvard Provides full cataloging.	Wesleyan Provides minimal level of cataloging.	University of Washington Catalogs SACAP music materials based on the cataloging information provided by SACAP.

Subject Specialization of the Librarians

Most of the libraries have South Asian subject specialists and not necessarily South Asian music specialists.

Conclusion

After analyzing the survey results, I found that the libraries generally collect South Asian music material in all formats based on the current research needs of the students and faculty. It is essential, however, to also plan for the future needs of the users. Librarians require a clear vision of the possibility of substantial growth of interest not just in South Asian classical music but also in popular music and in the new musical trends in the Diaspora, invented by youth. A formulation of a collection development policy covering all genres would address the future needs and expand the scope of the collection.

The ethnomusicology archival collections could be expanded by collecting the field and concert recordings of not just classical but also other musical genres as well. The inclusion of ethnomusicology collections in the main catalog would increase accessibility to these collections. However, in reality, high costs and constrained budgets are obstacles, preventing the library to acquire acquiring important resources that address the current and future needs of the users. Libraries can form consortiums for co-operative acquisitions and digitization to combat the above mentioned challenges. Each member library can build an in-depth printed collection in one area and depend on the other libraries for other areas/ genres. This would be an effective strategy to avoid duplication of printed resources. A national bibliography of all the resources in academic institutions produced collaboratively by the music librarians will prove beneficial to all the users of these resources. Effective outreach programs, library workshops, instruction sessions might promote the music collection to the intended users.

Recruitment of motivated librarians who are very knowledgeable in this area can help build a rich collection. These librarians, with the capacity to visualize the changing technology and research needs of the users and initiate new projects and ideas, can serve as role models for positive changes in the libraries.

References

Diethrich, G. (2000). Desi Music Vibes: The Performance of Indian Youth Culture in Chicago. *Asian Music*, 31(1), 35-61. Retrieved November 12, 2006, from *JSTOR*.

Farrell, G. (1997). *Indian Music and the West*. New York: Oxford University Press.

Gautam, M. (1980). *The Musical Heritage of India*. New Delhi: Abhinav Publications.

Iyengar, B.R.C. (2003). *Raga Sudha: Understanding Carnatic Music*. Hyderabad: Vaivee.

Jairazbhoy, N. (1971). *The Ragas of North Indian Music: their Structure and Evolution*. Middletown, CT: Wesleyan University Press.

Karnani, C. (2005). *Form in Indian Music: A Study in Gharanas*. New Delhi: Rawat Publications.

Neuman, D. (1976). Towards an Ethnomusicology of Cultural Change in Asia [Electronic version]. *Asian Music*, 7(2), 1. Retrieved November 10, 2006 from *JSTOR*.

Samantha, A., & Bhatnager, C. (1998). Groovin' South Asian Style [Electronic version]. *Hues*. from Proquest (582069371).

Trimillos, R.D. (1972). Expanding Music Experience to Fit Today's World : A Conceptual Approach to Ethnic Musics Offers Students Valid Alternatives. *Music Educators Journal*, 59(2), 90-94. Retrieved November 18, 2006, from *JSTOR*.

Part III
National and Public Libraries

12

Founding of the National Library of Bangladesh: Post Colonial Experience

ABULFAZAL M. FAZLE KABIR

The national library of a country can be called a reflecting mirror of the profile of that nation. The history, the social trends and changes, national achievements, good times, bad times and other facts can be traced and understood by looking through the collection of a national library of a country.

Beginning with the role of the Bibliotheque Nationale of France, called the first national library of the world, hundreds of national libraries have been established in different countries of the world. However, the establishment of national libraries proper did not begin in many countries that were under colonial rule almost until the mid-twentieth century. The Indian subcontinent, the crown jewel of the British Empire, is one of these. The colonial rule of India under the British monarchy started in 1857. Before that the East India Company of England obtained royal charters from English government and carried on the administration of the country.

In 1947, India became independent of colonial rule and the British created two self-governing countries, India and Pakistan, on the eve of independence. The newly created Pakistan was comprised of two segments—West Pakistan and East Pakistan, separated by Indian Territory in the middle. Later, in 1971 the then East Pakistan emerged as an independent country and nation. This break-up was rooted to political incompatibility.

The Beginnings of the National Library

India, like many other countries under colonial rule, did not have any national library proper. However, there was an organized infrastructure that helped India to establish its national library sooner. The newly emerged Pakistan, on the other hand, had to start to plan for a national library from the rudiments, because of the geographic separation of its two segments/wings and the serious lock of an organized infrastructure. Because of the division of British India, the larger country India had the advantage of marshalling a plan for its national library.

Against this backdrop, Pakistan established a government central library in the capital of East Pakistan, Dhaka. It was designated as the copyright Book Depository Library. This library was established under the relevant section of "Delivery of Books and Newspapers" in the 1962 Copyright Ordinance of Pakistan. This Dhaka based central library was called Delivery of Books and Newspapers Branch of the Central Library of Pakistan, Dhaka. This branch continued to exist until after the emergence of Bangladesh in 1971.

After liberation, the need for appropriate mechanisms, legislation and avenues was voiced by all concerned, particularly the professionally educated librarians in Bangladesh. The opportunity for professional education for librarians had been available at Dhaka University, since late 1950s. This group of professional librarians created an impact on the Bangladesh government, by voicing their concern about the absence of a full-fledged national library for Bangladesh.

Later, in 1975, the Government of Bangladesh published three Gazette Notifications, LB/IL-13/75/385, LB/IL-13/75/386, dated August 8, 1975, and LB/IL-13/73/546, dated November 8, 1975, on developing a national library for Bangladesh.[1]

According to these Gazette notifications, the library, which was functioning as the Delivery of Books and Newspapers Branch of the Central Library of Pakistan, and might also be called the nucleus of a national library, would be developed as the National Library of Bangladesh. The National Library and the Bangladesh National Archives are stated to be working under the guidance of the Ministry of Cultural Affairs, Government of People's Republic of Bangladesh. Thus, by the mid-seventies the stage for the projected founding of a national library for Bangladesh was set.

Later, the Bangladesh government published in its Bangladesh Gazette Extraordinary, The Act Number XXVII of 1995, establishing a National Book Center to be henceforth called the National Library.[2]

In Bangladesh, the Legal Deposit System is the backbone of the National Library for the development of a national collection. It creates an archive of the country's creative and intellectual printed works. The Legal Deposit System of Bangladesh is governed by the Legal Deposit Regulations, as incorporated in the country's Copyright Law. The Legal Deposit Regulations promulgated in 2005 are at present in operation in Bangladesh. The Regulations had made the National Library of Bangladesh, the country's single depository, for the first time.[3]

Bangladesh also has a recent copyright law. The earlier Copyright Law of (Pakistan), 1962, was replaced by the Act of 1974 and amended by the Copyright Act No. 28 of 2000, which came into effect in November 2000.

The National Library Today

The National Library is now located in its own building in the locality called Agargaon, Sher-e-Banglanagar, in Dhaka.

The online encyclopaedia, Banglapaedia, gives a detailed resume of the role of the National Library of Bangladesh—The principal functions of the National Library of Bangladesh are as follows:

(1) to collect and preserve all publications within the country in accordance with the Bangladesh Copyright Act, 1974 (amended 2000), to manage them properly and make them available to the readers and researchers;
(2) to prepare and publish a national bibliography;
(3) to act as the guardian of all the libraries in the country;
(4) to make contact with all the libraries home and abroad and share and exchange resources and information with all of them;
(5) to prepare and publish an index of all the editorials and important articles published in the national dailies;
(6) to assist and co-operate for the development of the library science and information service;
(7) to prepare and publish a library directory;
(8) to allocate International Standard Book Numbers (ISBN); and
(9) to prepare and publish a Union Catalogue for Bangladesh.[4]

The National Library of Bangladesh has several sections, namely the Bibliography Section, Library Section, Binding Section, Processing Section, Computer Section and Microfilm Section. It has undertaken an automation program for its collection and information through Foxpro, Visual Foxpro and CDS/ISIS systems.

A computer scanning program has also been adopted for preserving many rare books and documents. The library has also undertaken a microfilming program for conserving rare materials especially the old newspapers. For this purpose it has very recently acquired a modern microfilm unit with computerized camera, a data processor, microfilm reader and printer.

The National Library has a collection of some 400,000 books including rare books and manuscripts and about 100,000 copies of learned journals collected from various sources. The collection of journals is one of the major items of its acquisition program. The Library has also received a large collection of rare books, journals and manuscripts from individuals as donations. It has also collected old daily newspapers, books and magazines from various government agencies and foreign sources like UNESCO, World Bank and ILO.

The Library has a good collection of Urdu, Arabic and Persian books as well as manuscripts and a large number of old maps of Bangladesh and that of the Indian subcontinent.

All the collections of the National Library are preserved in a seven-storied air-conditioned stack block equipped with modern facilities.

The National Library has various reader services and other facilities. It has four large Reading Rooms covering an area of some 743.22 sq. m. It also has a temporary Exhibition Hall and a 300-seat capacity air-conditioned auditorium.

The National Library organizes special exhibitions, seminars and symposia for all kinds of readers and users of the library, both children and adults, on a regular basis. In addition, it takes part in all national book fairs as well as in other relevant exhibitions within the country.[5]

The process of developing a national library for Bangladesh has gone through many measures, steps and plans. Such an elaborate process is experienced by most nations when these become independent of colonial rule.

It has definitely taken a little longer time for the Bangladesh National Library to assume a fuller role as the national library of the country. However, several factors have been helpful for Bangladesh in founding its national library: The role of UNESCO, working examples of the national libraries in other countries, the availability of trained professionals and the voices of concern about the need for a national library for the country. As of now, the library is functioning for posterity and the life of the nation it serves.

Notes

1. Encyclopaedia of Library and Information Science. s.v. "Bangladesh, National Library of." (by Mohammad Shahabuddin Khan), Vol. 40, Supplement 5, (New York: Marcel Dekker, 1986).
2. Heidelberg Bangladesh Law Translation Project, "Act No. XXVII of 1995: An Act Made to Establish a National Book Centre." Heidelberg University, South Asia Institute. http://www.sai.uni-heidelberg.de/workgroups/bdlaw/1995-a27.htm (accessed November 29, 2006).
3. Md. Shahabuddin Khan, "Legal Deposit System: Bangladesh." *CDNLAO Newsletter*. No. 56 (July 2006). http://www.ndl.go.jp/en/publication/cddnlao/056/562.html (accessed November 29, 2006).

4. Banglapaedia: National Encyclopaedia of Bangladesh. s.v. "National Library." (by Sharif uddin Ahmed). (Dhaka: Asiatic Society of Bangladesh, 2003). http://banglapedia.org/ (accessed November 29, 2006).
5. "National Archives and Library of Bangladesh." Department of Archives and Libraries of Bangladesh. http://www.nanl.gov.bd/ (accessed November 29, 2006).

13

New Choices for Bibliographic Services in a Wired Planet: Reflections on the National Library of India

R.K. SHARMA

Introduction

Symbiosis between knowledge society and libraries is crucial. Knowledge societies today have more choices and more free-of-charge alternatives than ever. Libraries have been important institutions of continuous learning throughout the world and serving essentially the same social functions as they have served in the past. Beyond this reality, we have already entered in the era of on-line community which has posed a great challenge to the existence of traditional libraries. The existence of future libraries will depend on high quality and tech-based services to the end users. To meet this obligation the librarians and libraries will have to retain their place, however, by renewing themselves. Undoubtedly, modern libraries have to trigger a new dimension to the electronic library movement by re-engineering the scope of responsibilities and services.

The State of Public and National Libraries in India

It is difficult to draft a single approach that would suit the Indian situation considering the diversity of Indian Library System which is at various stages of development. Though Dr. S.R. Ranganathan's original contributions to library science have put India on the top of the world in the field of library science, but in terms of library movement and library service, India is far behind most of the developed countries. Despite the progress made in library movement in India, the country is far from becoming a land of libraries as in the case of the US and other developed countries. Due to efforts of Dr. Ranganathan and Madras Library Association, Madras (now Chennai) was the first state in India to pass a library legislation to provide free public library service to its clients. Influenced by Madras Library Act, similar Library Acts have been passed in several other states: Andhra Pradesh (1960), Karnatatka (1965), Maharashtra (1967), West Bengal (1979), Manipur (1988), Kerala (1988), Haryana (1989), Mizoram (1993) and Goa (1994). Unfortunately, most of the states in India are yet to pass such Library Acts.[1] At present public libraries are neither up-to-date nor modern; neither are they well staffed nor well equipped. The public libraries have to become the ideal institutions for imparting education to public. Public libraries could serve as the backbones of Literacy Missions especially in developing countries.

National Library, Kolkata and the Three Recipient Public Libraries namely: Delhi Public Library (DPL), Connemara Public Library, Chennai and the State Central Library, Mumbai have primarily become the depository of the printed cultural heritage of India under the Delivery of Books Act, 1954 as amended in 1956 (DBA). In this context the National Library has a great importance in conserving the rich linguistic heritage of the country. Thus, there has to be a nexus and organized co-operation between all the four libraries with National Library at the top of the hierarchy. This is possible only when the libraries are well equipped with modern technology and compatible systems to ensure resource sharing and networking.

Developmental efforts must be guided by a well defined national policy and backed by various government plans and programmes for necessary infrastructure supports. Many attempts have been made by the Government of India (GoI) for developing good infrastructure of library and information services in the country during the last five decades. To highlight some of the achievements, the country now has four national libraries, viz. the National Library, Kolkata, the National Science Library, Delhi and National Medical Library, Delhi and IARI Library, Delhi considered as the National Library for agriculture. The main challenge would be to bring out close co-ordination between all these national level subject libraries and National Library of India.

National Library of India

The origin of the National Library can be traced back to 1836 with the opening of the Calcutta Public Library, which merged with the Imperial Library in 1903. Lord Curzon, the then Viceroy who helped in converting the Calcutta Public

Library into a national institution by merging it with the East India College Library and departmental libraries to give it a form of the Imperial Library. The Imperial Library Act of 1948 established the new National Library of India which is an institution of National importance under the Department of Culture, Ministry of Tourism & Culture, Government of India. The words of Lord Curzon are valid even today—"it would be a library of reference, a working place for students and a repository of materials for the future historians of India, in which as far as possible, every work written about India at any time can be seen and read".[2] The library's primary function is as a repository and conservator of printed material produced in India and materials about India produced in foreign countries. Production of bibliographical records and standardization of cataloguing procedures is also a mandate of the library. The library is designated to collect, disseminate and preserve the printed material produced in the country with the following aim:[3]

(i) Acquisition and conservation of all significant national production of printed material, excluding ephemera.
(ii) Collection of printed material concerning the country, no matter where it is published, and as a corollary, the acquisition of photographic records of such material that is not available with in the country.
(iii) Acquisition and conservation of foreign material required by the country.
(iv) Rendering of bibliographical and documents services of current and retrospective material both general and specialized.
(v) Acting as a referral centre purveying full and accurate knowledge.

Bibliographic Control

Role of National Bibliographies

The national and trade bibliographies are invaluable tools for the selection of both current and retrospective publications. There is a very large number of subject bibliographies, which provide information about retrospective publications in a particular subject area. National bibliography is list of books published in a given country. It is the record of books produced in the languages of one country, or of books produced in the country whatever their languages. It is almost a complete record of printed output in a given country, accepting no limitations in the subject fields, nor in the form of literature.

The aim of a national bibliography is to provide a complete listing of recorded knowledge on a national basis, and by cumulation for the whole world. Its educational purpose is to serve as a source of book selection. For instance, like many other countries, India and UK bring out their national bibliographies of current publications regularly. The US is publishing no such bibliography. Some trade bibliographies of the US serve as the national bibliography of America.[4]

Role of Central Reference Library

The CRL functions today as a separate subordinate office of the Department of Culture, Ministry of Tourism and Culture. It has no collections or library other than working as the National Bibliographic and Documentation centre. The CRL is mainly responsible for achieving the goal of Universal Bibliographic Control through effective development of the National Bibliographic Control. This library mainly responsible for the compilation and sale of the Indian National Bibliography (INB) in Roman script and in fourteen language scripts based on the receipt of books at the National Library under Delivery of Books Act, 1954 (as amended in 1956) and compilation and sale of Index Indiana (Roman Script) an Index to selected articles appearing in current Indian language periodicals.[5]

Among one of its main objectives is to publish the India's National Bibliography (INB). INB is a classified list of current Indian publications in 14 Indian languages, received at the National Library under the DBA. The categories of publications excluded are: (i) Musical scores, (ii) Maps, (iii) Periodicals and newspapers, (iv) Keys and guides to text books, and (v) Ephemeral items.

INB remains excellent book selection tool for current Indian publications, however, it suffers from two limitations: (i) the time-lag in its publications and (ii) the availability of records of all publications in regional languages in Roman script which many readers do not understand and this makes it difficult for them to use INB.

Collection and Bibliographic Services

The National Library, the repository of a huge literary wealth, numbers more than 3 million items plus additional 6 million copies of back issues of serials and pamphlets. The library has a priceless collection of 10,000 rare books and manuscripts besides a large number of microforms, maps, atlases and photographs. National library receives books and periodicals in almost all the Indian languages. These are received under the Delivery of Books and Newspapers (Public Libraries) Act, 1954 as amended in 1956. The library has separate Indian Language division for all languages recognized by Constitution of India. English books published in India are also collected under DBA.[6]

A bibliographic service centre makes available information on—information material issued within the territory it serves and other information materials included in the libraries and collections of the territory it serves. Bibliographic service centres have existed in some form or other almost as long as there have been any large national libraries. Development in the next few years seems to follow subject rather than national or regional patterns. The creation of projects like the MEDLARS search centres of the National Medical Library (USA)—to meet the growing needs of specialization, by limiting their field of action to a known discipline, and to provide greater depth and intensity of information.[7]

The National Library, Kolkata also provides Bibliographic Services to research scholars, government agencies, universities and national level institutions. Selected lists of reading materials or bibliographies are prepared by the library on request. Special bibliographies are prepared to augment the exhibitions, which the National Library holds. Compilations of exhaustive bibliographies on special topics, like Indology, are underway. The library provides bibliographies and/or bibliographic statistics to the national and international organizations. The library provides supports the Central Reference Library, Kolkata in compiling the Indian National Bibliography.[8]

As we know that the National Library has to play a major role as resource centre of dissemination of knowledge. It must act as channel for information transmission with variety of information services to support knowledge hunters (writers, thinkers, researchers, academic and research organizations etc.). User satisfaction should be an important yardstick for evaluating the services of the libraries on regular basis. However, barring a few libraries in India, the quantity and quality of information services provided even by National libraries have a long way to go to meet the ever-growing needs of the society.

Due to several reasons such as ineffectiveness of Document Delivery Act, to ensure inclusion of every title of Indian publications in the National Library holdings and low library budgets, weak procurement system and lack of acquisition policy and planning that there is no comprehensive national resource centre for all the documents produced in India and abroad. Many documents produced prior to independence find no mention at all. Not only there is procedural flaw but also the documents which are mailed to designated repositories are often left unpacked for indefinite period and also the documents received free of cost are given least priority. There is lack of organization, indexation and publicity of social data resources in any source directory. This left a considerable part of our national resource unutilized. However, the specialized institutes are better organized and efficient due to the demand for service.[9]

Libraries to go High Tech: Challenging Future

As keepers of the Books, libraries have traditionally been responsible for preserving historically and culturally valuable materials for posterity. At that time information was considered as merely a subsidiary support service and libraries were considered as the local center of information, making all kinds of knowledge and information readily available to its users. Advances in the new technologies, new techniques and new systems, had expanded the role of information. The use of the latest technologies such as *Internet* has brought changes in the information management. Technological innovation and the electronic provision of information continued to be priorities for us. The integrated Library Management System which brought together all major library operations, would reduce duplication of work; increase staff productivity; improve control over administrative and financial processes; and enhance satisfaction through a user-friendly retrieval system.

Some Facts about Internet[10]

The *Internet* is enabling a global revolution in scholarly communication. For the first time in history, we have an infrastructure that can deliver information any time and any place. This could change our society and global culture as dramatically and unpredictably—as did once the printing press and the automobile.

- ➢ There are 580 million people in the world with Internet access, or roughly, one in six people.
- ➢ China has the second largest Internet population in the world, after the US, and accounts for 6.6 per cent of all global Internet traffic.
- ➢ There are 3.2 million new Internet pages every 24 hours.
- ➢ There were 200 million Internet users in 2000, 600 million in 2002, one billion by 2005.
- ➢ In 1990, there were 300,000 Internet hosts, by January 1991, 171 million.
- ➢ Developing countries' share of Internet users: two per cent in 1991, 23 per cent in 2001.
- ➢ In 2001, there were six billion e-mails sent globally.

Breathtaking developments in telecommunications have made the whole world a global village. The confluence of these developments has brought about the emergence of cyber libraries and information networks. The cyber library, in contrast to the traditional library will be packed with digital documents—talking books, video series, and reference books on optical disks and CD-ROMs. The library will be linked to local, national and global networks. This will enable a reader to browse the contents beyond the actual contents of its own library and look up information that he needs instantly. He will have the option to browse print or download the information as he pleases. The library will have multimedia and CD-ROMs to supplement the knowledge he can get from the networks with local search facility. Books, encyclopaedias, manuals, directories and dictionaries will all be available in the form of CD-ROMs, encyclopaedia Britannica, one of the most valuable encyclopaedias of the world is already available, both in the form of CD-ROM and database on the internet.

India has become independent and entered the jet-age. Internet and IT industry have become the buzzword. In spite of it, the spirit of effective library service to the common man demonstrated by the library system is a far dream for most of citizens especially living in remote areas of the country. Even the cities do not have a proper library system, in line with their counterparts in the west.

The challenge of the digital divide goes to the heart of the mission of libraries to provide equitable access to information for all regardless of the information format. The mission of libraries, as well as their associated services, programmes and technologies is a key reason that libraries are indeed central to digital divide solutions and partnership. Efforts are being made to promote the centrality of libraries in the digital divide solutions and to counter a growing sentiment that the electronic libraries must be regarded as essential to economic and social growth, well being and quality of life.

Bibliographic Information on the Web

It is evident that bibliographic issues have emerged due to the growth of the Internet. In general context of continuing organizational and technological change, bibliographic services required in any library normally aims to be client-centered. Client-centered organization is one which continually improves and redesigns its services and products around the changing needs of its clients.

In early 1990s CD-ROM were popular for their storage capacity. Entire indexes were placed on CD-ROMs which allowed for rapid and far more complex searching than paper indexes. However, with the rise of online databases and their enormous storage and searching capabilities, CD-ROMs are nearly gone or play a much smaller role in the library services.

Librarians have traditionally been keepers of the Books. Their focus has been on building collections—for society, for scholarship, and for future generations. It has long been recognized that only 20 per cent of any given print collection is actually used with much frequency, but since no body can predict which materials will constitute that 20 per cent, libraries have always gone about collecting what they could. Now libraries have expanded their services to include information in electronic form—texts or indexes on CD-ROMs and commercial online databases. But libraries are finding that users prefer to use these new digital materials over print; in effect, the digital materials are directly competing with the strongest 20 per cent of the libraries' print collections.

Professional education for librarians is rapidly changing to meet new demands. Less emphasis is placed today on skills for managing books on shelves, papers in files, and references in indexes; rather, students are expected to master a wide range of new technologies and resources. Traditional methods for cataloging books and journals are to some extent being superseded by international standards for Web materials.[11]

The British Library's National Bibliographic Service[12]

The British Library Automated Information Service (BLAISE) was officially launched in December 1977. Blaise web is now well established as a high quality bibliographic service on the WWW. Blaise is seen by library world as a premium bibliographic service offering a wide range of databases and search facilities and being the bibliographic tool for information professionals.

The launch of OPAC 97 is one step forward towards the fulfilment of digital library by providing as it does free and simple access to library catalogues *via* WWW. Although most British Library Catalogue records are now automated, there are still parts of the collections that do not yet have automated records and this be will added soon.

The British National Bibliography (BNB) 1950, Library of Congress 1968 and British Books in Print 1965 are good examples of the British Library databases.

The People's Network (http://www.peoplesnetwork.gov.uk) is a national online library. It links every public library to the Internet and is a major provider of e-learning and e-government access point. There are more than 30,000 computers in more than 4,000 UK public libraries. The National Grid for Learning (http://www.ngfl.gov.uk) is a portal to educational resources. Launched in 1998, this counterpart to the People's Network is aimed at students and educators rather than library users and librarians. NGFL arose from a government strategy for information and communications technology (ICT) in education and lifelong learning.[13]

Library of Congress Bibliographic Services[14]

The Library of Congress with the immense collection of 119 million items is the world's foremost repository of accumulated knowledge and wisdom of humankind. It is part of legislative branch of United States government with primary mission to serve the Congress. Over half of its books and serial collections are in languages other than English. Its universal collections, which support research in all subjects except clinical medicine and technical agriculture, are also developed for and open to scholars from all over the nation and the world.

LC Digital Collections and Programmes: Out of millions of documents held by the Library, only a small fraction are in digital form. The American Memory, the flagship of the Library's digital services now offers more than 7.5 million digital items from more than 100 historical collections.

The Library's Prints and Photographs Online Catalog (PPOC) provides access through group or item records to about 50 per cent of the Division's holdings. About 90 per cent of the records are accompanied by one or more digital images.

There is large information available in the fields of law and legislation. It provides the THOMAS system, which offers full text of bills and congressional records. The library also co-operates internationally to collect digitized laws, regulations and other complimentary legal source in the Global Legal Information Network (GLIN) project.

NIDIIPP: The Library of Congress has a leadership role in the National Digital Information Infrastructure and Preservation Program, authorized by Congress in December 2000. It runs in co-ordination with other federal agencies and organizations in information community. It aims at developing national stretegy to collect, archive and preserve the materials in digital format for current and future generations.

Digital Reference: LC initiated an "Ask A Librarian" service, in June 2002. It is called Ask a Librarian service wherein the reference specialists and resources are brought into the contact of researchers and the general public beyond library walls. Patrons may access it from Library home page and then submit their questions to the reading room they feel is most likely to be able to answer it.

The Library of Congress launched the Ask A Librarian project using Question Point reference software that was developed in collaboration with the Online Computer Library Center (OCLC) of Dublin, Ohio. The software allows libraries to manage their reference traffic centrally, generate activity reports and statistics, and refer questions to colleagues in-house and experts elsewhere using a shared interface and a dedicated network. Question Point enables reference librarians to take their expertise out onto the web, and to build a worldwide collaborative network of librarians and resources.

The Digital Reference Team (DRT), is the group which has been recently formed comprising reference specialists who are dedicated to exploring the ways in which online tools may be used to promote and enhance the LC programmes and services. The DRT responds to reference questions about the Library's online resources, creates electronic pathfinders and bibliographies, maintains the Virtual Reference Shelf, writes and edits historical features for the Library's website, and presents a variety of electronic and in-person workshops for members of Congress, educators, librarians, historians and others.

Web Preservation: The MINERVA Web Preservation Project was established to initiate collection and preservation of worlds cultural and intellectual output which is presently created in digital format and does not exist in physical form.

Standards: To support its digital collections, the Library of Congress uses a variety of standardized metadata. The METS schema is a standard for encoding descriptive, administrative, and structural metadata regarding objects within a digital library, expressed using the XML schema language of the World Wide Web Consortium. The standard is maintained in the Network Development and MARC Standards Office of the Library of Congress, and is being developed as an initiative of the Digital Library Federation.

It is worth mentioning that the Bicentennial Conference on Bibliographic Control for the New Millennium was held in 2000 primarily to develop an overall strategy to enhance better bibliographic control of Web resources. Every objective of the LC Action Plan acknowledges the importance of partnership between libraries and other groups: metadata producers, standard developers, system and software developers, national libraries etc.

Role of International Organizations

International Organizations such as UNESCO, IFLA, FID, UNIDO plays a major role in developing international standards, organizing professional training programmes, promoting international cooperation, R&D in the field of libraries and brings out valuable publications. It is, therefore, National Libraries should explore all technical and financial help from these international agencies for upgrading their infrastructure and services.

Rethinking Copyright

Copyright is a legal concept that governs the ownership and use of intellectual property in the marketplace. How copyright is enforced for information in electronic form and on the Internet will directly affect functioning of libraries in the coming years. The social justification for copyright protection varies between legal systems of countries.

As interpreted in the United States, copyright protects the specific arrangements of words or images or musical notes that express an idea. Owners of the expression of that idea may prevent others from making copies, distributing, performing, or displaying their work without permission. However, copyright does not protect the idea itself, nor does it protect any other methods, systems, or facts underlying that expression. Indeed, those underlying ideas can be taken by others and built upon or expressed differently and these new expressions, in turn, are likewise protected under copyright.

The Digital Millennium Copyright Act (DMCA) that resulted in 1998, called by some "the most comprehensive reform of copyright law in a generation," established a number of complicated rules, the implications of which are still unclear. By ensuring stiff penalties for piracy and for the violation of encryption mechanisms, the legislation intended to encourage publishers to make their works available on CD-ROMs, DVDs, and online. However, more of these works will be licensed on a pay-per-view basis.

Distance education has emerged as another major battleground. Educational institutions point out it is extremely difficult to obtain approval for using copyrighted works in online courses; that it is often hard to identify who owns materials that are needed; and that licensing fees are unrealistically high. Under current laws, content providers would seem to have the upper hand, though the Copyright Office is studying the problem.

Implications for the National Library

The Government of India should draw inspiration from the pioneering efforts of Dr. Ranganathan to make India a true land of libraries and knowledge. However, in India, in particular where technologies of all ages are operating, needs a complete transformation in information policy to pave the way to digital library era. Following are several areas requiring attention, which have implications for the existence of National Library:

- Establish a national library development policy and work constantly for its implementation. National development plans should give a due recognition to an "Information Sector" as they do to other sectors of economy, such as agriculture, industry, education, S&T, trade and culture. The Government of India had framed a National Policy on Library and Information System (NAPLIS) during 1980s which could be used as model for preparing a new policy.
- Strive towards achieving a national network of public libraries, university libraries, IITs, IIMs, National Laboratories and industrial and specialized libraries. INFLIBNET is a step forward in this direction, though it has to go a long way.
- There has to be a complete re-examination of traditional information policies and strategies so that our National and Public Library System can meet the technology challenge.

- Create a working group of legislators and library leaders from all communities with a responsibility to provide clear vision plan for the electronic library system in the country including defining goals for statewide cooperative library activities, analyzing successful models of other states and providing recommendations for proper funding, structure and governance issues concerning electronic library culture in the country.
- An Internet service should be considered a public utility service just like basic telecommunications services, water, and electricity, with public service institutions, such as schools and public libraries, being allowed concessional rates for Internet users. In this context, the right to access information for all remains a fundamental right to be upheld with greater efficiency and imagination in a spirit of equity, justice and mutual respect.
- Spreading the culture of information literacy. Information literacy has many implications e.g. in teaching, learning, research work, publishing, and decision-making. As the society need lifelong education to acquire knowledge for transformation, electronic public libraries could become ideal institutions for meeting information needs of the citizens.

All this will offer a powerful, integrated knowledge grid as a vital resource and stimulus for research, development, growth and all round development of the country. Undoubtedly, National Library of a country should serve as a national resource centre and take lead responsibility for library movement in the country.

Computerized Bibliographic Services for a National Library: Strategies for Improvement

National Library of India which operates as a part of Department of Culture and Tourism, Government of India is really a well recognized library serving its clientele in the most effective and efficient manner. Following are some suggestions which would optimize the library's ability to respond to the changing needs of present knowledge society by providing best services:

- *Expansion of National Library website and offering value-added services.* Libraries are being asked to provide access to information regardless of whether it is physically located in the building or somewhere out on the Internet. At many libraries, the existing online catalog of holdings is being integrated into a Web site that provides information about a library's services and collections along with lists of links to Internet resources of relevance to local users. Libraries will have to compete with the new Web technology like *Web Portals/Gateways*. Straightforward sites that provide links to related databases, catalogues, websites through a variety of access methods will play a vital role. Librarians should aim at becoming knowledge navigators. Their professional ability of handling in-house collections and sources on the Web will help them to understand questions and finding their answers quickly.

- *Change over to Digital Reference Service*: The obvious advantage to this technology is that it allows users to access reference services and assistance, regardless of distances involved and perhaps time of day. Homepage on the web with "Ask the Librarian" link should be designed for providing e-mail reference service.
- India is a multi-lingual country and modern libraries are suppose to handle literature in various languages otherwise universal knowledge will be restricted to the elite familiar with one of the major languages of the world. Availability of information in electronic format would be the best answer to this problem.
- A national library could be tasked with developing a comprehensive collection of *grey* literature in all subjects. It could be a legal depository centre for receiving, repackaging and promoting this type of literature. In this way, the national bibliography would also include a comprehensive listing of *grey* literature. In USA, for instance, the Library of Congress has an aggressive policy of collecting *grey* literature from developing countries.
- New global digital network environment creates special problems and strains on the traditional system of copyright. One of the strains is that national boundaries have become almost meaningless in the digital world. It is difficult to recognize a work of authorship distributed on the Internet. And it is almost impossible for a nation to protect the intellectual property rights that are represented by it.
- The National Library should take steps to sponsor research projects so as to study various topics such as mechanisms that enabled computers to handle Indian languages and scripts. This has created a big gap between Indian languages and languages written in Roman script. The only national effort in this direction has been initiated by DELNET under the National Bibliographic Database pilot project.
- Network technology allows the traditional functions of a library, such as reference service, cataloging, collection development, and licensing of databases, to be handled by networks. Even the advent of growing digital information, books and journals will continue to be published on paper,

and librarians will still be needed to select, acquire, and manage these resources.

- National library should adopt the international standards for creating bibliographic records compatible for national or international exchange standards. The design of IFLA's UNIMARC exchange format has provided a new approach. On the other hand, efforts are being made for reaching a common MARC format for bibliographic exchange between USMARC, UKMARC and CANMARC formats. Metadata standards such as the Dublin Core have been designed for describing digital and physical materials in today's networked environment. Formats like XML are much more appropriate for digital libraries than proprietary formats such as Microsoft Word or PDF. For archives of grey literature, it may be more practical to support multiple formats.

Conclusion

Any country, which has poor management of information with its surrounding environment, will become increasingly detached and gradually stagnate. The information age has already brought great changes in the international information environment and in library technology itself: microform and other programmes rather than hard copy collection, computerized bibliographic search and databases rather than card catalogues, and information science education rather than traditional librarianship training.

These trends and their impact will certainly accelerate production of high quality information tools and their use in the society. A process of careful information exchange, and awareness and use of appropriate new technologies, is highly warranted, so that libraries which are main resource centers for information handling can continuously adopt their desired information dissemination role and serve their organizations with adequate information at affordable costs. Each library or information center should continually consider the concerns emerging out of the changing information needs of the society and play a more proactive role in fostering information and communication technologies and encouraging technology cooperation.

References

1. Kamaruddin, Abdul Reahman (21 November, 1999). Information Supermarkets. *Deccan Hearld (Sunday Hearld).*
2. http://pib.nic.in/feature

3. http://www.nlindia.org
4. Prasher, R.G. (1999). *Developing Library Collections*. New Delhi: Meddalion Press, pp. 84-95.
5. http://www.crlindia.org
6. http://www.slais.ubc.ca/courses
7. Murthy, Sunita K. (1999). Bibliographic Control and Standards. In. Kaul. H.K. (ed). *Library and Information Networking (NACLN 99). New Delhi: DELNET.*
8. http://www.nlindia.org
9. Mukhopadhyay, A. (1990). A Social Science Information System and Information Technology: Problems and Possibilities. In. Binwal, J.C. and others (ed). *Social Science Information: Problems and Prospects*. New Delhi: Har-Anand.
10. *Choices: Human Development Magazine*, (December 2003). NY: UNDP.
11. TIAC White Paper (Thomas Baker).
12. Lowery, John. (1997). Online Bibliographic Services from the British Library's National Bibliographic Service. *Information Services and Use*. 17(4), pp. 273-75.
13. Ashling, Jim. (2003). Bibliographic Databases in a Changing World. *Information Today*, 20(9), pp. 1-5.
14. http://www.loc.gov/rr/international and http://www.lcweb.loc.gov/catdir/bibcontrol/actionplan.html

Other References

1. World Information Report, (1997/98). UNESCO, Paris.
2. Mangla, P.B. (March 2002). The Dag Hammarskjold Library: Role in Bridging the Information Gap with particular reference to the Developing Countries (Paper presented in the 40th Anniversary of DHL: Legacy of the Secretary General, United Nations, New York).
3. Dasgupta, Kalpana (August, 2000). Libraries and Librarians in India on the threshold of the 3rd Millennium: Challenges and Risks (Paper presented at 66 IFLA and General Conference, Jerusalem, Isrărel).

14

Bangladesh's Frustrated Librarians: Formidable Barriers to Information Exist

RON CHEPESIUK

In April, hundreds of angry Bangladeshis protesting the Anglo-American invasion of Iraq marched in downtown Chittagong, a major port city in this densely populated country of 133.3 million, past the entrance to the Independent University of Bangladesh (IUB). Inside, I sat with Syeda Nahida Akhter, director of the American Corner, discussing the role that her institution was playing in providing resources to an information-starved country. The American Corner, established in January, is a satellite office of the Information Resource Center (IRC) of the US Embassy's Public Affairs Section in the capital, Dhaka.

The Corner operates much like a branch library and provides a small number of American magazines, newspapers, documentary videos, and reference books on American history and culture, as well as vital information about getting admitted to universities in the United States. There are also two computer terminals that IUB students and the public can use for word processing and to surf the Web at a cost of about 90 cents per minute. (To read about other American Corner libraries, in Russia, see pp. 56-58)

"We plan to operate much like an American public library and develop a lot of programs that will allow us to reach out to all types of Bangladeshis," Akhter explained. "We want to promote an understanding of the policies, values, culture, and society of the United States."

In the wake of the war in Iraq, giving a positive spin to the American experience is a hard sell in Bangladesh, the world's third-largest Muslim country, just as it is in other Muslim countries. Though Saddam has been ousted, the overwhelming majority of the Bangladeshis opposed the war and how the United States conducted it. "Bush killed a lot of innocent civilians for nothing," said one librarian, who didn't want her name used because she fears it might jeopardize her chances of getting an American visa someday. "Did the US find any weapons of mass destruction? Did the war help the US in its fight against terrorists?"

Four police officers are posted inside the entrance door to the IUB, but no attempts have been made to march on the American Corner, nor has its staff been threatened. And despite Uncle Sam's growing presence in the Muslim world, many Bangladeshis expect the Corner to have a positive impact on Chittagong, Bangladesh's second-largest city.

"The fact is, many Bangladeshis who want to get educated or who want information for their schooling or jobs need access to the American Corner and the country's other European cultural centers," explained Golam Sarwar Chowdhury, professor and chair of the American Studies Department at the University of Chittagong.

In 1955 and 1956, the IRC opened branch libraries in four additional cities. Each grew to include about 4,000 books, but the US government closed them all in the 1970s. The European centers that Chowdhury referred to are the British Council, the French Alliance Center, and the German Goethe Center, each of which has branches in Dhaka and Chittagong.

The European Presence

By far, the largest and most dynamic cultural center is the British Council, which has about 8,000 books in Dhaka and another 3,000 in Chittagong. In comparison, the IRC in Dhaka has a collection of only about 2,000 books. The two British Council resource centers differ in their content because each caters to local information needs. For instance, the British Council Library in Chittagong focuses on veterinary science, reflecting the needs of faculty and students at the Chittagong Government Veterinary College, whereas no such collection exists in Dhaka.

"When ordering books, we make a special effort to contact university departments and other organizations with a special interest in our stock," explained Mark Bartholomew, the British Council's deputy director and library manager. "We attempt to give up-to-date information on publications in print to these organizations so they can choose the works most relevant to their faculty, students, and staff needs."

The Alliance Française, which is under the aegis of the French Embassy, also has offices in Dhaka and Chittagong. "Our libraries are lavishly stocked with French magazines, newspapers, and books, with a total collection of about 5,000," said Gurupada Chakraborty, the Alliance's secretary. "In addition, we have a video club with more than 150 VHS cassettes that Bangladeshis can borrow."

As is the case with the German and British cultural centers, one has to be a member of the Alliance to use the collection. Yearly fees are about $10 for student members and $15 for the public.

Disorganization is the Rule

The foreign cultural centers serve the big cities of Dhaka and Chittagong and don't reach the vast numbers of Bangladeshis who live in rural areas. The Department of Public Libraries oversees the government public libraries but its responsibilities are fragmented. It does not manage the nongovernmental public libraries, which do not have any permanent financial support and operate with the help of member fees and government grants. "That support is paltry," said S.M. Abu Taher, deputy librarian at the University of Chittagong library. "It can't pay the salaries of the library staff, let alone the book budget or the building's maintenance."

As the non-existence of a viable public library movement shows, Bangladesh faces formidable—or perhaps more accurately, overwhelming—challenges in providing adequate library services. There is no automation, no climate control, no security procedure to protect against the theft of library materials, no adequate salaries to attract quality recruits to the library profession, no electronic databases, and no adequate funding. In short, Bangladesh has one of the world's most underdeveloped library systems.

"The libraries in Bangladesh are in a disgraceful condition," said Taher. "I wouldn't know where to begin to explain the tremendous barriers we face."

It has been that way long before Bangladesh became a nation in 1971. "During British rule some philanthropists and social leaders established some personal and public libraries," Taher explained. "After the independence of India and Pakistan in 1947, present-day Bangladesh [then East Pakistan] was deprived of its rightful share of libraries. The libraries were managed by untrained personnel and the situation was deplorable."

After independence, the Pakistan Library Association, which was formed in 1956, was renamed the Library Association of Bangladesh. Two IRC librarians were founding members. The association introduced a one-year post-graduate diploma course in 1989 and then established an Institute of Library and Information Science in six divisional headquarters in Bangladesh to meet the growing needs for library professionals. In 1993, Dhaka and Rajshahi Universities introduced a three-year honors course in library and information science.

American librarians want higher salaries, and rightly so. But in Bangladesh, salaries provide a subsistence wage, not a living one. And forget about benefits we take for granted like health insurance or a retirement plan. Mohamed Abu Khaled Chowdhury, an assistant librarian at the IUB library and a graduate of the three-year honors course, earns about $200 a month, while his assistant, also an honors course graduate, earns half that amount. "It's almost impossible to support a family on my salary," laments Chowdhury, who is married. "Sometimes, I am amazed at how far I am able to make the money go."

Golam Sarwar Chowdhury says the low salaries in the library profession show how misguided the country's priorities are. "In Bangladesh, people who work in education and related fields are not respected," explained the professor, who is a former Fulbright scholar and master's graduate of the University of Texas at Dallas. "In this country most of the money goes to the military, but let's be serious. Who will in Bangladesh go to war with?"

The working conditions in Bangladesh libraries leave a lot to be desired. On a sweltering and humid day in March, Taher and I were soaked in sweat as we toured the library. I saw a few fans but no air-conditioning. Taher explained that the university's administration had installed air-conditioning in the rare book section and the computer room. "We don't have the funding to set up air-conditioning in every area of the library," the deputy librarian revealed.

Both faculty and students at the University of Chittagong complain that some library books are missing or have pages ripped out, and many of the books that remain aren't particularly useful. With a lack of adequate shelving, moreover, a substantial number are lying on the dusty and dirty floor.

Tainted Transactions

What's happening at Chittagong reflects the crisis facing the country's library system. The core problem is corruption. The Berlin-based Transparency International, which monitors corruption worldwide, has ranked Bangladesh the world's most corrupt country for the past two years. As I know from firsthand experience, corruption affects every aspect of Bangladesh society, including libraries. I have seen cops extort money from cab drivers in broad daylight as throngs of people pass going about their business. Sources tell me kickbacks are provided to bureaucrats in government when books are purchased. Books are listed as bought that really haven't been. The record will often show many journal subscriptions that are non-existent.

"The problem with university libraries is that we don't have professional librarians running the show," explained Golam Chowdhury. "The libraries are usually headed by a professor who is a crony of the university vice chancellor or a flunky of some powerful individual close to the university administration." Chowdhury provided a telling anecdote to make his point. "A few years ago, we had a university librarian who never bought one book for the library. Instead, he returned the book budget money to the vice chancellor to please him."

Given the corruption, many academic departments in Bangladesh universities don't trust the university administration, so they build their own departmental libraries. The American Studies Department at Chittagong has a collection of 5,000 books. "The way universities care for their library collections is a joke," Chowdhury said sarcastically.

Despite the enormous challenges, there are some glimmers of library modernization. For instance, mobile library service has been introduced—an important development because most Bangladesh libraries and all of the foreign cultural centers, with the exception of the British Council, do not allow readers to take books home. The World Library Center in Dhaka has a bus-based library operation that now serves 5,000 members. Rajia Sultana Rosy, a woman who uses the service, told China Radio International news in June 2001 that "the introduction of the [mobile] library has been a blessing for women, especially housewives and young girls for many of whom it is quite difficult to visit a library regularly because of family restrictions and general disapproval in society of women coming out of the house."

Going Digital in Dhaka

Bangladesh libraries have taken their first tentative step into cyberspace, and local librarians see the Internet as the future of their profession. "Building a library filled with books and paper and microfilm is expensive," said Mahtab Uddin Ahmad, director of the IRC. "The technology that can help our people access the Internet's fabulous resources isn't expensive. As a developing country struggling to grow, Bangladesh needs up-to-date information quickly. That's why we see our future in virtual libraries."

Once again, the foreign cultural center libraries are taking the lead. In addition to providing Internet access to the public, the IRC library offers online database searching. Its most recent acquisitions include Master File Premier, which provides the full text to more than 2,700 periodicals in all subjects, and Business Source Elite, which covers more than 1,100 journals in business and economics.

The British Council has a Cyber Center located in its Dhaka library, which provides a basic monthly Internet training course for new users, as well as access to the Internet for a nominal fee. "Many resources traditionally available in print are now only available online," explained Bartholomew. "This poses a big problem for Bangladesh because many otherwise competent Bangladeshis lack IT literacy."

Then, in a nutshell, Bartholomew pinpointed the challenge facing all the libraries in Bangladesh: "We are reaching out, but our resources are limited. So, sadly, we are only reaching the tip of the iceberg."

15

Public Library System and Services in Andaman & Nicobar Islands of India: The State of the Art Report

SUNIL KUMAR SATPATHY and Y. GANESH

Introduction

A public library is a dynamic, living force and the intellectual nucleus of the community it serves. It is an institution of the public and for the public. Therefore, they must be open to all, without any hindrance. A public library must provide to its users the world's best thought giving reliable information in an unbiased and balanced way to satisfy individual's personal, professional or political aspirations. Thus public libraries are vital for individual's liberty and freedom of thought, the bedrock of modern democracy.

The purpose of a library may be a public academic is to provide the right information to the right type of reader at the right time in the right way. This implies that the libraries have to plan, develop and organize their resource and services in such a way that it should be facilitate easy retrieval of the desired information in quick time and with a minimum effort.

The Public Library system and services all over India is neither systematic nor proper. Which has badly affected the educational, socio-economical progress of the country. Hence it needs proper planning. Further, Andaman & Nicobar Islands of India needs special attention due to its complex geo-morphological condition, cultural and linguistic diversities.

Objectives of the Study

The objectives of the proposed study are to access the existing public library system and services of Andaman & Nicobar Island, identify the lacuna inherent in it and to find out the remedial measures for its development.

Scope and Limitation of the Study

The scope of the study is exclusively limited to the public libraries of Andaman Nicobar Islands. It includes the State library, District libraries, Zonal libraries and mobile library services. The present study excludes the academic and special libraries of the Islands. Further, the study is also restricted to developmental plan of public libraries only.

Methodology

In the present study, questionnaire method was used for survey and collection of data. On the basis of the objectives of the study, a pre-oriented structured questionnaire was prepared. These were mailed to different public libraries, which are geographically scattered throughout the UT. However, the investigator personally visited most of the public libraries to fill up the questionnaire and also to get first hand knowledge on existing public library system and services of the island. In order to make the resulting analysis meaningful and sound, statistical methods like percentage, mean, etc. were applied.

Geo-morphology of Andaman & Nicobar Islands

The Andaman & Nicobar Islands, situated in the Bay of Bengal with Port Blair as the capital were treated as a penal settlement till early forties. After the independence of India, these were accorded "Part D" status of state of the Union. With the reorganization of state in 1956, it acquired the status of a Union territory under the administration of a Lieutenant Governor.

Location

The Andaman & Nicobar Islands are situated in between 6° to 14° North latitude and 92° to 94° East longitude. These islands which comprise a group of 572 islands/islets lies in the Bay of Bengal. There are 36 inhibited islands including 24 in Andaman and 12 in the Nicobar Districts.

Land and Area

The Andaman and Nicobar Islands comprising 323 islands and 248 rocks with a total area of 8,249 square kilometres. Out of total area of these islands, forest covers 7,171 square kilometres.

Administrative Structure

The whole islands have been divided into different administrative units. For administrative purpose, the islands have been divided into two districts such as Andaman with Headquarters, at Port Blair and Nicobar with Headquarter, at Car Nicobar. The Andaman District consists of two Sub-divisions, i.e. Mayabunder and South Andaman and five Tehsils, i.e. Diglipur, Mayabunder, Rangat, Port Blair and Ferrargunj. The Nicobar district consists of two Sub-divisions, i.e. Car Nicobar and Nancowry. Both islands have 204 numbers of Revenue villages and 547 numbers of census villages.

People and Population

The Andaman and Nicobar Islands are the land of a large variety of peoples, among whom the aboriginal inhabitants are very ancient. The people of this island can be broadly of two types such as permanent settlers consisting of tribal and non-tribal and floating population.

As per census of India 2001, the total population of the UT is 3,56,152 out of which the male and female population is 1,92,972, and 1,63,180 respectively. Further as per census 2001, total ST population of the state is 29,469 out of which the male and female population is 15,127 and 14,432 respectively. There is no SC population in the islands.

Languages

Since the major portion of population are non-tribal and have come from different parts of the country and also from different countries, almost all scheduled languages are used in Andaman and Nicobar islands. Also many non-scheduled languages are also used among the tribals.

Education

The Education Department of Andaman and Nicobar Islands has ensured quality education for the Union territory (UT). The different types of school in the UT are:

School Name	Andaman District	Nicobar District	Total No. of Schools
Ashram School	x	02	02
Pre-primary School	x	03	03
Primary School	01	31	32
Middle School	01	09	10
Secondary School	01	09	10
Senior Secondary School	x	05	05
Total	03	59	62

Besides, there are four colleges and two technical institutions to impart higher education and technical education respectively. The Education Department also provides non-formal education in these islands to ensure continuous education and also to make people literate. There are 83 Shikshan Nilayams for the age group of 15-35 and 68 non-formal education centers for the dropouts. The literacy rate is 81.18 per cent as per 2001census. The literacy rate continuously growing in these islands.

Public Libraries in A&N Islands: The Present Scene

During British rule, though various types of works and surveys were conducted in these Islands, no library was set up. Even the British officers were reluctant to set up a library here. They were perhaps apprehensive of the obvious security risks involved in nurturing the patriotic zeal of the literate revolutionaries with the news of the freedom struggle in the mainland of India and other parts of the colonial world. Revolutionaries were even denied the access to any newspaper. But in the early 1930s, a small library was set up in the cellular jail and the political prisoners were allowed to read books, newspapers and magazines in the library. That was the beginning of library service in the Andaman and Nicobar Islands. Prior to this the British Government for the use of Government officials set up a Library at Ross Island, the then capital of Andaman and Nicobar Islands.

After the independence and the settlement of refugees (from the East Pakistan, now Bangladesh) in different Islands, the Government started to establish educational institutions to impart basic education to the settlers and took initiative in establishing school libraries. An information center was set up at Port Blair in the year 1957. In 1964 this information center was converted into District Library and later on considering the public interest, this Library was enlarged and reorganized into the state library in 1977.

The State library is run by the Department of Education and financed by the Andaman and Nicobar Islands administration. The Department of Education has framed two committees such as the State Library Planning Committee that is standing body for book selection and the Language-wise Sub-Committee for the smooth functioning of the library.

Under the Education Department different libraries were set up in this Union territory such as State Public Library, District Public Library etc. Besides few Tehsil/Zonal Libraries were established in different islands with the spread of education and to fulfil the demand of the local population and to encourage the reading habits among local people. Also many school libraries were set up in many schools to give the school going children an extra facility to read books of their choice and interest.

With the passage of time, the Department of Education has taken steps for spreading education through the libraries. Accordingly, the department had increased the number of Zonal Libraries under different plan periods. At present fifteen Zonal Libraries, which are functioning in different islands, such as Mayabunder, Rangat, Kadamatala, Manpur, Long island, Hut Bay, Neil, Havelock, Kamorta, Campbell Bay, Deglipur and Car Nicobar. In 1997, the Zonal Library of Car Nicobar was upgraded to District Library. Besides, Secondary and Senior Secondary schools and the higher educational institutions have their own libraries. Also all the important departments like Agriculture, Health, IP&T, Botanical and Zoological Survey of India, Electricity, Industry and AIR etc. have established their own department libraries at Port Blair. The number of libraries in the islands can be summarized as follows:

Table 15.1 : Llibraries of the Islands

Library	No.
State library	1
District library	1
Zonal library	12
School library	70
College library	3
Technical library	2
Research library	2
Department library	12

Data Analysis and Interpretation

The data collected through the structured questionnaire was organized, tabulated and interpreted with the application of suitable statistics. The findings of data analysis can be summarized as follows.

A good number of libraries were established between 1971 to 1980, 1981 to 1990 and 1991-2000. But after 2001, the growth rate of public libraries has not been maintained as per previous decade.

Table 15.2 : Libraries by Year of Establishment

Year of establishment	# of Libraries	Percentage
Before 1960	1	5.3
1961-1970	0	0
1971-1980	4	21
1981-1990	5	26.3
1991-2000	6	31.6
After 2001	3	15.8
Total	19	100

Above table shows that before 1960, there was only 1 library (5.3%) and between 1961-70, 1971-80, 1981-90 and 1991-2000, the number of libraries established were 0(0%), 4(21%), 5(26.3%) and 6(31.6%) respectively. It also shows that after 2001, only 3(15.8%) libraries were established which indicates a slow and negative growth of public libraries in the Union territory.

Library professionals do not head all libraries and the recruitment policies are neither consistent nor proper.

All libraries do not have their own library building, most of them housed in a room of some other building, which hampers the effective services of the library.

Regarding collection of library materials most libraries have only book collections and also below 10,000 in number. It shows that the library collection is not adequate as per the target population of these libraries.

Table 15.3 : Library by Collection of Books

S.No.	# of Books	# of Library	Percentage
1.	1-10,000	15	79
2.	10-20,000	2	10.5
3.	20-30,000	0	0
4.	30-40.000	0	0
5.	40,000 and above	2	10.5
	Total	14	100

Above table reveals that maximum libraries, i.e 15, out of 19 (79%) have their collection of books between 1-10,000; followed by 2 libraries (10.5%) have collection between 10-20,000 and above 40,000. Further, analysis shows that most of the libraries only possess some popular magazines but they do not possess any subject journals, which indicates that these libraries can serve the information needs of researchers to a little extent.

None of the libraries subscribes subject journals, which is highly essential for study and research. These libraries mostly subscribe to some popular magazines and newspaper.

The library books are centrally procured by the Government of UT and then are supplied to different libraries. Thus libraries have little scope to purchase library book directly. It indicates that the individual taste and demand of the locality cannot be met through this centralize mode of acquisition.

Table 15.4 : Mode of Book Acquisition

S. No.	Mode	Greate Extent	Small Extent	Not at all	Acquisition
(i)	Purchase	23	14%(10.5)	(15.9)	(73.6)
(ii)	Donation	02	17%(0)	(10.5)	(89.5)
(iii)	RRMRL foundation	35	11%(15.9)	(26.3)	(57.8)
(iv)	Govt. Supply	116	2%(57.9)	(31.6)	(10.5)

The mode of book acquisition has been presented in Table 15.4, which shows that main mode of acquisition is Government supply, followed by assistance from Raja Ram Mohan Roy Library Foundation, purchase and donation.

Table 15.4(i) reveals that the mode of acquisition through purchase is to a great extent in 2 libraries, out of the 19 libraries (10.5%), followed by to a small extent in 3 libraries (15.9%) and not at all in 14 libraries (73.6%).

Table 15.4(ii) states that regarding donation as a mode of acquisition out of 19 libraries, none libraries (0%) to a great extent; followed by 2 libraries (10.5%) to a small extent and not at all in 17 libraries (89.5%).

Table 15.4(iii) observe that out of 19 libraries the mode of acquisition through Raja Ram Mohan Roy Library Foundation to great extent in 3 libraries (15.9%); followed by in 5 library (26.3%) to a small extent and not at all in 11 libraries (57.8%).

Table 15.4(iv) brings out that, out of 19 libraries, the mode of acquisition through Government supply is to a great extent in 11 libraries (57.9%), followed by to a small extent in 6 libraries (31.6%) and not at all in 2 libraries (10.5%).

Regarding visitors of the library, mostly it belongs to general public and to some extent students. It indicates that these libraries are unable to maintain required information/document of some specialized group of society such as farmers, businessman etc., thus unable to attract them towards the library.

Table 15.5 : Types of User Visit the Library

S. No.	Types of users	Great Extent	Small Extent	Not at all
(i)	General Public	18	10%(94.7)	(5.3)(0)
(ii)	Govt./Pvt. Employees	04	15%(0)	(21)(79)
(iii)	Businessman	03	16%(0)	(15.8)(84.2)
(iv)	Farmers	00	19%(0)	(0)(100)
(v)	Students	24	13%(10.6)	(21)(68.4)

Table 15.5 indicates towards the types of users who visit the libraries.

Table 15.5 (i) shows that out of 19 in 18 Libraries (94.7%), General public visit the library to a great extent, followed by in 1 library (5.3%) to a small extent.

Table 15.5 (ii) observes that in none library, out of 19 libraries (0%) Government/Private employees visit to a great extent; followed by in 4 libraries (21%) to a small extent and not at all in 15 libraries (79%).

Similarly, Table 15.5 (iii) reveals that in none of the libraries, out of 19 libraries (0%) businessmen visit the library to a great extent; followed by 3 libraries (15.8) to a small extent and not at all in 16 libraries (84.2%).

Table 15.5 (iv) indicates that farmers are not at all visit the library and Community Information centers.

Table 15.5 (v) reveals that in 2 libraries out of 19, students visit to a great extent (10.6%), in 4 libraries (21%) to a small extent and in 13 libraries (68.4%) students not all visit the libraries.

The average number of users to these libraries is only 35, which is very low. It indicates that these libraries are unable to attract the users due to poor system and services.

Most libraries are managed by only one library professional even without any non-professional staff.

The main source of library finance is the assistance from central government. There is no provision for library cess in the Union Territory.

All libraries perform some basic technical works such as accessioning, classification of documents. But surprisingly most libraries do not have their catalogue, which indicates that the library collections of these libraries are not properly displayed to users.

All libraries provide some basic services such as lending, reading room etc. but none of the libraries except one provide reference service. Further, only one library, which provides reference service, and current awareness service only. It indicates that this is one of the reasons for poor attendance of users in these libraries.

No libraries have provision for community information service, neither they prepare any community information products. Therefore these libraries have failed to attract all sections of the community. It also resulted in the establishment of separate community information centers, which is also a threat to the existence of public libraries.

The main reasons for poor library condition in the Union territory are less finance, poor library collection, lack of library automation programs, lack of infrastructure facility, untrained library staff and also geo-morphological condition of the islands.

Proposed Structure of the Public Libraries System for the Islands

The proposed structure of Public Libraries System should be a five-tier structure as follows:

Tier I	State central library and information center	1 no.
Tier II	District public library and information center	2 nos.
Tier III	Tehsil public library and information center	7 nos.
Tier IV	Village public library and information center	67 nos.
Tier V	Mobile public library and information center	as per requirement.

However, the existing Public Library, Community Information Center etc. can also be changed to the Libraries of proposed Public Library and Information Center system instead of opening new Public Libraries.

Functions of Propose Public Libraries

State Central Library and Information Center

The State Central Public Library and Information Center should perform following functions:

- To be the apex of the entire Library and Information system in the Islands.
- To act as the repository of books published in the Union territory and received under the provision of the Delivery of Books Act, 1956.
- To maintain State Union Catalogue of books, periodicals, non-books materials, databases etc.
- To act as the agent for arranging Inter-States and International Inter-Library loans.
- To initiate and promote cooperative acquisition of library materials through consortium.
- To be the nodal center for Adult Education Programmes, Literacy programme, other library extension services of the Union territory.
- To provide training to Library staff of Public Libraries and Information Centers of the Union Territory.

Function of District/Tehsil/Village Public Library and Information Center

The various functions of District/Tehsil public libraries and Information Center should be as follows:

- Provide reading materials to people for home reading.
- Provide reading room service, reference services etc.
- Organize seminars, group discussions, dramas, and other cultural activities on various topics of public interest.

Proposed Public Library Network

The proposed network should provide minimum facilities and services in its initial stage and it should add new services and facilities every year to be a functional network. These are:

Hardware and Software Facilities

Set standards for member libraries to standardize activities such as communication format for interchange of bibliographic data, input output format, bibliographic description, classification and subjects headings, forms of heading, data input for abstracting and indexing, search/command language etc.

Create database of books, periodicals, CD-ROMs etc. and should be available online to all its member libraries. Besides, other services like electronics mail, retro-conversion of catalogues, maintain referral center, setting of document delivery center etc. should be provided.

It should organize various lectures, seminars, workshop and training programmes for the professional development.

The Network Services Center (NSC) should be located at State Central Library Port Blair with nodal centers at all participating libraries. A governing body consisting of technical experts, computer scientist and eminent library professional, should also manage the network.

Suggestions

The present study reveals a gloomy picture of existing public library system and services. Therefore, for its all-round development, the researcher has made following humble suggestions:

- Library legislation should be enacted in the Islands for the planned development of public libraries and information centers.
- The development of public libraries should be in a phased manner and should be a five their structure at State, District, Tehsil and village level.
- There should be a separate Directorate for its proper administration and management.

- A nominal library cess should be imposed on public so that they will realize the value of libraries and information centers and the services offered by them.
- Professional librarian should head all libraries and should be recruited properly as per requirement.
- There should be separate library building for all libraries and the location be in a central place, so that maximum people can use it.
- The library collection should include few books but also pamphlets, rare books, non-books materials like film, cassettes, CDs, DVDs etc.

Instead of centralized acquisition of books, it is better to provide that financial grants to individual libraries, so that they can purchase library material as per the users demand of that locality which differs from place to place. Further, assistance from Raja Ram Mohan Library Foundation should be properly distributed to all libraries.

The library collection and services be designed as per needs of all sections of people including farmers, businessmen etc. so that the basic aim of establishing these centres will be fulfilled.

Besides reading room services, other services which include community information services such as price list of communities, procedure and beneficial aspect cultivation, farming etc., general awareness on various diseases, government plans and programmes etc.: reprographic services; translation services should be provided by these libraries.

A Public Library Network should be established among the libraries and information centers of the islands.

Conclusion

The present study reveals a sad panorama of public libraries and community information centers pertaining to their system and services. The results also show that the existing public libraries and community information centers are not properly housed with necessary facilities to provide required services.

Hence, the humble research work mutatis-mutandis connotes: careful and thorough research on existing public libraries system and services of the islands particularly in the changing library situation: enactment of public library act in the Union Territory; setting up an Public library network for the planned development of public libraries and information centers of Andaman and Nicobar Islands. Therefore, it is concluded that immediate steps should be taken to remove the impediments lies in the existing public libraries system and services and to adopt and implement a best conceivable developmental plan for public libraries and community information centers of Andaman and Nicobar islands.

References

Augustine, C.A. and Devarajan, G. (1990). *Public Library System in India.* Ess Ess Publication; New Delhi. p. 135.

Directorate of Economics and Statistics. Andaman & Nicobar Islands (2001). *Basic Statistics. 2000-01.* Andaman and Nicobar Administration.

Directorate of Tourism, *Andaman and Nicobar: the Emerald Islands.* A&N Administration, Port Blair.

Ram, S. (Ed.) (2001). *Andaman & Nicobar Islands: Past and Present.* Akansha Publishing Houses, New Delhi, 1st, p. 238.

Sen, N.B. (Ed.) (1985). *Development of libraries in New India.* New Book Society of India; New Delhi. p. 82.

Part IV
Special Libraries

16

Regional Collaboration in Science and Technology Among South Asian Countries

B.M. GUPTA, MUJOO MUNSHI and P.K. MISHRA

Introduction

The present day South Asia, known previously as the Indian subcontinent, comprises the states of India, Bangladesh, Bhutan, Maldives, Nepal, Pakistan, and Sri Lanka. It represents 3 per cent of the world's area, but houses 22 per cent of the earth's population. It accounts for 1.65 per cent of the world's GDP and 1.12 per cent of global trade during 1995. The importance of developing S&T and its applications to meet the economic, industrial, trade and societal challenges has been recognized in most South Asian countries, as is evident from the emphasis placed in their development plans and policies. In national endeavors for developing S&T, importance has also been accorded to the creation of wide spectrum of S&T infrastructure in terms of research laboratories, R&D institutions, and in-house units in industry covering several disciplines. Yet the scale of S&T activity in most South Asian countries measured in terms of proportion of national income spent on R&D activity or the proportion of population engaged in its R&D activity is marginal, if at all significant.

South Asian countries have recognized the importance of international collaboration as a major factor in their development of science and technology capabilities. There is a wide scope of cooperation and collaboration in science and technology among South Asian countries. Each country can share with others the advantage it has in its S&T base and knowledge. The collaboration among

South Asian countries is being undertaken through bilateral, regional and multilateral agreements[1]. Among bilateral collaborations, India has taken the maximum initiatives and has signed bilateral agreements in science and technology with Bangladesh (1982), Pakistan (1983), Sri Lanka (1975) and Nepal. A majority of actual collaborations are undertaken under the umbrella of regional and international cooperation, through various agencies of the United Nations and other international organizations in the form of training of S&T personnel, exchange of scientists, and conduct of joint research and development projects.

The idea of regional cooperation was also conceived under the South Asian Association for Regional Cooperation (SAARC). India played a major role in promoting collaboration under SAARC. At present there are twelve areas of cooperation under SAARC, which include agriculture, communications, environment, health and population activities, and science and technology[2]. Regional cooperation is also fostered through other international agencies and their regional programs. These agencies and programs are playing significant role in exchange of information, training of technical personnel and scientists, and conducting of joint research and development projects among developing countries, including those pertaining to S&T.

The collaboration among South Asian countries has resulted in different kinds of outputs, which include joint research publications, technology development and transfer and development of products and processes. The joint research publication is an important indicator of the strength of research collaboration and its impact on different fields. This particular information on collaborated output is comparatively well documented in printed and computerized databases. However, there are hardly any sources through which other outputs of these collaborations could be easily documented and studied.

Some studies have been undertaken in the past on the collaborative linkages of Indian science, using publication data from Science Citation Index. The study by Nagpaul[3] was focused on the analysis of the transnational linkages of Indian science in eleven scientific fields, with 35 most significant partner countries during 1990 and 1994. The author in collaboration with his colleagues[4-5] has conducted a number of studies analyzing India's collaborative linkages, both at bilateral and multilateral level, with Russia, South East Asian countries, China, and Australia. The present study also looks at the collaboration linkages among South Asian countries.

Objectives

The main aim of the study is to study research collaborations among South Asian countries with following objectives: (i) To study the nature of collaboration in

S&T, as reflected in co-authored research papers, (ii) To identify the subject areas of collaboration, (iii) To evaluate the impact of collaborative research, and (iv) To identify the major institutions involved in these collaborative research activities and programs.

Databases and Methodology

The data for the study was culled from the *Web of Science (Expanded SCI)* database from 1994 to 2004 (11 years). This database covers around 6,000 significant journals of the world in all major fields of science and technology. However, it covers only a few domestic journals published from the South Asian countries. The journals covered by *Web of Science (Expanded SCI)* represent the mainstream science and technology. As a result, the study is restricted to the co-authored articles generated from collaboration among five South Asian countries. The articles were classified under 13 major disciplines and sub-disciplines, according to the classification scheme suggested by ISI, Philadelpia, USA. In this scheme, each article is classified into a main discipline and a sub-discipline using the subject title of the journal in which it is published. For impact factor data, we have used the *Journals Citation Report* brought out by Institute of Scientific Information (ISI) annually. Since the minimum and maximum value of IF varies across broad subjects, we have normalized the impact factor data using the methodology suggested by Nagpaul.

S&T Research Output of South Asian Countries

Table 16.1 presents the publication data for five South Asian countries from 1994 to 2004, as reflected in the *Web of Science (Expanded SCI)* database.

Table 16.1 : S&T Research Output of South Asian countries, 1993-2004

Year	India	Bangladesh	Pakistan	Sri Lanka	Nepal
1994	15,652	299	499	134	58
1995	16,373	349	615	136	84
1996	16,486	337	581	130	68
1997	16,269	355	537	122	83
1998	17,740	368	671	150	108
1999	18,726	398	637	189	125
2000	17,501	389	648	205	132
2001	19,339	433	613	186	154
2002	20,405	454	759	212	168
2003	23,135	532	862	310	181
2004	23,336	507	1024	281	178

It is clear from Table 16.1 that there is a wide gap between the research output of India and other South Asian countries. The normalized average number of publications per year from these countries during 1994 to 2004 was: 20,496 for India, 744 for Pakistan, 442 for Bangladesh, 355 for Sri Lanka, and 134 for Nepal. There is no consistency in the publication output of these South Asian countries. The number of publications, however, remained within a particular limit.

Collaboration in S&T Among South Asian Countries

The collaboration among South Asian countries during 1994 to 2004 has resulted in 466 co-authored papers in different fields of science and technology. The average number of co-authored papers (42) per year is very small as compared to the scientific output of all these five countries. These papers have appeared in different formats: research articles (394), review articles (17), letters (17) and the rest as letters to the editor, notes, meeting-abstracts, editorial material and discussion.

Of the five countries of South Asia, India has played a central role in encouraging collaboration among themselves. In 466 co-authored papers among South Asian countries from 1994 to 2004, India's collaboration with all the other four countries was the largest, with the joint output of 410 papers. It has 222 co-authored papers with Bangladesh, followed by Nepal (97), Pakistan (67), and Sri Lanka (53). The exclusive collaboration among Bangladesh, Pakistan, Nepal and Sri Lanka was, however, very small and resulted in only 56 co-authored papers. Table 16.2 presents the distribution of collaborative papers among South Asian countries.

Table 16.2 : Collaborative Papers Among South Asian Countries

Country	Number of Co-authored Papers				
	India	Bangladesh	Pakistan	Nepal	Sri Lanka
India	—	222	67	97	53
Bangladesh	222	—	27	19	8
Pakistan	67	27	—	10	20
Nepal	97	19	10	—	7
Sri Lanka	53	8	20	7	—
Total	410	251	106	116	78

Of the 466 co-authored papers among South Asian countries, only 136 (29%) papers were under bilateral collaboration and 330 papers under multilateral collaboration. A comparative stronger bilateral collaboration exists between India and Bangladesh and India and Nepal, which accounts for 32 per cent and 37 per cent, respectively of all co-authored papers. In contrast, India's co-authored papers with Pakistan and Sri Lanka involve mainly multilateral collaboration, which accounts for 91 per cent and 88.7 per cent, respectively of their total co-authored papers. Except with India, Bangladesh has strong multilateral collaboration with Pakistan, Nepal and Sri Lanka, accounting for 96 per cent, 95 per cent and 87 per cent of their total co-authored papers. In case of Pakistan, it has comparative higher bilateral collaboration with Nepal and Sri Lanka and strong multilateral collaboration with India and Bangladesh, accounting for 91 per cent and 96 per cent, respectively of their total co-authored papers. Nepal has comparatively higher bilateral collaboration with India and Pakistan, but strong multilateral collaboration with Bangladesh and Sri Lanka, accounting for 95 per cent and 86 per cent of its total co-authored papers.

The break-up of 466 co-authored papers under 13 major disciplines indicates the following picture. Basic life science and clinical medicine had the largest and almost equal number of co-authored papers (19%) each, followed by biomedical research 46 (9.9%) papers, chemistry 45 (9.6%) papers, physics 41 (8.8%) papers, agriculture 41 (8.8%) papers, engineering 37(7.9%) papers, and earth and environment science 27(5.6%) papers. Rest of the subject disciplines were contributing less than 5 per cent papers.

As compared to other countries, India's collaboration with Bangladesh is more widespread across all major disciplines. It indicates: (a) larger collaborative efforts in basic life science accounting for 25 per cent of their co-authored papers; (b) modest size collaborative efforts in clinical medicine, physics, engineering, biomedical research and agriculture, accounting for 14 per cent, 12 per cent, 11 per cent, 10 per cent and 8 per cent, respectively of their co-authored papers; (c) smaller collaborative efforts has been observed in all other disciplines. In contrast, India's collaborative efforts with Pakistan, Nepal and Sri Lanka are focused in few disciplines, namely clinical medicine, basic life sciences, biomedical research and agriculture.

The impact of these co-authored papers was analyzed through the impact factor of journals in which these papers were published. Considering all co-authored papers, the normalized average impact factor per paper was observed to be 0.83. It was 0.46 for bilateral papers and 0.98 for multilateral papers. Except for multidisciplinary sciences, which had exceptionally high normalized average IF per paper (3.86), the normalized average value of IF per paper under various disciplines, in terms of ranking were: 1.53 for clinical medicine, 1.03 for basic life sciences, 0.85 for biomedical research, 0.44 for biology, 0.40 for physics and agriculture each, 0.37 for chemistry, and 0.34 for earth and environment science, social sciences (0.29), engineering (0.20), computer science (0.17), and mathematics (0.10).

The highest normalized average value of IF was 2.33 under Nepal-Sri Lanka collaboration, followed by 1.43 under India-Pakistan, 1.22 under India-Sri Lanka, 1.17 under Pakistan-Nepal, 1.06 under Bangladesh-Sri Lanka, 0.96 under Bangladesh-Pakistan, 0.90 under Bangladesh-Nepal, 0.75 under India-Bangladesh, 0.60 under India-Nepal and 0.59 under Pakistan-Sri Lanka.

There were 194 journals in which these 466 collaborative papers were published. Of these journals, 194 journals have published only 1 paper, 53 journals 2 papers, 24 journals 3 papers, 4 journals 4 papers, 8 journals 5 papers, 2 journals 6 papers and 12 and 14 papers 1 journal each. A list of journals in which more than 5 collaborated papers were: (i) Journal of Clinical Microbiology (14 papers), (ii) British Medical Journal (12 papers), (iii) Lancet (6 papers) and (iv) Leprosy Review (6 papers).

In all, 412 institutions from South Asian countries were involved in the collaborative research during the period under study. Of these, 202 were from India, 68 from Bangladesh, 49 from Pakistan, 60 from Nepal and 33 from Sri Lanka. The names of major South Asian institutions along with their individual collaborated publications were as follows:

- *India*—(i) National Institute of Cholera & Enteric Diseases, Kolkata (49 papers), (ii) Jadavpur University (28 papers), (iii) All India Institute of Medical Sciences, New Delhi (25 papers), (iv) Banaras Hindu University, Varanasi (18 papers); (v) Society of Applied Sciences, Kolkata (16 papers), (vi) Christian Medical College, Vellore (12 papers), (vii) Indian Agricultural Research Institute, New Delhi (11 papers), (viii) Indian Institute of Technology, New Delhi (11 papers), and (ix) Indian Institute of Technology, Kharagpur (10 papers).
- *Bangladesh*—(i) International Centre of Diarrhoeal Disease Research (ICDDR), Dhaka (78 papers), (ii) University of Dhaka (38 papers), (iii) Jahangirnagar University, Dhaka (13 papers), (iv) University of Chittagong (12 papers), and (v) Rajshahi University (11 papers).
- *Nepal*—(i) Tribhuvan University, Kathmandu (33 papers) and (ii) B.P. Koirala Institute of Health Sciences, Dharan (12 papers),
- *Pakistan*—(i) Aga Khan University, Karachi (18 papers), (ii) University of Karachi, Hej Research Institute of Chemistry (18 papers), and (iii) International Water Management Institute, Lahore (10 papers).
- *Sri Lanka*—(i) University of Colombo (20 papers), (ii) International Water Management Institute, Columbo (16 papers), and (iii) University of Peradeniya (15 papers).

Bilateral S&T Collaborations Among South Asian Countries

Bilateral collaboration among South Asian countries had resulted in 136 co-authored papers. India's collaboration with South Asian countries had resulted in 120 co-authored papers. The maximum (72) papers were published through the collaboration of India with Bangladesh, followed by with Nepal (36 papers), Pakistan (6 papers), and Sri Lanka (6 papers). Of the remaining 16 bilateral co-authored papers among Pakistan, Bangladesh, Nepal and Sri Lanka, Pakistan collaboration with Nepal and Sri Lanka resulted in 4 and 8 papers each. Bangladesh bilateral collaboration with Pakistan, Nepal and Sri Lanka resulted in only 1 co-authored paper each.

The 136 bilateral co-authored papers were in 13 major disciplines and 50 sub-fields. The subject-wise and country-wise break-up of these papers is given in Table 16.4 along with their normalized average IF values. The largest number of papers was published in the area of chemistry (23), engineering (23 papers), and physics (22 papers) and the least in social science (1 paper).

It was observed that the normalized average impact factor per paper based on bilateral co-authored papers was 0.46. The highest normalized average value of IF (1.60) was under India-Pakistan, followed by 1.01 for Pakistan-Nepal papers, 0.93 for Bangladesh-Sri Lanka papers, 0.59 for Bangladesh-Pakistan papers, 0.47 for India-Bangladesh papers, 0.33 for Pakistan-Sri Lanka papers, 0.28 for India-Nepal papers, 0.26 for Nepal-Sri Lanka papers, 0.24 for Bangladesh-Nepal papers and 0.10 for India-Sri Lanka papers. It was also observed that India-Bangladesh bilateral co-authored papers had the highest normalized average values of IF in six disciplines: multidisciplinary sciences (3.40), computer science (0.22), social sciences (0.21), engineering (0.18), earth and environmental science (0.17), and mathematics (0.15); India-Nepal bilateral co-authored papers had the highest normalized average values of IF in three disciplines: biomedical research (0.63), physics (0.45), and engineering (0.18); Pakistan-Sri Lanka bilateral co-authored papers had the highest normalized average values of IF in two disciplines: agriculture (0.49) and biology (0.31); Bangladesh-Pakistan, Bangladesh-Sri Lanka and Pakistan-Nepal bilateral co-authored papers had the highest normalized average values of IF in one discipline each: chemistry (0.59), basic life sciences (0.93), and clinical medicine (2.44) (Table 16.4).

Multilateral S&T Collaborations of India with South Asian Countries

Of the 330 multilateral co-authored papers, 305 involved the participation of at least two South Asian countries and one or more other countries outside the

South Asian region. 23 papers had the participation of three South Asian countries simultaneously and one or more other countries. 2 papers had the participation of five South Asian countries simultaneously and one or more other countries. As a result on counting the total number of co-authored papers under 12 subjects, it comes as more number than the actual total. Among multilateral collaborative papers, the largest contribution (150 papers) was from India–Bangladesh, followed by India–Pakistan (61 papers), India–Nepal (61 papers) and India–Sri Lanka (47 papers), Pakistan-Bangladesh (26 papers), Bangladesh-Nepal (18 papers), Pakistan-Sri Lanka (12 papers), Bangladesh-Sri Lanka (7 papers), and Pakistan-Sri Lanka (6 papers) (Table 16.5).

The 330 multilateral co-authored papers were in 12 major disciplines and 75 sub-fields. The largest number of papers was published in the area of basic life sciences (77 papers), followed by clinical medicine (75 papers), biomedical research (42 papers), agriculture (31 papers), earth and environment science (23 papers), chemistry (22 papers), physics (19 papers), engineering (14 papers), biology (13 papers), social sciences (7 papers), multidisciplinary sciences (5 papers), and mathematics (2 papers). The subject-wise and country-wise break-up of these papers is given in Table 16.5 along with their normalized average IF values.

The normalized average impact factor per paper based on multilateral co-authored papers was 0.98. The highest normalized average value of IF was 2.33 under Nepal-Sri Lanka collaboration, followed by 1.42 under India-Pakistan, 1.37 under India-Sri Lanka, 1.29 under Pakistan-Nepal, 1.08 under Bangladesh-Sri Lanka, 0.97 under Bangladesh-Pakistan, 0.93 under Bangladesh-Nepal, 0.89 under India-Bangladesh, 0.79 under India-Nepal, and 0.76 under Pakistan-Sri Lanka.

It was also observed that India-Bangladesh and India-Pakistan and India-Nepal multilateral co-authored papers had the highest normalized average values of IF in three broad disciplines each: India-Bangladesh in biomedical science (1.04), agriculture (0.64), and mathematics (0.05); India-Pakistan in multidisciplinary sciences (9.85), basic life sciences (2.05), and physics (0.81) and India-Nepal multilateral co-authored papers had the highest normalized average values of IF in two broad disciplines: biology (0.58) and engineering (0.36). Similarly India-Sri Lanka, Pakistan-Nepal, Pakistan-Sri Lanka and Nepal-Sri Lanka multilateral co-authored papers had the highest normalized average values of IF in one broad discipline each: social sciences (0.46), chemistry (1.25), earth and environmental science (0.59) and clinical medicine (3.31).

In all 123 countries participated in multilateral collaborated papers, of which 118 countries were from outside South Asian region. These countries participated in various combinations, ranging from 3 to 61. Around 37.27 per cent of the multilateral collaborative research papers emanated from the team efforts of

3 countries. The participating teams comprising 11 to 61 countries accounted for about 9.39 per cent of the total multilateral papers.

In these papers, there was a noticeable involvement of international and regional organizations/centers, such as World Health Organization (29 papers), International Rice Research Institute, Manila, Philippines (10 papers), International Atomic Energy Agency (6 papers), UNFPA (7 papers), UNICEF (6 papers), International Maize & Wheat Improvement Center, Kathmandu (5 paper), World Bank (3 papers), CIMMYT, South Asia (5 papers), International Center for Agricultural Research in Dry Areas, Aleppo, Syria (2 papers). There was also an active involvement of international organizations located in South Asian countries, such as International Center for Diarrhoeal Disease Research, Dhaka (19 papers), International Water Management Institute, Columbo (11 papers), International Water Management Institute, Lahore (6 papers), ICRISAT, Patancheru (4 papers), International Center for Integrated Mountain Development, Kathmandu (5 papers).

The influence of different regions and countries on the collaborations was also analyzed. In these papers, the USA had participated in maximum 199 (60.30%) papers, followed by The United Kingdom (96 papers), Japan (91 papers), China (63 papers), Thailand (45 papers), Switzerland (37 papers), Indonesia (35 papers), South Korea (34 papers), Italy (34 papers), Philippines (29 papers), Malaysia (28 papers), Canada (25 papers) and Australia (22 papers).

The number of institutions collaborating per paper from various participating countries in multilateral papers ranged from 3 to 55. The participation of 3 institutions was in more than 32.60 per cent (30 papers) of the total papers. On the other hand, the participation of 11 to 55 institutions accounted for 15.22 per cent (14 papers) of all papers. Only in one multilateral paper, the number of participating institutions was 55. The number of participating institutions was less than 21 in other papers.

Areas for Future Cooperation

There are many areas of science and technology where cooperation among South Asian countries would be mutually beneficial. These include food and fermentation technology, ore processing, metallurgy, glass and ceramics, paints and plastics, fine chemicals and leather. Other common areas could be: utilization of common eco-system, preserving region's rich genetic bio-diversity, hydropower resources and transmission of the generated electricity; maintaining surveillance on seismic, climatic and other environmental changes for sending advance warning against draught, flood and other environmental changes; undertaking joint space programs for the survey of natural resources and sharing of traditional knowledge in different subject areas. In addition, complimentary technological relations are necessary to sustain commercial relations, recognizing that technology would dominate the development challenges in the 21st century. A SAARC study group on economic cooperation has also prescribed regional technological cooperation to meet the requirement of global competitiveness. India—contributing 78 per cent of the total manufacturing value in the region—has an unmistakable technological superiority in both capital and intermediate technology. Compared to western technologies, India's expertise would be more suitable to South Asian countries[6].

Conclusions

A study on S&T collaboration among five South Asian countries (India, Bangladesh, Pakistan, Nepal and Sri Lanka) has been presented through the analysis of joint co-authored research papers published during 1994-2004 in journals covered by Expanded SCI under Web of Science database. As an outcome of these collaborations, a total of 466 joint co-authored papers were published in which only 136 under bilateral collaborations and 330 under multilateral collaborations. In all 412 institutions from South Asian countries were involved in the collaborative research during the period under study. Of these, 202 were from India, 68 from Bangladesh, 49 from Pakistan, 60 from Nepal and 33 from Sri Lanka. Amongst India's collaborations with fellow South Asian countries, India-Bangladesh joint collaborative research produced maximum number of papers through bilateral (71 papers) as well as multilateral (47 papers) research. The most prefered area for collaboration has been found to be "basic life science", "clinical medicine", and "biomedical research" both in terms of joint research output and citation impact, probably because of marked growth in the research in health-related problems world over and application of these research results for solving environmental health hazards during the last decade. However, under bilateral collaboration, the preferred areas of collaboration were chemistry, engineering and physics. USA, as expected, had the maximum share amongst participating countries outside the South Asian arena in all co-authored papers. The need for further cooperation has been indicated in areas such as biotechnology, biodiversity, environment, floods and droughts, etc., and above all, in traditional knowledge on medicines and healthcare of the region.

Notes

1. Das, Suranjan (2 December 2000). Regional security through constructive bilateralism: Prospects for South Asian stability. *Economic and Political Weekly*, pp. 4349-59.

2. Gupta, B.M. & Dhawan, S.M. (2003). India's Collaboration with People's Republic of China in Science and Technology: A scientometric analysis of co-authored papers during 1994-99. *Scientometrics* 57(1), pp. 59-74.
3. Gupta, B.M., Dhawan, S.M. & Walke, Rajpal (2002). Indo-Russian Collaboration in S&T: An analysis through co-authored publications, 1995-99. *Current Science* 82(9), 1075-77.
4. India, Department of Science and Technology, Technology Information, Forecasting and Assessment Council (1995). *Status of S and T in India.* New Delhi.
5. Nagpaul, P.S. (2000). International collaboration in Indian scientific papers. *Scientometrics* 48(3), pp. 381-402.
6. Thomas, Jibby (2000). Science and Technology Cooperation in SAARC. In. B.C. Upreti, ed. *SAARC: Dynamics of Regional Cooperation in South Asia* (225-265). Vol.2. New Delhi: Kaling.

17

Collaboration Patterns Among SAARC Countries in the Area of Medicine: Status and Challenges Ahead

RAMESH KUNDRA and DIVYA SRIVASTAVA

Introduction: SAARC Its Origin

The South Asian Association for Regional Cooperation (SAARC)[1] was established when its Charter was formally adopted on December 8, 1985 by the Heads of State or Government of Bangladesh, Bhutan, India, Maldives, Nepal, Pakistan and Sri Lanka. SAARC thus provided a platform for the people of South Asia to work together in a spirit of friendship, trust and understanding. These countries comprise an area of 5,127,500 km^2 and a fifth of the world's population. Afganistan has recently joined. The aim was to accelerate the process of economic and social development in Member States.

At the inception of the Association, the Integrated Programme of Action (IPA) consisting of a number of Technical Committees (TC's) was identified as the core areas of cooperation. Over the period, number of TC's were changed as per the requirement.

The current areas of cooperation under the reconstituted Regional Integrated Programme of Action which is pursued through the Technical Committees covered are:

- Agriculture and Rural Development;
- Health and Population Activities;

- Women, Youth and Children;
- Environment and Forestry;
- Science and Technology and Meteorology;
- Human Resources Development; and
- Transport.

Aims and Objective

India's strength among the SAARC countries lies in the establishment of large number of R & D institutions and their research output in which it competes not only with SAARC nations but also with many developing countries. Health and population problems being one of the major areas of commonality, needs strong cooperation. This paper discusses the present status of cooperation and collaboration among the SAARC countries after 12 years of its inception. Papers published during 1997 and 2002 from these countries and Indexed in PubMed database have been used for the study and the following issues are discussed:

- The pattern of publication of SAARC countries in areas of medicine.
- The pattern of collaboration in SAARC countries.
- Total contribution of SAARC countries in different areas of medicine.

This is a pilot study and analysis for only two years (1997) and (2002) was carried out. The authors propose to carry out a more extensive study of the SAARC countries for a longer period. The purpose of the study is to highlight that these countries are focused more towards the areas being covered by developed countries. The SAARC countries having common health problems and often affected by same natural calamities and epidemics do not attempt for a common minimum program to overcome the same. SAARC countries continue to be guinea pigs for the MNC's first it was in the case of tropical diseases and now it is in cases such as Cancer, HIV/AIDS, Metabolic Diseases, Tuberculosis and Diseases relating to pollution, etc. Apart from these, attempts have been made to reflect the collaboration pattern of the authors and the areas in medicine reported by them through publication pattern of these countries.

Health and Population Activities (the theme of this paper) is one of the key issues figuring in the cooperation among the SAARC countries. The health indicators (Table 17.1) reflect lot of commonality among these countries in terms of population growth, mortality rate and in, input to health sector in terms of expenditure especially among nations bordering India. Maldives and Sri Lanka are few exceptional cases reflecting different social and health indicators among the SAARC countries.

Table 17.1 : Health Indicators of SAARC Countries

Health Indicators	Year	India	Pakistan	Bangladesh	Bhutan	Nepal	Maldives	Sri Lanka
Total population (000), 2003	2002	1,065,462,000	153,578,000	1,46,736,000	2,257,000	25,164,000	318,000	19,065,000
Annual population growth rate (%), 1993—2003	2002	1.7	2.6	2.2	2.5	2.3	3.0	0.9
Dependency ratio (per 100), 2003	2002	61	82	70	84	78	85	46
Percentage of population aged 60+ years, 2003	2002	7.8	5.7	5.1	6.5	5.9	5.2	10.3
Child mortality m/f (per 1000)	2002	85/90	98/108	68/70	85/85	80/85	67/77	17/13
Adult mortality m/f (per 1000)	2002	283/213	225/198	251/258	261/202	290/284	165/146	235/120
GDP per capita (Intl.$ 2002)	2002	1,568	1920	1734	1700	1219	5301	3540
Total health expenditure per capita (Intl $, 2002)	2002	96	62	54	76	64	307	131
Total health expenditure as % of GDP (2002)	1997	5.3	3.8	2.9	3.6	5.4	6.5	3.2
	2002	6.1	3.2	3.1	4.5	5.2	5.8	3.7
General Government expenditure on health as % of total expenditure on health, 2002	1997	15.7	27.2	33.7	90.4	31.3	81.9	49.5
	2002	21.3	34.9	25.2	92.2	27.2	87.7	48.7
General Government expenditure on health as % of total general government expenditure, 2002	1997	3.2	3.8	5.6	10.1	9.3	10.9	6.0
	2002	4.4	3.2	4.4	12.0	7.5	13.3	6.0
Private expenditure on health as % of total expenditure on health, 2002	1997	84.3	72.8	66.3	9.6	68.7	18.1	50.5
	2002	78.7	65.1	74.8	7.8	72.8	12.3	51.3
External resources for health as % of total expenditure on health	1997	2.3	2.7	10.0	32.1	10.6	4.2	3.2
	2002	1.0	1.8	13.5	18.7	9.0	3.4	1.9
Social security expenditure on health as % of general government expenditure on health, 2002	1997	NA	43.9	0.0	0.0	0.0	0.0	0.0
	2002	4.6	42.9	0.0	0.0	0.0	23.8	0.0
Papers published (PubMed)	1997	2895	150	86	0	34	0	59
	2002	5914	252	107	0	59	0	85

South Asia region[3] is one of the most populated area and has about 22 per cent of world's population, with 33 per cent births annually, about 37 per cent of annual global child mortality (CM), and the second highest maternal mortality ratio (MMR). Among the SAARC countries India has the highest proportion of births. Where as Sri Lanka has the highest female literacy of 87 per cent, followed by India with 38 per cent. Female literacy for the whole region together is only 36 per cent.

Pakistan

Pakistan is a country with a population growth rate of 2.6, the highest among the SAARC countries and has a quite closed health policy system. Most of the R&D on health issues are reported from medical educational institutions and five research institutes, namely: Central Drugs Laboratory; Pak Medical and Research Council, under Ministry of Health, Islamabad; Pakistan Medical and Dental Council, Islamabad; Pakistan Nursing Council (NIH), Islamabad; Pharmacy Council of Pakistan, Islamabad; and PIMS Islamabad.

India

The health sector in India is characterized by: (i) a government sector that provides publicly financed and managed curative and preventive health services from primary to tertiary level, throughout the country and free of cost services to the consumers (these account for about 18 per cent of the overall health spending and 0.9 per cent of the GDP), and (ii) a fee-levying private sector that plays a dominant role in the provision of individual curative care through ambulatory services and accounts for about 82 per cent of the overall health expenditure and 4.2 per cent of the GDP.

India has a long history of biomedical research including health systems research. In several instances research results have directly influenced programme policies or led to modifications in programme strategies. These areas include emerging health problems like HIV/AIDS, other important communicable diseases like tuberculosis, leprosy, filarial and diarroheal diseases, malaria, Japanese encephalitis, non-communicable diseases like cancer, cardiovascular diseases, metabolic disorders, contraception, MCH and nutrition etc. Efforts have been made to develop a bibliographic database on HSR. With WHO support, nearly 400 HSR studies have been abstracted and a database was developed by the NIHFW in 1996 and efforts are on to cover other areas also.

Nepal

A National Health Policy (NHP) in Nepal was formulated in 1991 with the objective of enhancing the health status of the population, 86 per cent of which is rural. The NHP is a comprehensive policy that addresses service delivery as well as the administrative structure of the health system. The 8th Health Plan (1992-1997), 9th Health Plan (1997-2002) and Second Long Term Health Plan (SLTHP) (1997-2017) were developed in keeping with the NHP. The Nepal Health Research Council is the main body for planning and coordinating research activities related to bio-medical and operational research. The provision of grants is a means for promoting young researchers, research programs of the institutions of medical education and activities of selected NGOs specializing in research.

Maldives

In Maldives health is considered a basic right of every citizen and the government emphasizes the goal of *health for all* based on the primary health care approach. The island nature of the country poses a major challenge to providing equitable access to health care. A number of researches have been carried out in the recent past, mainly to assess prevailing situations in reproductive health, nutrition and some other disease conditions, along with assessing knowledge, attitude and practice. Almost all these researches have been carried out with expatriate technical assistance, as the country does not have appropriately trained personnel. Focus has not been given to clinical based research mainly due to lack of appropriate resources and manpower. However, this is an area the country needs to focus.

Bhutan

Bhutan has enjoyed peace and political stability since the present line of hereditary monarchs was established in 1905. Bhutan's approach to health care has been the delivery of an integrated health service package to its population scattered across a difficult mountainous terrain. It has made significant strides after adopting the primary health care approach in 1978. Substantial financial allocation has been earmarked for development of research capacity within the Health Division. Future strategies will also include collaboration with research institutes in other countries.

Sri Lanka

Sri Lankan policy, irrespective of the government in power, has always regarded education and health as crucial to socio-economic development, while the concept of equity and social justice in favour of the underprivileged has also been a feature of state policy. Institutions and organizations involved include the National Institute of Health Sciences which is the focal point for HSR, the Medical Research Institute which is mainly involved in biomedical research, the Faculties of Medicine of the Universities, operational units of the Ministry of Health such as the Family Health Bureau, Epidemiology Unit, etc., professional organizations such as the Sri Lanka Medical Association, other ministries and institutions, NGOs and the Traditional Medicine Institute. The main constraints have been inadequate funding, minimal health research utilizing a multidisciplinary and intersectoral team approach, and the absence of a mechanism for adequate dissemination of information and utilization of research findings.

Methodology

For the study we downloaded papers indexed in PubMed[2] for the year(s) 1997 and 2000, from the SAARC countries—Pakistan, India, Nepal, Maldives, Bangladesh, Sri Lanka, and Bhutan. The PubMed covers most of the core primary journals published from these countries. PubMed is available *via* the NCBI Entrez retrieval system, and has been developed by the National Center for Biotechnology Information (NCBI) at the National Library of Medicine (NLM), located at the National Institutes of Health (NIH), USA. Entrez is the text-based search and retrieval system used at NCBI for services including PubMed, Nucleotide and Protein Sequences, Protein Structures, Complete Genomes, Taxonomy, OMIM, and many others. PubMed also provides access and links to the other Entrez molecular biology resources.

Analysis and Discussion

As mentioned earlier this is a pilot study (to be extended later) to observe the pattern of papers published from SAARC countries. Almost all the countries are geographically placed as the neighbours of India. Any comparison among these countries carries no meaning as R&D activities in most of the smaller nations (Bhutan, Maldives) are either missing or are at its infancy. The year selected for the study coincides with the data reported by WHO statistical health figures for the year 1997 and 2002[3].

Growth of SAARC Publications

Table 17.2 indicates that in 1997, 5312 total papers were reported by other nations on SAARC countries while 3224 papers were published by SAARC researchers in health related areas. A total of 6417 papers were published by SAARC countries and 10036 total papers were published on SAARC countries by other nations in 2002. The rise in total papers on SAARC countries was at an average of 47.1 per cent and in case of papers by SAARC countries only, it was 47.9 per cent. A substantial increase in the publication activity by all the SAARC countries, from 1997 to 2002 was witnessed except for Bhutan and Maldives.

On Bhutan or by Bhutanese no papers were published during 1997 or 2002, it could be presumed as a result of lack of any research facilities in medicine. In Maldives only one paper was published in 2002. The maximum rise in total papers was seen in Nepal (52.8%) followed by India (48.2%) while after Bhutan the least rise was seen in Bangladesh.

Table 17.2 : Trends of papers published from SAARC countries (1997, 2002)

Countries	Total Papers on SAARC 1997 to 2002	Papers by nations of SAARC 1997 to 2002	% increase of total papers over five year period 1997 to 2002	% increase of papers over five year period 1997 to 2002
1. Pakistan	268 430	150 252	37.7	40.5
2. Bangladesh	143 188	86 107	23.9	19.6
3. Bhutan	0 1	0 0	100.0	0
4. Maldives	0 0	0 0	0	0
5. Nepal	67 142	34 59	52.8	42.4
6. Sri Lanka	96 131	59 85	26.7	30.6
7. India	4738 9144	2895 5914	48.2	51.1

International Collaborative R & D Activities on SAARC countries

Table 17.3 projects the total papers on SAARC countries and by SAARC countries during 1997 and 2002. Scholars from rest of the world have shown a substantial interest on health problems of Sri Lanka (61.5%) followed by India (61%) and Bangladesh (61%) during 1997, while in 2002 the focus was on Nepal (58.5%) followed by Bangladesh (43%). There is substantial percentage increase of interest in SAARC health activities over the last five years. As a result one may assume that SAARC forum has drawn attention to other forums such as ASEAN, SAF, OECD, OPEC and the developed countries. The lower percentage of interest by scholars from outside SAARC on India and Pakistan during 2002 compared to 1997 may reflect a strong local R&D activities. In 1997 the international collaboration with scholars of SAARC nations was 39.3 per cent while in 2002 it decreased to 37.1 per cent. Thus, it could be assumed that there was an increase in activities of local scholars working on SAARC health problems within the SAARC region only.

Table 17.3 : International Collaborative R&D Activities on SAARC Countries

Countries	Total Papers on SAARC (TP)	Papers by nations of SAARC (P)	% of Papers by other Countries
	2002-1997	2002-1997	2002-1997
1. Pakistan	430-268	252-150	41.4-56.0
2. Bangladesh	188-143	107-86	43.0-60.1
3. Bhutan	1-0	1-0	100-0
4. Maldives	0-0	0-0	0-0
5. Nepal	142-67	59-34	58.5-50.8
6. Sri Lanka	131-96	84-59	35.1-61.5
7. India	9144-4738	5914-2895	35.2-61.0
Total	10036-5312	6417-3224	37.1-39.3

SAARC Collaboration Pattern

Table 17.4 indicates the pattern of collaboration among the scholars of the respective SAARC nations which may be referred as national collaboration for the year 1997 and 2002. In 1997 a total of 2852 (85.3%) co-authored papers were reported and 6050 (94.3%) were there in 2002. The single authored papers were 14.7 per cent in 1997 and reduced to 5.7 per cent in 2002. Most of the decline in single authored papers and the drastic increase in co-authored papers was as result of Indian co-authored papers with an increase from 78 per cent to 88.1 per cent. Similar trends were visible among other SAARC countries.

Table 17.4 Collaborative Papers of SAARC (2002)

Countries	Total Papers	Collaborative Papers (%)	Single Author papers (%)
	1997-2002	1997-2002	1997-2002
1. Pakistan	150-252	85.3-92.8	14.7-7.2
2. Bangladesh	86-107	91.9-95.3	8.1-4.7
3. Bhutan	0-1	0-0	100-0
4. Maldives	0-0	0-0	0 0
5. Nepal	34-59	83.3-81.3	16.7-18.7
6. Sri Lanka	59-84	78.0-88.1	22.0-11.9
7. India	2895-5914	84.8-94.6	15.2-5.4
Total	3224-6417		

The growing professionalisation in the area of health studies is an indicator of this trend. Before coming to a major conclusion one needs to carry out a major and extensive study.

Major Health Issues of SAARC Countries

Table 17.5 presents the analysis of the 2002 papers pertaining to health issues faced by SAARC member states. For analysis purposes five major areas of the region have been identified and further discussed. The areas have been identified through personal observations and expereinces of the authors of this paper who are the *bona fide* citizen of one the SAARC member countries. The issues pinpointed are: Local Health, General Medical Practices, Tropical Diseases, Cancer and HIV/AIDS. The purpose is to reflect the issues that are of interest and are favourite to the scholors of SAARC countries. Pakistan (71.4%) and Bangladesh (65.4%) contribute maximum papers to local health issues while percentage share of papers on Tropical diseases problems were, Pakistan (15.9%), Bangladesh (15.0%) and Sri Lanka (13.1). India and Nepal contributed maximum papers towards studies reltaed to the area of Cancer and in AID/HIV. The overall contribution of India and Sri lanka was maximum papers during 2002. In General Medical Issues, the topics covered were experiments to test certain medical equipments, drug analysis, tradtional and medicinal plants related experiments, etc. Sri Lanka lead (48.8%) the list followed by it. India contributed papers in all the five identified areas significantly, instead of concentrating anyone of the areas being discussed here. Although India has a strong medical research base and can certainly lead in any of the issues reflected in the study, but the present data does not support this, this may need further exploration.

Table 17.5 : Papers Published by SAARC Countries During 2002 on Health Issues

Countries	Total Papers (2002)	Local Health Problems	General Medical Issues	Tropical Diseases	Cancer	HIV/AIDS
1. Pakistan	252	71.4	9.9	15.9	2.8	0.0
2. Bangladesh	107	65.4	17.8	15.0	0.0	1.8
3. Bhutan	0	0.0.	0.0.	0.0.	0.0.	0.0
4. Maldives	0	0.0.	0.0.	0.0.	0.0.	0.0.
5. Nepal	59	57.6	22.0	15.3	5.1	0.0
6. Sri Lanka	84	34.5	48.8	13.1	1.2	2.4
7. India	5914	40.6	44.0	10.1	4.2	1.1

Another observation that can be made is the poor interest of the researchers in the issues relating to tropical diseases which SAARC nations are facing from time to time. Tropical diseases such as Malaria, Filaria, Cholera, TB, etc. has not been wiped out from this part of the continent but continue to ruin the economy of these countries.

Conclusion

The following conclusion can be drawn from this study:

- Health related R&D institutions in SAARC countries, needs to be more focused towards studies related to tropical diseases.
- Closer cooperation needs to be established among the SAARC nations dealing with local issues and tropical medicine.
- An extensive collaboration study of the SAARC countries needs to be carried out of wider scope, maybe for the period of 1995-2005. The international collaboration among the SAARC nations and other countries need to be carried out in detail.
- PubMed subject classification should be followed for subfield studies.

Notes

1. South Asian Association for Regional Cooperation from Wikipedia, the free encyclopedia (Redirected from SAARC).
2. PubMed, available *via* the NCBI Entrez retrieval system, was developed by the National Center for Biotechnology Information (NCBI) at the National Library of Medicine (NLM).
3. World Health Organization Regional Office for the Western Pacific 2005: Country Health Profile.

18

ABIA South and Southeast Asian Art and Archaeology Index Project at IGNCA, New Delhi

RAMESH C. GAUR

IGNCA—An Introduction

The Indira Gandhi National Centre for the Arts (IGNCA)[7], established in the memory of former Prime Minister of India Late Smt. Indira Gandhi, in 1987, is visualised as a centre encompassing the study and experience of all the arts—each form with its own integrity, yet within a dimension of mutual inter-dependence, inter-relatedness with Nature, the social structure and cosmology. The IGNCA's view of the arts encompasses a wide area of studies, such as creative and critical literature, written and oral; the visual arts, ranging from architecture, sculpture, painting and graphics to general material culture; photography and film; the performing arts of music, dance and theatre in their broadest connotation; and all else in festivals, fairs and in lifestyles that has an artistic dimension. It is in the Centre's agenda to explore, study and revive the dialogue between India and her neighbours, especially in the South and South East Asia, in areas pertaining to the arts. The IGNCA manifests its academic, research work in its publications, international and national seminars, conferences, exhibitions and lecture series. The principal aims of the Centre are:

- To serve as a major resource centre for the arts, especially written, oral and visual;

- To undertake research and publication of reference works, glossaries, dictionaries and encyclopaedia concerning the arts, the humanities and cultural heritage;
- To establish a folk arts (including those of tribes) division with a core collection for conducting systematic, scientific studies and for live presentations;
- To provide a forum for creative and critical dialogues between and among the diverse arts—traditional and new, through performances, exhibitions, multi-media projections, conferences, seminars and workshops.
- To foster dialogues between the arts and contemporary ideas in philosophy, science and technology, with a view to bringing the gap that often occurs between the modern sciences on the one hand and the arts and culture, including traditional skills and knowledge, on the other;
- To evolve models of research programmes and arts administration more appropriate to the Indian ethos;
- To elucidate the formative and dynamic factors in the complex web of interactions between and among the diverse social strata, communities and regions;
- To promote awareness of and sensitivity to historical and cultural linkages between India and other parts of the world;
- To develop a network of communication with national and international centres of arts and culture, and to affiliate with universities and other institutions of higher learning within India and abroad, for the purpose of expanding the knowledge base in the arts, the humanities and the cultural heritage.

IGNCA as an Organization

To fulfil the objectives[7] outlined in the Conceptual Plan of the Indira Gandhi National Centre for the Arts and its principal aims, its functions are organized through five divisions that are autonomous in structure but inter-locked in programming.

The *Kalanidhi* Division comprises a Reference Library of multi-media collections, which includes printed books, slides, microfilms, photographs and audio-visual material, a conservation laboratory, a multi-media unit and the Cultural Archives. The *Kalakosa* Division undertakes fundamental research and investigates the intellectual traditions in their dimensions of multi-layers and multi-disciplines. As a research and publication division, it endeavours to place the arts within the integral framework of a cultural system, combining the textual with the oral, the visual with the aural, and theory with practice. The *Janapada Sampada* Division complements the programmes of *Kala Kosa.* Its focus shifts from the text to the context of the rich variegated heritage of the rural and the small scale societies. Its activities focus on the lifestyle study programmes comprising of the *Loka Parampara,* which revolves around a community, and the *Ksetra Sampada,* which revolves round a region. It has developed (a) a core collection of material and documentation of folk arts and crafts including those of tribes; (b) several multi-media presentations; and (c) launched multi-disciplinary lifestyle studies of tribal communities for evolving alternative models for the study of the Indian cultural phenomenon in its totality and the inter-webbing of environmental, ecological, agricultural, socio-economic, cultural and political parameters. The *Kaladarsana* Division provides a forum for inter-disciplinary seminars, exhibitions and performances on unified themes and concepts. The *Sutradhara* Division provides administrative, managerial and organizational support and services to all the other Divisions.

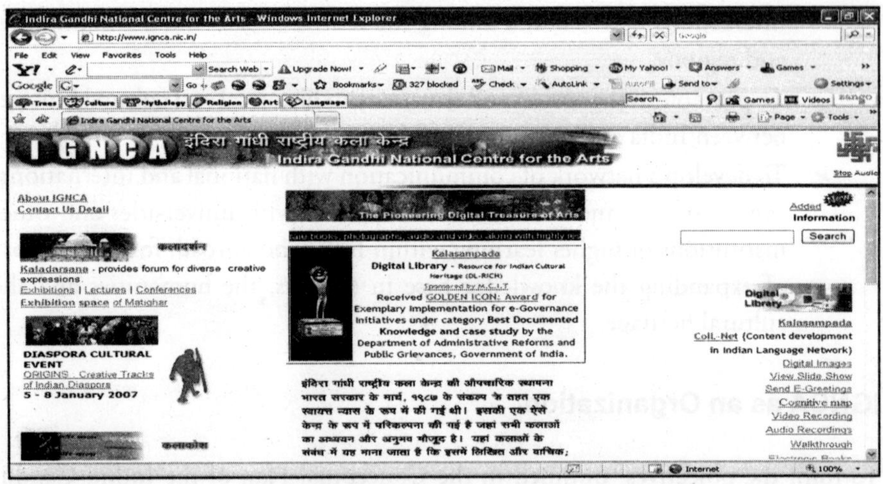

IGNCA-KALANIDHI: A Cultural Knowledge Resource Centre

Kalanidhi[8], a National Information system and Data bank, consists of the Reference Library of print collections, a large library of Microfilms/Microfiches, collection of slides, Cultural Archives and photo documentation in the disciplines of Archaeology, Anthropology, History, Philosophy, Literature, Language, Arts, Crafts, etc. on Greater India, South Asia, Southeast Asia and West Asia. A cultural archives consisting of precious collections, a well-established conservation laboratory and the multi-media unit also form part of the Kalanidhi. The basic objective of Kalanidhi is to support research objectives of different divisions of the centre and to help researchers and scholars from other academic institutions.

Programme A

The Reference Library: It has a large collection of reference material for the users in the forms of printed books, journals, slides, microfilms audio and videotapes and digitized format. There is also a dedicated bibliography section. It has acquired a vast resource of about 1,30,000 of books. The major activities of Reference Library are:

- *Rare Books*: It has acquired books published in 18th and 19th centuries. Most of them have been digitized to minimize the physical handling of the books.
- *Personal Collections*: A unique feature of the IGNCA Library is the personal collection of eminent scholars and artists. Some of them are: Prof. Suniti Kumar Chatterji, Hazari Prasad Dwivedi, Thakur Jaideva Singh, Krishna Kripalani, Maheswar Neog, Narayana Menon, Dev Murarka, Lance Dane, Heeramaneck and Dr. Kapila Vatsyayan. Most of these collections have been received as gift. In some extraordinary cases a few collections are purchased also.
- *Series and Catalogues*: The library is concentrating on building a complete corpus of printed material on the Catalogue of manuscripts of Indic and Asian origin, published in all parts of the world. So far besides the Catalogues Catalogum, it has acquired catalogues of major Sanskrit, Persian, Arab manuscripts from libraries/research institutions of India, UK, USA, Germany, France, Italy and Japan. The series acquisition programme includes the LD series; Ecole de France, Institute of Indian Studies, Pondicherry Series; KP Jayaswal Research Institute, Patna; Satapitaka, series and Bibliothique National series.
- *Journals*: The Reference Library subscribes to 235 journals in various subjects confirming the aims and objectives of the IGNCA. In order to create a strong research collection, the Library is also acquiring back volumes of several journals.
- *Area Collection*: The Library proposes to develop area collections

particularly on South, South East and West Asia. It plans to extend its scope to Latin America and Africa in the next phase of its development.

- *Annotated Bibliography of Arts, Culture and Archaeology*: An outline Database of annotated bibliography covering the subjects—arts, culture and archaeology, performing arts—will be developed. Select portion of the bibliography will also be brought out in print form.
- *Microfilm/Microfiche*: A unique feature of Kalanidhi is the reprographic compilation of unpublished manuscripts in Indian and foreign collections from private and public libraries. A pioneering attempt has been made to bring under one roof primary sources of the Indian tradition lying scattered, fragmented, inaccessible or worse, in danger of extinction. The Microfilming Unit has acquired 20,000 rolls of manuscripts from various libraries covering about 2,50,000 manuscripts. Some of current microfilming projects are (1) Government Oriental Manuscripts Library, Chennai; (2) Rajasthan Oriental Research Institute, Alwar; (3) Dr. U. V. Swaminathan Iyer Library, Chennai; and (4) Oriental Research Institute, Mysore.
- *Photography and Slide Collection*: A concerted effort is being made to establish a large photograph and slide library. Here also the focus is on developing a resource centre where documentation on Indian and Asian art is easily accessible. At present over one lakh visual images are available both in slides and digital form. Photo documentation of six museums in northern India in collaboration with the National Museum Institute is under planning. The slide unit collection has swelled to over 1,25,000.
- *Sound*: A library of sound tapes discs will be established. This will comprise spoken work, Vedic intonation, poetry recitation and music of all genres. Sound Library will concentrate on materials from India, South East Asia, West Asia, Africa and Latin America.

Programme B

Programme B of Kalanidhi has been divided into two sub-programmes (1) *National Information System and Data Bank* in the Humanities and the Arts and the Cultural Heritage of India. The National Data Bank will provide for computerized storage retrieval and dissemination of information on all aspects of arts and cultural heritage through multi-media storage and retrieval systems. (2) *Library Information System*: (WEB OPAC): This includes cataloguing information about all the books and periodicals available in the IGNCA Library.

Programme C

- *Cultural Archives*: Under this programmes the IGNCA collects, preserves, classifies and disseminates the original and reprographic materials. The acquisitions are made under the categories of literature (*sahitya*), architecture (*vastu*), sculpture (*silpa*), painting (*chaya pata*), music (*sangita*), dance (*natya*). The cultural archives of IGNCA also acquired paintings, which are rare and reflect India's culture and aesthetics. Many scholars, artists and art enthusiasts, over the last decades, have carefully and dedicatedly collected materials of their interest ranging from literature and personal histories, recitation, painting, music to folklore and tribal arts. Some of these rare collections of ethnography and audio/visual documentation of old masters and rare art forms have been acquired by the Cultural Archives. Ethnographic films and documentation of communities done under specific research projects are the highlights of the Cultural Archives. An audiovisual library of all the film documentation, made under the series of "Great Masters" and other field and research projects, documentation of legendary artists, films of lifestyles and interviews of eminent personalities done by Dr. Kapila Vatsyayan are some of important collection under audio video library. Two of the IGNCA's film productions *'Yehou Jagoi'* by Dr. Aribam Shyam Sharma and 'Wangla *of the* Garos' by Shri Bappa Ray have won National film awards. The paintings and graphic arts of the late Brunners, the mother and daughter from Hungary who made India their home and painted its people, landscapes and captured the spiritual aspect of the country in their works are the latest addition to Archival holdings. Late Elizabeth Brunner has bequeathed 852 oil and water paintings to the IGNCA.
- *Preservation and Conservation*: The Conservation Lab of Kalanidhi caters to the conservation and preservation needs of works of arts housed in the IGNCA, conducts awareness campaigns and training programmes. It is the designated manuscript conservation centre of the Delhi region under the National Mission for Manuscripts (NMM). The IGNCA proposes to set up a centre for excellence in conservation.
- *Photo Documentation*: Photo Documentation on various in-house and outside activities in the areas of interest of the IGNCA is being carried out on regular basis.

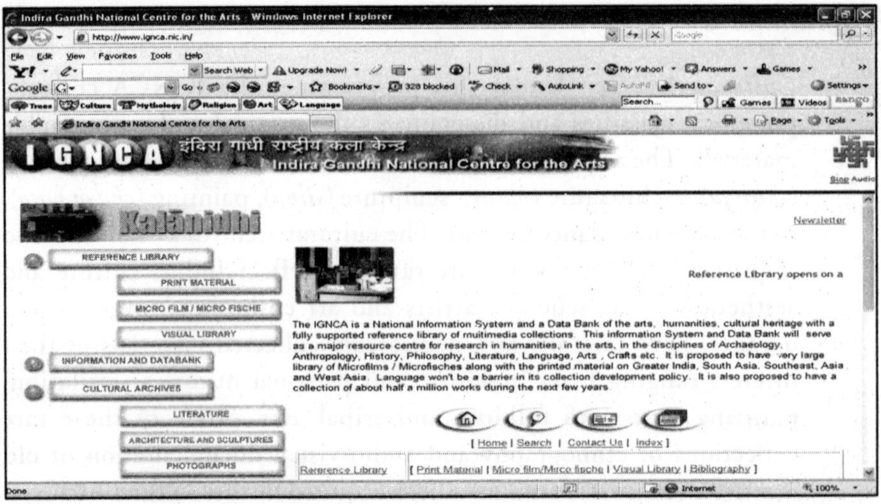

The ABIA Project: Genesis

The ABIA project is a global network of scholars co-operating on an annotated bibliographic database for publications covering South and Southeast Asian Art and Archaeology. The project receives scientific support from UNESCO also.

ABIA stands for Annual Bibliography of Indian Archaeology that was published by the Kern Institute in Leiden during 1926-73. The ABIA is a unique and ambitious scheme of annotated bibliographic compilations on Indian Arts and Archeology, which used to be brought out annually by a group of Dutch Scholars from the early part of the twentieth century. The ABIA was the brain child of Professor J. Ph. Vogel, one of the most notable Indologists of the 20th century. The name ABIA was coined by a group of Dutch Scholars, who started this series in 1926. For about half a century the ABIA publication dominated the world of Bibliography and scholars the world over depended on it to know what has been published and where on India's past? Running for about half a century and publishing several volumes of annual and random numbers, the ABIA rendered unique service to Indian studies between 1926 and 1984 and kept scholars engaged on Indian arts and archaeology under great debt. Perhaps the loss of colonies in South East Asia and such other factors led South Asian Scholars in the Netherlands to face a crisis in the 80s, ultimately resulting in the suspension of ABIA publication in 1984. This loss was immensely felt by everybody as there was nothing of the kind to fill the vacuum caused by its exit.

Though suspended for about a decade in the late eighties and early nineties, this pioneering effort was revived in 1995 mainly through the efforts of scholars from the International Institute for Asian Studies (IIAS), the Netherlands. The Dutch again found willing and enthusiastic partners in Sri Lanka, Thailand and Indonesia in 1995. The Dutch created a special fund for running the ABIA Office in Leiden to publish the annual number to input of information on the net and to run the electronic mail coordinate the work carried out by the participating units in South and South East Asia, and to meet the cost of the annual workshops, advisory broads and the editorial committee meetings, some funds were also provided by them to assist centers in South Asian and majority of South East Asian countries.

In 1996, the International Institute for Asian Studies (IIAS), Leiden put forward a proposal to resume the bibliography. The new bibliography is called ABIA South and Southeast Asian Art and Archaeology Index, briefly ABIA Index. The new ABIA had to keep pace with the time, widen its net to include both South Asia and South-East Asia plan not only the annual numbers in print comprising the most significant researches, but also accommodate every bit of information on line and made the information immediately available to anyone anywhere in the world accord to the independent position and status to the participating partners in the project earn the respect of Orientalists in Europe, America, Australia, Russia and China, and at the same time retain the basic character of the 1926 ABIA, making India the largest publishing nation of Oriental studies in the world.

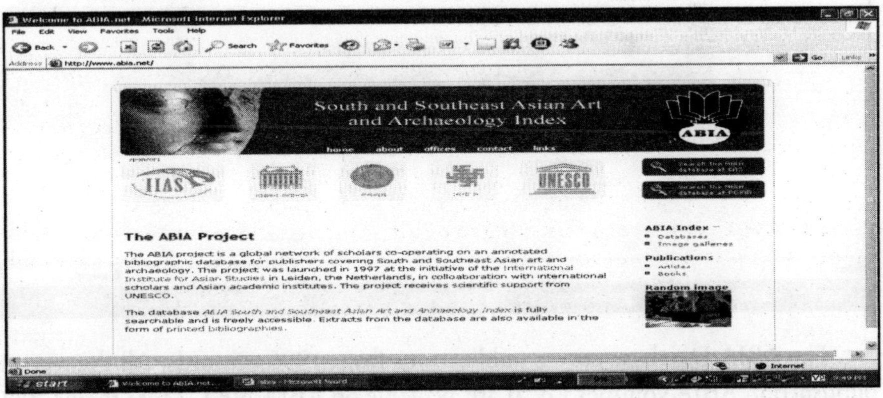

The ABIA Index: Objectives

The basic objective[6] on ABIA project is to compile and maintain a bibliographic electronic online database which supplies annotated records, covering the subject pre- and pro-history, historical archaeology, ancient and modern art history, material culture, epigraphy and paleography, numismatics and sigillography. An Annotated

Bibliography extracted from the database is published annually in a printed version in addition to CD-ROM Version of ABIA Index.

The database ABIA South and Southeast Asian Art and Archaeology Index is fully searchable online and is freely accessible at http://www.abia.net. Extracts from the database are also available in the form of printed bibliographies. Two volumes have been published so far, containing approximately, 3,350 annotated and key word-indexed references to publications between 1996 and 2001. More details are available at http://www.abia.net for upcoming publications.

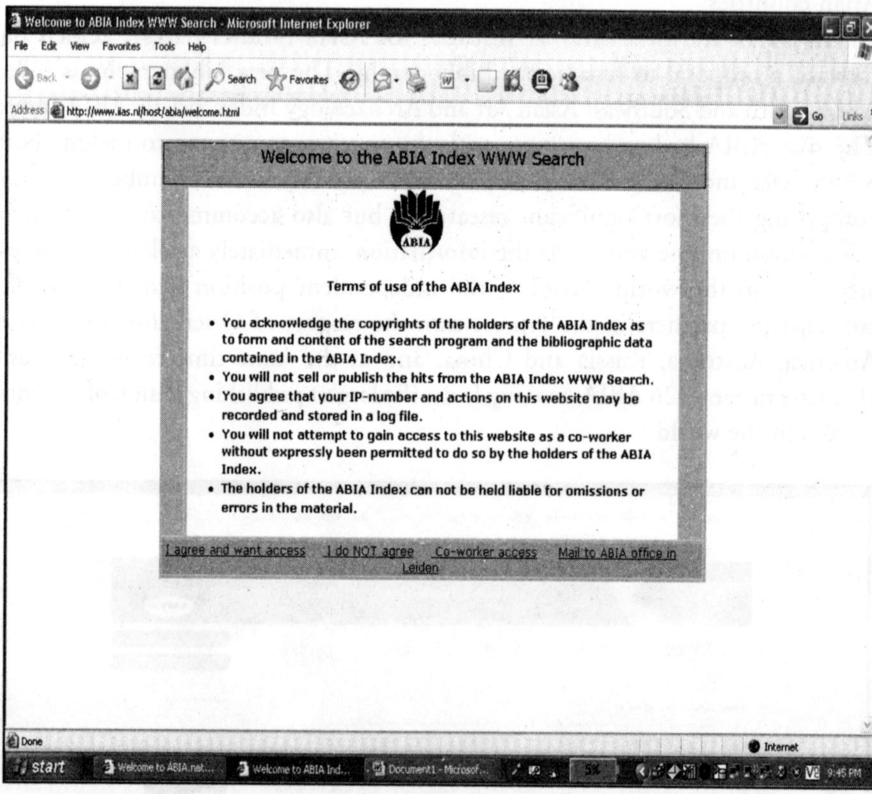

The ABIA Database covers publications from 1996 onwards. All the records published in ABIA volumes I & II are available on ABIA NET. More than 12000 records are available in the online database. One may search with terms, e.g. author's name; words from the title, ISBN number etc.

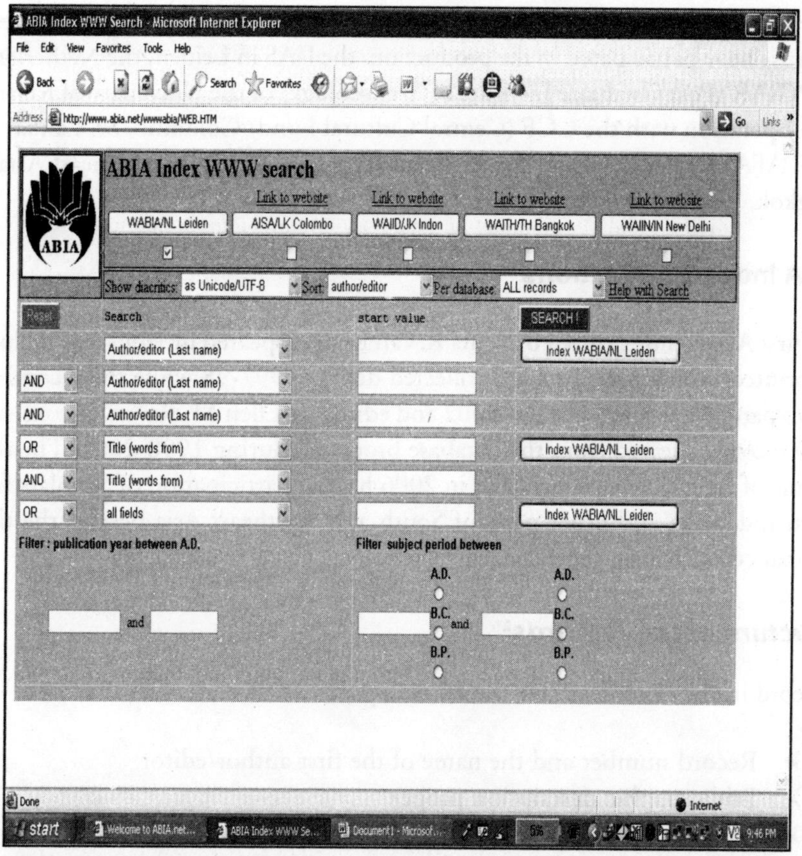
ABIA Index WWW Search - Microsoft Internet Explorer
http://www.abia.net/wwwabia/WEB.HTM
ABIA Index WWW search
Link to website
Link to website
Link to website
Link to website
WABIA/NL Leiden
AISA/LK Colombo
WAIID/JK Indon
WAITH/TH Bangkok
WAIIN/IN New Delhi
Show diacritics: as Unicode/UTF-8
Sort: author/editor
Per database: ALL records
Help with Search
Search
start value
SEARCH !
Author/editor (Last name)
Index WABIA/NL Leiden
AND
Author/editor (Last name)
AND
Author/editor (Last name)
OR
Title (words from)
Index WABIA/NL Leiden
AND
Title (words from)
OR
all fields
Index WABIA/NL Leiden
Filter : publication year between A.D.
and
Filter subject period between
A.D.
B.C.
B.P.
and
A.D.
B.C.
B.P.

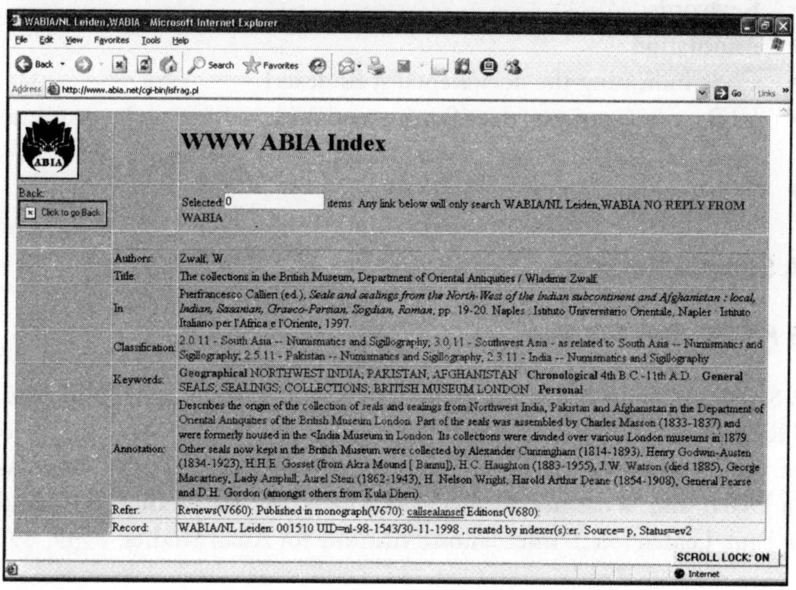
WABIA/NL Leiden,WABIA - Microsoft Internet Explorer
http://www.abia.net/cgi-bin/isfrag.pl
WWW ABIA Index
Back:
Click to go Back
Selected 0 items Any link below will only search WABIA/NL Leiden,WABIA NO REPLY FROM WABIA
Authors: Zwalf, W.
Title: The collections in the British Museum, Department of Oriental Antiquities / Wladimir Zwalf
In: Pierfrancesco Callieri (ed.), Seals and sealings from the North-West of the Indian subcontinent and Afghanistan : local, Indian, Sasanian, Graeco-Persian, Sogdian, Roman, pp. 19-20. Naples : Istituto Universitario Orientale, Naples : Istituto Italiano per l'Africa e l'Oriente, 1997.
Classification: 2.0.11 - South Asia -- Numismatics and Sigillography; 3.0.11 - Southwest Asia - as related to South Asia -- Numismatics and Sigillography; 2.5.11 - Pakistan -- Numismatics and Sigillography; 2.3.11 - India -- Numismatics and Sigillography
Keywords: Geographical NORTHWEST INDIA; PAKISTAN; AFGHANISTAN Chronological 4th B.C.-11th A.D. General SEALS; SEALINGS; COLLECTIONS; BRITISH MUSEUM LONDON Personal
Annotation: Describes the origin of the collection of seals and sealings from Northwest India, Pakistan and Afghanistan in the Department of Oriental Antiquities of the British Museum London. Part of the seals was assembled by Charles Masson (1833-1837) and were formerly housed in the <India Museum in London. Its collections were divided over various London museums in 1879. Other seals now kept in the British Museum were collected by Alexander Cunningham (1814-1893), Henry Godwin-Austen (1834-1923), H.H.E. Gosset (from Akra Mound [Bannu]), H.C. Haughton (1883-1955), J.W. Watson (died 1885), George Macartney, Lady Amphill, Aurel Stein (1862-1943), H. Nelson Wright, Harold Arthur Deane (1854-1908), General Pearse and D.H. Gordon (amongst others from Kula Dheri).
Refer: Reviews(V660): Published in monograph(V670): callsealansef Editions(V680):
Record: WABIA/NL Leiden: 001510 UID=nl-98-1543/30-11-1998 , created by indexer(s):er. Source= p, Status=ev2
SCROLL LOCK: ON

Since the re-start of the Project, in January 1997 three regional Centres of expertise have participated in the production: the IIAS in Leiden, the Netherlands; the PGIAR (Post Graduate Institute of Archaeology) of the University of Kelaniya in co-operation with the CCF (Central Cultural Fund) Colombo, Sri Lanka; and the SPAFA (Regional Centre for Archaeology and Fine Arts in Southeast Asia) in Bangkok, Thailand.

ABIA Index Publications

The first ABIA Index edited by Karel R.Van Kooij appeared in 1999 that included the printed bibliographic record collected during 1997-98 while the second one in two parts was brought out in 2002 and edited by Ellen M. Raven. It consists of 2050 records selected from the database processed during 1998-2001. The third volume of ABIA Index is expected in 2006 having participation of Scholars from India, Indonesia and other parts of South and Southeast Asia besides the three regional coordinating centres.

Structure of the Records[2]

A record in the book contains the following elements:

- Record number and the name of the first author/editor
- Bibliographic description proper
- Language code
- Keywords
- Annotation
- Code indicating the documentalist (indexer)
- UID code (=unique identification code) identifying each record in the database and the book
- References to related publications

ABIA Sample Record[2]

1308 Kooij, Karel R. van

ABIA South and Southeast Asian Art and Archaeology Index, volume one /ed. by Karel R. van Kooij, Ellen M. Raven (coord. ed. for South Asia), Marijke J. Klokke (coord. ed. for Southeast Asia), S. Settar and Doris Yapa (eds. for South Asia), Hasan Djafar and Wilasinee Thabuengkarn (eds. for Southeast Asia). London: Kegan Paul; Leiden (etc.): International Institute for Asian Studies, 1999, 597 p., ill. (Studies from the International Institute for Asian Studies). ISBN 0-7103-0625-3. (eng).

South Asia; Southeast Asia; ABIA: bibliographies; archaeology; arts; modern art; material culture; epigraphy; palaeography; numismatics; sigillorgraphy

Annotated and key-word indexed bibliography covering the prehistory, archaeology, arts, material culture, epigraphy, palaeography, numismatics and sigillography of South Asia, Southeast Asia and regions culturally linked to those areas (Afghanistan, Southern Central Asia, and Chinese Silk Road area. Tibet and South China). Includes over 1300 references to publications from 1996 and 1997 mostly. Also includes an essay by Karel R. van Kooij on 'meaning in early Buddhist art', and by Edi Sedyawati on 'research by Indonesian archaeologists between 1976 and 1977'. Successor to the 23 volumes of the Annual Bibliography of Indian Archaeology (ABIA) that were compiled at the Kern Institute of Indology, Leiden between 1926 and the middle of the 1970s, covering the period 1926-1972.

(IND=er) (UID code+-99-1561/19-01-1999)

Indexes[2]

Author Index

The author index lists the standardized form of the names of authors, editors and others involved in a publication and mentioned as such on the title page or header of an article.

Geographical Index

The Geographical index contains names of mountains, rivers and river basins, plains, lakes etc., and of villages, sub districts, districts, provinces, countries and larger regions.

Subject Index

The subject index contains general descriptive terms or keywords including: fields of study—

- Scholarly approaches,
- Archaeological and art historical terms,
- (Pre-) historic periods,
- Kingdoms,
- Dynastic names,
- Cultures,

- Ancient cities,
- Architectural structures,
- Works of art, etc.,
- Motifs,
- Gods and goddesses,
- Sites,
- Texts,
- Artifacts,
- Forms of material culture, and
- Languages (rendered without diacritics).

Annotation[2]

The annotation attempts to be concise and to elucidate the context, the inherent interest and the potential value of the publication. Its maximum size is circa 1,000 characters (circa 150 works). Although at times the editors borrow from abstracts supplied in the publications themselves, the style of the ABIA abstract conforms to a format optimized for database searches *via* keywords from thesauri.

If the title of the publication is not in English, the first sentence of the annotation provides a translation of the title in Italics. In the annotation, titles of texts and terms in languages other thank English have also been put in Italics.

ABIA Index Coverage[2]

The regions, subjects and materials covered by the ABIA, South and Southeast Asian Art and Archaeology Index are the following:

Regions

- *South Asia*: Bangladesh, Bhutan, India, Nepal, Pakistan, Sri Lanka and the Maldives.
- Southwest Asia.
- Central Asia and East Asia as related to South Asia.
- *Southeast Asia*: Brunei, Darussalam, Cambodia, Indonesia, Laos, Malaysia, Myanmar, the Philippines, Thailand and Vietnam.
- East Asia and the pacific as related to Southeast Asia.

Subjects

- Pre and protohistory.

- Historical archaeology.
- Ancient art history.
- Modern art history.
- Epigraphy and Palaeography.
- Numismatics and sigillography (seals).

The performing arts and ancient history are not included.

Materials

- Monographs,
- Articles in monographs,
- Articles in periodicals,
- Unpublished Ph.D. theses,
- Any 'grey' literature of an academic level.

Revised editions and translated publications are included, but unaltered reprints are not.

Languages[2]

The language of the database is English. However, it is our aim to process information on publications in any language. In practice, the ABIA Index covers publications in those languages with which the ABIA editors and annotators are familiar or for which they receive help from others than English include a translation of the title at the beginning of the annotation.

Software

The bibliographic data are documented with the help of CDS/ISIS, a text retrieval programme designed and distributed by UNESCO.

Classification Code[2]

The ABIA Index Database and books use a broad classification with three digit numbers.

- The first two digits indicate the geographic region.
- The third digit refers to the form of the publication, or its subject matter.

Geographical Classification

1.0	South and Southeast Asia	6.0	Southeast Asia
2.0	South Asia	6.1	Brunei Darussalam
2.1	Bangladesh	6.2	Cambodia
2.2	Bhutan	6.3	Indonesia
2.3	India	6.4	Laos
2.4	Nepal	6.5	Malaysia
2.5	Pakistan	6.6	Myanmar
2.7	Sri Lanka	6.7	Philippines
2.8	Maldives	6.8	Singapore
		6.9	Thailand
		6.10	Vietnam
3.0	Southwest Asia as related to South	7.0	East Asia are related to Southeast Asia (e.g., South China)
4.0	Asia (e.g., Afghanistan, Iran)	8.0	The Pacific as related to Southeast Asia (The region of Austronesian culture).
5.0	Central Asia as related to South Asia (e.g., Uzbekistan and Tajikistan)		
	East Asia as related to South Asia (e.g., the region of Tibetan culture)		

1. ABIA: South and Southeast Asian Art and Archaeology Index—Volume 1 edited by Karel R. van Kooij.

Geographic spread of records printed in ABIA Index 1

On South and Southeast Asia general	39
On South Asia and its periphery	635
On Southeast Asia and its periphery	632
Total number of records	1306

2. ABIA: South and Southeast Asian Art and Archaeology Index: Volume 2

Geographic spread of records printed in ABIA Index 2

On South and Southeast Asia general	64
On South Asia and its periphery	1336
On Southeast Asia and its periphery	650
Total number of records	2050

Source: introduction to *ABIA Index* 2, p. xxvii

ABIA Index 2

Classification + Country		Record no. in Book	Amount
1	S&SE Asia	1307-1370	64
2.0	South Asia	1371-1577	207
2.1	Bangladesh	1578-1620	43
2.2	Bhutan	1621-1626	6
2.3	India	1627-2205	579
2.4	Nepal	2206-2286	81
2.5	Pakistan	2287-2420	134
2.7	Sri Lanka	2421-2523	103
2.8	Maldives	2524-2526	3
3	SW Asia	2527-2587	61
4	Central Asia	2588-2622	35
5	East Asia	2623-2706	84
6.0	SE Asia	2707-2787	81
6.1	Brunei, Darussalam	2788	1
6.2	Cambodia	2789-2859	71
6.3	Indonesia	2860-3065	206
6.4	Laos	3066-3077	12
6.5	Malaysia	3078-3102	25
6.6	Myanmar	3103-3162	60
6.7	Philippines	3163-3189	27
6.8	Singapore	3190-3195	6
6.9	Thailand	3196-3263	68
6.10	Vietnam	3264-3348	85
7	East-Asia	3349	1
8	Pacific	3350-3356	7
Total			2050

ABIA Index Volume 2—Contributing Sources of the Records[2]

(as indicated by library origin)

Library/annotator	Processed at	Amount Contributed to V2	Records on various countries in V2 (joint effort)	
			S&SE Asia	64
			South Asia general	207
Sri Lanka	Sri Lanka	215	Sri Lanka	103
Sri Lanka	Sri Lanka		Maldives	3
India	Sri Lanka	106	India	579
Bangladesh	Sri Lanka	29	Bangladesh	43
Pakistan	Sri Lanka	5	Pakistan	134
Nepal	Sri Lanka	11	Nepal	81
Bhutan	Sri Lanka	1	Bhutan	6
Leiden	Netherlands		SW Asia	61
Russia	Netherlands	37	Central Asia	35
Leiden	Netherlands		East Asia	85
Leiden	Netherlands		Pacific	7

(*Contd.*)

Library/annotator	Processed at	Amount Contributed to V2	Records on various countries in V2 (joint effort)	
Leiden	Netherlands		SE Asia general	81
Leiden	Netherlands		Brunei Darsussalam	1
Leiden	Netherlands		Cambodia	71
Indonesia	Netherlands	70	Indonesia	206
Leiden	Netherlands		Laos	9
Malaysia	Netherlands	23	Malaysia	25
Leiden	Netherlands		Myanmar	60
Leiden	Netherlands		Philippines	27
Leiden	Netherlands		Singapore	6
Thailand	Netherlands	9	Thailand	68
Leiden	Netherlands		Vietnam	85
Netherlands	Netherlands	1441		
NL in France	Netherlands	12		
NL in UK	Netherlands	81		
Total	2050	Total	2050	

ABIA Index: Its Benefits

It is in this way, ABIA Project is a collaborative effort of many countries in South and Southeast Asian regions. To open an international network for this academic field is not a luxury but a necessity to keep our Archaeological and Art historical memory in order to make it accessible to future generation. It is expected that the new ABIA South and Southeast Asian Art and Archaeology Index will fulfil its special assignment and make the scholarly world familiar with the art historical and archaeological work that is being done at academic institutions and by scholars all over the world. The ABIA Index database is useful for art historian, archaeologists, Asia specialists, anthropologists, numismatists, historians and epigraphists. It should also appeal to librarians, curators, educational service staff and collectors of Asian art and coins.

ABIA Project at IGNCA

Publication of Bibliographies and the development of bibliographic databases are some of the basic objectives of IGNCA. Under these programmes a number of bibliographies have been published. The participation of IGNCA to ABIA project is to fulfil the above objectives as well as to strengthen International co-operation amongst Arts and Archeology institutions in South and Southeast Asia.

In ABIA Project, Indian activities started with Prof. Settar, Dharwad, India, probably in 1998. In December 2001, Indira Gandhi National Centre for the Arts is able to associate itself with the ABIA project and assist in getting the required entries on Indian publication. MOU signed between IGNCA & PGIAR in October 2002 to continue the work. From 1st January 2007 IGNCA has become the coordinating office for ABIA Project for next five years. Under this project it is planned to establish a regional network of individual scholars and institutions in India to gather information on various publications in the area of interest of ABIA Project. Apart from the contributions of records to ABIA, this project will also help in strengthening IGNCA's Bibliographic activities. IGNCA will be planning, publication of ABIA volume IV within next two years of this project.

Other Participating Countries[2]

International Institute for Asian Studies

The International Institute for Asian Studies (IIAS) is a postdoctoral research centre based in Leiden and Amsterdam, the Netherlands. Its main objectives to encourage the study of Asia and to promote national and international cooperation in this field. The geographic scope of the institute covers South Asia, Southeast Asia, East Asia and Central Asia. The institute focuses on the humanities and the social sciences and, where relevant, on their interaction with other sciences.
Email: http: www.iias.ni

Postgraduate Institute of Archaeology

The Postgraduate Institute of Archaeology (PGIAR) is a coordinator, national institution engaged in archaeological education, training, research and popularization. It was established by ordinance in 1986 and is one of the two postgraduate institutes of the University of Kelaniya. A Board of Management that has *ex-officio* representation from all institutions in Sri Lanka directly or indirectly engaged in archaeology administers the PGIAR.

The Seameo Regional Centre for Archaeology and Fine Arts—SPAFA

The SEAMEO Regional Centre for Archaeology and Fine Arts is the coordinating unit in a Bangkok of a project, under the aegis of the Southeast Asian Ministers of Education Organization (SEAMEO) that aims to cultivate awareness and appreciation of cultural heritage, to promote and help enrich archaeological and cultural activities in the region, and to further professional competence in the fields of archaeology and fine arts. SEAMEO-SPACA operates as an autonomous, International institution hosted by the Government of Thailand.
Email: http: www.seamco.ora/centre.spafa.htm

ABIA project also represented by some individual scholars and institutions from following countries:

(1) Bangladesh
(2) Bhutan
(3) Cambodia
(4) Indonesia
(5) Malaysia
(6) Nepal
(7) Pakistan

ABIA Workshops

In January 1997 the project officially started with the first ABIA workshop which was hosted by the PGIAR in Colombo (Sri Lanka). A second workshop followed in August 1997 hosted by SPAFA in Bangkok (Thailand). The third one took place in December 1998 at IIAS in Leiden (the Netherlands). The fourth workshop at Dharwad in Karnataka (India) was followed by the 5th Workshop of ABIA at Kediri (Indonesia). The 6th ABIA Workshop was hosted by IGNCA in New Delhi (India) on December 1-2, 2003. 7th Workshop and Seminar of ABIA was arranged at PGIAR, Colombo, Sri Lanka during 30th July to 2nd August, 2004. The 8th ABIA Annual Workshop and Seminar on "Asian Earth Ceramics of South and Southeast Asia" held at International Institute of Asian Studies, Leiden University, Leiden, the Netherlands during 11th January to 13th January, 2006. These international meetings are being held regularly to strengthen the communication lines between editors and offices, henceforth 9th ABIA workshop has been organized at Dhaka, Bangladesh during February 12-13, 2007.

Notes

1. ABIA: South and Southeast Asian Art and Archaeology index, Vol.1/ed. by Karel R. van Kooij.—http://www.iias.nl/host/abia/node/12
2. ABIA: South and Southeast Asian Art and Archaeology Index, Vol.2/ed. by Ellen M. Raven and Helga I. Lasschuijt.—Leiden: E.J. Brill, 2002
3. On the history of the ABIA Index software/Anton van de Repe
4. Jean Philippe Vogel: a Dutchman who went Indian/Gerda Theuns-De Boer in *IIAS Newsletter* 22(2000); http://www.iias.nl/host/abia/node/72
5. A giant's step to Sri Lanka: ABIA's chair transferred/Ellen M. Raven in *IIAS Newsletter*, 27th March(2002); http://www.iias.nl/host/abia/node/10
6. www.abia.net
7. IGNCA Brochure
8. Kalanidhi Brochure

19

Libraries and Information Centers on Women's Studies in India

PARUL ZAVERI

Introduction

Awareness regarding women's issues in India has been created due to the setting up of research centers on women as part of the university system or as independent units, women's programme units within the governmental system and intergovernmental agencies, women's activists groups and forums and grassroots level organizations. The Government of India has made special provision for funding of research on women related issues. Also it provides support for setting up of women's studies departments.

These libraries collect all types of information related to women's issues.

Women's information is interpreted as information about women, for women, and by women. For this paper women's information and women's studies information is used interchangeably. Women's information is interdisciplinary in nature and is required for various purposes by different groups. For example, women's groups may require information for action, advocacy, empowerment and welfare, whereas a researcher in women's studies may want it for research, evaluation and theoretical development. The government may want it for policy formulation, developing programmes for women etc. Women themselves require information so that they will be able to make informed decisions and choices, participate in political processes, and engage with institutions of civil society, and influence governance and development. Poor women, rural women, non-literate women and literate women—all have the right to access information.

This information is available in various physical formats from print to digital. The peculiarity of women's information is that apart from traditional formats like books, journals, audio-visual and digital formats like CD-ROM, it is also available in grey literature formats like pamphlets, diaries etc. There is a vast amount of information which is unpublished and lying in individual collections or with women's groups, as reports. The lack of proper bibliographic control and secondary sources makes it difficult to locate this information.

To make this information available easily, the Indian Association of Women's Studies, in the 1980s, suggested development of a clearing house for women's information, providing bibliographic and documentation services. This has been supported by establishment of research centers on women's studies, specialized women studies libraries, and special collections of women's groups having special collections. Women's universities also have specialized collections on women's studies.

Women's information is being collected and made available in various types of organizations which can be categorized as follows:

- Libraries and Information Centers belonging to Women's Organizations.
- Women's Library Collections within the Academic Systems.
- Women's specific collections within the University Libraries.
- Women's collections of the Women's Studies and Research Centers set up under the universities.
- Collections in the Women's Colleges having Women's Cells or Women's Development Centers.
- Special collections on women with Social Science Research Institutions with an interest and focus on women's studies.
- Collections with various national agencies and documentation centers.

Libraries and Information Centers belonging to Women's Organizations

Different women's groups and organizations exist in India, which focus on diverse activities related to women. These organizations have libraries which have collections of women's studies literature. They try to collect literature in published as well as unpublished forms including books, journals, pamphlets, newspaper clippings, brochures, reports, conference papers as well as audio-visual materials. Libraries also collect digital material.

Many organizations have made efforts to build women's collections in India. Some examples are:

- *Jagori*—Jagori (meaning 'awaken woman') at Delhi is a women's training, documentation, communication and resource centre that was established in 1984 on issues related to women's rights, to meet the information and analysis needs of other women's groups, NGOs, researchers, media, and other regular users.

- *ISST*—ISST (Institute of Social Studies Trust, Delhi) library and documentation centre, was started in 1984 with the aim of providing information and documentation support to the scholars, researchers, planners and development agencies through sharing and exchange of information resources in the field of gender studies. The library has a collection of books, conferences/seminar papers, research reports, journal articles, brochures, annual reports, newsletters and government publications. ISST provides library services like reference and information dissemination, inter-library loan, current awareness service, and newspaper clippings service on gender issues.
- *Nirantar*—Nirantar at Delhi is a resource centre for Gender and Education and has a large collection of books and resource materials on gender, education, violence, health, *panchayati raj* (local government) and other development issues. It also includes reports, NGO publications, policy documents, as well as educational resource material.
- *Akshara*—Akshara at Mumbai has a collection of materials including books, journals, videos, posters etc. with a gender perspective. A unique, customized classification system, The Akshara Classification System is developed for organizing the women's collection. It also conducts trainings on setting up and running a feminist documentation and information centre.
- *Vacha*—Vacha at Mumbai functions as a women's resource center, and has a library and cultural center where researchers as well as non-academic women could also visit to borrow books, to look at magazines and journals, to view videos and to attend talks and lectures and other events. Vacha creates outputs accessible to literacy-deprived women.
- *Streevani*—Streevani at Pune does documentation on women's issues.
- *Olakh*—Olakh at Baroda is a feminist documentation resource and counselling Centre.
- *SPARROW*—SPARROW (Sound and Picture Archives on Women) at Mumbai was set up in 1988 and has a unique collection of archives for women with print, oral history and pictorial material.
- *Swayam*—Swayam at Kolkatta is a women's organization working on violence against women. It has an in-house library and documentation center and produces resource materials like posters, booklets, fact sheets, short documentary films, music cassette, research studies and resource directories.

- *Chetana*—Chetana Information Documentation Centre at Ahmedabad was established in 1984 with a small collection of books. Today, it is a storehouse of worldwide information on health and development of women, adolescents and children. The collection also includes reports, manuals, video films, slides, flip books, posters, information kits, photographs, brochures, CDs, transparency-sets on various subjects and languages.

Similarly other organizations involved in documentation work for women are Kavya for women—Bangalore; Alochana—Pune; WINA Reference Library—Mangalore; Sanhita Gender Resource Centre—Kolkata; Uma: A Resource Centre for Women and Panchayati Raj—Bangalore; and a Resource Centre on Trafficking Against Women by UNIFEM in New Delhi are specialized information resource centers. All these centers are involved in working for creating awareness regarding women's issues in society. Most of these centers have started with an individual's vision and have grown into full-fledged organizations. Normally they are supported by private or government funds and are totally dependent on donor's support. Many of them were established about ten to twenty years back and over the years they have been able to build qualitative collection in women's studies. Main activities of these information centers are collecting, organizing, documenting and disseminating information on women's issues at regional, national and international level. It is interesting to note that many organizations in India working on women's issues have a small in-house libraries and their collection include publications of their own as well as other Indian and International publications in women's studies. One such example is Majlis—a legal and cultural resource centre in Mumbai has a small reference library. All these libraries and information centers are either managed by professional librarians or women activists. Collections in these centers are organized either by standard or in-house developed classification schemes as per their convenience. Their collections mainly focus on issues and activities related to women for which those organizations have been established.

Women's Collections within the Academic System

In the University System in India special women's studies collections exist in—

- Women's Universities,
- Women's Studies Departments in the Universities,
- Women's Studies Research Centers,
- Women's Colleges.

Most of the university libraries have women related material from India as well as from other countries. The collection includes books, journals and digital materials. University Grants Commission, India has provided momentum to this by promoting women's studies within universities in the country. Also the Department of Scientific and Industrial Research and other Government departments have provided special funding for research in women related areas. They provide grants to academic institutions as well as other research organizations for research on women's issues. Women's Universities like SNDT Women's University, Mother Teresa Women's University, Padmavati Mahila Vishwavidyalaya, Avinashlingam Institute for Home Science, Higher Education for Women have substantial collections in Women's Studies. SNDT Women's University which was established in 1916 with five women students has today thousands of students. The Library is committed to play a proactive role in the empowerment of women through dissemination and use of information and knowledge. The University Library has developed a strong collection on women's issues and established a tradition of service. The library's collection of books, journals, theses and dissertations, audio-visual material, newspaper clippings, reprints and electronic materials as well as indigenous databases and other retrieval tools, add value to the collection. The library provides documentation and reference service in women's studies. The National Information Centre established at the University Library during 1986-1997 developed a database 'Suchak' which included bibliographic references on women's studies published in English and other Indian languages—Hindi, Gujarati and Marathi. The Centre is no more functioning.

Mother Teresa Women's University Library was started in 1984 and has a unique and rare collection of books. The Library has a good collection of reports and subscribes to journals on women studies. Documentation work has been carried out on women related issues. Similarly, other women's universities and general universities do have collections on women's studies.

With support of University Grants Commission, India, many universities have set up women's studies centers and women's studies cells, which have small libraries and documentation centers attached to them. They promote women's studies through teaching and research, curriculum development, extension services, documentation and dissemination. Women's studies being interdisciplinary in nature, many of these centers work collaboratively with other departments of the university. These centers collect a variety of materials like conference and workshop papers and publications, projects, research and evaluation reports, pamphlets, posters, brochures and audio-visual materials. Many of these centers provide newspaper clipping services. These centers especially collect information pertaining to women for the regions where they are situated, as well as in regional languages.

Some of the examples are Research Centre for Women's Studies at SNDT Women's University, Mumbai; Sarojini Naidu Centre for Women's Studies at Jamia Millia Islamia University at New Delhi; Women's Studies Unit, Tata Institute of Social Sciences, Mumbai; Anveshi—Research Centre for Women's Studies at Osmania University at Hyderabad; School of Women's Studies, Jadavpur University, Kolkata; Women's Studies and Development Centre, University of Delhi and the Resource Centre or the Study of Women, Households and Development (WHODSIC) at Women's Studies Research Centre, Vadodara.

Fatima College, Madurai; Loyola College, Chennai; Patna Women's College, Patna; and Women's Studies Resource Centre at Janaki Devi Mahila Vishwavidayalaya are examples of institutions which have built up small collections on women's studies. These centers, however, are not supported by University Grants Commission, India.

Social Sciences and Development Research Center's Collections

The Indian Council of Social Science Research (ICSSR) has various general social science and development studies research institutions and centers which also integrate women's issues in their collection. The Centre for Women's Development Studies (CWDS) which was established under ICSSR in 1980 is devoted to building up and expanding the theoretical and empirical base on gender issues, and combines research concerns with action and advocacy. Over the years the centre has developed a very good collection in women's studies and is regularly bringing out current awareness bulletins, thematic reading lists and bibliographies. The Centre in collaboration with other institutions has organized various international and national workshops and conferences. The Centre has started an e-discussion forum 'BOL' to create a common interactive forum on gender issues.

Collections of National Agencies

Some of the national and sectoral centers in India contain collections on women's issues. National Library of India, NASSDOC (National Social Science Documentation Centre), CORD (Centre on Rural Documentation, National Institute of Rural Development), NCERT (National Council of Educational Research and Training), The Indian Council of Agriculture, National Labour Institute, and National Institute of Health and Family Welfare are some of the examples. Women's studies items form a small part of the collections of these centers.

There are various national level agencies, organizations and commissions which are involved in women's welfare activities. Some of them have their own libraries. An example is the National Commission on Women which has its own library with a collection of books, journals and newspapers relating to women's advancement. The National Resource Centre for Women under the Department of Women and Child Development, Government of India, provides access to women related resources.

Others worth mentioning are The Network of Women in Media, India (NWMI), which is an informal, non-hierarchical organization comprising women journalists and others working in or on the media and one of its focuses is to provide access to and information about online, offline and research resources through its website—http://www.nwmindia.org

Common Issues Related to Women's Studies Libraries

Considering that women form half the Indian population, India has a very few libraries and information centers on women's issues. Many of them are facing a financial crunch and surviving mainly on donations from government and other welfare agencies. Though there are various schemes declared by the government for welfare of women, not enough support is provided for growth and development of libraries and information centers on women's issues. Scope of women's information has expanded and has become more interdisciplinary in nature, but these centers are not able to cope with the growing demand for women's information.

Many of the libraries and information centers especially in academic institutions which have very strong collection on women's studies mainly focus on serving scholars and academics in women's studies. There is no proper effort by them to reach women activists working in remote areas, illiterate women and grassroots level activists working for women.

Collections on women's studies in many universities either have a separate section in the main library, or the women's studies collection is merged with the regular collection. The latter makes it difficult to locate resources on women.

Apart from traditional forms of publications like books and journals, a lot of women's information is available as grey literature lying with women's organizations, or with activists in women's studies, and it is difficult to locate this information and make it accessible to a larger audience.

There is no proper effort to organize these collections in libraries. Standard classification schemes are not very useful and many of these libraries have their own system of retrieval of information. Akshara, Mumbai has developed its own classification scheme to organize its material and this has been adopted by some organizations.

As information published on women's studies is scattered, not enough effort has been made to have bibliographic control of these publications. This results in difficulty of acquiring these resources by libraries. There are very few publishers from main stream press specializing in women's studies. Poor networking and cooperation among these libraries and information centers, result in duplication of many activities.

Other problems faced by these libraries are non-availability of proper resources on women, lack of current information, inconsistency of information between different sources, absence of information in Indian context, lack of information in Indian languages and very few reference sources exclusively on women. For example, statistical data on women in India is scattered in different resources and many times it has been observed that there is inconsistency of data in these resources.

Due to lack of a trained professional staff, libraries in the smaller organizations are commonly managed by paraprofessional staff and this does not provide a healthy environment for development of women's studies libraries.

Information technology is not yet used to its full strength for library activities in women's studies centers. E-resources especially in multimedia format need to be brought out more.

In spite of the problems faced by these libraries and information centers, they have continued serving for the growth of women's studies. They can still serve the community better by improving their collections and services.

Making Women's Studies Libraries More Efficient: Some Suggestions

In general and especially among women, information need is an unfelt need, so effort should be made to raise information consciousness among them. Apart from traditional library services, libraries should also look into other methods of information delivery like lively informal, oral and interactive methods. Objective of libraries should be not only to provide access to information but also to encourage women's ability to use it to leverage their positions.

Though these libraries and information centers are focusing on women's issues, the users can be from any gender, who is working in women's studies areas. However, main groups of users are women with different levels of education, from different communities, from different geographical locations and with different language backgrounds. So Libraries and Information Centers must cater to this special group. Libraries should provide special ambience for women so that they feel comfortable to visit and pursue their knowledge and information. Libraries should provide outreach services to reach women who may not have time to visit the libraries. Libraries should plan out collaboratively with women's organizations to satisfy the information needs of these women.

Many women's organizations bring out their publications which may not be available through regular channels. Also many of these grassroots level women are creators of information which may not be published in a book form. Apart from collecting books and journals, libraries should make a special effort to collect publications which may have not been found important and neglected by the mainstream press. Libraries should also collect regional language material and material in various physical forms which can be accessed by women with literacy or without literacy.

India should develop an active public library system located at every village, which would be accessible by women in their free time. Women's studies libraries and information centers should work collaboratively with public libraries in local areas and reach out to all women.

Gender information networking is necessary and can be achieved in following ways:

- A collaborative bibliographic control of published and unpublished material in English and Indian languages would be an extremely useful service to women's studies.
- A union catalogue of periodicals, audio-visual materials and grey literature like annual reports, project reports, brochures etc. will help in locating actual documents.
- Resource sharing and cooperation among libraries will be useful in sharing of resources among the libraries.
- A consortium of libraries on women's issues needs to be explored as this will help in overcoming the financial crunch faced by many of these libraries for subscription of journals.
- There is a need to create indigenous databases and digital libraries on women's issues, which can be accessed, by libraries and information centers through networking. Gendwaar was one such attempt by SNDT Women's University and Centre for Women's Development Studies. Gendwaar is a gateway to enhance access to gender studies information in South Asian Region. However, the project could not continue due to financial problems.
- Women's movement around 1970s, International Women's Year and International Women's Decade celebrated in 1980s by United Nations

created awareness and support for women's rights. This resulted in formation of various women's organizations, publications on women's issues and setting up of women's resource centers globally. As described above India also has seen setting up of women's studies departments, libraries and information centers. These centers are actively supporting and contributing to the improvement in quality of women's life. Women's studies libraries and information centre are playing a major role in this.

References

Akshara—A Women's Organization. Retrieved on November 20, 2006 from http://www.aksharacentre.org

Centre for Women's Development Studies. Retrieved on November 15, 2006 from http://www.cwds.org

Chetana—Centre for Health Education, Training and Nutrition Awareness. Retrieved November 5, 2006 from http://www.chetnaindia.org

Gandhi, Nandita (n.d.). Let a Thousand Flowers Bloom: Creating Alternative Classification Systems. Retrieved on November 5, 2006 from http://www.aksharacentre.org

ISST—Institute of Social Studies Trust—A Documentation Centre. Retrieved on November 10, 2006 from http://www.isst-india.org

Jagori—A Women's Training and Documentation Centre. Retrieved November 15, 2006 from http://www.jagori.org

Kalkoti, G.K. (2003) Disseminating women's information and knowledge. In: *Empowering Women Through Information and Knowledge: From Oral Traditions to ICT*. v.1 (pp. 187-196). Mumbai: SNDT Women's University.

Mother Teresa Women's University. Retrieved on November 5, 2006 from http://www.motherteresauniv.org

National Commission on Women. Retrieved on November 15, 2006 from http://ncw.nic.in

National Resource Centre for Women. Retrieved on November 15, 2006 from http://nrcw.nic.in

The Network of Women in Media, India—an Organization of Women Journalists. Retrieved on November 20, 2006 from http://www.nwmindia.org

Nirantar—A Centre for Women and Education. Retrieved on November 15, 2006 from http://www.nirantar.net

Outline of the Akshara Classification System (n.d.). Retrieved on November 5, 2006 from http://www.aksharacentre.org

Parekh, Harsha (2003) "Dissemination of Women's Information in India" A Conceptual and Historical Framework. In: *Empowering Women Through Information and Knowledge: From Oral Traditions to ICT*. v.1 (pp. 144-150. Mumbai: SNDT Women's University.

SNDT Women's University. Retrieved on November 5, 2006 from http://sndt.ac.in/

Shah, Parul and Ranganathan, Hema (2003) Reference Queries at SNDT Women's University Library: An Analysis 207-215. In: *Empowering Women Through Information and Knowledge: From Oral Traditions to ICT*. v.1 (pp. 207-215). Mumbai: SNDT Women's University.

Shukla, Sonal and Manorama, Swatija (2003) Documentation and Dissemination for the literacy deprived. In: *Empowering Women Through Information and Knowledge: From Oral Traditions to ICT*. v.1 (pp. 125-131). Mumbai: SNDT Women's University.

SPARROW—Sound and Picture Archives for Research on Women. Retrieved on November 5, 2006 from http://www.sparrowonline.org

Swayam—Ending Violence Against Women. Retrieved on November 5, 2006 from http://www.swayam.info

Vacha—Voice of Women—A Women's Organization. Retrieved on November 20, 2006 from http://www.vachaforwomen.org

Vyas, Anju (2003) Making women's information visible: Women's knowledge and Information Repositories in South Asia. In: *Empowering Women Through Information and Knowledge: From Oral Traditions to ICT*. v.1 (pp. 109-115). Mumbai: SNDT Women's Universty.

20

Organization and Dissemination of Social Science Research Information: Indian Scenario

P.R. GOSWAMI

Introduction

Research methods and information seeking behaviour or scholarly communication in social sciences is a complex subject. In natural sciences, research is described as a brick laying process, each new development is built upon earlier accepted findings; where as in social sciences scholars tend to examine, evaluate, accept or reject ideas, beliefs and findings of the peers. Published scientific literature in the form of learned periodicals, patents, conference proceedings, reports, etc. are major sources of learning and dissemination of new findings; they play a cementing role in the development of science. Similarly, in social sciences too, published material plays an important role for the advancement of research in the field. Social scientists communicate with each other with the help of different types of printed and other sources of information transcending the boundaries of space and time.

Before discussing the content and structure of different genres of social science research information, one needs to define this complex and wide subject. Social scientists generally examine issues which generate public and social discussion. And this factor expands the scope of their literature or source material for research. Many general books and periodicals written either for laymen or for polemic purposes come under the purview of social scientists. In their analysis and commentary on social life, the scholars in the field use as data a large variety of written records such as newspapers, annual reports, memoirs, governmental records, oral histories, statistical compilations, etc.

Even election manifestoes released by different political parties in their constituencies form a part of social science research literature. In fact, information about state policy and its consequences is costly and confusing. By providing members with relevant information about state activities and by acting as an organized conduit to governmental decision making, political parties have traditionally performed this task of multiplier or agency. It has been rightly said that the literature on social sciences is much wider in scope than literature written by social scientists.

The proliferation of research in social science disciplines particularly in development economics had an impact on the growth of social science literature and establishment of special libraries and documentation centers. In order to make informed decisions, the government conducted several surveys and censuses through specialized agencies. A number of scholarly periodicals such as *Economic and Political Weekly, Contribution to Indian Sociology,* and *The Indian Economic and Social History Review* later came into existence. Learned societies and autonomous institutions produced a large body of literature as research results that could be used by the scholars. Similarly, statistical system of the government started collecting data on a large number of socio-economic variables.

The purpose of this paper is to provide a backgrounder on promotion of social science research in India highlighting the progress made in organization and dissemination of different categories of print and non-print sources of data and information which include:

(a) Grey literature
(b) Government reports
(c) Statistical publications

In addition, the efforts made so far to achieve bibliographic control over the vast myriad of social science publications; and a recent initiative by the National Social Science Documentation Centre (NASSDOC) to start a resource sharing activity among major social science libraries have also been discussed.

Social Science Research in India: A Background

After independence, India recognized social science research as a necessary constituent of its socio-economic development plan. The Planning Commission of India which was set up by the government to act as a "think tank" for the entire plan process that included the five year plans, had a research cell. The idea for the formation of Indian Council of Social Science Research (ICSSR) germinated in this cell. The stalwarts in the field such as Dr. V.K.R.V. Rao, D.R. Gadgil,

M.S. Gore, Ramkrishna Mukherjee were primarily responsible for starting this autonomous body (i.e. ICSSR) in 1969. The decision to establish the ICSSR was taken on the basis of recommendations of a committee which said that there was a need for "coordinated and balanced distribution of research over different disciplines, different regions and different categories of research"; and also observed that the unsatisfied stage of social science research (in India) is due to absence of any central or national organization which could not only bring the social scientists together and provide a forum for exchange of views between them; but also as a spokesman for social science research and elicit support and recognition by government.

The governing board of the ICSSR, known as the Council prepared a policy document, i.e. Statement of Policy on the *Role, Responsibility, Functions, Programmes and Organization of the ICSSR.*

The following were enumerated as the major programmes of the ICSSR (Ghosh 2006):

(1) Research Surveys,
(2) Identification and Development of Talent: Study Grants, Doctoral Fellowship, Post-Doctoral Fellowships, ICSSR Research Fellowships, National Fellowships,
(3) Research Grants: Teachers' Awards, Research Projects, Research Programmes, Secondary Analysis,
(4) Assistance to Indian Social Scientists for Research Abroad,
(5) Contacts with Overseas Social Scientists,
(6) Asian Research,
(7) Professional Contacts Between Indian and Overseas Social Scientists,
(8) Publication Grants,
(9) Training in Research Methodology,
(10) National Social Science Documentation Centre, New Delhi,
(11) Regional Social Science Documentation Centres,
(12) Union Catalogue of Social Science Serials,
(13) Source Material for Social Science Research,
(14) Bibliographical and Documentation Services: Data Libraries,
(15) Clearing House Services (including Publications),
(16) Contacts with Overseas Organizations,
(17) Publication Services (Newsletters, Information Brochures, etc.),
(18) Professional Organizations of Social Scientists,
(19) Dissemination and Utilization of Social Science Research,
(20) Social Statistics, Social Indicators and Social Report.

The programmes enumerated at serial numbers 1, 10, 11, 12, 13 and 14 were primarily aimed to consolidate library and documentation related works and to achieve bibliographic control over social science literature published in India. The policy document also recommended creation of a Social Science Documentation Centre (SSDC) as a unit of the ICSSR. Later, SSDC became NASSDOC or National Social Science Documentation Centre whose primary objective was to provide information support service to social science researchers and to take care of certain programmes of the ICSSR. However, the regular activities of NASSDOC have been revised from time to time. Apart from creating a number of retrospective bibliographical tools, indexing and abstracting services, and union catalogues in social sciences, NASSDOC is presently running several other programmes. They include

I. Library and Reference Services,
II. Literature Search and Bibliography on Demand Service,
III. Preparation of abstracts and indexes of major social science periodicals,
IV. Compilation of an Events Calendar Incorporating Details of Forthcoming Conferences, and
V. Document Delivery Service.

In addition to these, NASSDOC sponsors bibliographical and documentation projects and provides financial assistance to scholars for collection of research material from libraries and archives located in different metropolitan cities/towns of India (Goswami, 2003).

Union Catalogue and Bibliographical Projects: NASSDOC's Experiment

As a national body, NASSDOC is expected to provide access to social science periodicals holdings of Indian libraries. A major project was started by NASSDOC in 1970 to compile a *Union Catalogue of Social Science Periodicals*. The work was completed in 1973. The holdings data were published in several volumes. Each volume containing data pertaining to a state/or a group of states and Union territories.

NASSDOC is also expected to achieve bibliographic control over Indian Social literature that is published all over the country in a dispersed manner. A project was undertaken by NASSDOC in 1970 to compile retrospective indexes of Indian social science periodicals. Prior to this, two publications *Guide to Indian Periodical Literature* and *Index India* (Rajasthan University, Jaipur, India) were catering to the needs of social scientists. Another publication *Index to Indian Economic History*, jointly compiled by the ICSSR and the Gokhale Institute, Pune, India, released in 1965 is considered to be a reliable source on the subject. Two volumes containing articles appearing in Indian Periodicals in Education, Psychology and Sociology have been included in these compilations. Another similar compilation, i.e. *Indian Social Science Periodicals Literature (INSPEL)* has been recently released in the electronic form (CD-ROM) containing bibliographic data from Indian periodicals in economic and political science. The coverage is similar to two earlier print publications, i.e. since the inception of the journals to 1970.

Recent Initiatives: ISID Database

As regards the bibliographical control of Indian Social Science Literature, the Institute for Studies in Industrial Development (ISID), New Delhi, a ICSSR supported institution, has done pioneering work in the field of indexing and abstracting of social science journals and newspapers. Initially, the ISID developed a user friendly literature search facility for the journal *Economic and Political Weekly (EPW)* during the 1980s. This index has been updated from time to time and it has been gradually expanded by including references from journals relevant for various social science disciplines like economics, finance, management, demography, health, education, political science, sociology, history, gender studies, etc. The number of social science journals covered in this database is 105. This database has been named as Online Index (OLI). Apart from this, the institute has indexed newspapers, which contains articles on public sector, management, economics and other subjects. At present, 14 English languages newspapers, mostly published from the national capital are scanned and classified under 60 heads to facilitate easy search and retrieval. The press clippings are now stored as images in computer and they are linked to the search software. The number of entries in the Online Index is approximately 1,40,000 and the records in the press clipping index has reached 8,40,000. Recently published *ISID Online Database Users Network* (1999-2006) says that this database has 4000 registered users from India and other countries of the world.

In addition to these retrospective indexes, NASSDOC has compiled quite a few other bibliographical tools/research aids in the form of abstracting journals, surveys of literature, etc. Even today, no proper feedback on their use and value is available. After examining their structure, content, and timeliness, one can say that their limited scope, time-lag, frequent change in choice of subject headings, lack of publicity and the quality of information included have reduced their utility as tools of research.

Grey Literature: Government Reports and Institutional Publications

As a matter of fact, various categories of published and unpublished reports compiled and under the aegis of certain government departments such as the Planning Commission, Ministry of Commerce, Ministry of Industry or regulatory bodies like Department of Economic Affairs and Reserve Bank of India are considered primary sources of information by social scientists. Many of these reports are neither made available through book trade channel, nor are they acquired regularly by prominent social science libraries. There are uncoordinated fragmentary collections of government reports in most of the libraries. As a result, the collection remains underutilized and their reference value remains low. A close look at the present state of government reports publication and distribution mechanism would reveal the following:

(1) Most of the committees/commission reports, working group/task force/ expert group recommendations and administration reports (i.e. annual reports on the working of different government bodies) are official documents and they are not made available to the research institutions and their libraries through book trade channel.
(2) Priced reports are supplied to the "libraries as and when published" basis by the agents. In the absence of a reliable publisher's catalogue, it becomes difficult for a library to identify the gap in its report collection. Moreover, inexplicable format of government reports add to the woes of libraries.
(3) Utility of a report is closely intertwined with the timeliness of its release. Timeliness means both speed and punctuality. The meaning of speed is that the government reports are made available to the users soon after the period of time to which they refer where as punctuality means that the reports are made available near to the dates of their release which have been decided and made public in advance.
(4) There is wastefulness in government reports publishing. Free mailing lists are maintained on the basis of requests received, and priority users are identified on the basis of seniority of a person or an organization. As a result, many priority users turn out to be non-users. At the time of their 'transfer' or retirement, many government reports which have 'reference value' for social science researchers are thrown out of their rooms and sold as waste papers (Goswami, 2002).

However, the utility of government reports can be enhanced with the help of IT based dissemination programmes. National Informatics Centre (NIC) has developed websites of government agencies and some of the government agencies like the Planning Commission and Reserve Bank of India (RBI) have put their flagship publication (including annual reports on the working of the organization) on their websites. A Mumbai (India) based NGO, i.e. Society for Service to Voluntary Agencies (SOSVA) has planned a web based library housing all economic, social and political studies reports prepared with government, bilateral or multilateral aid. One can have access to previous research work with the help of this web based library. In fact, recent advances in IT and declining cost of data storage and communication has led to an explosion in the volume of available electronic information. Many other government agencies are now willing to provide electronic versions of their publications at a nominal cost. However, the research institutions are required to have a close liaison with publication units of prominent planning and policy making units of the government. And they can collectively launch a project to compile a comprehensive annual catalogue of official reports which can take the form of users' guide for researchers in social sciences.

Statistical Data and Social Science Research

In recent years, there is an emphasis on empirical research in social sciences. It has been said that in older days, people derived their understanding of society mostly from history, literature and personal experience. Now they want to base their conclusions on numerical evidence. As a result, economists have become more econometric, political scientists more numerate and sociologists more systematic (Forman, 1987).

A cursory search of the *Econlit* database turns up hundreds of empirical studies published in referred journals. Needless to say, statistical system of a country provides knowledge base to such empirical studies. In India, there is a well organized statistical system that generates data on a large number of socio-economic variables. Major statistical agencies are:

(i) Central Statistical Organization (CSO),
(ii) National Sample Survey Organization (NSSO),
(iii) Office of the Registrar General of India (RGI),
(iv) Directorate of Economics and Statistics, Ministry of Agriculture (DES), and
(v) Directorate General of Commercial Intelligence and Statistics (DGCIS).

Following are the major statistical operations in India which produce national and state level data on a number of variables:

- Census of India,
- National Sample Survey,
- Agricultural Census,
- Annual Survey of Industries,
- National Accounts Statistics.

Apart from these, regulatory agencies such as DGCIS, Reserve Bank of India, Ministry of Industry, Department of Economic Affairs, Ministry of Finance publish a number of important data series which are basically aggregation of administrative records.

It is often said that the government spends a large amount of money for collection of statistical data but this is generally not effectively used by researchers partly due to the fact that tabulation, analysis and dissemination of this data in a convenient user-friendly made is not considered important by the government. Also the collection, processing and dissemination of micro-level data by state statistical agencies are downward unsatisfactory. Only a few out of 27 states and 7 Union territories are able to publish their data series on a regular basis.

Recently there has been a change in government's policy regarding dissemination of data. According to the new National Policy on Dissemination of Statistical Data, researchers can access unpublished data in electronic form available with the official agencies. In order to maintain privacy or confidentiality provision, unit level data is made available after deleting the identification mark. NSSO, one of the major statistical agencies in India, has decided to make available primary data on CD-ROM on variables like education, literacy, employment/ unemployment, landholdings, consumer expenditure, etc. This change in government policy has necessitated many other agencies like CSO, RGI, DGCIS, Labour Bureau, etc. to develop computerized databases for speedy and timely dissemination (Goswami, 2001). As a result, social science research libraries are now required to collectively negotiate with statistical agencies for a user-friendly mode of dissemination.

Social science researchers also use data provided by the statistical offices of other countries and also by international organizations. Macro economic data are contained in the *World Development Indicators* from the World Bank. However, the problem with the data provided by international organizations is that they are often reconstituted rather than directly observed. The reconstruction is often cruder with more guesswork than analysis. These derived data are contained in publications like *World Development Report (World Bank), The State of World's Children (UNICEF)* and *Human Development Report (UNDP).*

There are enough arbitrariness in these figures to make the purists shrink at thought of touching such data. In fact, given the scarcity of reliable primary information, the purist position can almost lead to abstinence from empirical work altogether. Similarly, economic data contained in the quarterly, or monthly publications of statistical offices of transition economies are often misleading. Thought these data are readily available from the statistical offices and Central Bank websites, they are to be used intelligently. The sources, coverage and quality of macro-economic data in transition economies have varied dramatically over the past decade.

Access to Social Science Information: Network for Resource Sharing

Social science literature produced in India is vast and it also includes research material produced in regional languages. Similarly, scholarly periodicals published in the West that are used by the Indian researchers are quite large in number; and it may not be possible for a single library or institution to acquire all periodicals. A recently published report *Social Science Research Capacity in South Asia* (a study sponsored by the Social Science Research Council, New York) has said that access to an unbroken series of periodicals is one of the most pressing needs of social scientists in all of South Asia and mounting costs have forced most libraries to terminate their subscription to most international journals. As a remedial measure, clusters of libraries belonging to a particular discipline, have now joined hands and started library networks. One of the major programmes envisaged under a 'network' is to start consortium based subscription to electronic journals. One of the most prominent example is INFONET programme under the INFLIBNET (i.e. Information and Library Network), an initiative by the University Grants Commission of India. Another notable example is INDEST consortium, under the aegis of Ministry of Human Resource Development, Government of India.The primary objective of this initiative is to provide access to electronic journals in the areas of science and technology which include management and allied subjects. The beneficiaries are Indian Institutes of Technology (IIT's), Indian Institute of Science (IISc), Indian Institutes on Management (IIM's), National Institutes of Technology (NIT) and several other engineering colleges.

As a concept, a network is deemed as an inter-institutional arrangement intended to break information isolation. It is also a form of social capital which facilitates coordination and cooperation. One of the recent initiatives by the ICSSR is to launch a Social Science Libraries Network (SSLN). It is basically a capacity building initiative directed to enhance LIS infrastructure in the ICSSR supported research institutions and regional centres. Some of the prominent social science libraries are expected to join this cooperative venture.

The term 'network' has become important in recent years due to advances in IT. Earlier the prevalent term was 'resource sharing', now libraries and resource centres mostly rely on information services and programmes that are made available in a networked environment. The organization having good IT infrastructure now expect seamless, prompt and effective access to a range of networked information services and products (Jain, 2003). In a broad sense, the proposed SSLN can do the following to achieve their organizational objectives:

- Share staff expertise.
- Share library resources in print and digital form that may include books, periodicals, statistical publications, government reports, institutional publications like monographs, occasional papers, working papers.
- Pursue joint purchasing agreements for web-based services like full text e-journals and other databases (e.g. bibliographical and indexing/abstracting services).
- Encourage cooperative development and deployment of information resources and technologies (e.g. use of open source software).

The purpose of this network would be to provide access to information rather than single ownership of documents. However, copyright and intellectual property right (IPR) issues are to be taken care of while planning the activities of a network. An important factor for this network would be adherence to a 'standard' by all members of a network; as without a standard, a technology or a process cannot become ubiquitous, particularly when the technology is part of a larger network. At present, there is a willingness on the part of IT professionals to go for open standards that allow inter-operability. These open standards are not controlled by vendors and they are usually developed by virtual communities of volunteer programmers.

Since SSLN would be a large network encompassing more than 30 libraries, it would be worthwhile to follow open standards that are widely used and understood. The value of a technology does not just depend on its quality but also on the number of users. And positive feedback from the users can help a software firm to dominate the market. Apart from IT related standards, members of the SSLN are required to follow certain other uniform rules and procedures in their day to day work. All members are expected to follow a particular cataloguing code or scheme of classification/list of subject headings.

Under the SSLN, the following activities and services have been envisaged:

- Cooperative cataloguing,
- On-line catalogue of holdings of periodicals (i.e. union catalogue),

- Social science LIS forum,
- Staff exchange programme,
- Training programmes and workshops,
- Open archives and grey literature,
- Consortium subscription to e-journals,
- Union catalogue of books and government publication/reports, and
- On-line directory of library professionals and social scientists.

The overall coordination of network activities is to be the responsibility of NASSDOC. Perhaps two most important programmes under the aegis of SSLN would be creation of a database of Indian social science periodicals' literature and an exhaustive record of government published reports and other forms of grey literature. Some of the Indian social science journals are irregular and it is difficult to keep a track of their publication date. Moreover, the quality of papers published in some of the journals from the university departments is below average. In a recently published paper on social science research in *Economic and Political Weekly* it has been said that some academies have successfully persuaded university authorities to launch department journals to inflate their own publications. This has been done under the cover of promoting research talent. Instead of promoting the journals' reputation as a credible and peer reviewed scholarly publication, these academics publish their own articles showcasing their own stock of publications. As a matter of fact, it becomes difficult to select 'most reputed' research journals published in India on social sciences. It would be better if the task achieving bibliographic control over Indian social science periodical literature is confined to indexing of articles that have research value. And for selection of articles, voluntary academic intervention of social scientists would be necessary.

In other words, one of the objectives of the SSLN would be management of knowledgeable people and to study building and use of knowledge networks. Needless to say, a network of free thinking learned persons would create more knowledge than these same learned persons would do without a network.

Concluding Remarks

The diversity of the Indian social literature is a challenge for the LIS sector; and proper organization, and dissemination of this vast myriad of print, non-print, digital information would largely depend on the concept of resource sharing; and cooperation among major institutions and their libraries.

Social science research libraries in India must change from collection oriented institutions to service oriented organizations and LIS professionals have to change from custodian of books and documents to information managers and disseminators. In this changing scenario, IT will play an important role. However, while taking advantage of the different components of IT, the libraries and information centres will have to ensure the following:

(i) Take stock of the actual need of the library and its users.
(ii) Consider both preservation and access as vital components of library service.
(iii) Development of library professionals to cope with the new environment.
(iv) Marketing of library and information services.
(v) Utilization of knowledge management (KM) principles for organization and dissemination of research information.

The SSLN planned under the aegis of ICSSR-NASSDOC primarily for the purpose of resource sharing among major social science institutions' libraries in the country, is basically an effort towards better organization and utilization of research material by the social scientists. It is a capacity building endeavour in the area of LIS using state of the art IT infrastructure. The success of this project would largely depend on those at the helm of affairs at the ICSSR and member institutions. Since public fund available for social science research in India is limited, use of a part of this limited budgetary allocation for enhanced access to knowledge may not get adequate support from the decision makers.

The proposed SSLN would be largely a virtual network in which the coordinating body, member institutions and recipients of various services need not be present in the same place at the same time. But a shared commitment to the cause (i.e. high quality service) still requires personal contacts and sharing of experiences to make it real. A mission-oriented objective of the SSLN should be to bring people closer so that they can form a 'human network' to develop mutual trust and belongingness.

References

Forman, Nigel (1987). What role for the social sciences? *Policy Studies* 8(1), 44.

Ghosh, Partha S. (2006). Social science research in India: an institutional analysis of the ICSSR experiment [unpublished]. School of International Studies, Jawaharlal Nehru University.

Goswami, P.R. (2003). NASSDOC's new initiatives. *ICSSR Newsletter*. 34(2), 17-18.

Goswami, P.R. (2001). Statistical databases in India: Towards a better dissemination. *Internatinal Information and Library Review*. 33, 181-196.

Goswami, P.R. (2002). The application of leadership and management principles and strategies to a library and information service. In Wei Wei etc. Ed. *Leadership and Management Principles in Libraries in Developing Countries*. New York, Haworth Information Press.

Institute for Studies in Industrial Development, New Delhi (2006). ISID Online Databases Users' Network, May 1999—August 2006. New Delhi, Institute for Studies in Industrial Development.

Jain, P.K. (2003). Indian Council of Social Science Research (ICSSR) maintained research institutes' libraries in India: Towards digitalization and networking. *International Information and Library Review*. 35, 217-232.

Parekh, Harsha (1977). Social science literature: size, use pattern and bibliographical services. *Economic and Political Weekly*. 12, 1423.

Part V
Information Systems and Networks

21

Information Technology Enlivens: Chaos and Creation of Life Needs

M.A. GOPINATH

Informatively: Chaos

— Information Needs Logic Regimentation is a False confusion; It needs Maps for chaos, Eros, and Galore.

— Smallest of the small sustains largest of the large maintains equal of the equals lives crisis of crisis calls for New Information Consists Interfaces.

— When choas sits on Fire Creation Captures Cognition Eros maps domain Speciality Galois Kinmites them to use.

— Such is the lead for life organization; Information Lemmas chaos to Eros; Galors pulls chaos and Eros to creative use.

— Then the world goes through a revolution for Newness.

— Maps of domain speciality always kinetic; It can revolute the map to newness, for change is order and order is change.

— Map guidelines has to be flexible to the matchings of user needs and thus create a transient frame of mind to flexes.

— Recall what a computer virus can do. The ones that are most familiar to people are those that on some appointed day may destroy all records on any computer that has been affected by virus. Chaos Information.

CREATION FOR KNOWLEDGE EXPERIENCES FOR USES: CHAOS AND CREATION

The Jungle of Life

There happens life in sudden corridor of homes and hospitals. While everyone may be happy that a life newly arrived to add to complexity, there can be a solution in chaos and creation. Panini, said a life born is a boon given by god. But when the boon reaches, 3, 5, 15, 20 years we may have to slowly forget about life. This the principle of chaos and creation over time. Life keeps coming, world keeps growing because we measure time. Majority of people don't measure time.

Here is an episode: I had finished three cups of water and my captors were getting impatient. Then for the first time, the officer seemed to realize. I was a soldier and examined my "Uniform". I was wearing an old pair of Kampong-made sheet rubber shoes and *khaki* trousers and shirt. On the shoulder-flaps of the latter were leather crowns and as soon as he read that I was major, he jumped to his feet and saluted—surely the height of Japanese politeness. (F. Spencer Chapman, *The Jungle is Neutral*, p. 144)

There goes a mannerism that was in chaos but an army culture jumped a Japanese to be polite. That is, is a military custom. Chaos sometimes generates false systems and its politeness. Thus can be computerized and picturised. A drama of life of false politeness. Other things automatically follow to a fountain. It is a system articulation in diplomacy of public relations. There are many false factors in civilized living. Otherwise, one tries .... the other for no course. In a hidden treasures humans are worse than animals. Beastie boys and Gorilla-Dirty Hurty.

Regimentation of Chaos Creation

Mind articulates many thoughts to train studios. They walk through a social .... and cohesion. There are multiple .... Leading sets of chaos in clash of creativity. Every brainstorming has an unalloyed flows of thoughts as daft punks. One time more is what chastens brain storming. A backyard of chaos us on information system. That begins to regulate a pattern in a language. The parsimony is a knowledge .... through communications and its involutes.

That leads ....: An all round knowledge settings go differentially into an integral cocoons of epigrams. They then settle to point of need requirements. That becomes a mind-modeller. It then begins to help that which is mind-entertainer or catch word thoughts. They emerge in smalls, like children and gain growth potential like .... Tree. Then it growth to a youthful of knowledge potencies. They grow then into an experienced wisdom. But it not be helpful to currents as situation changes context. It runs like sun-dial. Then sunlights begun to thoughts to ...... for suave communication metaphased like swans.

Guidelines and pathfinders:

(1) All kinds of troubles are removed and sanguined for sourcings.
(2) Niche times new by Arietels of annarphoras.
(3) Life of great feels and ...... Generate chaos for new creations.
(4) A source of creators, prevaricators, and destructors all combined for action and activation spreadation for world economic, social and political needs.
(5) A three times of day that preyrates a ...... tonasim services. That means innovations. That leads to invention.
(6) That lives of an earth get their solutions by mind earth through a goddess mission for chaos and creations.
(7) Resources after are sampuned for collection, distribution, resourcing and consummation as an ordrain of Goddess providers.
(8) Never be sorrowful or resentful of what you get and what you gone they are all two sides of the same coin.
(9) A flower mixes flights of human mind just like bee builds a beehive.
(10) Reproductive values of human for chaos and creation.
(11) The fishes resources themselves in spite of fisher nets and other baits.
(12) This is natural symphony and sympathy of chaos and creation. The fish nets loose their values after same; and reversal always happens to fish resourcing; chaos engines creation.
(13) There are many hurdles control systems for chaos engine systems to loose their own control for new creations and further chaos.
(14) Every creature in nature resource, reproduces, relives, re-engines, recreates an ... of power sectors of chaos to creation. $f(\text{chaos})^2 = (\text{organization})^2 + (\text{operation})^2 + (\text{arguments})^2$.
(15) There can be bad dreams that will be vanished by presence chaos devices and their creations.
(16) Thus, emerges a ...... which is more powerful than system and thus leads to a power chaos.
(17) The health of all natural objects including human beings services in chaos and creation. For every ......these is chaos in cure and creation.
(18) Even .... Objects such as stars help chaos creation and its impacts on world and its living and non-living objects.

Creation as Resources of Digestive Modes

Knowledge grows in entitlement. It gets need-consumed for some purposes. Otherwise it stagnates to starvation every piece of knowledge gets valued to a destination is to consume and digest every bit of it for utility creativity get boosts of congenital .... support. Therefore, life is full of creations that are digestable. It resources, produces, distributing, consummates customized knowledge: *Karma Yoga.*

The playmate is yourself and your other self of contentment's. "In Japanese organizations, the *Sempai-Kohai* relationship helps achieve this kind of learning. ·The Japanese focus on the relationship, whereas the West's boss-subordinate terminology tends to focus on each individual in his role. The Japanese unabashedly acknowledge that the *Sempai-Kohai* relationship is made up of emotional as well as functional ties and they harness both senior and junior are seen as inescapably linked; ones failure or success necessarily affects the other. The *Sempai-Kohai* relationship is not a hierarebical imperative to be endured, but something of mutual benefit—a force that binds. One's *Sempai* in Japan is usually outside of one's direct reporting relationships. In this respect, one's member-mentor's is like an organizational "God father". However, the pattern behaviour is so deeply embedded that it influences the manner in which direct reporting boss-subordinate relationships are conducted. They are generally closer and more supportive than in the west". (Richard Tanner Pascale and Anthony G. Athos, *The art of Japanese Management,* p. 136)

Thus, is an extra-official, extra-curricular relationship. They produce different kinds of team relationship. Thus, plays an organization and unusual happenings for runs, contingencies for ...... operands of work-doing-temperaments. It is difficult to step back from such a remarkable man and his management implications that can be drawn from his specific case. Whether you judge his genius as malign or benign, whether you would have liked to work for him or not, the "unshakeable fact" remains that Geneen—and at times extreme contrasts between Information Technology Transfer (ITT) and *Matsushita*—can teach us something important. Thus, a recupe for management is *Sempai-Kohai* and its relational four....

$$S_K^F = (\text{NH})^2 + (\text{ITT})^2 + (\text{Matsushita})^2$$

Assuming that there is a production control manager, he will receive in his office the instructions to put an order in hand. Before these instructions reach him, they will have been considered by the production manager who will have satisfied himself that the work can be done, how it can best be done, what alterations will be necessary to factory layout and in fact, will have given his attention to all the technical considerations surrounding the production of the job. Where appropriate, his notes on the job will be attached to the instructions when they reach the production control manager. This latter individual, therefore, has before him all he needs to know in order to get the wheels turning, plan the work and progress it through the factory, however many processes may be involved. (M. Gilbert Frost, *Teach yourself management*. Ed. 3, 1968, p. 112). Thus, a chaos has to be managed humanly. Creations come from humans all defecations that happens around it comes from a strange circumstances which is the home chaos. It plays-recognition of trivial that makes anew and ever anew.

Radicals of Chaos for Creations

Run a missile, it targets a point and dwells a chaos called terrorism you have to control chaos. You call men and women to support and overcome chaos by some means. People produce organized chaos. More firemen die a martyr death. This has addition to chaos want only organized. Thus has been happening in the world. For the sake one person war has been promoted all in this world. According Greeks even Gods fight for simple person. And never trace that person anywhere. But it leads to anonymity everywhere. Now radicalism lies in chemistry. Like aromatic radicals and benzene rings. Anyone of the sly position is occupied by a carbon atom of the Hexaging indicate destabilization. The radical is in potentially kinetic state. Say, the single radical is phosphorus (Pw) or Mercury (Hg) or Chlorine (Cl) or Hydrogen (H). The destabilization takes faster and the ring dissolves itself into several compounds. Thus radicalism beginning with strangeness and ...., home, village, township, city, mega city and world as a whole. An earth quake is inner radicalism of Benzene Rings for outlets and new inlets. A natural phenomena chaos, creation, Eros.

There Appears P-anova Leading Smokes and Later to Openness

A chaos beginning for goodness: due to freedom. But it grows out of proportion to a largesse that may lead to further distriction. At that time the ocean tantalizes the entropy into intropy. Then the chaos has made inroad of victory to sustainment ocean, sky and earth. There happens to be social elevation of thoughts to tides. It always settles in middle of rushes in a homeostatic of minds, ... Going radicals to a quiet places .... We have to self.... around resourcefulness of self to others and others. Thus, otherness is fingers points. Thus, it moves in multitasking and multiple ....management. All these radicalism are to have pleasant .... to settlements. The world's humanities surges on socialising and associating sagas of livelihoods. Then leads to power sectors of knowledge spreads to utility and *vice versa*. It all ends in social goodness. It is a person—sharehood principle to live with surroundings. When change occurs, fear of unsettlement always dashes tomonosphere of mind creates a radicals' disturbance. That destroys the surroundings always. A computer interfacial them leads to ca…, cinema and to life. Thus, chaos created disturbance and its distribution.

Seciets of Chaos and Creation

When you are in openness, burn the bottom, churn the tops; set a challenge to the middle. You see lotus. Here is an episode: "Two of the boys were glasses, curiously enough the same kind tiny, old-fashioned, with round steel rions. The larger of the two-end he was quite large-well over six feet—was dark-haired, with a squase jaw and coarse, pale skin. He might have been handsome had his features been less set, or his eyes, blind the glasses, less expressionless and blank. He wore dark English suits and corned umbrella (a bizarre sight in Hampden) and he walked stiffly through the thrŏngs of hippies and beatniks and preppies and punks with self-conscious formality of an old ballerina, surprising in one so large as he. "Henry Winter" said my friends when I pointed him out, at a distance, making a wide circle to avoid a group of bongo players on the Lawn (Donna Tar, *The Secret History*, p. 17). Thus, dress, manners magnitude, managers are secret ployts of presale to the future through a past. Thus chaos of creation is secret agent of time to tide. Resourcings strangeness to familiars. When we floats openness, ones ….is others creation; taken together they recreate procreation. Thus, nature ….many to many and two to one. A theorem of Alohraham and Eve. An unseen….nature is its wholeness which changes periodically to ….and … in imagination—BASE. It is finally something must said of the need for periodical self-examination by the office manager. It is his job constantly to have in mind the aims of simplifying office procedure, developing usefulness of work, economizing efficiency, and increasing sufficiency. He can best satisfy this requirement by taking opportunity every six months to weigh up what has he achieved, what he is achieving, and to compare this with what he wants to achieve. Try rations: 12/6 $(\theta+\theta 1>\theta 11)(x.y.z)\Sigma$. Someone will tell him sooner or later if he is not den…. … office and it is far better that he should one to tell him self and to do something about it (M. Gilbert Frost, *Teach Yourself Management*, p. 03). Self-management is self-evaluation chaos to creators.

Vectors of Chaos Creation

Fourier of results prevailed for self-attainment: Chaucer's. There is always a swan court to settle simple punishments. We can bring chaos of creation to principle of protection as well as ultimately of destruction. All happens in cyber palaces; Then we get a learnability packages for life long learning; Then you will getting whitened in pose of legging seat arrangements of stomach fills. That will bring a message of goodness to sto....needs and self needs; Then you will have benefits of audio in sound sangunated instrumental sofistication of music mantalizations. Then we get to learn more from matured learning modems to you and to computers a model of HCI and then you can become ambitions to yourself irrespective of others. That will help scriptology in all languages in all climes, in all times, in all ways, and always. Then you keep singing yourself until this starvation. For even Unresolves Food Sanchain to people which is in addition to what religion does. However, these natural disaster spread a permanent starvation by no money texts and food poisoning contexts.

Holism of Chaos to Creation

All chaos stood for creation, if then prondes data of .... A holism leads it to Recreation: "I remember" the inspector pulled open the drawer, handed the all of string to his superior, and, more circumspectly, using his handkerchief, tricked up the scissors, in their case, and stood waiting for sargent .... Take it from him. Chaos of creation is an assistant problem. Like a ... to skey an assistant tries to snowball chaos and spread message of creation. The Boss sets creation to procreation and then to recreation chaos to creation is recreation. Chaos might create mazes. Here is another episode of thoughts "The inspector looked down the nose." That is how he seems to me and its what I have been given to understand. But the butler and Mrs. Haddington's personal maid, both state that seat on—carew was after miss Cynthia Haddington which was not at all what Mrs. Haddington Wished, for he was old as she was, and, what's more, he was very intimate with her. But that added him to austerely is uncorroborated gossip". (Gorgette Beyer, *Duplicate Death*, p. 58). The presence of a concept of detection is putting up curtains on a focused thought which is only probable in least confidence intervals; but it might happen.

The Development Pull an Organic Chaos to Systems

"The application of indiffinition in its varicus forms requires skill. Our discussion identifies some of the vagueness in organizational life and suggests that more skill is needed. Our perspective is that organizations are organic, not mechanical or even hydraulic. We try our best to work with them effectively, to make decisions and implement change effectively. But there is often unpredictability in the system.

One solution is Geneem's. He sought to reduce uncertainty, ambiguity and imperfection, enormously though double cheeks, obsessive controls, quantification, and ...concentration. Another approach is to recognize that only certain amount of what an organization can accomplish is attainable directly, and the rest is obtainable with a flute in hand". (Richard Tanner Pascale and Anthony G .... *The Art of Japanese Management.* pp. 144-45).

Thus a world of chaos has an organic strength to create new approaches to sustain chaos out of system. But chaos build predictability with time series—

$$f(\text{chaos})^{2t} = (\text{systems}^1, \text{systems}^2, \text{systems}^3)\ (xt_1 + xt_2 + xt_3) = z^2 + u^2 + \mu^x$$

where z is genius control, u^2 is geographics, μ^x = ... of all.

We build chaos in minds by story telling. If brain storms every mind to a creation of newness. It is like horse riding and holding the reigns for direction. We also put blinkers to horses eyes. Then we have problems devilishness ....the mind for target operandis. Then we pass a Bayesian Algorithm for protection, production, destruction and marketing consignments. In such situations hardware provide hands on facility for helpful operations. That kind of platforms would help fight chaos for creation through alround adapting expertise and development. This will provide a knowledge corridor for learning and understanding. These operation have to be energized as well as synergies for chaos production, creative resurgence and ....of world image processing. Thus, we have to develop routes and roots for chaos ....and its play as impact of growth it is just like using ...the atmosphere for rains, rainbows, mirrorages of astrals in the media of wind/water to the earth. But all the time aerodynamics and fluidics remain in dynamic state of presentation and preservation. Chaos is a necessity for human health care and also veterinary health care. They depend on trees, forestry and jungles.

A build of metaphors focus a chaos to an analogue. It can digital set to operate. For example, python can model chaos in several different ways. It can all be attributes of its different qualities. It can be like a Japanese giant in trouble. It produces ill effects and well effects simultaneously and ... It provides blurred images of pearl's shines. It can provide a box-fox arrangement of model control of chaos and its reversal. It can produce a sovereign site of Information Technology Transfer. They produce Genen's US which will continuously produce a probabilistic wellness of pythons. The eschew knowledge flow in the air of contentment's. Chaos have several chaotic systems; they survive as computational systems without any specified limits. It has an edge base of systems. Chaos have relevance to Brain functions; Analogue computations are designed for chaos; Several computational procedures such bottom up and top-downwards system are chaotic. The digital computations control a family of computations, discrete non-stopping computations also create new knowledge and new interface. The action of brain, classical modelling of brain, computational modelling of brain, connectionist models of brain, dualistic view points of brain natural selection in brain, involved consciousness and its organization are sets development of chaos and creation. The chaos is contigent ....with three different worlds. One is self, the other not of other self, the third against world of sativa, non-sativas. Then the destruction of administration for just a gala same of selfish cowardice. There happens solution of learnedness and its balance to surge. But depressions discretes life of good and theft, murder, cowardice goes in mesh, an alter ego chaos. Then only a God who can handle terrorism by terrorism that pervades world to save from disaster. Even great spiritual souls cannot survive. Evil designs, ghost constellations for any purpose. Tolerance, totalitarianism, tempetulations are of psyche portent and are meaningless to them. Even Sovereign Gold is surrendered by evils to do ... others. There is wholesome awareness of bad and evil struggling to survive with bad resources which runs a plenty. If evil provides funds and so evil can survive but none is happy or safe. Evil doess are cowards who never face reality. Hide behind arcades and facades. Destruction is the only way to meet distraction and demolish evil to another evil. The power of energy from Goddess should blind evil doess, to their self-negation bun in cowardice forever. The energy burns evils to their own Detroit of life. It is chaos and creation compute.

Example from Education

Mapping Domain Specialities Retrieval Systems try to play tandem to Human computer Interactions: Interfacial. The main purpose of such education is to build interlinking, adoption, and adaptation of the existing general map of domain specialties of knowledge. In every chaos development a renewed effort is called for developmental research in mapping knowledge structures. If modification is needed then it has to be based on the guidelines for mappings. Such guidelines are computicated by an events constellation and constitution leading to knowledge base. Equation which is stated thus:

$$f(k): f(\text{chaos}) \rightarrow f(M) + f(G) + U^x$$

where K is knowledge, M is Mapping, G = Guidelines for Mappings, U^x is power to understanding for transactions. The development of a mission (Information Access) information system calls for the examination of capability of mapping language. There happens to be decision in chaos of mapped links. The decision is to be made on the variety of users' background. It has to be .... By depth, variety, volume and structure of subjects as represented by the information systems. Galois builds Eros through chaos. This calls for need. The need for understanding the nuances in human interface and concentrating on developing such interface dances leads to product development with user-friendly features. In this context, an Information Professional learns the process of structures of expressions of subjects from chosen mapping delineations of domain specialities. This provides scope for learning the flexibility of mapped representations at end use. The computers have progressively reduced map represents to a meaningful metaphors at the end use interfacial. Thus choas and Eros run in Galois. These, we are always in dynamic change in nature. The world's interest always keep changing and it is that which changes representation of ideas in terms and notations. This is a chase of charms for each one them have to produce informatively in single shows or in collective protections. The flex of chaos always settles in ideas. Many times, it does not go any farther. But the chances of spill overs projects into terms in natural languages. They then selves charm into a multiple shades of meanings. It varies in synonyms, homonyms. This process is called polysems. They intertwine into contexts of broader terms and harmers. Besides these there can tacit antonyms and its variants. We phonetic variants, morphovariants and megaphoneal variants. We can have .... in common gossip language sementies, ..., denotations, representations and revelations. Thus, what is a chaos is a forum of Eros which are nearer to human understandings. There are many songs where transmit Eros as primordial of language presentations. To put this in consistency and contexmality of multiple meaning and uniform control notations generated by even domain speciality is symphonated by computer interfaces leading to patterns of knowledge and semaphores.

THESES GAIN METAPHORS. THUS, PATTERNS OF KNOWLEDGE, LOGIC AND LUMPS TO GEOCOONS OF DEVELOPMENTS

Introductions

First order logic is summative and their consequent events. Logic is predictive as well as indicative. Humans are different because of logic. It is done thing subject (noun>abject) and verb and adverb as predicates. It is also made of computational loops, and breaking of loops to reduction calculus. A logic base is differential calculus and its summation is integrative calculus. It is built on Modulus of 'Meta M-thesaus and hypothesis. It is all stage dynamics of static's. It has Mach-Zehender inferences meter and interferences meter. It is built of light comes Las the basis of interference and inference and thereby interpretations. It has tilting of cones, degree of tilts, non-compatibility and observational e....... for light cents. There are stages of interpretations composition of light is a base for logic.

$$\$(\text{Logic}) = \frac{dx}{dy}\,(\text{ideas } 1) + (\text{ideas } 2) + (\text{ideas } 3)$$

Many worlds of true polity is ever its interpretations. That is a grammar of language

$$s(\text{Language}) = \frac{dx}{dy}\,(\text{grammar}) + (\text{brains})$$

Thus, a knowledge emerges out grammar metaphors to knowledge. These arguments of language has two brains: computers: Humans. Events casually influenced and space-like separated produces patterns of logic. ......evolution are then lead to universe of knowledge. Domain speciality of knowledge provides halting problems. They produce lumps; crystalline lump forms a domain speciality. A decay of lumps provide many short-term speciality such as missions of voyages lumps of fluids is a generator of fluidics and its calibration spherical lumps are areal of domain knowledge. Microtubules act as cellular ......of knowledge which is semantics of logic and language.

A set of circumstances build in a consciousness as a ....Microtubules trigger consciousness, computing, organizing center, quantum coherence in microtubules spreads nino-speciality domain constructions. Quantum oscillations in microtubules dynamics the movement of cogon in logic domain formations. Foundations of these issues provide mathematics; Fruitfulness of math's meanings of concepts, perception of truths, philosophy mathematics and role of success produces patterns of knowledge, simple, cumulative and complex grammars of meanings to end use. The appearances are sowed deeply in mind to neuron segments.

Neurons as Patterns of Knowledge

Computers have a neuron architecture of systems. Creative neurons produce a life newness of logical thoughts. They absorb.... and set patterns of knowledge for consummation. Dangers in technology of computers is in logical boundary. It goes as data field theorems game playing computers by logical deviation produce puzzles of knowledge. It has a parallel serial strengths and weakness of computers. Viruses and neurons deflate entire computer records for nothing: conformations, confrontations, conflicts, conjurors, criteria, communications etc.

These are all Neural Necessities

Neurons are for understanding. Lack of understanding is settled by computer interfacial. Mathematical algorithm possibilities increase understanding in multi-fold and multi-tasking. Artificial intelligence procedures delineate relevance of understanding. Simulation of knowledge algorithm is understanding procedures simulation of "by-unsound algorithm" may give aroseul to barriersis understanding. But mental quality of understanding is an adaptive developments. Simulations of values of understanding is tacit to many and one to others. Unitary evolutions (U) is linearity of learning, understanding and assimilating Notion of probability is a universe of long bang-and its origins. Universe of compositions is non-computation model but metaphor models Decadence meaning is 10/1:1/10 = 1 only one. The universe states and neuronal pattern of knowledge. Thus is basis vector space algebra guiding external experiences. Complex vectors have dimensionality. It is nature of water to become multi-mediaions wane functions and its collapse unitizes ....meaning different confidence intervals understanding.

Knowledge is in several substrates. Each of them cue others to cognition. ....of active knowledge degrees of consciousness. A neuron is an emergence phenomenon of patterns of knowledge. The external manifestations of global nature of knowledge. The mathematical meaning of knowledge is set pattern of logics. Passive sensory phenomenon of physical descriptions and quantum measurements. The quantum .... Needs understanding patterns and time sensations. Conservation laws, consistency under systems and formal nature, constructive view points, continuous parameters and continuous hypothesis, conjectures, comm.... quietness, conservation and conversation are ...... by neuronal patterns of knowledge. Correct quantum gravity and correspondence gravity and correspondence principle counterfactuals and cryptography and cubes are pattern numbers. Cubic cytoskeletons and anaesthetics were control centers of organizations. Neurons as magnifying device and significance of microtubules for neuro transmitters, quantum interferences in neutrons and neuron transmitters it is all knowledge of nucleus formations and its turbulences in external mediation. Numbers complex, complex conjugates, geometrical representation of ratio pairs of pattern of knowledge quantums. Concepts of influence on physical brain. Mind models for physical basis of Minkosuskils space pattern. Momentums of angular, displacement, of a particle. Morality of Mozart's of musical dice let μ operation leading absorption of knowledge and its patterns. Half silvered mirrors protective of negatives and positive simultaneously leading logical mysterism. Measurement commute patterns, enteraction free measurement problems, as central X-mystery of quantum theory's non-commuting null partial premieres of Bayesian yes/no models of measurements.

Management of Patterns of Knowledge

Mind plays openness. But of management has a pattern. The most usual group bonus scheme, applied to the whole factory, takes a starting point of standard level of production. This may be the average for a certain number of preceding years or may be calculated in relation to a standard preceding years or may be target of production. Then comes transfers to market to sales. A further difficulty arising out with group schemes of this kind is that of dealing with persons who join or leave the company during the year. This, like others is pattern of knowledge management.

A factory a model set for management of production. Since factory proper is a part of the production function, it will come under the control of the specialist executive responsible for that function. He will probably be known as the works manager, factory manger, general works manager, or production manager. His titles matter little.

What does it matter is that he shall be possessed of technical skill in the processes employed in the factory and additionally, that he shall be adept at management. His job, as we have seen, will be to set of model patterns to receive broad instructions as to what policy from the managing director and instruction as to what is required from either the Board or the sales office. These instructions he will convert into finished goods at a cost such that the sales policy can be achieved. In addition, a specialists in production, he will advise his colleagues and the Board, through the manager director, on all technical matters relevant to his function and in the case of batch production, will initiate this himself. Thus management modulates pattern of knowledge by supervision as well as documentation of metaphors.

Natural Language and Robots

Natural language processing techniques can be used in identifying key words (noun phrases) from document titles which are expressed in a Natural Language. That sets pattern of knowledge not for the books but also readers. Formalison can then be developed on the basis of a pattern of knowledge that readers and teaching the information. Thus document space in digital system becomes digital diaphora. This can be iconed as the user want in multr-fasting modulated environment for neuronal understanding of knowledge patrons etc.

There can be spurts of .... In organization of knowledge. Quantum states of Natural Language set entangled knowledge pattern. It has measurement quantum of knowledge. A normalized quantum state brings in its orthogonal complement. It then gets superposed measurements of state vectors of knowledge dimensions.

Quantum theory is exposed by basic rules f (quantum) = $A^2+B^2+\mu^x$. These are the fundamental ingredients of a natural language. It has always incompleteness as growth factors. It has needs for changes to state vector diagrams of $A^2+B^2+C^2+D^2+E^2+\mu^x$ = f (quantum states)^2. It has....patterns of knowledge.

They are Computable to Meaningful.

Robots of natural language has ascertains and ascertainalities for prepotence. It has an attainment of mathematical belief structures. Governments of robots have an ....of pattern of knowledge. There are also chances of factors affecting evolution of robots of natural languages. Evolution of Robots have behaviour mechanisms of patterns of knowledge. Contributions concerning possible circumventions of Robots of Automata. It leads to cellular automata of Language patterns of knowledge systems. They are metaphored for fast perceptions of attributes.

Space-Time and Spin State of Knowledge Patterns

Spin of classical objects entertains a game of physics to mind. It is the turn of events that provides a description to mental orientation of synapheclefts. The quantum theory provides a quantum theory of spin down and spin ups and intermediate oscillation with a halving centers. They can be modulated to space spin of ±7. It is states of orthogonality between states of mind. It can have states squared modulus rule and a squirrel metaphor for gathering knowledge and its extension in time of use. Space-time curvature of diagrams of spin states leads to superimpositions of geometrics say x = y cos. It can go on to several states of θ revolutions. It is built $f(\theta)2 = f\{\theta_1 + \theta_2 + \theta_3 + \theta_4 + \theta_5\}^2$. Thus an elasticity of rubber sheet is what is the ductility of the pattern knowledge that visualizes in a dynamic state as well as potential states. Singularities merge with two-dimensional space time management f(s, +) = $f(I_n^2)$. Where n is an positive integer reaching ±7 or less. Thus we get finite sets of patterns of knowledge with infinite ranges appearing as factors 1/12 where 1 tends to do.

Thus, if you go out of 1/12 (Family) you have to live with 1 tends to ∞. Patterns of knowledge then set themselves to schrodingers picture leading to unitary evolution and lineants of paged patterns of knowledge. The statements are reduced to continuous, gravitations of Hilbert space representation of rate of real physical phenomena of digital spheres of patterns of knowledge representations. That is sealer representations begin nigh ends of Helbert's space $(1 \rightarrow 7) + (7 \rightarrow 1) = 1$. States of vectors thus generate by texts of reversibility in a knowledge patterns appreciations. Backward-evolved and forward evolved reduced to bracketed vectors of two states of patterns of knowledge. It can ket Vectors. Such as μx where x is left to right.

Pre states of knowledge gets into an anomalous state. The anomaly is a recognition of the need for externals of stimulation. It may lead to contemplations. It is a search state for mind stimulations using sources of information and its relevancies. The mind filters the resources available outside. Just a nature, as Newton' explains fall of apple as a gravitational physics. It is biophysics because a tree releases as matured atoms of its complete states to externals. The human mind has thus two states: Release and absorption of knowledge states.

This is simulated in computer by expert system metaphors.

When main states of stories of knowledge gets to prismatic state of presentation and power pointedness of patterns of knowledge presentation. The general user and applications of hyper texts in a patterns of evolution of knowledge packages arrive with:

(a) Library browsing presentations,
(b) Information Retrieval Systems,
(c) Electronic Documents Publishing,
(d) Expert Systems Variables,
(e) Knowledge Patterns Professionally,
(f) User-absorptions of Stimulate,
(g) Neuronal Processing in Brains,
(h) Two-value Memory States of Cognitions: Learn to ....

Jumping of mind is controlled (Ket Vectors) for finite proportion of patterns of knowledge propagations probability mix fire get to orthogonal states $f(R)=f\{\theta_1+\theta_2+\theta_3+\theta_4+\theta_5+\theta_6\}(t)$. Reality of object transfer information is two state patterns of knowledge based such beginning "1" to "7" unstable quantum states of knowledge run in .... Creativity falling into knowledge patterns $f(1+7)+(7+1)$ quantum states, vector mediation and reduction takes place by framing all knowledge in postulated pattern of seven states such as $E=f(e_1+e_2+e_3+e_4+e_5)$. Then we can success orient operators in Matrix of 7/7 of "e" states of knowledge which is learnability, understandably, assimilation ...., resources, and consummations for use. It a .... And super fluidity conductors besides normal fluidity of patterns of knowledge for communication purposes. It is linear brain conductivity to end use problems, changes, chances ......, cohesion, containability, ... To contexts, and commands-package for any time use of knowledge patterns .... It will be dynamic in an internet context for information interfacials producti........

The images of decision making that we have been discussing exert considerable influences on executive thinking. It is simply less acceptable for a normal decision makers that spin states of knowledge sets patterns of realism over space and time relevance to decision making. It is a superfluous to normal and ... states of patterns of knowledge. It is a flow within to flow out and …….. area controls of activation of surroundings to a changed states. That is a "manager" state of mind to external needs of inter operability's.

Market Segmentation

A market is a marvel of products' exchange to money and also other way mind. An idiot has to become rascal in order to become PASCAL. There happens a kind of hooliganism exchanged civilization and its mous sell false for ……… and …….. satisfactions. That becomes a pattern of knowledge and domain specialities. That satisfy an elephant metaphor which is a consumer for every producer and transporters of ………… Consignments of self…. bestial naturals. Some generalizations can be made out this platforms and operations. Patterns of knowledge behave like two headed janus. One it adopts to social necessity in any ……..correlations. The other is it models novelty in social culture by ……. ……..of new products. Stainless steels, Plastics, and Computer technologies, Information technologies are all products of preferred patterns of knowledge various in affordability. Unless the method of use of product is obviously, simple than that of the product which seeks to replace then these will be no resistance to it ….. In many cases the key words is "affordability to utility". For example, a dutch company once installed an electronically operated humidifying plant in a Rhodesian textile factory. It was far superior to the anbquated system, which its replaced, and apparently very simple to control. The control panel consisted of four coloured lights, beneath which there were buttons of corresponding colours. If a light switched on, it was an indication that an adjustment was necessary, and this could be set in motion by pressing the buttons of the same colour. If a light switched all went well in all nights except me. The native foremen noticed green light flicks. That was an appropriate choice electrically set.

Thus a utility connects to type of market segmentation to knowledge powers:

(1) Products which are bought largely because of their "national" characteristics will usually be sold in an unmodified form. Examples as Scotch Whiskey, French Perfume, and Swedish glassware and Chinese brassware. Even so, individual markets require variations in pack, size, volume, labelling and general presentation.

(2) Companies lacking the financial capability promote an unmodified product in a market where it will not be readily acceptable in its existing form, must normally adopt a policy of market segmentation. Possible exceptions, for this form of patterns of knowledge, occur when such a

small share of the market is required that it might assumed that there are an adequate number of indictable, willing purchases. The workings of patterns of knowledge, woollies to other patterns in continuity of time, space energy, matter and personality to a domain speciality consignments. Very often, however, such a view turns out later to be wishful thinking. Which shadows a mind meaning fabrics of knowledge to external presentations and attractions. In an industrial sector possible customer are usually undetectable because they are non-existent. For consumers goods minute minority tastes abound markets. The difficulty is to convince a shopkeeper that he should invest in slow moving stock against the possibilities of accessional purchase. Patterns of consumers.

(3) When the products fall within a common place category, its strangeness to end users, lyres unfamiliarly due to patterns of knowledge influences, variances in design features and its main promotional asset is its attractively low price, then product differentiations is often the most expedient strategy cheap tape-recorders and cassette players would come within this description. Unfamiliarities can be produced by variations of patterns of preferred knowledge packages. Thus patterns sell commonality on a consumer preferences of intuited patterns of .... of mends and their knowledge counterparts.

(4) Industrial products are of generated know-hows with effectiveness of operational ..... which depends on the nature of power source, or the physical characteristics, or the level of knowledge intelligence in faceted modernization of mind combinations to material accesses. The intelligence operators, must usually be sold under the umbrella of market segmentation set in uniques patterns of knowledge consumptions. This is a power point of umbrella strategy of transfer knowledge preferences. It is clearly impossible to sell machinery powered by a motor tuned to the appreciation vatages. Equally, a computable position of control levels in matrix 99 contingencies and switches demand ergonomic modifications and new processor or unusual methods of operation may necessitate the provision of service forces of patterns of proffered knowledge to consumptions.

(5) Patterns of knowledge manifested in industrial products, which are precisely the same as those of several competitors may, however, often best be sold by product differentiation. There are for example many, man-made textile fibres which are exactly similar as regards physical and chemical properties. The design textures exudes a professional profferings of patterns of knowledge for purchasing. Terylene, Dacron, Trevira and

Tetron are all brand names given to the same polyester fibers. Modification of the product to meet the needs of a particular maker, even its is feasible, would be costly and undesirable. However, affordability can be generated using statistically variances and ANOVA modelling to market consumers. Sales for all these brands is, however, created by various promotional nature guided by a pattern such as $f(E)=f(E_1+E_2+E_3+E_4+E_5)$ t. This structures space in a domain consumptions.

(6) Products of knowledge with a high decorative style or fashion content, which is not uniquely in any natural characteristics are likely to regulate to required market segmentation strategy. Clothing materials have a classification with relevance to preferred patterns of knowledge variances.

(7) If its knowledge product itself, or the usage of that product, is affected by variations in climate or attitude, then again market, segmentation is an appropriate pattern of manifests. Modification may be limited to the packaging or may have an essential fántasy score to make affordable to an ANOVA sales. Beyond these generalization, there is a further aspect to be borne in mind and its modelling to an ANOVA pattern of knowledge variances. There are four characteristics, one or more of which may be made into invisible college of consciousness of mutual transactions. The inherent in the product as it is offered in the home market, builds transmigrations to international market segmentations. The life of patterns of knowledge is variances of products in different market segmentation. The ANOVA of these variances builds an affordability and its utilization for humans.

Agency of Patterns of Knowledge and on the Domination of the West: Geopolitical Economics

Agencies of knowledge patterns build domain specialities last three centuries say beyond industrial revolution. There is dominance of western concepts which are good to West and strange to the East, North and South. While there can be collectivision that West propagates but individualism is brighter in the East. North and South for individuals have contributed social developments. For example, religion in non-West concept is largely individual and tolerant. But Western interference in this has been brutal military misadventures: war, pestilence, destruction and non-development.

The basic wars in last three centuries have been a process of money grabbings by brutal hooliganism. It became large scale operations. It demigrates non-Western civilization. So much so Greece had to refuse any developments from West or any other country. Peace in knowledge of Greece lies competition of living with their own intelligence. The political intelligence West does not have any relevance to others but it is a superimposition. India and similar countries in popular contexts are overcoming Westminster political economics and are ....the metropolis as market segmentation for rural economics. There needs to organization revenues flow to government to organize people intelligence to generate better returns to people. There happens a subconscious evolution of knowledge economics which prevails beyond Western superimpositions. The argument Western knowledge patterns is that Non-West markets with the West, the basic concepts of monitization of money lies in the West and has become Universal. East, North, South have used their intelligence to play with Western money for so called development. It is indeed multivariate economy that is surging in Non-West that subtains all includes West.

These and many factors similar contribute to the frenzied need for many governances at all levels including family homes. Many salesmen ....scurry through their work, only to return home to say "I could have done with twice as long as there". A perusal of trade directories have strange P-ANOVA of small, less small, big and less big mix for money measurement in .... success measures. The trade directories go beyond human peripheries which facilitate product movements in the ...... of buying geographic. But agriculture products remained same wherever they moved. But agriculture technology and Food Technology combined Medicine have produced product varieties which have dissimilar patterns controlled by geopolitical economics. Thus alls for an agency pattern with geopolitical governance. This may be running subconscious but it wan't development unless governments attempt to cognitive the money values not for market but for political governance. They are beyond management concepts. Management is plan process for factory ....

These coverage may be tuned to presentation of three patterns of knowledge to salesmanship.

(i) The availability and the presentation of simples,

(ii) The habits of negotiation product-pattern building and their consumptions,

(iii) Competitive act only as affordability, governance and P-ANOVA, M-ANOVA, and N-ANOVA where M the money plays the middle resources. Money is a mediator of resources, exchange and producer resources. Development of patterns of knowledge must be closer to political economics and more fames.

Conclusions

A pattern of knowledge is a cluster of specialists and their neighbourhood ...... They build chain of links with domain specialities and their influences. Then, it is a population that frenzies of knowledge pattern into emergence of knowledge evolution. They come out of thought processes. It has impacts of education, environment and livelihoods. The latter creates specialities. It can be occupational, professional, out-of-professional by geocooned for earnings, livings and let-livings. A socio-economic—......of thoughts that cocoons a pattern of knowledge. Human minds and its natural equivalents have to reduce tycoons to cocoons and its inter-operabilities. It is a need for minds alterations to certain occupations vocations, and professionalism. It then leads to an expertise by constant application of know how, do how and show haves. The leads to new productions, new standards of living, new Gross National Products and new Gross Development Products. In many countries of this world this contexts are invisible and immeasurable. They do not have informatively but have incognivity. ....cannot measure it. That is a process of appealing to information that .... of invisibility.

INFORMATION APPEAL TO SALESMANSHIP: A CONJURE OF POLITICAL ARRANGEMENTS

Introductions

There are several touts that forays information to quarters of salesmanship. It engines a human mind and its alter egos to float towards product utilities and its value addition to the life a person or a company were can we find people who like what we happen to produce? Rather than asking "How can we build permanent and growing markets by identifying and producing what people like? There goes an information corridor for salesmanship.

Advertising

An advertisement is an assessment of rough objectives and relationships. It has competitive weapon and international spill over to catch customers for products and *vice versa*. Planning information research of product utilities gain sales control of agents and appointment agents. If controls flow of relevant information to a purchase contingencies of choice products. It has guarantees as ....services base, credit terms to immediately contain the finance problems training operations to usage of products. Then enhance use multi-tasking. Thus maximize the sales of products. Information base news beneath every product and its sales. People are the other arguments for the information links and aptitudes. It has a cost of exhibition. Its follow up and inquires gain satisfaction through samples and standard designs. It has sales literature built for complete concise of information flow to products. There can be sales club, to promote products, information and customers. It needs intensive distribution of quality, quarterly of products > people and people > products reach agreements for sales and its utility to speak value additions. Distribution of agents, agreements, briefing, commission agents, control and motivation of agency chains, reports, sales forecasts, selection aids are all information intensive in appealing for decision-making of product sales. It has negotiation, manipulation, ..., and bargains set in a continuing packages of knowledge resources to information people of products and the cost-benefit ratio of their sales for socio-economic living in neighbourhoods. Environment sales of products is cajole, capture, contain, co-.......and correlate information appeal resources. They are varieties of poly-ANOVA ....to plenty of sales.

Japanese Reflections: Reflections are Mirror Images

Japanese are ultra modern. They produce automobiles in Europe and USA besides many other countries and arrange the sales of it all over the world. There are Japanese everywhere even in Russia, ...and China and Australia. They hence bargained knew how and do-how but geo-climate the products to the needs of different countries. The shapes and sizes of automobiles are so neatly grafted that even six line traffic congestions can play automobile chip electronics and game theories to survive, surge and reach targets. Even the ten sheets can be safe. This has been reflected in India everywhere and every city produces automobile comfortable to their geodesies. Even finely can be varied in near .... bio-gas can be a comfortable transport fuel. The scripts on the automobiles tell every comfort that can give to its users plus it helps computational information as guide to traffic managers. This is P-ANOVA fixed M-ANOVA leading to N-ANOVA. The whole thing then leads D-ANOVA. But the sales appeal...says all these mobiles have short fast life. Since today's human wants novelty there can be no second thoughts about one time utility. It this leads to business of second sales not for mobiles and automobiles. Use, vanish, and wear out is the principle of Japanese Reflections on India and likeway in other countries. This is already there in textiles. Our scripts say our bodies are like wearing our textiles. Therefore, regeneration is needed. Information appeals for salesmanship depends on a kit which begins with idiocy and moves rascalis. They it sets a star-galaxy to survive becomes pascalis. Then it programs the information to appeal to people who want new opera for defies pleasure sales literatures are reflections of want and self-appeal.

Thus we lead ourselves to compatibility markets. It is mixed economy of good and bad time scales. For guarantee bad is kept very low and almost not there. Screening of products by people is done in at least five segments to appeal for five …… and sixth advice by sales person. Market Research Press auxiliary services, calibrations, dimatic considerations, comparative attitudes for sales satisfactory, competitive of cost benefit ratios, ergo ….., danger zone safeties physical tastes of shape and size product pack values, product usage benefit ratios and purpose for resource operators.

These cocoons to play of personal profit, social cognition and mights. Culture designs builds culler-locales for sales. Designs are anthropomorphic to transports and environment-morphine traffic self-guidance and roods interoperability. Sales go by forecast planning agent manipulations, trips execution, pro…prevalences, sales di… qualities, post-sales assurances and follow up. Japanese build clienteles out of clistomers and *vice versa*. Indians build a constancy by repair facilitation with regenerative casket for existing shapes to transfer time for any product utility and services.

Price strategies are new here to purchase on monthly payments rather than one time payments. Product compatibility regulates livability. Colour, differentiation of comports, products manuals planned research product developments all depend on information appeal for salesmanship. It is an assurance for …..and that includes insurance state taxies all cumulated monthly payments for products. Banks provide wherewithal to reflective sales promotion and informatively generates information technology. That is a marvel of plenty to plenty without any penalty.

Focal Primalties for Information Appeals

Products have to be sold irrespective of origin of their production, every sales has to a personal and thereby appealing to individuals and their competitors. Since money is involved in sales and their benefits for self-economics. This centers around the concept of "Personal affordability". This was thought to be one time payment. These days every sale is a banking process. The installment prudence provides equal-payments for a period of time say 5 years. At the time of sales, the banks provide to both pasties a sales compatibility. And that is a focal primarily. Information in scales of the mind of the buyer to a relative advantage of installments buying for small interest rate. The decelerate economy where expenditure is rated against use provides the guarantee for product durability and sales contrasts. Thus, banks are the providence of salesmanship. The appeal is this transaction is well organized by all the parties of sales. Even here there can be competitions for affordability. It is a statistical connotation: f(statistics) # f(distribution) + f(profits).

The focus of sales is product-consummation. The second is cash-advance for continued production for markets. The other second provision is maintenance of the product for guaranteed period of sales agreement. The latter is the information appeal. It is provided in language for ... approval and tandem profit attainment. If the product duration less, the services contracts begin of eratees sales auxiliaries. And these are many outlets. It applies to product such as Refrigerators, Jewels, and even clothes and groceries. Commission agencies are market salesmen. They invest in clienteles as well as products. It is a kind of pull policy in terms of sales of products. It has built-in package costs. It recourse, to media publicities. Media selection is chain publicity procedures. It has always protection package. Strategies within market is to reduce inventory costs and storage costs product mobility is primary, focal priority. It may reduce profit to marginal costs. It then reduces to price locality and value addition. The product profits grows along with its usages.

That Usage is not Personal but Social in All Contexts

An equal duration payment sales spread profits for products as a partial payment of packaged sales. Thus, time plays affordability for customers as well as sales. These factors play tandem to informatively through Bank Services, Bill boards .... Awareness, brand intention, call/recall frequencies in time/money correlations, competitions of return values of used products although to a minimum scale values. Every product even when used has a timed reduction values or depreciations. This suggests an appeal to exchange old to new, but paying about 90 per cent of the new product costs: primality of .... This is called credit appeal transactions life is short or long but sales is of a duration. The third focal primality is durability. This loads to form of involvements in business, customs, say, is the investor in products concept, general philosophy of all production is end user pays, it leads to increased feasibility, legal constraints, economic implications, political implications, profile of products consistence, reasonable growth facilitating in spite expenditure leading reduced economy values. Product guarantee and that is the information appeal for ...... Multi ..... has a ....

Personality Factors in Sales Appeals

Personality is *in-vivo* and *in-situ*. "Heisenberg, to whom positivism was the greatest philosophical opponent, rejected it at the very outset. Positivism makes mistake of refusing, to see the overall connection and of wanting to deliberately keep them in dark". This means that a concept of positivism is difficult attain in the material world of product sales. Thus, positivism is replaced by "opportunism". And sales is such factor for personalities and their asp... "opportunity cost" is not measurable after sales although it is a normal need of the mind. Personality ... for opportunism is played in clearance sales values. It clashes with product sales value. The price we pay for any product is a timed factors many times people do not measure time-benefit in opportunity costs. This becomes part of an unreasonable effectiveness of mathematics. Information appeal turns to sales appeal. It provides a kind defection to gravitational wavelengths of price variations. It becomes a question for mind values to sales value, and product values. That is a poly-ANOVA of standardization of ill......... Poly-ANOVA is a prosperity distribution through dissemination. ANOVA is a basic concept of statistical variance of technology to products and its sales appeal. It is application novelties of operators of values aging. That builds .... to cost-benefit ratios of sales and its timings to end use consummations. It is a climate for a variety of possible problems posed by climatic variations. Sometimes they relate to the physical properties of the packaging itself-certain raw materials become ...... in conditions of extreme heat and humidity. Sometimes use only can prevent such corrosions of product values to social use. Non-inventory market sales is money-Anova of standard demotion of price values. Personalities of clientele—customer anovas is culler—local to mental of their environment. It is like occupations, family, geo-coons, economic distastes, combinational values for other product essentiality and peer values of the product estimations. Strong conviction are needed to decisions of buying products for self or sometimes of others. Usually a buyer has a team of valuers to assess needs/non-needs cybernetics. Since too many products begin to appeal personality to products-sales, it is now a computer-based evaluations of buying products and confirmations.

Cost-Benefit Catapulting

An information Appeal we are concerned always with: A buying as an investment of money in a product. Commonsense say, it is a growth money in product use. A return of benefit of that sort measures the material of make to function an durability and its renewal; at a lower cost when it goes to repair and re-function. That is a strategy based price. In essence, comparison of two previously established figures of price is not more than a guide to strategy. If the two are compatible then little strategic ingenuity is required. If there is a yawning gap there are two possible methods of bridging the gap. Firstly, it may be possible to employ a strategy which will permit further cost cutting and this permit a further price reduction. The availability of such a strategy is usually ascertainable in several different ways.

(1) Is large scale market feasible?
(2) Is product sustainable by high volume of advertisement?
(3) Could the product be sold cheap in spite of high cost products?
(4) Could be a physical climate of joining a poor population products?
(5) Are there sponsors to reduce the cost for end users?

There are Many a Step between the Cup and the Lip: Need for Cooperations

Secondly, it may be possible to justify the price because of competitions. Under cutting the price in competition for end use benefit. It may be less supply and high demand operative rather than *vice versa.* That may then be bought from a small industry for lowest cost production ratio. Alternatively, a competitor can be temperately by temporary reduction of product. As the competitor vanish the prices may grow in staircase data abstraction of values. Almost everywhere there is a customer containment in a .... $F(E) = (E_x + E_y + E_z)\, u^x$ of products.

New Methods of Use

Even when the customers are highly competent to buy on barter some products they would search for new applications. For example, the introduction of man-made fibers into many textile plants was, for example, delayed by their foremen dyers. Very often they were highly competent technologists, but they saw no reason to invite rebukes, or even endanger their jobs, by encouraging the development of yarns or fabrics, which they felt that they may fail to dye effectively.

Thus Invention is Mother of Necessity

On account of innovations the resistance was reduced by cost-ratio. But health hazards become visible in wearing man-made fabrics. The solution was to find dyes of naturals that can play natural experiences. It is, however, possible to build information appeal sales as important prediction developer. It can train a target market by exposing the convenience of new products over the old ones at a reduced cost. They may, therefore, be an important influencing factor on final market selection. This kind change product, change use is instructional appeal to sales by information alternations of appeals transactions.

Conclusions

The market has information for use information is not a commodity by itself but a commodity for commodities. They have to predict power to influence end user values. According to eminent British Psychologist of this century, R.D. Idins observed: "A child born today in the United Kingdom stands a ten times greater chance having more information than merely university education". This can be taken as an enhancement absorption of information appeals for decision alternatives for buying a product from the market: A social, ...

That is a market of heaps and auction: entropy for information

Information appeals through servicing agents should at once increase his role from that of an opinion-measurer to forecast information influences. As such, he has three tasks:

(i) To provide the agents information for value addition such as N-anova about the company values, product values, sales values, and use values.
(ii) To pass on an adequate degree of product of knowledge.
(iii) To observe and analyse the selling process and ensure information development ANOVA. Thus, informal appeals for predict and post ...... measure of U-ANOVA values to ends.

Information plays a selective dissemination of product values for purchase. Such a .... constructions for product appeals to end use can be done continuously by target-spaced-market information. It will help identification of important concepts of product ANOVA. The user statement of information sheet in which requirements analysis is made by agency. Value-ANOVA is basic to information appeals for sales management of product distribution for end use.

That Suites Itself for Dissemination Sales has to Grow for Multiples

Distribution function of a continuous random variable of information appeal for salesmanship tends such as:

$$Ix \rightarrow Kx \rightarrow Ax = y \cos \theta^3$$

That means Information variable, Knowledge variable and Action variable are all going by θ^3 and y cos θ^3. The functions of information leads to sale of y a product in 3-dimensional angle of buyer, seller, and products. The information tends to become knowledge appeal and action implementation happening as to y cos θ^3. This ....a 3-dimensional achievement of sales are possible by random variable of information distribution.

Information theorems have final values in sales transacts. A monotonic comergence of random variables of information provides a product sale. The orthogonal projection of information provides conjunctives towards a product catchments areas. Sampling books sales of products on the basic of mental appeals to product virtualities. It is then booked for purchase. Electronic entertainment shapes usually do sample books and take some time to product the requirements. The information appeal transforms itself to products numerical filters.

This leads to wave propagates of information appeals for sales. Thus, a theory of modulation of information appeals leads to products distribution is market segments. The average time value of a product sale can be converged sale-ANOVA. The information contingents adds reliability to information appeals for sales. However, transmission will be noisy and numerical. This is an operand of transmission medium to trial and success heuristics of sales operation. Variances of uncertainty get widened centre conditional variance operates for information flow set ups for sales.

Random variables of information starts from 0 to 100 on a confidence interval of S/I = > 1. The probability .... of a pair of random signals cooperates to generate sales of > 1. Products scalars and tensors set up .... in probability tans of $P = S^2: I^2 > 1$. Projection of uncertainties can be masked by information appeals. Propagations advances sales certainties and its quantification. Photo detectors confirms sample sale to quarterly. Power permite mean determine sales volumes of products.

Then their appears a programme of symmetry with momentums. Consider two real moment, the information appeal for sales s_1, and the sales happening is s_2 and the transaction happens at "t" time, then the moments pairs of random variables is $(s_1 + s_2)\ t = f(s)$. Thus, the variance of s_1 is the compact value of information appeal and the actual sale is variance of s_2. The total is variance of s_2. The total summitries is $(s_1t + s_2t) = f(s)\ t$. Thus, the valuation of random nets of sales is a probability law $f(P) = f(S) = f(s_1+s_2)^t$. Thus, the variance of these builds uncertainties of 1 to 100 at different confidence internals. Every sales counts 1. There $f(P) = f(S) > 1$ for choices.

In practice, the probability law f(P) is not in general known except when cue are concerned with ..... $f(p)_9 = f(s)_9 - u^x$. Where u^x is uncertainty variance where u^0 = sales happens at one time, u^1 = sales happens two times. We are content with knowledge of the means and co-variances, which are the moments of order 1 and 2 associated with the pair s_1s_2. This pair coincidence and co-variances is the u^x for information appeal for sales. Any two pairing in one hundred population to buy is treated as uncertainty gaining certainty of sales. That experience of u is sales.

Then we need to control uncertainties. To those neo-Keynesians who would counter such a change where uncertainty prevails in sales, the information appeal adds some more of it as planning plays solo to pairs of transacts. If Keynesians influence then government has to reduce uncertainty by certianing inflationary de-tends towards sales. If governments become mixed of markets the value has a guarantee of g^x where every uncertainty can be reduced to a confidence interval of 50150. The summates could $f(S) = f(p) = f(s_1+s_2)t + s^x + h^x$. If ......> 0. Then it can be say an integer running between 1 to 100 the $f(s_1+s_2) + s^{100} + u^{100}$ means there complete sale of goods in markets.

There is a paradox of sales. There are sincere and probably irreconcilable differences between those interested in buying a product and there are others who don't recommend the product to be brought. But though they may buy product in the end, there happens to .... Buying product. We defining it as $f(w) = f(w)_1$—$(w)_2 + w_3$. Then may be somebody buying for somebody else. This happens in book business very often. So also with computers. There happens a mandatory commission is the only difference that may have quantum variance in reality. There is often unreality with realities. Then the summations $f(w)$—$f(u) = f(w_1 + w_2 + w_3)^t$. You is an agency between the product and the buyer. There may be ideology difference buying, as wëll transactional difference in sales of a product. This difference happens everywhere. Nonetheless the removal this service removes information appeal for sales. Thus, there happen human politics which is beyond information this argument is not moral or material question. It is the principle human difference in sales transaction seller-product-buyer are in conjure of life experiences. Information appeal for sales is a capital supply planning. That has a chance factor of Scylla and Charibridis. The valley has a mountain in front of it capital has a bank loan in front of it. That is, a social economy. Intelligence of information says to be loan is the safest method for all times: good, bad and evil. It means live with time and produce sales for sales. An enticement: Developmental Information Economics.

22

Impact of Information Technology on Indian Library Sources and Services

H.S. CHOPRA

India is an ancient country like Assyria, Babylonia, Mesopotamia, Egypt, China etc. India was seen as a rich, culturally superior and an advanced civilization in a number of spheres unheard of in other parts of the World during the ancient times.

Since the days of Harappa and Mohenjodaro India is being invaded by a large number of foreigners whose only motive was to destroy the indigenous culture, monuments, manuscripts, educational institutions, and loot the costly things. After the slavery of thousands of years India became independent. Thus one can understand the economic, industrial, research and educational plight of the country.

In spite of all odds India is progressing in all sectors very rapidly, and has emerged as an Information Technology giant in the world.

Ancient Sources: Manuscripts

The manuscripts which are wealth of knowledge belong to the last 5000 years. These manuscripts are in different languages and scripts and on different types of writing materials like palm leaf, birch bark, wooden boards, cloth, stone, rock, paper etc.

Rigveda, Yajurveda, Shamveda and Atharvaveda, Puranas, Sutras, Samhitas, Brahamanas, Upanishads, Jain and Buddhist scriptures evidently exhibit the calibre of our scholars. Even till to day these scriptures are lighthouses for our ancient history, religion and other disciplines. Approximately 20 per cent of the total ancient literature of the world is available in India.

Manuscript writing continued till the advent of printing press in some states. However, it continued in Northern region till middle of the 19th century.[1] According to National Mission for Manuscripts approximately 5 million (50 lakh) manuscripts are available in India.[2] Individual efforts of preparing catalogues (printed form) or descriptive bibliographies are available but a complete database of manuscripts even in one language is still not available.[3]

Projects are underway at certain educational institutions and oriental libraries to digitize the manuscripts so that these are preserved for posterity.[4] National Mission for Manuscripts is holding seminars, conferences and giving financial aid to institutions for their digitization. Information technology has awakened the librarians, curators and custodians of our Oriental libraries to adopt the latest digital techniques. A union database of all manuscripts available in India, is being prepared by National Mission for Manuscripts after physical verification of the manuscripts.[5] So far as promote access is concerned through ready availability of database in a soon-to-be-established 'National Manuscripts Library' and eventually on Internet. The mission is improving access to the treasure of manuscripts.

Books

Millions of books had been published in India since the days of starting of printing press.[6] Sixty to seventy thousand books are published in India in English as well as other prominent Indian languages. English is the leading language for large number of publications. Process has started to bring out CDs of the books for the use of the readers by certain publishers in India.[7]

Because of various factors like humidity, acidity, dust, microbiological insects, pollution and natural hazards, these books are becoming brittle and fragile. With the passage of time these books will crumble and become a heap of dust. Inferior paper and tropical conditions aggravate the deterioration of books. Information technology has come as a great help for the preservation of books, research journals, backsets, and manuscripts. Hugh information in one CD is proving very useful to readers in India as the number of books purchasing population is insignificant. It is helping in saving space, manual upkeeping of books, circulation, price, availability etc. With these the library services are now in changed form.

Digitization process is limited only to books published in India and not to books published in other parts of the world because of copyright problem. Digitization process has been initiated by our President Dr.A.P.J. Abdul Kalam from the Library of Rashtrapati Niwas (Residence of President). Shortly these books will be put on Internet for freely accessing.

A large number of universities, educational institutions, oriental libraries have started process of digitization of books.

INFLIBNET an autonomous centre of University Grants Commission has prepared a database of books available in different universities. At present the number of books is approximately 70 lakh.

A11EBIP is the first electronic version of Indian Books in print by Sher Singh of the Indian Bibliographic Bureau, New Delhi. This database also lists thousands of books not found in Indian Books in Print, along with their prices, published from India in the fields of social sciences, humanities, science and technolgy.[8]

Research Journals: Online Scenario

In India approximately 11,000 research journals are published in various disciplines. Albeit few journals are covered by Science Citation Index, Social Sciences Citation Index, Medlars, Inspec, Biological Abstracts, Chemical Abstracts etc. yet it does not mean that rest of the journals are not research oriented. If 'Historical Abstracts', is analyzed it covers maximum those books which are published in U.S.A. or European Union. The books published in India are highly informative and relate to Indian history, politics, sociology and economics which may appear less important to the scholars of U.S.A. and other countries. Number of Indian Journals is rapidly increasing and improving their quality and standard day by day. The well established societies and associations are offering free access to journals as well as backsets archives.[9]

Journals

In spite of poverty, illiteracy, population growth, natural hazards and problems of multi-racial society. India is progressing almost in every field. So far as research publications are concerned in science and technology India stands at number 12 in the World publications. U.S.A. with 200870 research articles is on number one and Japan with merely 57420 stands at number 2.[10]

In India we have about 342 universities and 17,000 postgraduate and degree colleges, most of which cannot afford to subscribe the costly foreign research journals and databases.

INFLIBNET an autonomous centre of UGC at Ahmedabad (Gujarat) is providing free access to about 4500 foreign e-journals to the Universities so that the researchers and scientists can benefit from the research and development of advanced countries.

Most of the Indian journals cater to the needs of regional scholars. The fact is that India is a multilingual, multiracial, and multi-religious country. Every state is different from the other in a number of spheres. Therefore, these journals are very useful for the scholars, researchers and students of a particular region. To put them on-line may be an expensive venture, however, process of digitization and preservation in CD form has started all over India. Some of the institutions, societies and universities are giving free-access to their journals.[11]

Indian Academy of Sciences

The prestigious peer-reviewed journals of the Indian Academy of Sciences are available online free to all users. Publications cover the physical sciences, life sciences, physics, mathematics, chemistry, earth and planetary sciences, plant sciences, animal sciences, and modern biology, materials science, astrophysics and astronomy, genetics plus the journal resonance, aimed at improving the quality of science education and teaching. Access to all of these journals is free and open to all users.[12]

Journal of the Indian Institute of Science

The Journal is a multi-faceted publication with content likely to be of interest to research students as well as academic and R&D professionals. It provides free and open access to all articles for all users.[13]

Journal of Postgraduate Medicine

A multidisciplinary quarterly biomedical journal, is one of the oldest medical journals from India. The website of the journal provides free access to full text of articles from 1990. There is free access to all articles to all users, online.[14]

IndMED

India's contribution in the areas of biomedical research and health care has been significant and conforming to international standards. However, only a small fraction of it is available for reference through international bibliographic databases. In an effort to redress this imbalance, the National Informatics Centre of India has developed IndMED (database covering prominent peer reviewed Indian biomedical journal). Initially this site offers access to the tables of contents and abstracts of 75 leading Indian journals. More journals would be added to the list as their quality improves in coming years. Access to this database is free and open to all users.[15]

Indian Medlars Centre

Indian Medlars Centre is providing services like MedIND which consists of 38 full text journals. MetaMed is meta-search tool to search IndMED and PubMed with a single click. Union Catalogue describes the holdings of the major medical libraries of India. This center has been jointly set up by NIC and ICMR to cater to the information needs of the medical community of India.[16]

Indian National Science Academy

Indian National Science Academy plays a crucial role in promoting, recognizing and rewarding excellence. Another important task is to publish journals, organize scientific discussions and bring out proceedings and monographs. The Academy promotes public awareness and understanding of science. Acting as links between the scientific community and the planners, they advise the governments on critical issues. Importantly they serve as forums for interaction among scientists within and outside the country. Following journals are published by Indian National Science Academy:[17]

(1) Indian Journal of Pure and Applied Mathematics.
(2) Indian Journal of History of Science.
(3) Proceedings of the Indian National Science Academy.

Reference Sources

Digital South Asia Library has put:

Archaeological Survey of India. Western Circle Progress Report, 1898. Calcutta (Kolkata).

Hunter, William Wilson, 1840-1900, *et al.* Imperial Gazetteer of India, Oxford, Clarendon Press, 1908-1931.

Digital South Asia Library is providing access to on-line dictionaries of some Indian languages.[18]

ISID: An important component of the ISID research infrastructure is the On-line Index (OLI) to Indian Social Science journals and Press Clipping files (PCI) of national English dailies.[19]

Index to 105 Indian Social Science Journals enables users to search for references on the basis of string (series of characters) either for author's name, or words in titles for selected journals—most of them since their first volume. Press clipping files generated by the Institute, cover India's major 15 English Language Newspapers and the press clippings are categorised under 58 Subject Heads. These subjects cover not only economic news, catalogued industry and issue-wise, but also important news and information on political, social and other developmental issues. Important news items, articles, editorials and book reviews are maintained chronologically since 1980-81 in the form of bound volumes. Beginning from 1990, titles of important clippings in all subjects have been placed in a database.

The National Informatics Centre (NIC) has chosen ISID to host the NIC-ISID Center for Exchange of Databases. The Web page of the Institute provides access to two open databases on a round-the-clock basis to Internet users.

Newspapers and Magazines

In comparison to USA, India is a developing country. However, India is leading in the publication of books in English in Asia. There were 41,000 registered newspapers in March 1996 with a total circulation of 72.3 million. In 1994, there were 369 dailies in 18 languages with a circulation of 20 million.[20] In 2005 the number of circulation has increased drastically. Most of the newspapers in English are providing news, important articles etc. on Internet, which are freely accessible.

National Law School Article Index

It is an online public access catalogue. All the journals which are received by the library are indexed and brief bibliographic information is provided on the Internet.[21]

Ph.D. Theses

Continuous research work is going on in all the Universities in India. Number of Ph.D. theses in different subjects is also increasing year by year. INFLIBNET has claimed that so far their database has 1.35 lac entries. The number of theses is continuously increasing however the site does not have abstracts. It is useful for researchers to know the work already done on a particular subject. Before the advent of information technology, it was very difficult to obtain such information.

Vidyanidhi (Meaning 'Treasure of Knowledge' in Sanskrit) is India's premier Digital library initiative to facilitate the creation, archiving and accessing of doctoral theses. Vidyanidhi is an information infrastructure, a digital library, a portal of resources, tools and facilities for doctoral research in India. Vidyanidhi is envisioned to evolve as a national repository and a consortium for e-theses through participation and partnership with universities, academic institutions etc. Vidyanidhi enhances access to Indian theses and enlarges the reach and users for Indian doctoral research work.[22]

NISCAIR

National Institute of Science Communication and Information Resources (NISCAIR) came into existence on 30 September 2002.[23] One of the core activities of NISCAIR is to collect, organize and disseminate S&T information generated in India as well as in the world which has relevance to India S&T community. Under this programme, the institute is building comprehensive collection of S&T publications in print as well as in electronic from and disseminating through traditional as well as modern means benefiting different segments of the society. Major resources under this activity are National Science Library, Electronic Resources, Indigenous Databases and Raw Materials Herbarium and Museum.

DELENT (Developing Library Network) is providing the following database to the educational institutions. However, it is not freely accessible.[24]

Union Catalogue of Books	Union List of Periodicals
Union Catalogue of Periodicals	
Article's Database	Union List of CD-ROM's
Indian Specialist': A who's who	Union List of Videorecordings
Theses & Dissertations Database	Union List of Sound recordings
DEVINSA Database	Urdu Manuscripts
National Bibliographic Database	Engg. & Technology E-Journals: Table of Contents

Government Information Sources on Internet

With the advent of information technology and maximum use of Internet the geographical and other sources of India are being made available online. This information is freely accessible and one can down load the information.

National Library of India, Kolkata is also digitizing its important books and important documents. It has more than 5000 microfilms and one lakh microfiches. Scanning and archiving of rare and brittle books and other documents on compact disc has been undertaken. English books and documents published before 1900 and Indian publications of pre-1920 are considered for digitization. So far more than 25 lakh pages have been digitized.

National Archives of India which possesses very valuable records has also started microfilming rare manuscripts and books. However, the process to digitize the official records is yet to be finalised. It has two types of records one which can be shown to readers/scholars, the other is banned for consultation for a particular period. To put information of archives on Internet is a gigantic project. Its digitization will provide information to posterity.

National Information Centre: Its role in providing information relating to different departments of India and states is highly praiseworthy. It has ushered a new era of e-sources in India.

Information technology and telecommunication has changed the format of information sources and services in India. Almost every educational institution has prepared its databases of books, journals, backsets, manuscripts, newspapers etc. Use of e-journals, e-books Internet, e-learning, CDs, digitization, Edusat etc. has transformed the traditional library sources and services within few years. India has bright future for digital sources which will eventually change the services also. Undoubtedly, within few years India will be IT giant in the world.

Notes

1. B.S.Kesvan, *History of Printing and Publishing in India: A Socio and Cultural Re-awakening.* Vol. I, New Delhi, National Book Trust of India, 1985 p. 7.

   or

   Hazara Singh, Punjabi Printing and Publishing, Ph.D. Thesis, Guru Nanak Dev University, Amritsar. p. 91.

   or

   Emmett Davis, *Press and Politics in British Western Punjab, 1836-1947*, Delhi, Academic Publication, 1983. p. 22.
2. National Mission for Manuscripts, Report of the second year. p. 6.
3. In West Punjab (India) manuscripts are available in three Universities and some colleges there is lack of initiative to prepare unified catalogues of manuscripts.
4. National Manuscripts Library at the Indra Gandhi National Centre for the Arts, New Delhi is the central node.
5. National Mission for Manuscripts. *op. cit.*, p. 6. See also http://namami.
6. H.S. Chopta, *Preservation, Conservation, Restoration and Digitisation of Library Maternals*, Delhi, Independent. Pub. Co. 2004. pp. 122-150.
7. http://www.inflibnet.ac.in.
8. http://www.vedamsbooks.com/no 32986. htm.
9. 2005 World Development Indicators, the World Bank pp. 310-312.
10. *India 2006*; A reference annual, New Delhi, Publication Division, Ministry of Information and Broadcasting, 2006, p. 247.
11. http://www. inflibnet.ac.in
12. http://www.inasp.info/peri/free. shtml
13. http://www.inasp.info/peri
14. http://www.inasp.info/peri/free. shtml
15. http://indmed.nic.in
16. http://indmed.nic.in
17. http://www.insa.ac.in/html/home.asp
18. http://dsal.uchicago.edu/reference
19. http://isidev.nic.in/odb.html.

20. Barry, Turner ed., *The Statesman's Yearbook*, 2003, p. 830
21. http://www.nls.ac.in/lib/articles/index.html
22. http://www.vidyanidhi-Digital Library and E-Scholarship Portal
23. National Institute of Science Communication and Information Resources (NISCAIR) came into existence on 30 Sept. 2002.
24. Delnet (Developing Library Network) is providing the following database to the educational situ

APPENDIX

Indian Open Access Journals

Annals of Cardiac Anaesthesia (http://www.indegene.com/ijcd/indIJCDHome.html)
Bulletin of Materials Science (http://www.ias.ac.in/matersci/)
Current Science (http:/www.ias.ac.in/currsci/)
Endodontology (New Delhi) (http://medind.nic.in/eaa/eaam.shtml)
ICMR Bulletin (http://icmr.nic.in/bulletin.htm)
Indian Heart Journal (http://indianheartjournal.com/)
Indian Journal of Aerospace Medicine (http://www.medind.nic.in/iab/iabm.shtml)
Indian Journal of Anaesthesia (http://www.medind.nic.in/iad/iadm.shtml)
Indian Journal of Cancer (http://www.bioline.org.br/cn)
Indian Journal of Critical Care Medicine (http://www.ijccm.org/)
Indian Journal of Dermatology, Venereology and Leprology (http://www.ijdvl.com/)
Indian Journal of Gastroenterology (http://www.indianjgastro.com/)
Indian Journal of Human Genetics (http://www.bioline.org.br/hg)
Indian Journal of Medical Microbiology (http://www.ijmm.org/)
Indian Journal of Medical Sciences (http://www.bioline.org.br/ms)
Indian Journal of Nephrology (http://www.ijnephrol.com/index2.htm)
Indian Journal of Pediatrics (http://www.ijppediatricsindia.org/)
Indian Journal of Pharmacology (http://www.ijp-online.com/)
Indian Journal of Plastic Surgery (http://www.ijps.org/)
Indian Journal of Radiology and Imaging (http://www.ijri.org/)
Indian Journal of Surgery (http://www.bioline.org.br/is)
Indian Pacing and Electrophysiology Journal (http://www.ipej.org/)
Indian Pediatrics (http://www.indianpediatrics.net)
Journal of Astrophysics and Astronomy (http://www.ias.ac.in/jaa/)
Journal of Biosciences (http://www.ias.ac.in/jbiosci/)
Journal of the Indian Medical Association (http://www.jimaonline.org/jimastart.html)
Pramana: Journal of Physics (http://www.ias.ac.in/pramana/)
Proceedings of the Indian Academy of Sciences: Chemical Sciences (http://www.ias.ac.in/chemsci)
Proceedings of the Indian Academy of Sciences: Earth and Planetary Sciences (http://www.ias.ac.in/epsci/)
Proceedings of the Indian Academy of Sciences: Mathematical Sciences (http://www.ias.ac.in/mathsci/)

Sadhana (http://www.ias.ac.in/sadhana/)
Sankhya: The Indian Journal of Statistics (http://sankhya.isical.ac.in/index.html)
The Indian Journal of Chest Diseases and Allied Sciences (http://www.indegene.com/ijcd/indIJCDHome.html)

23

Multipurpose Community Telecenters: Transforming South Asian Societies into 'Information Societies'

BINH P. LE

Introduction

> "Many developing countries remain poor largely because they had let the Industrial Revolution pass them by. They can ill afford to miss the information revolution technology."
>
> —M.S. Swaminathan

In November 2006 hundreds of scholars, technology experts, and policy makers gathered in New Delhi for a series of conferences (Indian Telecenter Forum 2006, e-GovIndia 2006, and Digital Learning India 2006), all of which were devoted to the promotion of the development of multipurpose community telecenters (hereafter, telecenters) in India. In 2005, another conference on telecenters entitled "Content for Community Needs" was organized by One World South Asia (OWSA), in which the concept of 100,000 telecenters was introduced. Similarly, in 2004, according to the *Katmandu Post,* hundreds of delegates from the South Asian Association for Regional Cooperation (SAARC) countries (Bangladesh, India, Nepal, Pakistan and Sri Lanka) participated in another international seminar on telecenters in Kathmandu, the capital city of Nepal. This seminar was organized by the Nepal Library Association and the Nepal National Library, with the support from UNESCO. These and countless similar conferences have been held not just in the Indian subcontinent but also throughout the world since the establishment of the first telecenters in the farming communities in Sweden and Denmark in the middle of 1980s—for there is a consensus that telecenters might be a feasible alternative for meeting the information needs of people living in developing countries as well as a technical foundation for developing countries that want to transform their digitally backward societies into "information societies."[1]

Interestingly, endogenous impulses are not the only ones that push for the development of telecenters in developing countries, especially in rural and marginalized communities. In fact, exogenous forces, such as the G-8 Group (the 8 industrialized countries), the International Development Research Center, the United Nations, and the World Bank have been even more forceful in this milieu. For example, at the World Summit on Information Society (WSIS), held in Geneva in December 2003, world leaders declared:

> We, the representatives of the peoples of the world … declare common desire and commitment to build a people-centered, inclusive and development-oriented Information Society, where everyone can create, access, utilize and share information and knowledge, enabling individuals, communities and peoples to achieve their full potential in promoting their sustainable development and improving their quality of life, premised on the purposes and principles of the Charter of the United Nations and respecting fully and upholding the Universal Declaration of Human Rights.[2]

Besides the altruistic interests in extending the benefits of the digital revolution to all humankind, there is also an undeniable realization that "the benefits of the information technology revolution are today unevenly distributed between the developed and developing countries and within societies."[3] Consequently, the digital divide, as stated in the G-8's *Digital Opportunities for All: Meeting the Challenge*, "is threatening to exacerbate the existing social and economic inequalities between countries and communities."[4] Likewise, according to the international development experts who gathered at the conference on Internet and Security, held at Harvard University in 1998, the "uneven global spread of the Internet—highly developed in wealthier nations, patchy elsewhere—could aggravate inequality between the world's rich and poor."[5] They warned that "the costs of inaction are greater than ever before."[6] In response to these dire challenges, the leaders at the WSIS stated that, "We are committed to turning the digital divide into a digital opportunity for all, particularly for those who risk being left behind and being further marginalized."[7]

Subsequently, these factors have forged a strong aspiration for the need to develop means to bridge the north-south digital divide including telecenters. Unquestionably, the need to develop telecenters and their potential benefits are beyond any doubt. Firstly, telecenters can provide vital services such as e-education, e-government, e-health, and e-trade. Secondly, in order to realize these potential benefits, ways to deliver information to the people must be developed, especially where no such information services systems are available. It is particularly imperative where public libraries are either non-existent or in poor conditions, since public libraries have proven to be the main source for delivering information to people everywhere. Thirdly, there are favourable conditions for the development of telecenters such as the availability of low cost advanced telecommunications technologies (e.g., the $100.00 laptop developed at the Massachusetts Institute of Technology, wireless technology).[8] Fourthly, the availability of open-source applications and other valuable information resources such as free medical, educational, scientific databases which can be accessed if the means for accessing such information resources are available. Fifthly, South Asian countries possess diverse social, cultural, ethnic, economic, religious, political, and especially geographic conditions, which are ironically "suitable" for such endeavour. Lastly, the development of telecenters can be viewed as the first step towards the establishment of South Asia's "information societies." Besides the obvious benefits, the development telecenters will certainly raise the level of consciousness among the people in these societies on the necessity of being a part of the global digital revolution. Conversely, the cost of inaction can be worse. These countries can no longer afford to fall further behind in the race to join the global knowledge or digital-based economy.

Despite these potentials, the results of extending information technologies, including telecenters into developing countries including rural and marginalized communities, have been mixed. According to a study on the application of information and communications technologies in developing countries, commissioned by The United Nations Commission on Science and Technology for Development (UNCSTD) revealed that:

> There are many instances where the use of ICTs is bringing widespread social and economic benefits. However, there are as many instances where ICTs are making no difference to the lives of people living in developing countries or are having harmful effect.[9]

It is, therefore, important that before investing more of their scarce resources in the development of telecenters, developing countries ought to critically examine experiences from other countries in the design, implementation, services, sustainability of telecenters as well as the potential *harmful effect* in the introduction of information and communication technologies into traditional societies such as the ones in South Asia.

Background

The first telecenters were established in the farming communities of Harjedalen in Sweden and in Lemvig in Denmark in 1985. By the middle of the 1990s there were more than 200 telecenters in over a dozen countries worldwide, mostly in Western Europe. Today, because there are so many different types of telecenters, the exact number is difficult to determine. Nonetheless, there are perhaps thousands of them, most of which are located in the African and South Asian countries. Like their counterparts in developed countries, telecenters in developing countries have been established in rural or marginalized communities, where commercial development of information and communication technologies is not prevalent. Needless to say, it is not profitable for private enterprises to invest in those areas because people simply could not afford to pay for such services.

The term "multipurpose community telecenter" has been labelled by different names: electronic village hall, Internet kiosk, computer in tent, rural knowledge center, or simply telecenter. The goals of telecenters are to help rural and marginalized groups to harness the benefits of the digital revolution and serve as a vehicle for building social and economic equity. The digital revolution thus far has brought the rural population and marginalized communities few if any benefits, because they lack the necessary telecommunications infrastructures, equipment, skills, money, as well as suitable social infrastructures.

There is no agreed-upon definition for telecenters. However, there is certain consensus in defining them as "physical spaces that provide individuals, community groups and organizations with public access to the information and communication technologies in order to contribute to their educative, personal, social and economic development."[10] One of the most important services offered by telecenters is to provide access to local, regional, national, and international information or resources previously available only to a few.

To function as full-fledged telecenters, they are usually equipped with computers, printers, photocopiers, telephones, scanners, fax machines, and facilities for meeting, training, education, and other governmental, social and cultural activities. Each telecenter requires a staff of two or three people to operate.

The cost for establishing a telecenter varies depending on the geographical and economic conditions. According to UNESCO, it costs between US $50,000 and 75,000 to start a standard telecenter.[11] In some cases, it might cost far less. For instance, Ashok Jhunjhunwala of the Indian Institute of Technology has been setting up Internet kiosks at $1,200 (Rs. 55,000) per kiosk.[12]

South Asia's Preexisting Conditions

Except for some large cosmopolitan areas, most South Asian countries are economically underdeveloped and predominantly rural. With a population around 1.5 billion people, South Asia is one of the poorest areas of the world. Communities within each of these countries are separated by natural barriers such as soaring mountains and rugged, impenetrable terrains as well as by distinct artificial social, ethnic, linguistic, religious and political forces. Modern communication and transportation infrastructures are also in poor conditions or non-existent.

One of South Asia's biggest problems is illiteracy. In recent years, these countries have produced some small middle classes as well as highly skilled workforces, but the vast mass of the rural population remains illiterate and impoverished. The fact is that more than 40 per cent of the population is functionally illiterate, people who cannot even write their own name. The literacy rate of women, young and old, especially rural women is extremely low. For example, only 10 per cent of Pakistan's rural women are literate.[13] Similarly, in 6 of the 24 states, 25 per cent or less of the women in rural areas are literate.[14] In Rajasthan, less than 12 per cent of rural women are literate.[15]

In terms of information services, public libraries are virtually non-existent or are in appalling conditions.[16] The underdevelopment of public libraries can be attributed to the fact that the governments of these countries could not afford to fund the development of public libraries. These governments have to use their scarce resources on other urgent problems such as healthcare, defense, and economic development. Consequently, public libraries are the least of their concern.

These conditions are indeed abysmal. Ironically, these very factors might be viewed as "suitable" conditions or impulses for the development of telecenters. As noted, telecenters were conceived and designed to help the people who live under such environments. Today, besides the advent in telecommunication technologies which make geographical, physical and technological infrastructural barriers less significant, telecenters can be developed and tailored to meet the needs of these vast diverse communities, depending upon the religious, ethnic, political, social and cultural traditions as well as to empower marginalized segments such as rural women and young girls in the society.

Necessary Development Conditions

Recent efforts to bridge the north-south "digital divide" have been centered on the need to provide developing and marginalized communities throughout the world with essential communication and information technologies such as $100.00 laptop computers, wireless and broadband connectivity as well as to have free access to medical, economic and scientific databases. However, as researchers at the International Development and Research Center in Canada and many others who have been involved in the development of telecenters throughout the world argue that communication and information technologies is important, but they must be corresponded with the right kind of social infrastructures.[17] If telecenters can be useful as well as financially sustainable, the following issues must be considered: community participation, community's demand-driven information services, and financial self-sustainability.

Community Participation

According to UNESCO and a host of scholars one of the most fundamental requirements for successful construction of telecenters is "the participation and cooperation of a wide range of local organizations."[18] The problem, however, is that community involvement in the development of telecenters has thus far been rather limited. What has happened is that telecenters are often conceived and implemented by academic, economic, or political leaders at the national and international levels. They recognized the information needs of the communities as well as the enormous potential of telecenters and sought the resources, be it domestic or international, to build them. In the process, local leaders and civil organizations are often not consulted or involved in the development of telecenters.

There are other very important reasons for the lack of local participation.[19] South Asian countries, like many developing countries, are still very traditional, where local and tribal traditions are still the dominant forces in their society. In fact, in many of these societies, local and tribal traditions play a much more important role than that of the national's. This is especially true with regard to the newly modern national states that were artificially created by the decolonization process, for they share few if any similar national traditions. In many cases, national decrees might be subordinated to local and tribal traditions or simply ignored by local and tribal leaders.

Even today, nearly a half century after decolonialization, these forces are still in conflict. Principally, the conflict involves, on the one hand, local and tribal leaders who wish to retain their authority in the advent of the creation of the modern nation state. On the other hand, national leaders who desire to create a unified modern nation state, which requires, among many other things, the relinquishing of local and tribal political, religious, and economic autonomy. In the process, local and tribal leaders see the establishment of telecenters and other national development efforts, regardless of their intentions, as a direct challenge or threat to their own authority.

The establishment of telecenters or other forms of modern telecommunication technologies, such as the Internet, in these societies might be seen not only as a direct challenge to their political power but also a menace to their very own distinct social traditions. To begin with, for many living in these traditional societies, the Internet is seen as a destabilizing force to their traditions. In the political arena, for example, the Internet indeed contains all types of information including information on politics, which supply resources on democracy covering topics such as universal suffrage, human rights, gender equality, many of which are in direct conflict with their existing political and social orders. The Internet can also be a destabilizing force in many other areas as well. For example, the Internet is seen as a venue providing mainly entertainment sources, many of which are considered immoral and degrading.

The conflict of social forces resulting from the attempt to create modern nation states can also be seen with the emergence of many extremist political and religious movements such as Afghanistan's Taliban, Sri Lanka's Tiger rebels, and Nepal's Maoists, just to name a few, not to mention the assassinations of many prominent national leaders such Mahatma Gandhi, Indira Gandhi and her son Rajiv Gandhi.

Interestingly, telecenter planners might take note of Sri Lanka's experience. Ram Sharan Sedhai of the *Kathmandu Post* reported:

> The Sri Lankan government in an understanding with the Tiger rebels has set up numerous telecenters in war-wracked Jaffna province. And interestingly, the centers are more secure than others and have proved to be the most effective in informing the people.[20]

Community's Demand-Driven Information Services

The main goal of telecenters is to meet the information needs of the community. However, as many studies on usability have demonstrated, the usage of telecenters worldwide is low. For example, Mahmood points out on the usage of telecenters in Pakistan that after several months "the number of daily visitors declined with the passage of time."[21] Interestingly, a similar pattern can also be found on the usage of telecenters in developed countries.[22]

Several factors contributed to this phenomenon. Firstly, the information needs of people living in traditional societies is rather limited as their daily life is relatively simple. It centers mainly on subsistent and self-sustained agriculture, which requires little information or knowledge beyond what they can learn from or can be provided by their forbearers. For centuries, the people, except the ruling and intellectual elite, in these societies have relied on the elderly in the family or society to provide them with the information or knowledge they need to function in their daily lives. Today, despite the important role information plays in the people's daily lives, the need for information has not been widely articulated in these societies. Thus, before telecenters are being set up, it is essential that the people in the communities must be educated not just about the availability of information sources but also why they need information.

Secondly, even if they realize the important role of information in today's life, they cannot access or use the information available *via* telecenters or other means.

For too many people, the information available on the Internet has little or no use at all because the vast majority of the people in these societies are functionally illiterate. They simply cannot read or write. Added to this challenge, most of the information available on the Internet is in Western languages, especially English. Moreover, these sources of information are written by and for users in the developed world. It has been suggested that it might be better to provide information, not only in native languages, but also in audio or visual. It is especially appropriate where illiteracy and oral tradition are still prevalent.

Thirdly, in order to have access to the information, they must have some computer skills. The problem is that many of these people have never used computers in their life. To make the matter worse, there are not enough trained and skilled workers to assist people using these information accessing tools. A positive development by The National Alliance for Mission 2007 (India) is an attempt to forge a train-the-trainer program which hopes to build a pool of hundreds of thousands of skilled village knowledge workers.[23] It is worthwhile to point out that even in developed countries, the lack of computer skills by users has been considered one of the most serious factors in preventing people from accessing the information they need.[24]

Financial Self-Sustainability

Unlike the development of public access telecenters in developed countries where they were funded by governmental or public sources, in contrast, most if not all telecenters established in developing countries were financed by grants awarded by non-governmental organizations (NGOs). The problem with "donor dependent" telecenters is that when the initial money ran out, telecenters ceased operation. In fact, a larger number of telecenters were closed after a couple of years after establishment. For example, only 5 of the 23 telecenters established in Mexico operate after 3 years of establishment.[25]

It has been suggested that telecenters should be incorporated into other regular or existing programs or services such as hospitals, school, city, and libraries.[26] Telecenters can also generate their own finances by offering services such as telephone, fax, photocopying, resume writing, training desktop publishing, and word processing.

For instance, in India, some initiatives—like Jhunjhunwala's—have focused on making such outlets self-sustaining micro business enterprises, unlike other donor-dependent telecenters elsewhere.[27] One of the major problems in turning telecenters into business enterprises is that telecenters might stop "being focused on human development and democratization of technologies, and being instead turned into spaces just aimed at consumption and entertainment."[28]

Conclusion

Telecenters offer a wide range of opportunities for meeting the information needs of people living in developing countries, especially rural and marginalized communities. They can also be a social vehicle for empowering marginalized segments of the population, especially rural women, who constitute one of the largest, poorest, and least literate groups in the world. And of course, telecenters can also serve as a stepping stone in the process of transforming the digitally backward societies into "information societies," as well as an impulse in raising the level of consciousness on the necessity of being a part of the digital revolution, a revolution that they can no longer afford to ignore. Unfortunately, the results have thus far been less hopeful. It appears that a number of factors have contributed to this disappointment. First, the focus has been heavily on technical rather than on social infrastructures. As demonstrated, insufficient social infrastructures can be as detrimental as inadequate technical infrastructures in the development of telecenters. Second, the lack of essential social infrastructural elements such as literacy, computer skills, indigenous generated language information sources, etc., has severely limited the usage of telecenters. Thirdly, donor-dependent development of telecenters has failed in enabling telecenters to be self-supported. As it happened, most of the telecenters established in the past decade relied mainly on resources from international organizations, and they ceased operations once the grants ran out. It is important then for planners of telecenters to develop longer term financial self-sustainability, to involve active local participation, and to focus on community's demand-driven information services. Conversely, grant donors and governmental agencies might require telecenters' grant seekers to include these components in their grant proposals.

Notes

1. See, World Summit on the Information Society (WSIS). 2003. *Declaration of Principles: Building the Information Society: A Global Challenge in the New Millennium.* http://www.itu.int/wsis/docs/geneva/official/dop.html. (Retrieved 11/19/2006).
   See also: Digital Opportunity Task Force. 2001. *Digital Opportunities for All: Meeting the Challenge. A Report of the Digital Opportunity Task Force.* http://www.g8italia.it/-en/docs/STUWX141.htm. (Retrieved 8/22/2006). T. Tschang, M. Chuladul and T. Le. 2002. "Scaling-up Information Services for Development: A Framework of Increasing Returns for Telecenters," *Journal of International Development*, 14(1), p.129. S. Jorge. 2002. "Telecenter for Universal Access: Endangered Policy Options." http://isiswomen.org/pub/wia/wia2002/telecenters.htm. (Retrieved 10/10/2006).
2. Ibid., WSIS. http://www.itu.int/wsis/docs/geneva/official/dop.html. (Retrieved 11/19/2006).

3. Ibid., WSIS. http://www.itu.int/wsis/docs/geneva/official/dop.html. (Retrieved 11/19/2006).
4. Digital Opportunity Task Force.2001. *Digital Opportunities for All: Meeting the Challenge. A Report of the Digital Opportunity Task Force.* http://www.g8italia.it/-en/docs/STUWX141.htm. (Retrieved 8/22/2006).
5. D. Jellinek. 1998. "Computing and the Net: For Richer Not Poorer — Does the Net Reduce Global Inequalities or Exacerbate Them?" *Guardian*, May 28, p. 5.
6. Ibid., *Digital Opportunities for All.*
7. Ibid., *Declarations of Principles.*
8. J. R. Young. 2005. "MIT Researcher Revealed a $100 Laptop Designed to Benefit Children Worldwide,' *Chronicle of Higher Education*, 25(14), p. A41.
9. R. Mansell and U. When (eds). 1998. *Knowledge Societies: Information Technology for Sustainable Development.* New York: Oxford University Press for the United Nations Commission on Science and Technology for Development, p. 14.
   See also: R. Gomez. 1998. "The Nostalgia of Virtual Community: A Study of Computer-Mediated Communications Use in Columbian Non-governmental Organizations," *Information Technology & People*, 11(3), 217-34.
10. Cited in "In Depth: Telecenters," http://www.choike.org/nuevo eng/informes/3084.html. (Retrieved 12/15/2006).
    See also: R. Gomez, P. Hunt and E. Lamoureux. 1999. "Wondering about Telecenters: Can They Contribute to Sustainable Development in Latin America?" http://www.idrc.ca/enev-4343-201-DO TOPIC.html. (Retrieved 9/19/2006).
11. R. Fuchs. 2000. "Telecenters Share the Tools of the Information Age," *UNESCO Courier*, 53(3), p. 43.
12. "South Asia Mull Cost of Telecenter," http://newkarla.com/new4.php?action=fullnews&id=28047. (Retrieved 1/12/2007).
13. K. Mahmood. 2005. "Multipurpose Community Telecenters for Rural Development in Pakistan," *Electronic Library*, 23(2), p. 214.
14. V. A. Velkoff. 1998. *Women's Education in India.* Washington, D.C.: Department of Commerce/Bureau of the Census, p. 2.
15. Ibid., Velkoff, p. 2.
16. Ibid., Mahmood, p. 210.
    See also: M. Ghosh. 2005. "The Public Library System in India: Challenges and Opportunities," *Library Review*, 54(3), pp.181-2.
17. "Technology Tools: Instruments for Community Empowerment and Development," in *Connecting People-Changing Lives in Asia.* http://idrc.ca/IMAGES/ICT4D/PanAsia/PAN/chap3.html. (Retrieved 10/7/2006).
18. See: "Multipurpose Community Telecenters," http://porttal.unesco.org/ci/er/ev.phpURL ID=5341&URL DO=DO-TOPIC&URL-SEC... (Retrieved 1/11/2007).
    See also: T. Tschang, M. Chuladul and T. Le, 2002, p.139.
19. For an excellent theoretical discussion on modernization, see S. P. Huntington. 1968. *Political Order in Changing Societies.* New Haven: Yale University Press.
20. R. S. Sedhai. 2003. "Setting up 1,500 Telecenters during Tenth Plan Unlikely," *Katmandu Post*, December 31. http://www.nepalnews.com.np/contents/englishdaily/ktmpost/2003/dec/dec31/economy.htm. (Retrieved 1/4/2007).

21. Ibid., Mahmood, 2005, p. 211.
22. D. Ellen. 2001. "Bridging the Digital Divide: Access for All," *Assignation*, 18(2), p. 33.
23. B. Harris. "Training Seen as Essential for India's Rural Connectivity Plans," http://www.govtech.net/digitlcommunities/story.php?id=96943. (Retrieved 2/06/2007).
24. Ibid., Ellen, 2001, p.34.
25. "South Asia Mull Cost of Telecenter," http://newkarla.com/new4.php?action=fullnews&id=28047. (Retrieved 1/12/2007).
26. Ibid., Fuchs, 2000, p. 43.
    See also: Reilly and Gomez, 2001; and Gomez, et al. 1999.
27. "South Asia Mull Cost of Telecenter," http://newkarla.com/new4.php?action=fullnews&id=28047. (Retrieved 1/12/2007).
28. "In Depth: Telecenters," http://www.choike.org/nuevo_eng/informes/3084.html. (Retrieved 11/20/2006).

References

"From All Sides ...: How Effective or Otherwise Has the Warana Wired Village Project Been? It Helps to Take a Look the Picture from All Angles," *Businessline*, August 2, 2004, p. 1.

"Knowledge Sharing through Telecenters." (www.i4d.csdms.in)

Choike.org. "In Depth: Telecenters." (http://choike.org/neuvo_eng/infromes/3084.html)

Cooks, Linda and Kirsten Isgro. 2005. "The 'Cyber Summit' and Women: Incorporate Gender into Information Communications Technology UN Policies," *Frontiers*, 2005, Vol. 26, No. 1, pp. 71-88.

Digital Opportunities for All: Meeting the Challenge: *A Report of the Digital Opportunity Task Force*. Genoa Summit 2001. Genoa, 11 May 2001.

Ellen, Deborah. 2001. "Bridging the Digital Divide: Is Access Enough?" *Assignation*, Vol. 18, No. 2, 2001, pp. 32-36.

Ernberg, Johan. 1998. "Telecenters: Access for All," *Telecommunications*, Vol. 32, No. 4, p. 510.

Ernberg, Johan. 1998. *First International Conference on Rural Telecommunications: Universal Access for Rural Development from Action to Strategies*. (http://www.itu.int/ITU/univ_access/papers/NTCA_joh...)

Fuchs, Richards. 2000. "Telecenters Share the Tools of the Information Age," *Unesco Courier*, March 2000, 53, 3, p. 43.

Geoff, Naim. 1998. "European Telecenters Showcase for Remote Working," *Financial Times*, April 1, 1998, p. 17.

Ghosh, Maitrayee. 2005. "The Public Library System in India: Challenges and Opportunities," *Library Review*, 2005, Vol. 54, No. 3, pp.180-91.

Gomez, Ricardo, Patrik Hunt and Emmanuelle Lamoureux. 1999. "Wondering about Telecenters: Can they Contribute to Sustainable Development in Latin America?" (http://www.idrc.ca/en/ev-4343-201-1DO_TOPIC.html)

Harris, Roger. 2003. Rural Development with ICTs in Nepal: Integrating National Policy with Grassroots Resourcefulness. (http://www.developmentgateway.org/download/181374/v12p4.pdf)

Huntington, S.P. 1968. *Political Order in Changing Societies*. New Haven, CT: Yale University Press.

International Development Research Center. *Connecting People: Changing Lives in Asia*. (http://www.idrc.ca/IMAGES/ICT4D/PanAsia/PAN/chap1.html)

International Development Research Center. 2006. "Sri Lanka Telecenter Family Network Project." (http://idrc.ca/en/ev-98417-201-1-DO_TOPIC.html)

International Development Research Center. 2006. "Mission 2007 Participatory Curriculum Initiative." (http://idrc.ca/en/ev-98414-201-1-DO_TOPIC.html)

James, Jeffrey. 2001. "Information Technology, Cumulative Causation and Patterns of Globalization in the Third World," *Review of International Political Economy*, Vol. 8, No. 1, pp. 147-62.

Jellinek, Dan. 1998. "Computing and the Net: For Richer not Poorer Does the Net Reduce Global Inequalities or Exacerbate Them?" *Guardian*, May 28, 1998, p. 5.

Jensen, Mike and A. Esterhuysen. 2001. *The Community Telecenter Cookbook for Africa*. Paris: United National Educational Scientific and Cultural Organization.

Kanungo, Shivraj. 2004. "On the Emancipation Role of Rural Information Systems," *Information Technology & People*, Vol. 17, No.4, pp. 407-22.

Logan, Marty. 2005. "Rights: More Women Drivers Needed on the Information Highway," *Global Information Network*, p. 1.

Mahmood, Khalid. 2005. "Multipurpose Community Centers for Rural Development," *Electronic Library*, Vol. 23, No. 2, pp. 204-20.

Mansell, R. and U. When. Eds. 1998. *Knowledge Societies: Information Technology for Sustainable Development*. New York: Oxford University Press, for the United Nations Commission on Science and Technology Development.

Mrquez, Humberto. 2003. "Communications-Latam: Telecenters Aim to Narrow Digital Divide," *Global Information Network*, September 18, 2003, p. 1.

Mulama, Joyce. 2003. "Technology-Africa: Computers Still a Distant Dream for Women," *Global Information Network*, October 16, 2003. p. 1.

New Kerala.com. "South Asia Mulls Cost of Telecenters" (http://www.newkerala.com/news4.php?action=fullnews&id=28047).

Qvortrup, Lars. (no date). *A Mean to Social, Cultural and Economic Development of Rural Communities and Low-income Urban Settlements: Impact of Community Teleservices Centers on Rural Development*. (http://www.itu/ITU-D/univ_access/casestudies/_page.print)

Sharma, Milan M. 2003. "Industrial Policy, IEA, FITTA to be Amended," *Katmandu Post*, December 31, 2003. (http://www.napalnews.com.np/contents/englishdaily/ktmpost/2003/dec31/economy.htm).

Steinberg, James. 2003. "Information Technology & Development Beyond 'Either /Or'," *Brookings Review*, Spring 2003, Vol. 21, No. 2, pp. 45-49.

Tschang, Ted, M. Chuladul, and T. Le. 2002. "Scaling-Up Information Services for Development: A Framework of Increasing Returns for Telecenters," *Journal of International Development*, Vol. 14, pp.129-41.

UNESCO. 2004. "Networking Multipurpose Community Centers in South Asia." (http://portal.unesco.org/ci/en/ev.php-URL_ID=14161&URL_DO=).

UNESCO. *Ten Steps for Establishing a Sustainable Multipurpose Community Telecenters: User's Guide*. Bangkok: UNESCO.

United Nations and International Telecommunication Union. (no date). *World Summit on Information Society.* (file://c:temp\DEGM2J3U.htm)

Vergnes, Bernard. 2001. "Information Technology and Sustainability," *The OECD Observer*, Vol. 226/7, p. 16.

World Summit on Information Society. 2003. *Declaration of Principles: Building the Information Society: A Global Challenge in the New Millennium.* Geneva, 12 December 2003.

World Summit on Information Society. 2003. *Plan of Action.* Geneva, 12 December 2003.

World Summit on Information Society. 2003. *Shaping Information Societies for Human Needs: Civil Society Declaration to the World Summit on the Information Society.* WSIS Civil Society Plenary. Geneva, 8 December 2003.

World Summit on Information Society. 2005. *Tunis Commitment.* Tunis, 18 November 2005.

World Summit on Information Society. 2005. *Tunis Agenda for the Information Society.* Tunis 18 November, 2005.

24

DELNET—Developing Library Network: The Operational Network in South Asia

H.K. KAUL

Introduction

The information revolution that had begun to leave its impact in the 1980s on the libraries in India had mixed reactions from the library and information science professionals who manned these libraries. Some were oblivious to the new developments taking shape around the world and very few were concerned about its fallout. With no IT infrastructure in the libraries and with no training facilities for them in IT applications in libraries, the scenario was dismal. The librarians in Delhi were still progressive and were prepared to attend programmes where the importance of IT applications in libraries was discussed.

In the 1970s and 1980s, I had the privilege of visiting several library networks in Europe and the United States and was greatly influenced by their advantages for the users, library professionals and the institutions to which they belonged. Also, the libraries in Delhi had noticed that the budgets were inadequate, space in libraries was shrinking without any possibilities of additions and the costs of books and journals were regularly increased.

With this scenario we noticed at that time that several libraries in a vicinity subscribed to the same and similar journals and we could see that the rationalization of subscriptions would help them. It was also felt that it would help India as the foreign exchange reserves in the country were limited.

My advantage as Chief Librarian of the India International Centre in New Delhi was that I organized annual get-togethers of library professionals regularly during the last few decades in the first week of January. These get-togethers were quite popular as everybody would like to start the year with exchanging New Year greetings. On January 8, 1988, I organized a get-together of library and information science professionals like every other year but managed to follow the get-together by a panel discussion on networking of libraries in Delhi, especially for sharing of resources and rationalization of acquisitions. On the panel I had invited Dr. A. Lahiri, Director, National Information System for Science & Technology (NISSAT) besides other professionals in order to ascertain that if the proposal was approved by the library community and users there should be some agency to support this activity. NISSAT had already supported the establishment of a network of libraries in Kolkata in 1986 called CALIBNET. My proposal received full support from the professionals and Dr. A. Lahiri agreed to support it if any professional was willing to make it functional. My name was proposed by the audience to be the Convener and it was approved by everyone. This event laid the foundations of DELNET, the Delhi Library Network.

I had to get the approval of the India International Centre management before I could take up this additional work. The Board of Trustees headed by Dr. L.M. Singivi and the Director Mr. Eric Gonsalves approved the proposal and allowed me to work as Convener of DELNET. Before this, since the early 1970s, I had worked on several projects as Project Director and I had always got financial support from the Government of India for each project and had successfully completed those projects. This track record helped me in getting the approval for this important project quickly. NISSAT initially agreed to support DELNET on a project-to-project basis and we agreed to this arrangement.

The Projects

In 1988 eighteen libraries in Delhi agreed to cooperate and join DELNET.

The Library of the India International Centre (IIC) being the agency to initiate this work soon acquired a PC-AT and a printer. A training programme on computer applications for DELNET participants was organized in December 1988 with the financial assistance of NISSAT. This was the beginning of the creation of machine-readable catalogue of some books in the IIC Library using CCF and CDS-ISIS software.

In January 1989 the impact of information technology on social change in India was discussed at a panel discussion. Every participant felt that human life was influenced by IT in one form or the other and it would continue to be so in future. This gave a direction to the library professionals. They had to modernize their libraries and train themselves further. DELNET which was a year old had already converted special collections of the India International Centre Library into machine-readable form. NISSAT initiated the preparation of a feasibility report on DELNET and it was completed by CMC Ltd. in 1989. In pursuance of this report a Coordination Committee was constituted with Dr. S. Varadarajan, Director-General, Department of Scientific and Industrial Research, Ministry of Science and Technology as Chairman and Dr. H. K. Kaul as its Member-Secretary. A number of experts in library automation and networking including representatives of the University Grants Commission, Mahanagar Telephone Nigam Limited and CMC Limited were members of the Coordination Committee. Greater emphasis was laid on arranging training programmes. DELNET regularly organized such programmes for library professionals.

In 1990 I visited some of the operations library networks in Europe including BLCMP in Birmingham. As a result, I was able to collect extensive information on how such networks operated. In Delhi at that stage most of the librarians neither had direct phone connections nor had hardware and software in their libraries. We laid emphasis on helping the libraries in creating bibliographical databases. I wrote to the heads of institutions to provide hardware and telephone connections to them. The software CDS-ISIS was given free by NISSAT to the libraries. Under a special project, NISSAT gave modems to libraries with the minimum infrastructure as an inducement to get networked. Not only did we undertake projects to evaluate the time and cost involved in creating a catalogue record in machine-readable form but also arranged training in Anglo-American Cataloguing Rules II with the financial assistance of NISSAT.

Another project which was undertaken with the support of NISSAT was instituting Consultative Committees for Rationalisation of Acquisitions of Periodicals by the libraries in Delhi. In 1991 about Rs. 18 lakhs were saved as a result of the efforts made by the consultative committees. By 1992 the sum saved as a result rose to Rs. 40 lakhs.

In 1991 a courier service was started on an experimental basis, for timely exchange of periodicals. This was the first experiment which was not a great one but it gave the feeling that the use of a mobile van was necessary for the exchange of books and periodicals.

Also, in 1991 the E-mail service was started among the libraries with the use of X-400 software which was obtained by NISSAT from the Department of Electronics, Government of India. Initially it was operated from NISSAT.

Another project was the creation of a 'Union Catalogue of Current Periodical Acquisitions in Delhi Libraries'. This project was the first in the creation of a series of union catalogues by DELNET thereafter. In order to maintain standards in the creation of machine-readable catalogues, DELNET began offering guidance to librarians.

DELNET: A Society

The Initial Developments

With the confidence gained during the last four years we decided to go ahead in an organized manner. In June 1992, DELNET was registered as a Society. The India International Centre, were I worked as Chief Librarian, agreed to host DELNET activities for a period of three years and laid certain conditions within which I could work both as Director, DELNET as well as Chief Librarian of IIC. Dr. S. Varadarajan, the Chairman of the Coordination Committee became the President of DELNET.

With the registration of DELNET as a Society the work on the on-going projects was accelerated. The E-mail hub which was stationed at NISSAT was moved to DELNET in order to make the services more manageable. DELNET continued to undertake the rationalization of periodicals and saved another Rs. 25 lakhs in foreign exchange.

The Directorship of DELNET was assumed by me as a challenge and I resolved that DELNET should be a successful library network. In order to understand the functioning of library networks further I visited the library networks in the UK, USA and Canada. This was followed with the publication of a number of publications including *Library Networks: An Indian Experience*; *Library Resource Sharing and Networks; Library and Information Networking*.

DELNET also started the publication of "DELNET Newsletter".

The selection of the appropriate software for DELNET union catalogues and databases to be made available through the Web was difficult. We had no finances available with us and therefore, could not buy an imported software product. We got a free package from Frontier Technologies in Hyderabad and began working on it. This software was not very efficient and therefore within a year we had to discard it.

The Objectives

DELNET started with defining clearly its objectives as part of the registration of DELNET as a Society. The salient objectives were:

(i) to promote sharing of resources among the libraries by developing a network of libraries in Delhi, by collecting, storing and disseminating information and by offering computerized services to the users;

(ii) to understand scientific research in the area of information science and technology, create new systems in the field, apply the results of research and publish them;

(iii) to offer technical guidance to the member-libraries on collecting, storing, sharing and disseminating information;

(iv) to coordinate efforts for suitable collection development and reduce unnecessary duplication wherever possible;

(v) to establish/facilitate the establishment of referral and /or research centres, and maintain a central online union catalogue of books, serials and non-book materials of all the participating libraries;

(vi) to facilitate and promote delivery of documents manually or mechanically;

(vii) to develop specialized bibliographies, databases of books, serials and non-book materials;

(viii) to develop databases of projects, specialists and institutions; and

(ix) to coordinate with other regional, national and international networks and libraries for exchange of information and documents.

The Organised Network: The Hiccups

In 1992 after DELNET was formally registered as a Society, the registration of member-libraries started formally with the signing of the MOU and the presentation of the application form for joining DELNET. The basic principle adopted at this stage was that all types of libraries could join DELNET and also the admission fee and membership fee will be low and the same for all types of libraries, irrespective of their size or financial strength. Most of the libraries that had travelled with us since 1988 signed the MOUs and paid the registration fee and annual membership fee. This way we got small money. We did not have sufficient finances with us. NISSAT promised to give us support if we gave an undertaking that we would arrange training programmes and raise money to be returned back to NISSAT. NISSAT probably could not visualise that a library network needed regular finances to perform and to survive. However, in the initial stages due to lack of funds, for the survival of the network, I accepted the proposal but soon realized that DELNET could not grow as a viable network within these financial constraints and therefore, refused to accept NISSAT support.

The Role of the National Informatics Centre (NIC)

DELNET entered a new phase in 1992. As we were unable to accept the NISSAT offer of accepting financial support which had to be returned to NISSAT after organizing training programmes. I approached Dr. N. Seshagiri, Director-General,

National Informatics Centre (NIC) and explained to him how important the project was for the country and how a small financial support could save the project. He is a visionary. He accepted our proposal and thus NIC began giving project grants to DELNET for enhancing our facilities. Also, NIC provided entire hardware to DELNET. This support was later continued by Dr. N. Vijayaditya, Dr. Seshagiri's successor till 2006.

Membership

DELNET's membership has been growing steadily. The admission fee of Rs. 5,000 and annual fee of Rs. 5,000 was charged from institutions. In the year 2,000 the annual membership fee was increased to Rs. 7,500 and this rate still continues. The following graph describes how membership of DELNET grew since 1992.

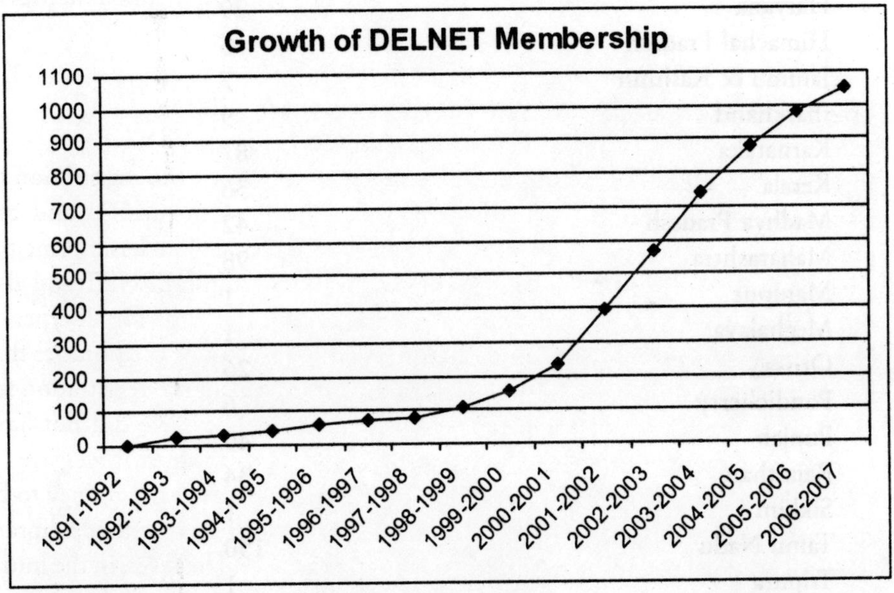

1991-1992	0	1999-2000	153
1992-1993	26	2000-2001	233
1993-1994	30	2001-2002	393
1994-1995	43	2002-2003	565
1995-1996	57	2003-2004	743
1996-1997	69	2004-2005	878
1997-1998	76	2005-2006	979
1998-1999	106	2006-2007	1051

The present breakup of DELNET membership is given as follows:

India

Andaman and Nicobar Islands	1
Andhra Pradesh	108
Arunachal Pradesh	1
Assam	6
Bihar	6
Chandigarh	5
Chhattisgarh	6
Delhi	172
Goa	6
Gujarat	28
Haryana	29
Himachal Pradesh	6
Jammu & Kashmir	7
Jharkhand	9
Karnataka	87
Kerala	36
Madhya Pradesh	42
Maharashtra	98
Manipur	1
Meghalaya	1
Orissa	26
Pondicherry	6
Punjab	40
Rajasthan	34
Sikkim	1
Tamil Nadu	150
Tripura	1
Uttar Pradesh	76
Uttaranchal	12
West Bengal	36
Total	1037

Other SAARC Countries

Nepal	2
Sri Lanka	3
Total	5

Outside SAARC

Oman	2
Philippines	1
United Arab Emirates	2
United States	4
Total	9
GRAND TOTAL	1051

Subject-wise Breakup

General	168
Science and Technology	743
Social Science	112
Humanities	28
Total	1051

Types of Libraries

Academic

Universities	53
Deptt./Centres	824
Research/Special	92
Public Libraries	5
Government Libraries	29
Libraries of Diplomatic Missions/UN Agencies	10
Miscellaneous including Trusts	38
Total	1051

The Standards

Till 1992, DELNET followed CCF, AACR II and LCH as the standards for creating machine readable catalogue-records. The reason being that NISSAT was supporting DELNET and also that NISSAT was distributing CDS/ISIS software mostly free to libraries. In 1992, we got into the debate about the MARC format and eventually when UK MARC, US MARC and CAN MARC were harmonized and MARC 21 came into force we began promoting the use of MARC 21. However, as CCF had penetrated deep into the minds of librarians and they had found it easy to operate and MARC needed more effort to understand and also reasonably good software support for creating MARC 21 records, we have been advocating the use of MARC 21 regularly. We did not have a punitive clause in our MOU. Even if we had, punishing libraries would have resulted in disheartening librarians from getting their libraries networked, reducing Inter Library Loan (ILL) and Document Delivery Services (DDS), and finally, in reducing DELNET membership which would have crippled our thin financial lifeline. However, while signing the MOU with every participating library, we specifically mentioned that they have to use MARC 21, AACR II and LCSH standards while creating their machine-readable catalogue records.

DELNET offered software support for creating MARC 21 records and gave guidelines for using the requisite international standards. However, libraries that used CCF or other standards joined DELNET and promised to upgrade their records. In order to promote ILL and DDS services DELNET made every effort to incorporate into its union catalogues all such records which were prepared by its Member-Institutions using ISO standards.

DELNET Databases

Union Catalogue of Books: CCF

DELNET maintains an online union catalogue of books available for its member-libraries. This union catalogue is continuously updated and is growing progressively in size. The information can be retrieved by title, author, subject descriptors, series, date of publication, place and publisher, corporate body, location code and ISBN. It has about 60,00,000 bibliographic records in it. The request for interlibrary loan can be placed online through the Web using the union catalogues.

Union Catalogue of Books: MARC

DELNET introduced the creation of records in MARC format by taking up National Bibliographic Database projects and some retro-conversion projects. The database presently has about 75,000 records.

Union List of Current Periodicals

DELNET has created the union list of current periodicals. It covers periodicals in all subjects including science and technology, social sciences and humanities. More than 1000 libraries are participating in this project. The database is available online to DELNET users. It now lists about 21,000 periodicals and is being updated regularly with new titles and locations.

Union Catalogue of Periodicals

DELNET maintains a union catalogue of periodicals, which contains full holdings data of periodicals available in its member-libraries. At present the union catalogue contains about 19,000 records.

Database of Periodical Articles

The database has articles on various subjects which can be searched under the title, author, compiler, name of the periodical, subject descriptors, date of publication, ISSN and location. The database is being extensively used by researchers and scholars. At present the database contains over 5,70,000 records.

Union List of CD-ROMs

The information about CD-ROMs available with the member-libraries have been compiled in this union list. The database has about 1,770 records.

Union List of Video Recordings

The union list of video cassettes available in member-libraries is also completed. The database has about 3,600 records.

Union List of Sound Recordings

This union list contains information about 750 audio cassettes available in member-libraries.

Database of Urdu Manuscripts

A database of Urdu manuscripts available in Delhi libraries was added as a sample. Though compiled in the 1970s, it contains a descriptive list of 210 manuscripts.

Database of Theses and Dissertations

A database of theses and dissertations submitted to the member libraries of DELNET conducting research, including the Universities was started. It covers various subjects. The database has 41,400 records.

Indian Specialists' Database: A Who's Who

DELNET had created a database of Indian specialists which is available online to member-libraries. The database now has profiles of 2,000 scholars. This database is considered very useful as search can be made by name, area of specialisation, subject interests, languages known, etc.

DEVINSA Database

DEVINSA (Development Information Network for South Asia) is a special database on socio-economic issues related to South Asia. It was prepared by IDRC/JNU and has nearly 20,000 records of periodical articles, books and unpublished material.

National Bibliographic Database

DELNET undertook the compilation of the National Bibliographic Database with the support of the Department of Culture, Government of India in 1998 as a Pilot Project. Fifty thousand records of books: 20,000 in English, 15,000 in Tamil and 15,000 in Punjabi were created at the Punjabi University, Patiala and International Institute of Tamil Studies, Chennai. Another fifty thousand records were also created at Andhra University Library, Visakhapatnam and Asiatic Society of Bombay, Mumbai in English, Telugu, Marathi and Sanskrit. We also created about 50,000 records at the Asiatic Society in Kolkata and Sahitya Academy Library in New Delhi.

DELNET Services

An Overview

With the high-speed Satellite Communication facilities of NIC spread across the country and the growth of Internet Service Providers, DELNET is finding itself in a better position now to let researchers, scholars and readers in the country access about 60,00,000 bibliographic records withholding data through more than 1050 libraries in India and six other countries. These resources are growing everyday as an increasing number of libraries join DELNET from different parts of India and outside India and as they send their records in machine-readable form for merging into the DELNET union catalogues.

The following is the breakup of the DELNET databases:

1.	Union Catalogue of Books	50,50,078
2.	Union Catalogue of Periodicals	19,289
3.	Union List of Current Periodicals	25,252
4.	Articles Database	8,84,115
5.	CD-ROM Database	2,281
6.	Union List of Video Recordings	5,000
7.	Union List of Sound Recordings	748
8.	Database of Theses and Dissertations	44,304
9.	Specialists' Database	2,000
10.	Urdu Manuscripts	210
11.	Union List of Newspapers	70
12.	DEVINSA	20,000
	Total	60,50,347

Important Links

DELNET offers links to Engineering & Technology E-Journals: Table of Contents, Cambridge Dictionaries Online, GISTNIC Databases, ENVIS: Environmental Information System, US Patents: Full Text, Networked Digital Library of Theses and Dissertations, MEDLINE and Other Database of NLM, SARAI: South Asia Resource Access on the Internet and Library of Congress Catalogues.

ILL/Document Delivery Service

Document Delivery Division of DELNET responds to ILL requests of member-libraries for books and periodical articles by delivering documents and photocopies at their institutions through courier/post. This service is provided for specially identified items by users while searching the databases online. The service is being offered to promote resource sharing at the national and international levels. DELNET has published ILL Guidelines for this purpose. Member-Institutions who make use of this service pay an ILL-Online fee of Rs. 4,000 per year to DELNET besides photocopying and postal/courier charges.

Training

DELNET arranges training programmes, lectures, workshops regularly in New Delhi and other parts of India. DELNET also started the organisation of the **National Convention on Library and Information Networking** (NACLIN) every year since 1998. The latest in the series has been NACLIN 2006 which was organized at the University of Jammu from October 27-30, 2006. In 2006 the word 'Knowledge' was added to the title thus making it the **National Convention on Knowledge, Library and Information Networking** (NACLIN). Special concessions are provided to the staff of member-institutions for participation in these programmes.

AICTE-DELNET MOU

We entered into an arrangement with the All India Council for Technical Education (AICTE) in 2001 to network all libraries of technical institutes /colleges approved by AICTE. Under the AICTE-DELNET MOU, it was considered that the modernization and networking of libraries of affiliated institutions of AICTE was important. It was hoped that it will go a long way in offering to the students and staff the best available information on the topics of their study, in introducing resource sharing among the libraries, in acquiring the latest technological inputs for modernising their libraries and in reducing expenditures on buying publications. DELNET has been networking the libraries of the affiliated institutes of AICTE. So far about 700 libraries of AICTE approved technical institutions have joined DELNET.

AICTE began by offering a start-up financial support in terms of admission fee of Rs. 5,000 and annual membership fee of Rs. 7,500 for the first year to each institution that joined DELNET. Details are available at delnet.nic.in and www.aicte.ernet.in

Software Development

In order to modernise and network libraries, DELNET prepared a number of software packages for creating MARC records and for library management purposes. The purpose of creating these packages was to introduce the creation of MARC records and to give software to those libraries that could not afford costly library management software. However, DELNET is not keen to compete with software agencies by introducing more and more features as DELNET is not a software agency. Our objective is help libraries so that they can cross the initial hurdles in library management and database creation work.

DELNET Building

The Jawaharlal Nehru University gave one acre of land to DELNET in 1994 for the construction of its building in JNU Campus. The Ministry of Tourism and Culture gave Rs. 100,00,000 for the construction of the building. In December 2001 the foundation stone for the proposed building was laid by Mr. Jagmohan, the Minister for Tourism and Culture and the function was presided over by Dr. Karan Singh, the Chancellor of Jawaharlal Nehru University. The plan was to construct an administrative block as well as a hostel block in the campus. In October 2005 finally the DELNET moved from the India International Centre to its own building in JNU Campus. By now the construction of the Administrative Block is completed and is operational. The work on the Hostel Block and the campus environs could not be completed owing to lack of finance. We hope to do so as soon as the necessary financial support becomes available for this purpose.

National Knowledge Commission

The Working Group on Libraries of the National Knowledge Commission that completed its report in 2006 recommended that DELNET should network about 25,000 libraries in the next few years. If the report gets the approval of the Central Government and the Planning Commission, we hope to network a large number of libraries.

Conclusion

DELNET has emerged as a major library network in South Asia. Its membership, resources and services are growing. It is an independent body and hopes to serve users associated with the libraries in South Asia and other parts of the world. We hope to make a major contribution to networking knowledge resources and making them available to users in the world.

25

Working together with AGRINET: Agriculture Information Network of Sri Lanka

I. MUDANNAYAKE

Introduction

Agriculture Information Network (AGRINET) was initiated as a sub-network of SLSTINET in 1982 with the prime objective of resource sharing among agricultural libraries in Sri Lanka. The coordination of AGRINET later from the year 1995 was entrusted to the Sri Lanka Council for Agriculture Research Policy (SLCARP) which is the apex body for agriculture research policy planning and funding in the country.

AGRINET over a period of twenty-five (25) years has proved to be effective and active in facilitating the agriculture information flow of the country. There is a great relevance in strengthening agriculture information provision in the country mainly because Sri Lanka is predominantly an agricultural country, although its contributions to the GNP (Gross National Product) in the past two or three decades is declining (from about 40% in early 1950's to 17% in 2005) (Central Bank, 2005) a high percentage (72%) of the total population live in rural areas and 45 per cent of them are engaged in agriculture as their main livelihood (Dharmawardena, 2001).

Further agriculture research pioneered scientific research in Sri Lanka, as the first research institutes which established in the country were for the three main commercial crops, tea (1922), rubber (1910), coconut (1928) and the establishment of the largest research institute in the country the Department of Agriculture in 1911 (Perera,1995).

It is a well accepted fact that agricultural scientists (95% of the total) are engaged in research (Mudannayake,1987) and at present all 517 scientists (100%) excluding universities, in the National Agricultural Research System (NARS) are engaged in research (INFORM, 2006).

All these facts emphasize the necessity and the potential of strengthening the agriculture research system in the country to ensure food security and improve agriculture export earnings and finally, add quality to the lives of the farming communities. Access to agriculture information is pivot to all these developmental efforts. In this context AGRINET can be viewed as a positive development in facilitating scientists to access to information through collaborative programmes of agriculture libraries in Sri Lanka.

Mission of AGRINET

To improve capacity of agricultural libraries for speedy access, exchange and delivery of information required by agricultural scientists in the country through collaborative programs.

Goals

- Promote resource sharing,
- Enhance information skills of the user community,
- Capacity building of library personnel within the network,
- Establishing linkages with national and international information networks.

The AGRINET membership consists of twenty-five (25) agricultural libraries including research and academic libraries which are noted below:

- Department of Agriculture Library
- Department of Export Agriculture Library
- Forest Department Library
- Tea Research Institute Library
- Rubber Research Institute Library
- Coconut Research Institute Library
- Hector Kobbekaduwa Agrarian Research and Training Institute Library
- Sugarcane Research Institute Library
- Veterinary Research Institute Library
- Institute of Post Harvest Technology Library
- National Aquatic Resources Research and Development Agency Library

- Sri Lanka Council for Agriculture Research Policy Library
- Agriculture Library of University of Peradeniya
- University of Colombo
- University of Ruhuna
- University of Sri Jayawardenapura
- University of Wayamba
- University of Rajarata
- University of Kelaniya
- University of Batticaloa
- Industrial Technology Institute
- National Science Foundation
- International Water Management Institute

Management of a information network is crucial for making all stakeholders including librarians, supporting staff and institutional heads to be committed and to extend the fullest cooperation for achieving the expected goals. The AGRINET is managed under three levels. AGRINET functions as a thrust area of the Sri Lanka Council for Agriculture Research Policy (SLCARP) and the Council library acts as the focal point. The AGRINET advisory committee consists of nine librarians, representing a good cross-section of agricultural disciplines such as animal science, forestry, food science and aquaculture. The advisory committee is responsible for coordinating, setting priorities, planning and reviewing the programmes of the network. All AGRINET librarians are responsible for managing AGRINET activities at local level.

AGRINET On-going Programmes

Selective Dissemination of Journal Content Page Service (SDCP)

Access to scientific journals is increasingly important for scientists to engage in research and development in terms of benefits to the national economy. Sri Lanka has a long record of experiences with stringent budgets for libraries and low funding for research which handicaps the research capabilities of the scientists and the research culture of the country.

At the time of the initiation of AGRINET, the outcome of a need survey for scientific journals conducted with scientists in eight leading research institutes revealed that only 25 per cent of the required journals were available in the country (Perera, 1982).

This situation led librarians to develop a mechanism to share the journal holdings available in the country and to increase access to information. The SDCP service was planned out by compiling a union list of journals and identifying journal requirements of each and every scientist in participating institutions. Librarians are responsible for exchanging journal content pages within the network and the content pages are directed to their respective researchers and document delivery or full papers are provided on the basis of requests.

There is a positive need to continue the journal content page service of AGRINET because the journal content page is the only source of current information for a substantial number of agriculture researchers who are stationed in remote areas where they have no or very limited access to libraries or the Internet for information.

At present about 400 journal titles are being shared by agricultural scientists in the country under this programme. The current union list of AGRINET periodicals with the publisher's URL's is placed at the web site of the SLCARP (URL http://www.slcarp.lk) for easy access to journal content pages for those who have the Internet connections.

The journal union list reflects a good cross-section of discipline-wise information needs of the agricultural scientists at national level, because scientists are involved with journal selections at their respective institutions.

The AGRINET SDCP service continues as a core programme with positive responses and the interests of the end users—the scientific community.

Bibliographic Utilities

The AGRINET has taken the leadership in the production of bibliographic utilities at national level, as a measure taken for consolidation and dissemination of scientific information generated within the country to all agricultural scientists.

The most important initiative undertaken by AGRINET is the compilation of the National Agriculture Bibliography of Sri Lanka.

A national bibliography is an archival record of intellectual activity of a nation. One of the common challenges faced by scientists in developing countries is the barriers to access to local contents. In Sri Lanka the research outputs and intellectual efforts of scientists are scattered and limited in accessibility. As an example the academic research is not widely spread among scientists in other institutes due to various reasons.

In this respect a national entry point to access local agriculture information cross cutting institutional boundaries is an essential initiative for strengthening the information flow of the country.

The National Agriculture Bibliography is compiled by incorporating all bibliographic data transferred by participating libraries in the network. All libraries are expected to send data to the AGRINET focal point, the SLCARP library in electronic format.

All libraries use a common library software (CDS/ISIS) developed by the UNESCO and a common data base format to exchange data within the network. The focal point library produces the National Agricultural Bibliography in print and in electronic format by merging all data together. The participating libraries receive the compilation (print and electronic versions) free of charge.

In addition, subject and commodity based bibliographic utilities are also produced by AGRINET in the same manner with the help of participating libraries in the network. Bibliographies on commodities which were on the national agenda for increasing production were chosen by AGRINET to produce bibliographic utilities.

AGRINET has produced commodity based bibliographies for tropical fruits such as banana, pineapple, papaya, mango and covering areas such as goat rearing, organic agriculture, drought and indigenous knowledge which has a national focus. These bibliographies are very helpful for researchers as full documents can be accessed within the country. The AGRINET is looking forward to make the bibliographic utilities accessible on the web.

User Seminars/Trainings for Agricultural Scientists

The AGRINET acts as a facilitator for promoting awareness on agriculture information available and accessible in the country and enhancing the information skills of the end users. The strategy adopted by the AGRINET on this is organizing user seminars at various agriculture research institutes targeting agriculture scientists in that particular area.

AGRINET has conducted user seminars in all parts of the country except North and East because of the conflict situation in the country. The seminars focus on facilitating the agriculture scientists to become aware of information bases available at AGRINET member libraries and how to access them. The seminars include CD-ROM and Internet demonstrations too.

An introduction to on-line access to scientific and scholarly information resources of the PERI (Programme for the Enhancement of Research Information) programme of the INASP (International Network for the Availability of Scientific Publications) has been a regular feature of the AGRINET user seminar agendas of recent times. INASP has been the most important web based information initiative for scientists in Sri Lanka, to increase access mostly to full texts of information across the world freely bridging the digital divide.

AGRINET is paying special attention in selecting venues for user seminars in recent times where they have good network connections specially because of providing hands on trainings to participants.

The hands-on trainings focus on effective use of different search techniques in different web based interfaces. The participants of the seminar are provided with information on how to get registered for PERI on-line information facilities.

The AGRINET user seminar has become an effective platform for scientists to interact with AGRINET librarians on their concerns and issues over access to information. The feedback of each AGRINET user seminar reveals that the seminars are very useful for the agricultural scientists to expand their knowledge and capacities on information. The main drawback to access on-line resources specially PERI initiatives in Sri Lanka is lack of infrastructure in agriculture research institutes located in remote areas and low funding for information.

Information Retrieval Services of AGRINET

The AGRINET focal point at the Sri Lanka Council for Agriculture Research Policy, subscribes to a number of costly CD-ROM data bases such as TEEAL (The Essential Electronic Agriculture Library) CABI CD-ROMS etc. for facilitating all AGRINET member libraries in literature searching and document delivery. Some of the costly CD-ROM databases are subscribed by the AGRINET member libraries for sharing the resources collectively.

Training of AGRINET Member Librarians

The AGRINET conducts training programmes for AGRINET member librarians specially on information technology for enhancing professional development of the members. The librarians are trained on handling and managing their library databases which were developed on a common software. The regular AGRINET meetings provide a good platform for librarians to interact with each other, discuss, exchange of ideas and opinion.

The twenty-five years experience in working together in a network helped all AGRINET librarians to evaluate the strengths and weaknesses of the information resources, services, infrastructure etc. available in their libraries as well as in other member libraries for optimization of information services. The success and the continuation of the network is due to the commitment and positive cooperation extended by all stakeholders of the network mainly the librarians, heads of institutes, and specially the Sri Lanka Council for Research Policy for the financial support given for all programmes. AGRINET is seen as a positive development with much potential in enhancing the agriculture information flow of the country.

References

Central Bank of Sri Lanka. (2006). *Annual Report 2005*. Colombo: Central Bank. Colombo: SLCARP.

Dharmawardena, H.S. (2001). *Sri Lanka: In Rural Tranformation in the Asia and the Pacific*, 234-253. Tokyo: APO.

INFORM 2004: Information for agriculture research managers (2006).

Mudannayake, Irangani (1989). Information needs and information practices of agricultural scientists in Sri Lanka. Peradeniya: PGIA. (PGIA occasional Publication; no.3).

Perera, M.J.C. (1982). Agriculture information network AGRINET in Sri Lanka. Unpublished.

—— (1995). Development of scientific information services in Sri Lanka: a perspective with special reference to Sri Lanka. *Sri Lanka Library Review* 9, no.1&2 (March): 43: 53.

Yapa, N.U.(1995). Library Neworks. *Library News*.16, no.3 (July-Sept.): 16-21.

26

Access to E-Resources and Scholarship: Role of Library Consortia in India

R.K. BHATT

Introduction

No library is an island, irrespective of its size and resources. Shared working practice has, therefore, emerged in the last few decades and it includes interlibrary loan arrangements and programmes to lend documents to other institutions for display/exhibitions and use. Libraries, thus, have a long tradition of working together. Collaborative arrangements for the acquisition and management of electronic information resources can result in lower prices and saving in terms of actual cost, time and staff. A most important development for academic libraries, thus, has been a change from organizational self-sufficiency to a collaborative approach. This trend can clearly be seen from a rapid growth of library consortia. The concept of "consortium" perhaps originated or evolved from the concepts of co-operation, co-ordination and collaboration. One of the purposes of the consortia is to reduce the cost of collection development, particularly the cost of electronic indexes and journals.

Library Consortia

Objectives examine and review national and international issues such as pricing policies and copyright law.

- Bring pressure on commercial publishers to reduce the "growth rate" in the cost of information and to bring down the unit cost of information.

- Encourage access and sharing of unique and special collection which are available in member libraries.
- Recognize few libraries, so that they can take the responsibility of developing and maintaining collection which are of archival value.

The ability of consortia to achieve these objectives entirely depend upon the co-operation and commitment from member libraries, of course, it also depends upon the co-operation and commitment from publishers, as well as on availability of funds. There is no single model for consortia approach. Models vary from a highly decentralized to centralized system. The library consortia, thus, may be grouped as:

- ➢ Large consortia concerned primarily with computerized large scale technical processing (like OCLC);
- ➢ Small consortia with user services and every day problems (for campuses); and
- ➢ Consortia based on a principle of "co-operation", with respect to special subject areas, interlibrary loan, reference service, etc. These are also referred to as limited purpose consortia.

Cooperation amongst institutions for sharing the library resources is being practiced for decades. Traditionally, primary purpose of establishing a library consortium is to share physical resources including books and periodicals, amongst members. However, the mode of cooperation has gone under a transformation with infusion of new information technologies from print-based environment to digital environment. The emergence of Internet, particularly the World Wide Web (WWW) as a new media of information delivery triggered proliferation of Web-based full text on-line resources. Increasing number of publishers are using the Internet as a global way to offer their publications to the international community of scientists and technologists. The technology provides an unparalleled media for delivery of information with greater speed and economy. The library and information centres, as heavy consumers of electronic journals and on-line databases, stand to benefit greatly from this technology driven revolution. The availability of IT-based electronic information products are exerting ever-increasing pressure on libraries, which, in turn, are committing larger portions of their budgetary allocation for either procuring or accessing Web-based on-line full-text search services, CD-ROM products and on-line databases. The libraries with their diminishing or at the best static financial allocations, have to consider new ways to consolidate global resources amongst them in order to maximize their limited financial resources. The combination of these developments have resulted in development of "Shared Subscription" or "Consortia based Subscription" to journals everywhere in the world.

A very high degree of correlation has been observed between the number of journals available to researchers in a given scientific organization and the scientific productivity of researchers and research organization in terms of numbers of research articles produced. Our country has witnessed a sharp and persistent decline in number of research journals subscribed by educational and research institutions across the country for past two decades. As a result, the total research productivity of the country, in terms of numbers of articles produced by our researchers has declined by more than 2 per cent in past one decade whereas the research productivity of other Asian countries like China and South Korea has actually increased by 2-3 per cent in the last one decade. It can be ascertained that these countries have increased their subscription base substantially in past two decades.

Shared Subscription or Consortia-based subscription to electronic resources through consortia of libraries, on the one hand, permits successful deployment and desktop access to electronic resources at a highly discounted rates, on the other hand, it meets with the increasing pressures of diminishing budget, increased user demands and rising cost of journals. The library consortia on the basis of sheer strength of numbers of institutions, offer healthy business growth opportunities to the electronic publishers and thus attract the best possible price and terms of agreement. With this welcome change, the libraries all over the world are forming consortia of all types and at all levels with an objective to take advantage of current global network to promote better, faster and more cost effective ways of providing electronic information resources to the information seekers. GALILIO (Potter *et al.*,1996), OhioLink (Kohl, 1997), TexShare (Martin, 1996), VIVA (Perry, 1995) and SUNY Connect (1999) are some of the well-known library consortia.

Library Consortia: Indian Scenario

The detailed description about the consortia that are in operation in India is described below:

- INDEST Consortium,
- UGC INFONET (UGC, Government of India),
- IIM Consortia (Consortium of all IIM institutions in India),
- CSIR Consortia (Consortium of all CSIR Laboratories in India),
- FORSA (Forum for Resource Sharing in Astronomy and Astrophysics),
- Consortium of Ministry of Communications and Information Technology Library and Information Systems for Resource Sharing and Creating a Digital Library,

- Rajiv Gandhi University of Health Sciences, Bangalore—Consortia,
- DAE Consortia (Department of Atomic Energy, Government of India Consortia),
- Indian National Digital Library in Engineering Science and Technology (INDEST)—AICTE Consortium (http://paniit.iitd.ac.in/ indest).

The Ministry of Human Resource Development (MHRD) has set-up the "Indian National Digital Library in Engineering Sciences and Technology (INDEST) Consortium" on the recommendation made by the Expert Group appointed by the Ministry under the chairmanship of Prof. N. Balakrishnan. This consortium consists 38 centrally funded government institutions including IITs, IISc, Bangalore, NITs, IIITs and IIMs. These 38 members are the core members of the INDEST consortium. Besides, 43 Government or Government-aided engineering colleges and technical departments in universities have joined the Consortium with financial support from the AICTE. The Ministry provides funds required for providing differential access to electronic resources subscribed for the consortium to the core members through the consortium headquarters set up at Indian Institute of Technology, Delhi. Moreover, the INDEST Consortium, as an open-ended proposition, welcomes other institutions to join it on their own for sharing benefits it offers in terms of highly discounted rates of subscription and better terms of agreement with the publishers. All electronic resources being subscribed are available from the publisher's Website. The Consortium has an active mailing list and a Web site hosted at the IIT Delhi.

The INDEST Consortium is the most ambitious initiative taken so far in the country. The benefit of consortia-based subscription to electronic resources is not confined to 38 major technological institutions in the country but is also extended to all educational institutions under its open ended proposition. 43 Government/ Government-aided Engineering Colleges are provided access to selected electronic resources with financial support from the AICTE and 60 engineering colleges and institutions have already joined the consortium under its open-ended scheme. The total number of members in the Consortium has now grown to 141. The INDEST Consortium, on the basis of sheer strength of numbers of institutions has attracted the best possible price and terms of agreement from the publisher. The Consortium subscribes to over 6,500 electronic journals from a number of publishers and aggregators. The INDEST Web site hosts a search interface to locate these journals and their URLs as well as their alphabetical list. Some of the advantages to using electronic journals are as follows:

- Consortium subscription allows remote access to its member institutes beyond their dream.
- More than one user at a member institute can use e-journals simultaneously.

- Multidimensional features of e-journals encourage the users to use them round the clock.
- E-Journals are flexible and do not require physical processing, storage space and even environmentally valuable.
- Access to archival issues is available and CDs are supplied to member institutes for future use also.
- Consortium member Institutes can create their own digital library and accessible e-resources can also made available besides their own digital collections to serve the end users.
- Facilitates member institutes to view full-text of articles online; send e-mail or photocopy request for an article of their choice, which is not available at their library.

Users of the member institutions can create their own TOC that alerts through them by e-mail the TOC for the latest issue of their favourite journals and selected journals of their choice can be added to their personal MyTOC profile.

Optimum utilization is guaranteed and thus more research and development activities are being geared up for the development of the country.

Major Activities of the INDEST-AICTE Consortium:

(1) To arrange subscription to identified electronic resources for member institutions;
(2) Identification of new resources;
(3) Interaction with member libraries to ensure optimal utilization of subscribed electronic resources;
(4) Ensure access to subscribed electronic resources to member libraries as per their subscription;

- Organize training programme for the member institutions on use of electronic resources;
- Initiate additional activities complementary to the present activities of the Consortium; and
- Encourage interactions amongst member libraries.

Electronic Resources Subscribed by the Consortium

Electronic resources subscribed by INDEST-AICTE Consortium can broadly be divided into Full text Electronic Resources and Bibliographic Databases. The member institutions are provided with differential access to these resources on their needs and activity profile.

Sl. No	Full Text Resources and URL	Accessible to
1.	ABI/INFORM Complete (http://www.il.proquest.com/pqdauto)	IITs, (Except IITG) IISc, IIMs, NITIE, IIITMs
2.	ACM Digital Library (http://portal.acm.org/portal.cfm)	IITs, IISc, NITs, ISM, SLIET, NERIST, IIMs, NITIE, IIITMs
3.	ASCE journals (http://.pubs.asce.org/journals/jrns.htm)	IITs, IISc, NITs, ISM, SLIET. NERIST
4.	ASME Journals (http://www.asme.org/pubs/journals/)	IITs, IISc, NITs, ISM, SLIET. NERIST
5.	Captaline (http://capitaline.com/intranet/INDEST_consortium.htm)	IITs,(Except IITG) IISc, IIMs,
6.	CRIS INFAC Industry Information Service (http:www.risil.com/)	IIMs
7.	EBSCO Databases (http://search.epnet.com/)	IITs, (Except IITG) IISc, IIMs,
8.	Elsevier's Science Direct (http://sciencedirect.com/)	IITs, IISc, IIMs, selected from NITs, ISM, SLIET, NERIST
9.	Emerald Full-text (http://iris.ermeraldinsight.com/)	IITs,(Except IITG) IISc, IIMs,
10.	Euromonitor (GMID) (http://www.euromonitor.com/gmid	IITs (Except IITG), IISc, IIMs,
11.	Complete IEEE/IEE Electronic Library Online (IEL) http://ieeexplore.ieee.org/	IITs, IISc, NITs, IIITs
12.	Indian Standards (Intranet version)	IITs,(Except IITG), IISc, NITs, SLIET, NERIST
13.	Insight http://www.insight.asianerc.com/	IIMs
14.	Nature http://www.nature.com/	IITs, IISc, NITs, ISM, SLIET, NERIST
15.	Proquest Science (ASTP) (http://www.il.proquest.com/pqdauto)	NITs, ISM, SLIET, NERIST, IIITs, IIITM
16.	Springer Verlag (http://www.springerlink.com/)	IITs, IISc, NITs, ISM, SLIET, NERIST, IIITs, IIITMs
	BIBLIOGRAPHIC DATABASES	
17.	Compendex Plus (http://www.ei.org/ev2/home)	IITs & IISc
18.	INSPEC on Ei Village: http://www.ei.org/ev2/home	IITs & IISc
19.	J-Gate Custom Content for Consortia (JCCC) (http://jccc-indest.inoformindia.co.in/)	NITs, ISM, SLIET, NERIST, IIITs and IITMs can have access to all the journals subscribed by all the IITs and IISc.,
20.	JET (http://jet.informindia.co.in)	AICTE supported (Selected)
21.	MathSciNet (http://www.ams.org/mathscinet)	IITs & IISc
22.	SciFinder Scholar (http://www.cas.org/SCIFINER/SCHOLAR/index.html) (access through a Z39.50 Client to be installed on each PC)	IITs & IISc
23.	Web of Science (http://isiknowledge.com/)	IITs & IISc

Governance

The Consortium operates through its headquarters at IIT Delhi, under a National Steering Committee consisting of members from amongst beneficiary institutions under the Chairmanship of Prof. R.S. Sirohi, Director of IIT Delhi. A National

Review Committee has also been set-up under the Chairmanship of Shri V.S. Pandey, Joint Secretary (Technical Education) with an overall responsibility for making policies, monitoring the progress, coordinating with UGC and AICTE for promoting the activities of INDEST Consortium.

UGC INFONET (http://web.inflibnet.ac.in/)

UGC-INFONET was formally inaugurated by the Hon'ble Prime Minister on 28th December, 2002. UGC is modernizing the university campuses with state-of-the-art campuswide networks and setting up its own nationwide communication network named UGC-INFONET. The UGC-INFONET will ride on ERNET infrastructure to provide assured quality service and optimal utilization of bandwidth resources. The project is being funded by the UGC with 90 per cent capital investment and 100 per cent recurring cost during the Xth Plan period. A Joint Technical and Tariff Committee (JTTC), consisting of leading experts in the country has been set up to guide and monitor the entire project. INFLIBNET Centre, an autonomous IUC of the UGC, is the nodal agency for co-ordination of the UGC–INFONET and facilitates linkage between ERNET and the universities. UGC INFONET will be a boon to the higher education system in several ways:

- It will become a vehicle for distance learning.
- It will be a tool to distribution of education material and journals to remotest of areas.
- It will be a resource for researchers and scholars for tapping most up-to-date information.
- It will form a medium for collaboration among teachers and students, not only within the country but all over the world.
- It will be on Intranet for university automation.
- It will establish a channel for globalization of education.

The Consortium has started offering its services from January 2001 onwards. Now 119 universities joined in the consortia get access to electronic resources and others are expected to join and the following are E-Resources subscribed by the UGC-infonet consortium.

Sl. No.	Full Text Resources	URLs
1.	American Chemical Society	http://pub.acs.org/
2.	Royal Society of Chemistry	http://www.rs.org
3.	Nature	http://www.nature.com
4.	Institute of Physics Publishing	http://www.iop.org/EJ
5.	Cambridge University Press	http://journals.cambridge.org
6.	Project Muse	http://muse.jhu.edu/journals
7.	Encyclopedia Britannica	http://www.britannica.com
8.	JSTOR	http://www.jstor.org
9.	American Institute of Physics	http://www.aip.org
10.	American Physical Society	http://www.aps.org
11.	Science Online	http://www.scienceonline, org
12.	Annual Reviews	http://www.annualreviews.org
13.	Springer Link Journals	http://www.springerlink.com
14.	Kluwer Online Journals	http://www.kluweronline.com
15.	Emerald Library Science Collections	http://www.emeraldinsight.com/fr
16.	Elsevier Science—Life Science Collection	http://www.sciencedirect.com
17.	Ingenta Gatway Portal	http://gateway.ingenta.com
18.	J-Gate Gateway Portal	http://www.j-gate.informindia.co.in
	Bibliographic Databases	
19.	Chemical Abstracts Service	http://www.cas.org
20.	BIOSIS: Biological Abstract	http://www.biosis.org

IIM Consortia (Consortium of all IIM Institutions in India)

Indian Institutes of Management (IIM) consortia was formed in the year 2000. The objective is to ensure among the IIMs, optimum utilization and enhancement of the resources and to minimize the expenditure by consortia based subscription to the commonly subscribed databases and journals. The idea is to approach the publishers of CD-ROM databases to begin with, as a consortia, for better prices and services. Eventually, other digital databases and journals are also planned to be covered by the programme.

In the case of journals, all the six IIMs put together subscribe to over 2550 scholarly titles of which around 1200 are duplications (overlapping titles). Among these, 33 titles are being subscribed to by all the IIMs. Having convinced on the dire need for a journals consortia, major publishers such as Elsevier (13), Kluwer (14) John Wiley (15), Blackwell (16), Taylor & Francis (17) and MCB University press (Emerald Full Text Intelligent Library) were approached and thay all now participate in the consortium. The end result has been highly praiseworthy and for over 777 E-journals IIMs are able to get online access, across all the IIMs, by paying a nominal additional amount.

IIM Consortium Resources

With the formation of the IIM Library Consortium since 2000, it has been strengthening year after year. The IIMs now have a strong digital information base in the light of the content license (electronic access) it has been able to obtain under the IIM Consortium. The IIM consortia has the following information base:

Two aggregated full text E-Journal databases, i.e. Business Source Premier of EBSCO (approx. 3000+ journals) and ABI/INFORM of Proquest (approx. 2000+ journals), having a wide journal coverage of around 4000 unique titles. (Now being provided through INDEST consortium).

About half a dozen bibliographic, Company/Industry (corporate) databases (national and as well as international), and value added information services.

Over 700 E-journals covering most of the outstanding publishers in Management such as Blackwell, Kluwer, Taylor & Francis, etc. are already under subscription and John Wiley is underway to take the number of titles to more than 1000 by 2005.

This scholarly resource base is a vast wealth of information and is highly vital, invaluable and voluminous that it is essential for the consortia to the future use by the IIMs. IIMs are also part of the INDEST Consortium. They subscribe to the following resources under this consortium:

- IEL Online Library (175 journals),
- ABI/INFORM complete (2004 journals),
- ACM Digital Library (30 Journals),
- CRIS INFAC,
- Asian Cerc/Insight,
- India Informer,
- EBSCO,
- Emerald Insight,
- Capitaline,
- Euromonitor,
- JCCC,
- Elsevier Science Direct,

CSIR Consortia (Consortium of all CSIR Laboratories in India)

Council of Scientific and Industrial Research (CSIR), is a society registered under the Society Registrations Act XXI of 1860 and is one of the largest government funded R&D organization in India with a chain of 38 laboratories spread across the country. CSIR has about 5000 active researchers, who are responsible for pioneering research in all aspects of scientific and industrial research covering broadly Chemical, Physical, Biological, Information, Environmental and Engineering Sciences and Technologies. CSIR's research output in terms of publication compares well with the leading scientific institutions such as IISc, Bangalore, TIFR, Mumbai and IITs. CSIR spends annually about 25 crores for journal subscriptions alone. Put together, all the 38 Labs of CSIR subscribe to as many as 3356 foreign research and scholarly journal titles annually. Most of the Library and Information centers of CSIR are well equipped with good IT infrastructure, network facility and high speed Internet connectivity.

The factors mentioned in the previous paragraph prompted for the creation of the CSIR consortia. The first ever consortia concept in the country was conceived at a meeting of Heads of CSIR Libraries and Information Centres held at NAL, Bangalore during 1993 itself. The purpose was to create exhaustive bibliographic databases covering major five disciplines of S&T using the rich journal resources of all CSIT—Library and Information centers. NAL took the initiative during 1999 itself to form a consortia "COMSAC (Consortia for Material Science and Aerospace Collections)" for giving access to 14 bibliographic databases of Cambridge Scientific Abstracts (CSA) covering the subjects Aerospace and Materials Sciences. This did not sustain for a long time as the consortia concept was new at that time and only three institutes paid their share.

Rajiv Gandhi University of Health Sciences, Bangalore—Consortia

The Rajiv Gandhi University of Health Sciences launched HELINET (Health Sciences Library & Information Network) Consortium, on the 15th of March 2003. HELINET is the first medical library consortium launched in the country.

The importance and the role of quality medical journals in medical education is known. Moreover, in a survey conducted in early 2002, the colleges of RGUHS were spending enormous amount of money to get only about 150 journals each, and even in those 150, many were duplicates. This spurred the need for reducing the cost while making the core medical journals more affordable and easily accessible.

Thus HELINET was born, with the twin objectives of (a) Networking the libraries in the colleges affiliated to the University to promote resource sharing, (b) To move these libraries gradually to digital main-stream. HELINET's mission is to network all the libraries under RGUHS for minimizing the cost of acquisition and maintenance of learning resources and maximizing their utilization, among the faculty, students and researchers the colleges and institutions affiliated to the University.

Under the HELINET scheme, the member colleges can get access to around 600 scholarly, international biomedical journals, from 24 leading publishers, at about one-third the price of their print subscription. Moreover, the member colleges can get all time access to the current journals as well as archives, i.e. the back-volumes of journals for a period of 7-10 years. The University has already spent Rs. 2 cores for establishing the consortium on a cooperative e-access model. For this purpose, the university has set up digital library infrastructure for managing and providing access to e-content. Electronic Resources for the Helinet Consortium are:

Elsevier's Science Direct (http://www.sciencedirect.com)
Ovid Biomedical Collection (http://gateway.ovid.com)
Annual Reviews-Biomedical Suite (http://arjournals.annualreviews.org/) Biomedicalsearch.dtl)
DAE Consortia (Deptt. of Atomic Energy, Govt. of India Consortia)

The Department of Atomic Energy (DAE) Consortia is funded and governed by Department of Atomic Energy, Government of India. Various centers which are covered under DAE Consortia are as follows:

Homi Bhabha Centre for Science Education (HBCSE), Mumbai,
National Centre for Radio Astrophysics (NCRA), Pune,
Computational Mathematics Laboratory (CML), Pune,
National Centre for Biological Sciences (NCBS), Bangalore,
TIFR Centre (Mathematics), Bangalore.

FORSA

Forum for Resource Sharing in Astronomy and Astrophysics is a consortium of Indian Institute of Astrophysics, Bangalore, Raman Research Institute, Bangalore, Inter University Centre for Astronomy & Astrophysics, Pune, Physical Research Laboratory, Ahmedabad, State Observatory at Nainital, Uttarakhand, Harish Chandra Research Institute, Allahabad. Currently, 23 Astronomy journals from Kluwer, and the journal "Nature" are accessed electronically, through the Consortium deal by the FORSA members. AIP journals and Blackwell Publishers for MNRAS are being considered by the FORSA.

IUC-DAEF

Inter University Consortium for Department of Atomic Energy Facilities is an autonomous institution of the University Grants Commission established in 1990. It is meant primarily for helping the University academic community in the utilization of major DAE facilities at Bhabha Atomic Research Center, Mumbai, Center for

Advanced Technology, Indore, Variable Energy Cyclotron Center, Kolkata, Institute of Physics, Bhubaneshwar, Tata Institute of Fundamental Research, Mumbai.

Suggestion and Conclusion

Besides the major activities, subscription and identification of new electronic resources; interaction with member institutions; organizing training programs; and encouraging interactions amongst member libraries, by both the INDEST Consortium and UGC-Infonet, and other Consortia, the following suggestions may be considered to ensure effective and optimal utilization of subscribed electronic resources.

Increased availability of computer systems and direct links to e-journals from the member institution's Library OPAC may be considered.

It would be desirable if studies are undertaken to evaluate the usage and usability of electronic resources in the member institutions Consortium and findings could be compared with each other's to know the issues and challenges.

Month-wise usage reports for electronic journals could be measured using log on file system by the Consortium to prove the statistics being provided by the publishers or Aggregators concerned to support future electronic resources building.

Information professionals have to conduct more awareness programs to market the new electronic journals services at their respective institutions. Information center Web-site, Intranet, Newsletters, Strategic pages of the institutions highlighting services responsive to user requirements may be created by placing articles, net based posters and notices about the electronic journal service.

Networking with thought leaders, influential persons in other departments and engaging them to spread the word about the electronic journals services may be considered.

Some E-resources are duplicated by Indian Consortia. The one of the concepts of Consortium subscription is to avoid redundant expenses and duplication of subscription.

In addition, Government of India also took special initiatives on citizen-IT Interface for which government has undertaken the re-engineering of their existing processes. Re-engineering of Government processes includes:

(1) India has already begun the process of re-engineering of the existing government processes and procedures essential to bring about transparency in working, reducing bureaucratic controls, increasing efficiency and productivity, reducing cost of service delivery, etc. Integration of projects across various departments to provide a single point of contract for citizens for delivery of services electronically is essential.

(2) In order to maintain the transparency in governance, India began to develop the Citizen charters of each and every government department and make it available over the Net.

(3) The Freedom of Information Act has been enacted thus ensuring right of citizen to have access to information.

(4) IT-Responsive State Governments have begun to utilize the concept of Business Process Re-engineering (BPR) to align the IT with business requirements of Government Departments, and focus of citizen as a customer to deliver one-stop integrated services.

(5) India has initiated a process of establishing a National Institute of SMART Government on all issues concerning IT-supported governance. Electronic Governance Institutes throughout the world are concerned with public policy, cyber law, economic development, delivery of services to citizens, constituency relationships and replacing industrial age institutions with the electronic art of governance, i.e. through digital age technologies and networks.

References

Ashok Jambhekar, Paul Pandian, and Dinesh K. Gupta, Partnership for Success: A case of IIMs libraries' consortia model, ALA Archive Site, http://archive.ala.org/work/international/jambhekar.html, accessed on September 21, 2004.

Charlton, G. Electronic Resources and documentary consortia: A survey of French scientific institutions. *Journal of Librarianship and Information Science*. 33(2) 2001; 85

http://www.google.com/CSIR consortium

Jagdis Arora and Ashok K. Rai, Indian National Digital Library in Engineering Sciences and Technology (INDEST) Consortium, Using Electronic Resources: A Compendium for INDEST Member Institutions, INDEST Consortium, IIT Delhi, New Delhi, 2004

Jagdis Arora and Pawan Agrawal, Indian National Digital Library in Engineering Sciences and Technology (INDEST) Consortia-Based Subscription to Electronic Resources for Technical Education Systems in India: A Government of India Initiative. http://dlist.sir.arizona.edu/archive/00000246/01/3.htm, accessed on September 12, 2003

Jagdish Arora, Indian National Digital Library in Engineering Science and Technology (INDEST): A Proposal for strategic Cooperation for Consortia-based access to electronic Resources, *Intl. Inform. & Libr. Rev.* (2003), 35, 1-17

Murthy, TAV, Access to Scholarly Journals and Database: UGC-Infonet E-Journals Consortium, *University News*, Vol.42, No.2, Aug 23-29, 2004.

27

Information Resources on South Asia: Printed, Online and Digital

TELLA RAMADEVI

Indroduction

South Asia is one of the prominent subcontinents that have attracted worldwide popularity. It consists of Bangladesh, Bhutan, India, Maldives, Nepal, Pakistan, and Sri Lanka. People in South Asia speak hundreds of languages, follow different religions, and have diverse costumes and foods. Because of its ancient history, civilization, variety of cultures and complex society, academicians from all over the globe are becoming more involved in teaching and research on various aspects of South Asia. Most recently, a number of universities in United States and Canada have experienced a tremendous increase in the enrollments by undergraduate as well as graduate students of South Asian ancestry that are taking courses dealing with their own heritage and traditions. To support teaching and research in the academic institutions, libraries have developed good collections of printed and microforms resources. In recent years there has been a huge proliferation of electronic and web resources on South Asia.

A number of online databases have been developed on South Asia, but most of these are in the area of science and technology. There is utmost need for more online resources in the areas of social sciences, humanities and arts. Efforts should be made to produce some qualitative web sites in various South Asian languages.

There are many web resources on South Asian Studies. I attempted to present herewith the resources useful for the academicians, research scholars who are perusing research on South Asian Studies. I have attempted to collect various Internet resources on South Asian Studies. I have also visited few of the South Asian Libraries in USA in the year 1999 and 2003:

Libraries with Major South Asia Collections,
http://www.columbia.edu/cu/libraries/indiv/area/sarai/LIBS.html
Database of and links to UK libraries with Asian Studies collections
(http://www.asiamap.ac.uk/index.php
India and Bangladesh Library Contacts (National Library of Australia)
http://www.nla.gov.au/southasia/contact.html
CONSORTIA of South Asia Libraries (SARAI)
http://www.columbia.edu/cu/lweb/indiv/southasia/cuvl/consort.html
British Library Oriental & India Office Collections
http://www.bl.uk/collections/asiapacificafrica.html
Cambridge University Centre of South Asian Studies
http://www.lib.cam.ac.uk/deptserv/manuscripts/collections.html
Cleveland Public Library,
http://www.cpl.org/sdi-special-collections.asp#Orientalia
Columbia University,
http://www.columbia.edu/cu/lweb/indiv/southasia/index.html
Cornell University, http://www.library.cornell.edu/Asia/sa.html
Harvard University, http://lib.harvard.edu/catalogs/hollis.html
Library of Congress, Southern Asia, Section
http://www.loc.gov/acq/devpol/colloverviews/south-asia.html
National Archives of India, http://www.nationalarchives.nic.in/
National Library of Australia, http://www.nla.gov.au/niac/libs/sasia.html
National Library of Bhutan, http://www.library.gov.bt/
Oxford University, http://www.bodley.ox.ac.uk/dept/oriental/iil.htm
School of Oriental & African Studies—SOAS (University of London),
http://www. soas.ac.uk/library/index.cfm?navid=306

South Asia Resources Database: The Australian Union Catalogue of South Asian Library Resources (via Curtin University)
http://recall.curtin.edu.au/ics-wpd/docssaru/sard.htm

(About 250,000 indexed bibliographic records from two files: main file of South Asia holdings in Australian libraries, and MARC records from National Library of Australia which don't have Australian locations. Site includes simple search as well as advanced boolean searching capabilities.)

SVK: Sundarayya Vignana Kendram (Hyderabad, India)
http://www.sundarayya.org/home.html

University of California—Berkeley,
http://www.lib.berkeley.edu/SSEAL/SouthAsia/wsacolle.html
University of Chicago,
http://www1.lib.uchicago.edu/e/index.php3
University of Hawai at Manoa,
http://www2.hawaii.edu/~asiaref/welcome.html#sasia
South Asian Collections of University of Illinois, Urabana-Champaign
http://www.library.uiuc.edu/asx/southwest.htm
University of Michigan Libraries,
http://www.lib.umich.edu/libhome/Area.Programs/South.Asia/
University of Minnesota, Ames Library of South Asia,
http://ames.lib.umn.edu/abames.html
University of Pennsylvania,
http://www.library.upenn.edu/resources/subject/area/southasia/librespenn.html
University of Texas, Austin,
http://www.lib.utexas.edu/subject/area/asia.html
University of Toronto,
http://utcat.library.utoronto.ca:8002/
University of Virginia,
http://www.lib.virginia.edu/area-studies/SouthAsia/sametb.html
University of Washington, http://www.lib.washington.edu/southasia/
University of Wisconsin—Madison,
http://www.library.wisc.edu/guides/SoAsia/
The Wellcome Library, London,
http://www.wellcome.ac.uk/404/404.asp?404;http://www.wellcome.ac.uk/en/old/HOMlib COL.html
South Asian Studies—Networks and Web Resources,
http://www.lib.virginia.edu/area-studies/SouthAsia/Lib/i/salin2004.html

Networks

SAARC—the South Asian Association for Regional Cooperation provides a platform for the peoples of South Asia to work together in a spirit of friendship, trust and understanding. Its documentation center and library, located in New Delhi, provides information services to Member States (http://www.saarc-sec.org).

SAN—the South Asian Network promotes the health and empowerment of people of South Asian origin living in California, and fills a critical service gap in the South Asian Community, which traditionally has been underserved by public interest organizations (http://www.southasiannetwork.org).

SARAI—the South Asia Resource Access on the Internet is hosted by the Columbia University, and is one of the best sources for finding web based information in South Asian studies. It provides useful links to reference and bibliographical resources, e-journals, e-news, e-books, and also International Directory of South Asian scholars (http://www.columbia.edu/cu/lweb/indiv/southasia/cuvl).

SARN—the South Asia Research Network has been created to promote the production, exchange and dissemination of basic research information in the social sciences and humanities. It provides links to electronic publications, research notes, abstracts, research centres, and conferences (http://sarn.ssrc.org).

SASNET—the Swedish South Asian Studies Network is a national network for research, education, and information about South Asia, based at Lund University. It encourages and promotes an open and dynamic networking process, in which Swedish researchers co-operate with researchers in South Asia and globally (http://www.sasnet.lu.se/sasnetf.html).

SAWNET—the South Asian Women Network is a useful medium of communication about South Asian women. It exists entirely in the electronic medium and its mailing list is run by a group of volunteer moderators that reaches over 700 women in four continents. (http://www.umiacs.umd.edu/users/sawweb/sawnet).

INFLIBNET—the Information and Library Network Centre is the product of Indian University Grants Commission, involved in creating infrastructure for sharing information among academic and research institutions. It is a good source for books, serials and theses databases available in university libraries in India (http://www.inflibnet.ac.in/index.jsp).

Projects

CSAL—the Center for South Asian Libraries—is an American overseas research center developed to facilitate scholarly research and teaching on South Asia through improved preservation of and access to the heritage of India, Pakistan, Bangladesh, Bhutan, Nepal, and Sri Lanka. It provides research support facility for American scholars by providing infrastructures and facilities to enhance research effectiveness and the exchange of scholarly information (http://dsal.uchicago.edu/csal).

DSAL—the Digital South Asia Library is a project of the Center for Research Libraries, and provides digital materials for reference and research on South Asia to scholars, public officials, and other users. This project has been funded by the Association of Research Libraries' Global Resources Program with support from the Andrew W. Mellon Foundation. Several languages dictionaries, reference books, and journals have already been digitized and are available free on the web to everyone (http://dsal.uchicago.edu/reference).

SALRP—the South Asian Literary Recordings Project records the voices of prominent authors from the region reading excerpts from their works. Recordings are available in Real media and MP3 formats (http://www.loc.gov/acq/ovop/delhi/salrp/about.html).

SAMP—the South Asia Microform Project is a cooperative program that acquires and maintains a readily accessible collection of unique materials in microform. Materials are collected both through the filming efforts of the project and through the purchase of positive copies of materials filmed by institutions and companies. It strives to cooperate with libraries and archives worldwide in preserving unique or endangered materials for the study of South Asia (http://www.crl.edu/areastudies/SAMP/index.htm).

Universal Library Project—is the result of collaborative efforts of professionals and educationists from India, China and United States. Digitization of materials in South Indian languages has already begun (http://delta.ulib.org/html/index.html).

Vidyanidhi—is a project of Indian doctoral theses database established to evolve as an online resource funded by the Ford Foundation and Microsoft (http://www.vidyanidhi.org.in/home/index.html).

Institutions

AIBS—the American Institute of Bangladesh is a consortium of U.S. Institutions involved in research on Bangladesh; development of educational institutions in Bangladesh; faculty exchanges; and sending U.S. graduate as well as undergraduate student to Bangladesh. (http://www.aibs.net).

AIIS—the American Institute of Indian Studies is a consortium of universities and colleges in the United States at which scholars actively engage in teaching and research about India (http://www.indiastudies.org).

AIPS—the American Institute of Pakistan Studies encourages and supports research on issues relevant to Pakistan and the promotion of scholarly exchange between the United States and Pakistan (http://www.pakistanstudies-aips.org).

AISLS—the American Institute for Sri Lankan Studies was established to foster excellence in American research and teaching on Sri Lanka, and to promote the exchange of scholars and scholarly information between the United States and Sri Lanka (http://www.aisls.org).

Associations

ACSAA—the American Council for Southern Asian Art is a useful source for the study and awareness of the art of South and Southeast Asia. In addition to periodic symposia, usually held every two years, ACSAA pursues these goals through various projects, including its bi-annual newsletter, bibliographies, a color slide project, a microfiche archive and outreach materials (http://kaladarshan.arts.ohio-state.edu/acsaa/hp.html).

ALIVA—the Asia Library & Information Virtual Association is the only virtual association of Asia's library and information professionals. The secretariat is located in Bangkok (http://aliva.org/html/about.html).

ANHS—the Association for Nepal and Himalayan Studies provides a platform for people with wide-ranging interests in the Himalayan region. It aims to raise the profile of the world's highest region, increasing awareness of the unequaled diversity of human and natural worlds within the Himalaya-Hindukush (http://www.macalester.edu/~guneratne/index.html).

BASAS—the British Association for South Asian Studies is the largest academic association in the United Kingdom for the study of India, Pakistan, Bangladesh, Sri Lanka, Nepal, Bhutan, Maldives and the South Asian Diaspora (http://www.staff.brad.ac.uk/akundu/basas).

CONSALD—the Committee on South Asian Libraries and Documentation has been created to develop, organize and coordinate information resources and services in Canada and United States (http://www.lib.virginia.edu/area-studies/South Asia/Lib/consald.html).

ISOSA—the Independent Scholars of South Asia provides an academic "home" for those with a passion for South Asia, a commitment to serious scholarship, and a career path without a tenure track academic position. (http://www.indiastudies.org/isosa).

SAAG—South Asia Analysis Group is a non-profit non-commercial think tank. Its objective is to advance strategic analysis and contribute to the expansion of knowledge of Indian and International security and promote public understanding (http://www.saag.org).

SACAP—the South Asia Cooperative Acquisitions Program is operated by the Library of Congress, New Delhi Office for the benefit of the libraries in Canada and U.S. It identifies, acquires selectively, catalogs and distributes a wide variety of library materials (http://www.locdelhi.org).

SAALG—the South Asia Archives & Library Group consists of representatives of libraries, archives and other institutions in the United Kingdom with specialization in South Asian Studies. Its aim is to acquire books, manuscripts and archival materials (http://www.bodley.ox.ac.uk/users/gae/NCOLR/salg1.htm).

SAJA—the South Asian Journalists Association foster ties among South Asian journalists in North America and improve standards of journalistic coverage of South Asia and South Asian Americans (http://www.saja.org).

SALTA—the South Asian Teachers Association is a professional organization with the mission to encourage a more effective cooperation among instructors and educators of South Asian languages, linguistics, and literatures in colleges and universities in North America (http://ccat.sas.upenn.edu/salta).

SSAS—the Society for South Asian Studies supports advanced research in the history, visual and material culture, ethnography, language, religion and literature. It publishes an annual journal, South Asian Studies. (http://www.britac.ac.uk/institutes/SSAS).

Subscription Databases

AIIEBIP—the All India Index to English Books in Print is the first electronic version of Indian Books in Print that lists thousands of books not found in elsewhere, along with their prices. A Directory of Indian publishers with complete addresses and contact details is also included (http://www.nisc.com/factsheets/qebip.asp).

BAS—the Bibliography of Asian Studies is on-line version of the Bibliography of Asian Studies that contains records on all subjects, especially humanities and social sciences, pertaining to East, Southeast, and South Asia published worldwide from 1971 to the present (http://ets.umdl.umich.edu/b/bas).

DELNET—the Developing Library Network provides a Union Catalogue of books, Union list of current periodicals, CD-ROM Databases, Database of Indian specialists, Database of periodical articles, Union list of video recordings, Urdu manuscripts' database, Database of theses and dissertations on India (http://delnet.nic.in/).

India Statistics—provides an oceanic depth of India-specific socio-economic statistical facts and figures culled from various secondary level authentic sources. Over half-a-million pages of statistical data have been qualitatively analyzed, condensed and presented in a user-friendly format (http://www.indiastat.com).

ISID—Index to Social Sciences Periodicals is the On-line Index to over one hundred Indian Social Science journals and press clippings files of national English dailies. (http://isidev.nic.in/odb.html).

Online Collections

Books—A list of online books available free on the web can be accessed at http://door.library.uiuc.edu/asx/online_books.htm.

Serials—Web based access to online journals can be found at (http://door.library.uiuc.edu/asx/serials.htm#Online).

SALIN—South Asian Libraries & Information Networks is an on-line journal that presents the review of South Asian libraries, information networks, programs and services—http://www.universitypunjabi.org/pages/dlis/salin/salin.htm.

There are two popular sites that provides links to all newspapers published in South Asia—http://door.library.uiuc.edu/asx/online_newspapers.htm, and http://oldsite.library.upenn.edu/vanpelt/collections/sasia/webpapers.html.

South Asian OPACs

As the result of modernization, several libraries in South Asian countries have provided access to their Online Public Access Catalogue (OPAC) from their web sites to benefit researchers from all over the world. A list of some libraries is available at http://www.infolibrarian.com/opac.htm, and http://www.asahi-net.or.jp/~gb4k-ktr/indexeca.htm.

Miscellaneous

Country Studies' site of the University of Illinois Library provides detailed links to South Asian countries (http://door.library.uiuc.edu/asx/country_studies.htm). Countries information can also be accessed at http://www.asiasource.org/profiles/ap_mp_02_southasia.cfm.

Languages Learning Resources (http://door.library.uiuc.edu/asx/languages_resources.htm).

NLSIU—the National Law School Article Index is an index of Indian articles from the current journals being received by the Library, and is available free on-line (http://www.nls.ac.in/lib/articles/index.html).

South Asia Virtual Library—is a directory that keeps track of web based sources for the South Asian section, and is a starting place for exploration, and can be accessed at http://www.columbia.edu/cu/lweb/indiv/southasia/cuvl.

South Asian Libraries & Information Centres—the site provides links to various libraries—http://door.library.uiuc.edu/asx/SA_libraries.htm.

Listing of US and Canadian Libraries with South Asian collections is available at—http://www.columbia.edu/cu/lweb/indiv/southasia/cuvl/LIBS.html

Portal to Asian Internet Resources (PAIR)—http://digicoll.library.wisc.edu/PAIR/

Committed to directing users to Asian area content in the Humanities and Social Sciences, the portal is supported by an impressive complement of area studies scholars, bibliographers and subject selectors based at the libraries of the University of Wisconsin, the University of Minnesota and the Ohio State University.

(*Source*: http://www.lib.virginia.edu/area-studies/SouthAsia/Lib/i/salin2004.html)

Search Engines and Web Directories for Country, Language, or Region-Specific Searches

Australia—Anzwers, http://www.anzwers.com.au/

GoogleAustralia, http://www.google.com.au/

WebWombat, http://www.webwombat.com.au/Yahoo!

Australia and New Zealand, http://au.yahoo.com/index.html?ver=800

Ansearch, http://www.ansearch.com.au/

Malaysia—Cari, http://www.cari.com.my/

Jaring, http://www.jaring.com.my/

New Zealand—Search NZ

http://www.searchnz.com/

Index NZ, http://www.indexnz.com/

China—Gateway2China, http://www.gateway2china.com/

Indonesia—Google Indonesia, http://www.google.co.id/intl/en/

Catcha, http://id.catcha.com/english.phtml

Hong Kong—Timway, http://www.timway.com/welcome.html

South Korea—KoreaInfogate, http://www.koreainfogate.com/

India—123India, http://www.123india.com/

Khoj, http://www.khoj.com/

Google India, http://www.google.co.in/Taiwan-Yam, http://www.yam.com/en/yam/

Afghanistan—AfghanNetwork, http://www.google.co.in/Afghana!, http://www.afghana.com/Afghanistan Online, http://www.afghan-web.com/

Pakistan—GooglePakistan, http://www.google.com.pk/intl/en/Pakistani-Portal, http://www.pakistani.com/PakAvenue, http://www.pakavenue.com/

Search Engine Colossus, (http://coombs.anu.edu.au/WWWVL-AsianStudies.html) Search Engine Guide, (http://www.searchengineguide.com/pages/Regional/) are comprehensive global master directories of local search engines for regional, country, or language-specific searches. Yahoo! provides country-specific, http://dir.yahoo.com/regional/countries/index.html regional, http://dir.yahoo.com/regional/regions/and official government site, http://dir.yahoo.com/Government/Countries/search options. Google offers a comprehensive

Language Tools Page—http://www.google.com/language_tools to search in specific languages or countries, translate text, change language interfaces, or link to country-specific Google sites.

Note: Also see the sections of this site specifically on Australia and New Zealand, http://www2.etown.edu/vl/countspe.html#

China, http://www2.etown.edu/vl/countspe.html#China

India, http://www2.etown.edu/vl/countspe.html#India

Japan, http://www2.etown.edu/vl/countspe.html#Japan and

Taiwan.http://www2.etown.edu/vl/countspe.html#Taiwan

Principal Portals, Web Directories, and Indexes

Asian Studies WWW Virtual Library, http://coombs.anu.edu.au/WWWVL

AsianStudies.html). At the Australian National University, this is a fine global collaborative project which provides access to networked scholarly documents, resources, and information systems in all aspects of Asian studies.

Asian Studies Search Engines, http://www.ciolek.com/SearchEngines.html

Asian Studies WWW Monitor, http://coombs.anu.edu.au/asia-www-monitor.html with searchable database.

Portalto Asian Internet Resources, http://digicoll.library.wisc.edu/PAIR/index.html.

An excellent portal site from the libraries of the University of Wisconsin, the University of Minnesota, and the Ohio State University that provides "more than six thousand professionally selected, cataloged and annotated online resources" about Asia, with tutorials on using Asian and Asian-language online sources.

Other Sites

Asia Business Today, http://www2.etown.edu/vl/asia.html: From the CitiGroup Foundation and the Asia Society, excellent source of information on many aspects of Asia, its role in the world economy, and U.S. relations with the region, with fine country pages and daily briefings by e-mail.

AsiaMedia, http://www.asiamedia.ucla.edu/: Media news and views from the Asia Pacific region, with archives, from the UCLA Asia Institute.

Asia News Network, http://www.asianewsnet.net/: News from a consortium of Asian daily newspapers from many countries, with archives.

Asia Observer, http://www.asiaobserver.com/: Useful and comprehensive site, with selected links and focus on regional news, politics, and economy, plus regional and country backgrounds.

Asia-Pacific Economic Cooperation (APEC), **http://www.apec.org/:** The premier forum for facilitating economic growth, cooperation, trade and investment in the Asia-Pacific region. Information about APEC, the international economics and trade of the region, latest news, official statements, agreements, and more. Hundreds of free publications for download.

Asia Pacific Management Forum-, http://www.apmforum.com/: Outstanding for news, research articles, columnists, and resources on Asian business, from the Asian business resources of Orient Pacific Century, Anbar Management Intelligence, and their business and academic partners. With market research guides by country and searchable links to other substantive online sources.

Asia Pacific Policy Program, http://www.ap.harvard.edu/index.html: From the John F. Kennedy School of Government, Harvard University, a comprehensive Web resource on Asia, with online regional and country material.

Asia Pacific Research Online, http://www.ciolek.com/: From Asian studies specialist T. Matthew Ciolek of the Australian National University, a superb compendium of links to scholarly information related to online research, teaching, and publishing about Asia and related regions and topics.

Asia Regional Information Center, http://aric.adb.org/: Searchable site set up by the Asian Development Bank to provide "an array of regularly updated information about the economic performance and prospects of 16 Asian nations."

Asia Society, http://www.asiasociety.org/index.html: America's leading institution dedicated to fostering communication between Americans and the peoples of Asia and the Pacific. See their excellent.

Asia Source, http://www.asiasource.org/: on culture, business, politics, history, news, reference, languages, experts, links, and Web search.

Asia Profiles, http://www.asiasource.org/profiles/ap_mp_04.cfm: allows you to compare statistical data across Asian countries.

Ask Asia, http://www.askasia.org/: is "an educational website for students and teachers."

Asia Times Online, http://atimes.com/index.html: Excellent, searchable source for news and reports on all aspects of Asia today from an Asian perspective, by country and topic, with archives.

Asian Business Watch, http://www.asianbusinesswatch.com/: Has news on Asian economies, stock markets, special reports and presentations, and business contacts, plus a regional search engine.

Asian Development Bank, http://www.adb.org/: Online data and publications are available from this multilateral development finance institution, including the statistics off the Economics and Statistics, http://www.adb.org/Economics/: Key Indicators of Developing Asian and Pacific Countries, http://www.adb.org/documents/books/key_indicators/.Regional and country data and analysis are available Regions and Countries, http://www.adb.org/Countries/page.

Asian Studies Network Information Center, http://link.lanic.utexas.edu/asnic/: At the University of Texas, with the main objective of assisting those interested in Asia to find information on the Internet about Asia and Asian Studies programs.

Association for Asian Studies, http://www.aasianst.org/: The scholarly professional association open to all persons interested in Asia. Note their Asia Resources on the World Wide Web, http://www.aasianst.org/asiawww.htmand Asian Studies WWW Virtual Libraries, http://www.aasianst.org/library.htm.

Association of Southeast Asian Nations, http://www.aseansec.org/: Information about this major IGO, its activities, its members, and the region as a whole, including its foreign relations.

Central Eurasian Studies World Wide, http://ceswww.fas.harvard.edu/: Large compilation of resources for the study of Central Eurasia, from the Harvard Program on Central Asia and the Caucasus.

Channelnewsasia, http://www.channelnewsasia.com/: Excellent site featuring constantly updated news exclusively from Asia, by category and with special reports, features, and interviews.

Comparative Connections, http://www.csis.org/pacfor/ccejournal.html: An online journal on East Asian bilateral relations from the Center for Strategic and International Studies'.

Pacific Forum, http://www.csis.org/pacfor/.

Council on East Asian Libraries, http://wason.library.cornell.edu/CEAL/: The organization for East Asian librarians in North America, with guides to research on East Asia and information about the Council.

Digital South Asia Library, http://dsal.uchicago.edu/: From the Center for Research Libraries, a compilation of resources for South Asian studies, including references, images, maps, statistics, bibliographies, indexes, books, journals, etc.

East and Southeast Asia: An Annotated Directory of Internet Resources, http://newton.uor.edu/Departments&Programs/AsianStudiesDept/index. From the Asian Studies program at the University of Redlands, excellent annotated links by regional topics and country directories, plus current hot issues.

East-West Center, http://www.eastwestcenter.org/: At the University of Hawaii, "an internationally recognized education and research organization established by the U.S. Congress to strengthen understanding and relations between the United States and the countries of the Asia Pacific region." Some publications and commentary on-line.

EurasiaNet, http://www.eurasianet.org/: News, country information, features, analysis, discussion forums, and weekly bulletin about the region of Central Asia, from the Central Eurasia Project of the Open Society Institute.

Far Eastern Economic Review, http://www.feer.com/: Leading newsweekly for Asian economic and business news and analysis, with searchable archives.

H-Asia Discussion Network, http://www.h-net.msu.edu/~asia/: Part of H-Net Humanities & Social Sciences On-Line, "to enable historians and other Asia, scholars to easily communicate current research and teaching interests; to discuss new articles, books, papers, approaches, methods and tools of analysis; to test new ideas and share comments and tips on teaching... [and] committed to discussing region wide, comparative and professional issues important to scholars of Asia."

Integrated Regional Information Network, http://www.irinnews.org/AsiaFP.ASP: From the UN Office for the Coordination of Humanitarian Affairs, providing searchable news items on crises in Asia.

Korean Studies Internet Resources: http://www.library.ucla.edu/libraries/eastasian/korea.htm#TOC: Useful directory from the Richard C. Rudolph East Asian Library, UCLA.

National Bureau of Asian Research, http://www.nbr.org/: A non-profit, non-partisan U.S. institution that conducts advanced research utilizing the world's premier specialists on Asia and Russia, and serves as the international clearing house on regional expertise and important policy issues. Selected publications online, including the NBR Bulletin.

Access Asia, http://www.satp.org/: for information on contemporary Asian affairs and policy-related issues, links, and a listing of thousands of Asia specialists.

South Asia Resource Access on the Internet, http://www.sawnet.org/: From Columbia University, one of the best South Asia resource gateways on the Web, which is also the World Wide Web Virtual Library for South Asia.

South Asia Terrorism Portal, http://www.satp.org/: From the Institute for Conflict Management, in New Delhi, "information, data, commentary, research, critical assessment and analysis on terrorism, low intensity warfare and sectarian strife in South Asia."

South Asian Women's Network, http://www.sawnet.org/: A forum for those interested in women's issues in the six countries of South Asia, with many topical subsections and a moderated mailing list, based at Concordia University in Canada.

South China Sea World Wide Web Virtual Library, http://community.middlebury.edu/~scs/: Part of the WWW Virtual Library system, "an online resource for scholars and policy-makers interested in South China Sea regional development, environment, and security issues."

Southeast Asian Studies: Online Resources, http://www.ala.org/ala/acrl/acrlpubs/crlnews/backissues2003/february1/southeastasian.htm: Annotated article on Internet resources in the topic, as of February 2003, in full-text and with hypertext links, from the "College and Research Libraries News" of the Association of College and Research Libraries.

United Nations Economic and Social Commission for Asia and the Pacific, http://www.unescap.org/: From the U.N., news, analysis, and statistics about development, population, environmental, and trade issues in Asia and the Pacific.

US-ASEAN Business Council, http://www.us-asean.org/: This organization represents the American private sector and posts business and general news and information about the countries and economic concerns of the Association of Southeast Asian Nations.

World Bank East Asia and the Pacific Information, http:// wbln0018. worldbank.org/eap/eap.nsf: Papers, discussion notes, and reports dealing with the full range of economic, environmental, and social issues facing East Asia and the Pacific today.

World Bank Europe and Central Asia Information, http:// web.worldbank.org/WBSITE/EXTERNAL/COUNTRIES/ECAEXT/0, menuPK:258604~pagePK: 158889~piPK:146815~theSitePK:258599,00.html Papers, discussion notes, and reports dealing with the full range of economic, environmental, and social issues facing Eastern Europe and Central Asia today.

World Bank South Asia Information, http://wbln1018.worldbank.org/sar/ sa.nsf: Papers, discussion notes, and reports dealing with the full range of economic, environmental, and social issues facing South Asia today.

World Wide Web Internet Guide for China Studies, http://sun.sino.uni-heidelberg.de/igcs/: Part of the WWW Virtual Library system, this Internet guide keeps track of leading information facilities on China and has an internal search engine.

Source: http://www2.etown.edu/vl/asia.html

Electronic Resources on South Asia from UW (Metalib), http://metalib.wisconsin.edu

A general listing of indexes and other databases helpful for South Asian Studies.

Subject Indexes

Anthropological Literature, http://digital.library.wisc.edu: (access restricted) is a bibliographic index to articles and essays on anthropology and archaeology, including art history, demography, economics, psychology, and religious studies.

ATLA, http://digital.library.wisc.edu/1711.journals/atlasfto: (access restricted) is a good starting place to look for articles on topics related to South Asian religion.

Bibliography of Asian Studies (BAS), http://ets.umdl.umich.edu/b/bas/ (access restricted) is perhaps the most helpful online index for research on South Asia as it contains citations to articles both from and about South Asia.

Historical Abstracts, http://digital.library.wisc.edu.web/historicalabstracts (access restricted) while quite broad in its coverage, does include many references to studies on South Asian history.

International Index to the Performing Arts (IIPA), http://www.library.wisc.edu/databases/connect/iipaconnect.html (access restricted) is a good starting place to look for articles on South Asian cinema.

Modern Language Association Bibliography, http://collections.chadwyck.com/marketing/index.jsp (access restricted) includes citations to critical works on literature, language, linguistics, and folklore.

Public Affairs Information Service (PAIS), http://metalib.wisconsin.edu (access restricted) indexes journal articles, books and government and IGO documents in the fields of public policy and the social sciences in general.

South Asia Specific Resources

India Office 19th Century Publications Catalog, http://dsal.uchicago.edu/cgi-bin/oioc.py National Bibliography of Indian Literature: 1901-1953,

http://dsal.uchicago.edu/cgi-bin/nbil.py Official Publications of India Catalog, http://www.lib.uchicago.edu/e/su/southasia/off-pubs.html

Religion in South Asia: a select bibliography, http://www.library.wisc.edu/guides/SoAsia/religion/index.html RojaMuttiahResearchLibraryCatalog, http://www.lib.uchicago.edu/e/su/southasia/rmrl.html

SAWNET (South Asian Women's NET), http://www.umiacs.umd.edu/users/sawweb/sawnet/South and Southeast Asia Video Archive, http://digital.library.wisc.edu.dl/SEAvideo

(This resource is no longer updated. For more current video holdings at UW, check Madcat.) South Asian Diaspora Bibliographic Guides, http://www.lib.berkeley.edu/SSEAL/SouthAsia/resource.html

South Asian Diaspora Literaturein English, http://www.lib.washington.edu/Southasia/guides/diaspora.html SouthAsian Women Studies

http://www.lib.washington.edu/Southasia/Women/Urdu Research Centre catalog, http://dsal.uchicago.edu/cgi-bin/urlc.py

Digital Projects

Digital Dictionaries of South Asia, http://dsal.uchicago.edu/dictionaries/

Digital South Asia Library (DSAL), http://dsal.uchicago.edu/

A global collaborative effort to make important and rare South Asian resources available to the international community. Included in DSAL are reference resources, images, maps, statistics, bibliographies, indexes and books and journals.

Guide to the Indexing of South Asian Periodical Literature: http://digicoll.library.wisc.edu/SouthAsiaIndex/ lists if a journal has been indexed and if so, both where and to what extent.

PAIR (Portal to Asian Internet Resources), http://digicoll.library.wisc.edu/PAIR/catalogs select web resources originating from Asia.

SARAI, http://www.columbia.edu/cu/lweb/indiv/southasia/cuvl/

Links to just about anything and everything one might want online regarding South Asia. Included here are bibliographic tools, job announcements, e-newspaper and e-journal links, a directory of scholars working on South Asia and more.

Tibetan and Himalayan Digital Library, http://www.thdl.org/publishes multilingual studies, multimedia learning resources, and creative works concerned with the area's environments, cultures, and histories.

Governmental Information

Governments on the WWW, http://www.gksoft.com/govt/ provides comprehensive lists of websites from South Asian governments:

Bangladesh, http://www.gksoft.com/govt/en/bd.html India, http://www.gksoft.com/govt/en/in.html including

Doordarshan,http://www.ddindia.gov.in/ ElectionCommissionofIndia,http://www.eci.gov.in/

Indian Parliament,http://parliamentofindia.nic.in/Ministry of Finance, http://finmin.nic.in/

Ministry of Home Affairs, http://mha.nic.in/includingtheCensus,http://www.censusindia.net/

National Human Rights Commission, http://nhrc.nic.in/

Supreme Court of India, http://supremecourtofindia.nic.in/

Nepal, http://www.gksoft.com/govt/en/np.html

Pakistan,http://www.gksoft.com/govt/en/pk.html including: Islamic Republic of Pakistan, http://www.pak.gov.pk/Lahore High Court, http://www.lhc.gov.pk/ National Commission on Status of Women, http://new.ncsw.gov.pk/index.php

Sri Lanka, http://www.gksoft.com/govt/en/lk.html

The U.S. Government also publishes information about South Asia online, if somewhat outdated.

CIA Fact Books

Afghanistan, https://www.cia.gov/cia/publications/factbook/geos/af.html

Bhutan, https://www.cia.gov/cia/publications/factbook/geos/bt.html

India, https://www.cia.gov/cia/publications/factbook/geos/in.html

Nepal, https://www.cia.gov/cia/publications/factbook/geos/np.html

Pakistan, https://www.cia.gov/cia/publications/factbook/geos/pk.html
Sri Lanka, https://www.cia.gov/cia/publications/factbook/geos/ce.html
LC Country Studies:
Bhutan, http://lcweb2.loc.gov/frd/cs/bttoc.html
India, http://lcweb2.loc.gov/frd/cs/intoc.html
Nepal, http://lcweb2.loc.gov/frd/cs/nptoc.html
Pakistan, http://lcweb2.loc.gov/frd/cs/pktoc.html
Sri Lanka, http://lcweb2.loc.gov/frd/cs/lktoc.html .
Source: http://www.library.wisc.edu/guides/SoAsia/

Conclusion

The Internet has changed the notion of a Library as a place into a virtual library. A variety of technologies are used for accessing the vast electronic information resources available on Internet and the Web. Internet, a medium as well as a scholarly communication system, is being heralded as the basis of economic salvation for developing nations. Internet has the power to cut across the social and geographical distances and provide free flow of information. It is a development communication tool. In many ways it is a 'leveller' of hierarchies and barriers making it possible to harness information on South Asia.

The coverage of Grey Literature on South Asia is very limited. Grey Literature is that the literature which is not available through regular trade channel and normally available for the limited people, limited persons and limited period such as study reports, case studies, success stories, committee and commission reports, occasional and working papers, proceedings of the workshops, seminars and conferences etc. There is a need to develop databases/electronic resources of Grey Literature which are very useful for the academicians, scholars, trainers and researchers to improve the quality of research and training.

References

Rajwant Chilana. A paper and report on South Asia Library Information Network, February, 2004, also published in the *Asian Studies Newsletter*
http://www.lib.virginia.edu/area-studies/SouthAsia/Lib/i/salin2004.html
http://www.library.wisc.edu/guides/SoAsia/
http://www2.etown.edu/vl/asia.html
http://www.columbia.edu/cu/libraries/indiv/area/sarai/LIBS.html

Part VI
Bibliographical Control

28

Bibliographic Control of Indian Language Publications

T.A.V. MURTHY AND M. KANAKACHARY

Introduction

India is a land of Languages. Language is an important instrument of human communication and interaction. It is a barometer of the cultural development and extension of influence of a community. India is multi-lingual country. According to 1971 census, 1652 mother tongues were reported in India. Out of which 340 are labelled as tribal and classified into 101 tribal languages. Over a 100 tribal mother tongues, which were registered under 1971, census remained unclassified into any tribal languages for want of adequate data. The tribal languages are rich in oral tradition. Some of them do not have any script. Of late, they have adopted for writing purposes either in the Roman script or the script of one of the major Indian languages. The written literature in most of these languages is very scanty.

Languages undergo metamorphosis. They are after all the medium of human interaction. Like humans, they are very rich in associations and enterprises and achievement and complex in their own being. Languages never stand still. They are always in flux, even in apparently dormant parts their lies a restless tic. There is constant change in their sounds, phonology, grammar, semantics and usage.

The Constitution of India has recognized the following 18 Languages for the compilation of Indian National Bibliography (INB).

1. Assamese
2. Bengali
3. English
4. Gujarati
5. Hindi
6. Kannada
7. Konkani
8. Malayalam
9. Manipuri
10. Oriya
11. Punjabi
12. Sanskrit
13. Tamil
14. Telugu
15. Sindhi
16. Urdu
17. Marathi
18. Nepali

But, the INB is running behind the schedule. It needs to be timely brought out and the fascicules in all the languages also need to be brought out and make it available on web-enable mode. So that the research community will be benefited more.

The Government of India has recognized the following 22 Languages for providing document delivery and other services, by the National Academy of Letters (Central Sahitya Academy), New Delhi.

1. Assamese
2. Bengali
3. English
4. Gujarati
5. Hindi
6. Kannada
7. Konkani
8. Malayalam
9. Manipuri
10. Marathi
11. Nepali
12. Oriya
13. Punjabi
14. Sanskrit
15. Tamil
16. Telugu
17. Sindhi
18. Urdu
19. Maithili
20. Dongri
21. Kashmiri
22. Rajasthani

There is an urgent need for effective coordination between Central and Sahitya Academies.

Growth of Publications

There is a tremendous growth of Languages and Literature Publications in India. The Directory of Periodicals published in India (1988) lists—Journals in Languages alone. There are about 200 Institutions/Libraries (Central/State/Semi Government/ Aided/Autonomous/Private bodies) engaged in the fields of Languages in India and in the production and distribution of information in Indian languages.

A list of some Institutions is given as Appendix-1.

Besides these organizations, there are about 300 Universities and 18000 Colleges (with over 8.00 lakh teachers) which offer at same level or other, curricula with a language and literature contents. A number of doctoral degrees are awarded for study, research in various languages in India. All these institutions and some individuals have brought out useful publications in the field. A list of select sources in the field is given as Appendix-2.

As far as English Language and Literature is concerned, the Central Institute of English and Foreign Languages, Hyderabad is providing services as a National Center in the country though Government of India has not recognized it as National Resource Center. As a sample CIEFL Library has been studied and the following information sources as far as Indian Languages and Literature publications are concerned and they can be seen at Appendix-3.

Keeping in view the above growth of publications in Indian Languages and the Institutions working in the field, there is a dire need to set up a National Information Center for Languages (NICL) to achieve the Bibliographic Control over the Indian Language Publications.

Need for the Bibliographic Control

Publications growth in the Languages is so extensive that there is a need for systematic Bibliographic Organization and Control, otherwise much information is lost.

- ➢ Languages users are not aware as to how and where to access information and publications.
- ➢ Locational-Access and directional tools are inadequate.
- ➢ Timely access to information and publications is of great importance to the linguistic scholar.
- ➢ A coordinating and channelling communication support system as available in other fields, is necessary for languages.
- ➢ Bibliographic Control of Language publications.

Bibliographic Control is listing of all the publications in the field of all the languages published in India. Bibliographic control of the publications in all the languages is essential if the information resources in India are to be properly utilized. To achieve these, there is an urgent need for setting up of a coordinating center at the national level which is not yet established.

The Aims and Objectives of the proposed NICL:

- To function as National Apex body in the field of Indian Languages for the proper communication and dissemination of the Language information.
- To identify the important researchz areas in the field of Indian languages and to sponsor research through individuals and organizations.
- To act as a co-operative agency in a National network comprising various institutions and bodies (both Government and Private) and to set up the necessary links at various levels.
- To bring within its purview all Institutions connected with generation, connection and retrieval of information and literature in the Indian languages.
- To provide the necessary Bibliographic control mechanisms and support.
- To arrange for adequate access facilities to users who require the Language Publications/Information.
- To provide services as a National level link with International agencies in the field concerned, the proposed NICL should be 3-Tier System with Regional Information Language Centers (RILC) and Local Information Language Centers (LILC). The diagrammatical representation of the proposed NICL is as follows:

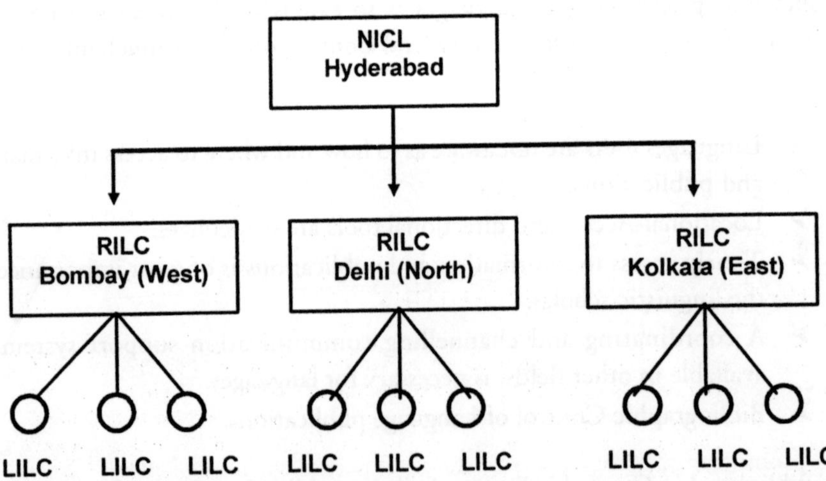

Fig. 28.1 : Tier System of National, Regional and Local Infromation Centres for Indian Languages

To work out for establishing the proposed 3-Tier System of NICL, it is suggested that a Working Group should be set up immediately consisting of some Language

Experts, Government Representatives, and Language Librarians so that the Committee would go into deep study and find out the feasibility and possibility in all aspects.

Therefore, there is an urgent need for setting up of such a center in India as were established in other disciplines like Science & Technology, Social Sciences etc. so that the center will coordinate a national resources sharing network and ensure its successful transfer and disemination to all those interested in its various branches of the field. The absence of such National center has been recognized by the Government of India and further it emphasized in its National Policy Document about its need for establishment. It reads as "The Committee on National Policy on Library of Information Systems appointed by the Ministry of Human Resources Development, Government of India, has recommended in its Report (1986) that "Special Libraries in Social Sciences and Humanities and in Sciences, Languages areas should be organized on similar systems as that of Science and Technology and databanks should be developed in the various subject areas. The report includes the following three points as its objects:

- Library and Information services are vital for all sectors of National activity. The availability of information, expeditiously and pin-pointedly, supports all decision-making processes at all levels. An informed citizen is an asset to a democratic system of Government of the proper utilization of information can improve too quality of citizens. The Government of India, there, realizes the value of coordination of upgrading of the existing Library and Information System and Sciences and initiating new programmes relevant to our National needs, taking advantage of the latest advances in Information Technology.
- To preserve and make known the Nation's Cultural heritage in its multiple forms.
- To set up adequate mechanisms for ensuring a rapid development of Library and Information facilities and services for meeting the information needs of all sectors and levels of the national economy."

Conclusion

The promotion, propagation and development of Indian Languages are major responsibilities of the Independent India to make the political independence viable and meaningful culturally and intellectually. Production is to make the languages function in new domains, propagation is to help the language learnt by more number of people and the development is to prepare the languages with adequate tools and materials for these two purposes. These three activities are performed by individuals as well as institutions. It is not sufficient for the Government alone to engage itself in them and to provide support to these activities. The voluntary organizations play an important role in this regard, and they do so more often out of cultural commitments to the languages.

Similarly, some of the Government and Private institutions in India particularly Central Institute of English and Foreign Languages (Hyderabad), Central Institute of Indian Languages (Mysore), Central Sahitya Akademy (New Delhi), Indian Institute of Language Studies (Patiala), International School of Dravidian Languages (Trivendrum), Institute of Kongu Studies (Salem), Pondicherry Institute of Linguistic Centre (Pondicherry) etc., have been providing documentation services like compilation of Bibliographies, Indexing, Abstracting, etc. But, there is no coordination between all these centers due to lack of a national coordinating agency. Further, some of these Institutions are computerized and some of the activities in some Institutions are partially computerized, but there is no network among those Institutions.

More over, UGC has set up INFLIBNET in Ahmedabad, in the year 1988, but so far INFLIBNET has not shown any special interest as far as information provision in the Indian Languages and Literatures are concerned. Even the UGC has set up Science Information Center at Indian Institute of Science, Bangalore, Social Science Information Center, UGC, Woman's University, Baroda. However there is an urgent need to set up Information Center for the Humanities which mainly includes Languages and Literatures.

In the absence of such a coordinating center at the national level, unnecessary duplication of work is taking place, which is leading to wastage of manpower, money, materials, machinery, etc. The consistency in the documentation services is also lacking.

In order to avoid all such duplicate efforts and to achieve Bibliographic Control, it is very much necessary and urgent to need to set up National Council for Indian Languages and Literatures (NCILL), on par with CSIR, ICSSR, ICMR, NCERT, etc. For taking up such activity, a Committee has to be constituted by Government of India, Ministry of Human Resource Development, as was already suggested in the above paras.

References

Director of Languages and Literature Institutions in India, Mysore: CIIL.

Kaur, Susheel, Comp. (1988) *Directory of Periodicals Published Guide, 1986-87*. New Delhi: Sapra & Sapra Publishers.

National Policy on Library and Information System (1987): CLIS Observer 4:3, pp. 134-35 &138.

Appendix-1

Institutions related to Indian Languages and Literature:

Academy of Sanskrit Research (Melkote)
Akhil Bharatiya Sanskrit Parishad (Lucknow)
Anand Ashram Sanskrit Sansthan (Pune)
Andhra Saraswtha Parishad (Hyderabad)
Anjuman-E-Islam Urdu Research Institute (Mumbai)
Anjuman-E-Taraqqi-E. Urdu (Delhi)
Arabic and Persian Research Institute (Tonk)
Arsha Sahitya Samshodhana Nayasa (Udipi)
Asian Manipuri Kala Academy (Cachar)
Asian Studies (Chennai)
The Assam Manipuri Sahitya Parishad (Juffirbund)
Assam Rashtrabhasha Prachar Samiti (Guwahati)
Assam Sahitya Sabha (Guwahati)
Bai Jerbai Wadia Library (Pune)
Bala Sahitya Bhavan (Kottayam)
Bangiya Sahitya Parishad (Kolkata)
Bangiya Vijnan Parishad (Kolkata)
Basu Research and Documentation Centre (Kolkata)
Bhai Vir Singh Sahitya Sadan (New Delhi)
Bharatiya Bhasha Parishad (Indian Languages Duvision) (Kolkata)
Bharatiya Sahitya Bhavan (Delhi)
Bhasha Sanchalanalaya (Directorate of Languages) (Mumbai)
Bhojpuri Sahitya Parishad (Jamshedpur)
Bihar Hindi Grandh Academy (Patna)
Bihar National Language Society (Patna)
Bihar Rashtra Bhasha Parishad (Patna)
Bihar Research Institute of Prakrit (Vaishali)
Bihar Sanskrit Vidhyapeeth (Patna)
Bihar Urdu Academy (Patna)
Bureau for Promotion of Urdu (New Delhi)
Central Hindi Directorate (Kendriya Hindi Nideshalaya) (New Delhi)

Central Institute of Foreign Languages and English (Hyderabad)
Central Institute of Higher Tibetan Studies (Varanasi)
Central Institute of Hindi (Hyderabad)
Central Institute of Indian Languages (Mysore)
Centre for Advanced Study in Sanskrit (Pune)
Centre of Advanced Study in Linguistics (Pune)
Christian Institute of Islamic Studies (Hyderabad)
Dakshina Bharat Hindi Prachara Sabha (Hyderabad)
Dakshina Bharat Hindi Prachar Sabha (Chennai)
Delhi Sanskrit Academy (Delhi)
Dhvanyaloka (Centre for English Studies and Indigenous Arts)
Directorate of Languages (Bhopal)
Directorate of Tamil Development (Chennai)
English Language Teaching Centre (Mysore)
English Language Teaching Centre (Solan)
English Language Teaching Institute (Bhopal)
English Language Teaching Institute (Allahabad)
French Institute (Pondicherry)
Ganganadh Jha Kendriya Sanskrit Vidyapeetha (Allahabad)
Gramanthara Bhasha Samsthan (Darinayakanapalya)
Gujarat Sahitya Mandir (Ahmedabad)
Gujarati Sahitya Academy (Gandhinagar)
Gujarati Sahitya Parishad (Ahmedabad)
H.M. Patel Institute of English Training and Research (Vallabh Vidyanagar)
Haryana Sahitya Academic (Chandigarh)
Himachal Academy of Arts, Culture and Language (Simla)
The Hindi Sahitya Samiti (Bharatpur)
Hindi Sahitya Samiti (Lucknow)
Hindi Teaching Institute (Dimapur)
Indian Institute of Advanced Study (Simla)
Indian Institute of Asian Studies (Mumbai)
Indian Institute of Islamic Studies (New Delhi)
Indian Institute of Language Studies (Patiala)
Indian Society for Commonwealth Studies (New Delhi)
Institute of Applied Language Sciences (Mysore)
Institute of Asian Studies (Hyderabad)
Institute of Asian Studies (Chennai)
Institute of Commonwealth and American Studies and English Language (Mysore)
Institute of Kongu Studies (Salem)
International Academy of Sanskrit Research (Mysore)
International Institute of Tamil Studies (Madras)
International School of Dravidian Linguistics (Trivandram)
International Telugu Institute (Hyderabad)
Jamia Islamia Arabia (Bhopal)

Jammat-E-Islamia Nind (Chennai)
Jammu and Kashmir Academy of Art, Culture and Languages (Jammu Tawi)
Kamarup Sanskrit Sanjibani Sabha (Nalbari)
Kannada Adhyayana Kendra (Centre of Kannada Studies) (Bangalore)
Kannada Adhyayana Samstha (Institue of Kannada Studies) (Mysore)
Kannada Sahithya Parishad (Bangalore)
Karnatak Prantiya Hindi Prachar Sabha (Bangalore)
Karnatak Provincial Hindi Prachar Sabha (Dharwad)
Karnataka Sahitya Academy (Bangalore)
Kerala Hindi Sahitya Academi (Trichur)
Konkani Bhasha Mandal (Goa)
Konkani Bhasha Prachar Sabha (Cochin)
Lalbhai Dalpathi Institute of Indology (Ahmedabad)
Language Bureau and Cell (New Delhi)
Languages Literary Centre (New Delhi)
Lexicographical Society of India (Trivandrum)
Linguistic Society of India (Pune)
Madhya Pradesh Hindi Granth Academy (Bhopal)
Madhya Pradesh Sahitya Parishad (Bhopal)
Maharashtra Rastra Bhasha Prachar Samiti (Pune)
Maharashtra Sahitya Parishad (Pune)
Manipuri Sahitya Parishad (Imphal)
Marathwada Sahitya Parishad (Aurangabad)
Mumbai Marathi Granth Sahitya Sangh (Mumbai)
N.D.K. Institute of Languages (Bangalore)
Nagaland Bhasha Parishad (Kohima)
Narmada Sahitya Sabha (Narmada Literary Society)(Surat)
National Sanskrit Institute (Jaipur)
Oriental Institute of Indian Languages (Mumbai)
Orissa Sahitya Academi (Bhubaneshwar)
Panjabi Sahitya Akademy (Ludhiana)
Peoples University of Literature, Arts, Crafts and Culture (Amravati)
Pondicherry Institute of Linguistic Culture (Pondicherry)
Rajasthan Bhasha Prachar Sabha (Jaipur)
Rajasthan Hindi Granth Academy (Jaipur)
Rajasthan Sahitya Academy (Udaipur)
Rajasthan Sahitya Samiti (Jhunjhunu)
Rashtra Bhasha Hindi Vidyapeeth (Indore)
Rashtra Bhasha Prachar Samithi (Wardha)
Rastriya Sanskrit Sansthan (New Delhi)
Regional Institute of English (Chandigarh)
Regional Institute of English (Bangalore)
Research Institute of Prakrit, Jainology and Ahimsa (Muzaffarpur)
Sahitya Akademi (National Academi of Letters) (New Delhi)

Sahitya Akademy (Chennai)
Sahitya Ratnalaya (Kanpur)
Sahitya Shodh Sansthan (Udaipur)
Sanskrit Academy (Hyderabad)
Sanskrit Academy (Madras)
Sanskrit Bhasha Prachar Samiti (Hyderabad)
Sanskrit Sahitya Parishad (Kolkata)
Sanskrit Sahitya Parishad (Tiruchirapalli)
School of Comparitive Languages (Lucknow)
Shree Dwarakadheesh Sanskrit Academy and Indological Research Institute (Dwaraka)
State Institute of English (Bombay)
State Institute of Languages (Trivendrum)
The Tamil Academy (Chennai)
The Institute of North-Eastern Languages (Guwahati)
Tamil, Sanskrit and other Indian Languages Research Institute (Chennai)
Telugu Academy (Hyderabad)
Telugu Bhasha Samithi (Chennai)
Tripura State Rashtrabhasha Pracjar Samiti (Agartala)
U.P. Hindi Grandh Academy (Lucknow)
Utkal Nagarilipi Parishad (Koraput)
Utkal Pratiya Rashtrabhasha Prachar Sabha (Cuttack)
Utkal Sahitya Samaj (Kolkata)
Uttar Pradesh Hindi Samsthan (Lucknow)
Vedic Sahitya Sadan (Hoshiarpur)
Vishveshvaranand Vishva Bandhu Institute of Sanskrit and Indological Studies (Hoshiarpur)
West Bengal Institute of Linguistics (Kolkata)
West Bengal Urdu Academy (Kolkata)
World Poetry Society Intercontinental (Chennai)

Apppendix-2

A Selective List of Language and Literature Publications available in the Institutions relating to Indian Languages and Literatures.

An Alphabetical Index of Persian, Arabic and Urdu Manuscripts in the U.P. State Archives (U.P. State Archives, Lucknow)

An Alphabetical Index of Sanskrit Manuscripts in the U.P. State Archives, (U.P. State Archives, Lucknow)

An Alphabetical Subject Wise Index of Sanskrit Manuscripts Available in the Andhra Pradesh Government Oriental Manuscripts Library and Research Institute (APGOMLRI, Hyderabad)

A Bibliography of Indian Folk Literature (Central Institute of Indian Languages, Mysore)

Bibliography of Indological Studies in 1953 (Asiatic Society, Calcutta)

Bibliography of Language Teaching Arts (Central Institute of Indian Languages Mysure)

Catalogue of Arabic Manuscripts (3 Vols.) (Arabic and Persian Research Institute, Tonk)

Catalogue of Arabic Manuscripts in the Collection of the Asiatic Society (Asiatic Society, Calcutta)

A Catalogue of Bengali Manuscripts in the Vrindaban Research Institure (Vrindaban Research Institute, Vrindaban)

Catalogue of Books in the Adyar Library, Madras (Vol. ii: Philosophy, History and Literature (The Adayar Library and Research Center, Madras)

Catalogue Catalogorum of Bengali Manuscripts in the collection of the Asiatic Society (Asiatic Society, Calcutta)

A Catalogue of Hindi Manuscripts in the Vrindaban Research Institute (2 Parts) (Vrindaban Research Institute, Vrindaban)

Catalogue of Persian Manuscripts (Salarjung Museum, Hyderabad)

Catalogue of Printed Books and Manuscripts in Sanskrit belonging to the Oriental Library of the Asiatic Society, Calcutta)

Catalogue of Rajasthani and Hindi Manuscripts (Jodhpur Collections-11 Parts) (Rajasthan Oriental Research Institute, Jodhpur)

Catalogue of Sanskrit and Prakrit Manuscripts (Chittorgarh Collections—2 Vols) (Rajasthan Oriental Research Institute, Jodhpur)

Catalogue of Sanskrit and Prakrit Manuscripts (Jaipur Collections—3 Vols.) (Rajasthan Oriental Research Institute, Jodhpur)

Catalogue of Sanskrit and Prakrit Manuscripts (Jodhpur Collections—17 Parts) (Rajasthan Oriental Research Institute, Jodhpur)

Catalogue of Sanskrit and Prakrit Manuscripts (Udaipur Collections—Vol. 1: Part 12) (Rajasthan Oriental Research Institute, Jodhpur)

Catalogue of Sanskrit Manuscripts (Vedic) (2 Vols.) (Asiatic Society, Calcutta)

A Catalogue of Sanskrit Manuscripts in the Vrindaban Research Institute (5 Parts) (Vrindaban Research Institute, Vrindaban)

Catalogue of the Adyar Library, Madras (Part 3: Atman in Pre-Upamisadic Veidic Literature) (the Adyar Library and Research Centre, Madras)

Classified Bibliography of Linguistic Disscrtations of Indian Languages (Central Institute of Indian Languages, Mysore)

Concise Descriptive Catalogue of the Persian Manuscripts in the Collection of the Asiatic Society of Bengal (Asiatic Society, Calcutta)

Cumulative Index of Indian Museum Bulletin (1966-80)(15 Vols.) (Indian Museum, Calcutta)

Descriptive Catalogue of Government Manuscripts at the Bhandarkar Oriental Research Institute (19 Vols) (BORI, Pune)

Descriptive Catalogue of Persian Manuscripts of History (4 Vols.) (Arabic and Persian Research Institute, Tonk)

Descriptive Catalogue of Rajasthani Manuscripts (Asiatic Society, Calcutta)

Descriptive Catalogue of Prakrit and Sanskrit Inscriptions in the Epigraphical Gallery of the Indian Museum (Indian Museum, Calcutta)

Descriptive Catalogue of Sanskrit Manuscripts in the Adyar Library (13 Vols.) (The Ady Library and Research Centre, Madras)

Descriptive Catalogue of the Bengali Manuscripts in the Collection of the Asiatic Socie (Asiatic Society, Calcutta)

Descriptive Catalogue of the Pali Manuscripts in the Adyar Library (The Adyar Libra and Research Centre, Madras)

Descriptive Catalogue of the Vernacular Manuscripts in the Collection of the Asiat Society (9 Vols.) (Asoatoc Society, Calcutta)

A Directory of Institutions in Language and Literature in India (Central Institute of India Languages, Mysore)

Index of Tamil Manuscripts (The Oriental Research Institute and Manuscripts Librar Trivandrum)

Marathi Descriptive Catalogue (4 Vols.) (Tanjore Maharajah Serforji's Sarasvati Mah Library, Thanjavur)

A Preliminary List of Sanskrit and Prakrit Manuscripts in the Adyar Library (The Ady Library and Research Centre, Madras)

Sanskrit Descriptive Catalogue (23 Vols.) (Tanjore Maharajah Serfoji's Sarasvati Mah Library, Thanjavur)

Tamil Descriptive Catalogue (4 Vols.) (Tanjore Maharajah Serfoji's Sarasvati Mahal Libra Thanjavur)

Telugu Descriptive Catalogue (2 Vols.) (Tanjore Maharajah Serfoji's Sarasvati Mah Library, Thanjavur)

Appendix-

A selective List of Information Resources of Indian Language and Literature Publicatio available in CIEFL Library.

19th Century English Literary Review: A Bibliography of rare books available, India (197

A Bibliography of Bengal Linguistics (1986)

A Bibliography of Bibliographies on India (1975)

A Bibliography of Doctoral Dissortatics accepted by Indian Universities 1857-1970

A Bibliography of Dravidian Linguistics (1973)

A Bibliography of Indian Folk Literature (1977)

A Bibliography of Prakrit Language (1977)

A Bibliography of Sanskrit Language of Literature (1984)

An annotated Bibliography of Modern Tamil Grammars & Tamil Hand Books (1983

An International Bibliography of Dravidian Languages and Linguistics (1994)

Applied Linguistics: Selectively Annotated Bibliography (1992)

Bibliography of Studies on Hindi Language and Linguistics (1978)

Bibliography of Theses in the subject of Gujarati Language and Literature (1973)

Commonwealth Literature: A check list of Holdings in the CIEFL Library (1985)

Commonwealth Literature: A Hand Book of reading lists (1976)

Communicative Language Teaching: A Bibliographical Survey of Resources (1985)

.H. Lawrence Studies in India: A Bibliographical Guide with a Review Essay (1990)
nglish Language & Literature Teaching in India: A Bibliography (2000)
nglish as a second Language: A select and annotated Bibliography (1987)
unctional Linguistics: A Selective Annotated Bibliography (1991)
ndia in English Fiction: 1800-1970; An Annotated Bibliography (1973)
ndian English: A Bibliographical Guide to Resources (1988)
ndian Literature in English Translation: A Bibliography (1984)
ndian Resources to TS Eliot: A Bibliographical Guide to writings in English (1988)
anguage Planning: A Select Bibliography (1988)
anguage Testing: A Bibliography (1990)
Jational Union Catalogue of Incunabula in Indian Languages (1987)
unjabi Language of Linguistics: An Annotated Bibliography (1992)
exture of Literature: A Bibliography of Discourse Analysis, Semiotics and Stylistics (1990).
ndian Scholarship on W.B.Yeats. (2000)

29

Building Print Collection in India: Issues and Problems

S.P. SINGH and TARIQ ASHRAF

Introduction

Good collection forms the backbone of the library to provide good information services and answer to various types of queries. Type of collection will depend upon the type of library. However, with the change of time, things are changing very fast in libraries too but importance of print collection can never be undermined. Printed material will always remain in demand as a source of authoritative information in the libraries. Collection development occupies the most vital position as "It is the document collection that gives library a character more so than either staff or building".[1] Collection development is a dynamic process that should involve both the information professionals and the service community. It must be responsive to the total community's needs, not just to those of current or most active users. "It should be geared primarily to identified needs, both long terms and short-terms, rather than to abstract standards of quality". "Collection development", according to Magrill[2], "as a planning process, uses the methodology typically followed in planning: establishing mission and policy statement, describing present state of affairs, reviewing relative strengths and weaknesses, considering environmental influences and other current trends, setting goals, and designing strategies to reach these goals. Collection development operates within the constraints of certain conditions that vary from one place to another and from one time to another."

Factors Affecting Collection Development

Aims and objectives of the parent institution are of paramount importance in identifying the priorities of collection development. For collection development in any library, following factors should be kept in mind[3]:

(i) *Philosophy of the Organization*: Theoretically, all libraries claim to have a philosophy of collection development but practically it is difficult to locate some such document that can act as a working guide. Ideally, based on the aims and objectives of the parent organization, each library should have a written philosophy.

(ii) *Nature of the Community*: Nature of the user community is a governing factor in the collection development. Therefore, librarian should know who are the users, and what are their information needs because all libraries exist to fulfil the information needs of their users.

(iii) *High Standards of Intellectual Contents*: Libraries are committed for providing authoritative information. Therefore, documents acquired should meet high standards of quality in terms of authoritativeness, accuracy, effective expression and physical format. Dewey's principle of "the best reading material, for largest number of readers at the least cost" should be adopted.

(iv) *Content's Relevance*: Significance and relevance of the subject contents should be given due consideration. The material acquired should have greatest relevance to the user community to be able to ultimately fulfil the aims and objectives of the organization. However, information needs in allied areas should be met through networking or resource sharing.

(v) *Library Cooperation and Networking*: Due to the problem of financial constraints, most of the libraries today are entering into such economic ventures to expand their resources so that needful materials can be made accessible or available to the user community.

(vi) *Availability of Budget and Existing Resources*: In libraries cost may sometimes be a deciding factor, but priorities must be fixed always so that the available amount may be spent judiciously. Suitability and usefulness of material to be selected should be evaluated in the light of resources already available in the library.

Collection Development Policy

Collection Development Policy is a written statement prepared for the guidance of the librarian regarding planning, budgeting, selecting and acquiring the material in the library. It is an essential communication tool for managers to ensure some continuity and consistency in the collection development programme even with the change in staff and funding. Therefore, it is a good planning tool in the hands of the librarians to safeguard or protect them against any kind of biasedness, personal pressures or influences.

The policy is formulated keeping in mind the long-term view of organization's mission statement and the strategic plan. The policy should be linked very closely to the general and specific programmes of the organization. It should be capable of defining priorities to be meaningful both for policy, makers and policy-executors.

Elements of Collection Development Policy

The policy should take into account the aims and the factors stated above. In principle, the policy should begin with organization's mission statement and strategic plans. According to Perkins[4], "recommendations of clients and knowledge of their information needs are the key elements in deciding what to buy". According to Evans[5] a policy document should have:

(i) A brief general description of the community to be served;
(ii) Identification of specific clientele to be served;
(iii) A general statement regarding the parameters of collection, such as specific subject field and type of formats that the library will acquire;
(iv) The statement on general limitations and priorities that will determine how the collection will be developed; and
(v) Keeping in mind the library's role in cooperative collection development and networking, the policy should make it clear as to whether the basic philosophy is self-sufficiency or cooperation.

However, once a policy is framed, it should be followed strictly unless it proves wrong or better one is found.

Role of Indian Publishing Trade

The publishing trade is closely connected with library collection development programmes as bulks of the purchases relate to published works only. If publishers do not feel a responsibility to produce quality materials, a librarian will not be able to select quality material. Hence, the policies and procedures followed by publishers have a direct bearing on the acquisition process in libraries by way of affecting the numbers of orders fulfilled, time taken, and the cost involved. "The status of librarian's order and the amount of effort needed beyond the initial order, to get material into the library are again directly related with the publishing industry and its distribution network."[6]

The vibrant publishing industry in India generates a turnover of approximately Rs 70 billion annually (Rs. 7,000 crores). Around 16,000 publishers in India publish 70,000 titles (estimated) out of which 40 per cent are in English, which makes India the third largest English language publishing country in the world. Of this, school and higher education books account for Rs. 2,000 crore to Rs. 2,500 crore (about 25%-35%) while general publishing is in the range of Rs. 800 crore (about 12%). Exports have grown from Rs. 330 million in 1991 to Rs. 3,600 million in 2003. The industry is growing at between 10 per cent and 15 per cent annually.[7]

These figures may sound quite impressive but it is not so, keeping in mind the population of India. Though India publishes about 70,000 titles every year, it is still one of the lowest in terms of books per million of population at the rate of around 30 books per million as against 735 in Europe.[8]

Problems and Issues

Collection development and acquisitions, while not ordinarily perceived to be demanding or exciting activities, contain elements that bring great personal satisfaction to those who are involved in acquisition work. There is a distinct joy in knowing that one has contributed to building up of a fine collection of library books. It provides great joy and satisfaction to librarian when the material needed by a particular user can be placed immediately in his or her hand. But the work related to collection development is not hassles free. Librarians have to encounter innumerable problems in their acquisition work. The variety of peculiar problems that arise in purchasing library materials are so great that it almost defies categorization. A few of the common difficulties are mentioned below:

(i) *Publishers' Faulty Policies*: Publisher's system of release of new titles has become much more conservative in recent years. Many publishers announce a title well in advance of its publication, and take the decision to publish the title when sufficient numbers of orders are received. In recent years, the librarians as well as wholesalers have become concerned with the tendency of some publishers to sell "direct only" to the library market, thereby eliminating the element of choice otherwise available to librarians. As a result, librarians are forced to purchase books directly from the publisher. This problem is compounded by the fact that not all publishers have a sufficient library or educational sales force in place. "The cost, efficiency of services and the products themselves, i.e.

documents, are influenced by a complex set of factors over which librarians have little or no control. As publishers are increasingly finding it difficult to store books for longer times, books are going out of print more quickly".[9] Speed and accuracy of delivery, willingness to handle wide range of publications, a proven track record with other libraries constitute important ingredients of a book supplier. Indian book trade is not well organized. Most of the book-sellers want easy money. They hardly believe in good service. They take interest to supply only those publications which are easily available and give them higher margin of profit. Due to this reason, only a small percentage of the titles on order are usually supplied. The booksellers are keen to sell those titles, which they have rather than what is required. Such book-sellers are always keen to grab the orders, even though they may not be able to execute them. As a result, the libraries are made to wait for a long time, compelling them to indulge in rush purchase at the end of the financial year for the fear of budget cuts in the forthcoming years. In the bargain, these booksellers are able to push the sale of their unsold books which were neither on order nor required for the library.

(ii) *Lack of Distribution Infrastructure*: Another most crucial problem which occurs in building up a sound collection is lack of proper infrastructure. As a result, "the libraries located in metropolis and major cities are well served by bookshops while the libraries located in rural areas and even towns are not".[10] On top of that, bookshops tend to be very conservative in their stocking habits, preferring to sell international bestsellers or topical quickies or textbooks. Though Indian publishing industry ranks seventh in the world and third after USA and UK in the production of English titles, the industry still remains at developmental stage given the size of the population. Furthermore, Indian publishing industry, in the post-independence era has been beleaguered by the problems of an overall shaky economic base. The basic problems of all publishers are primarily the lack of capital, paucity of printing paper at reasonable price, lack of effective distribution channels, high postal rates, heavy railway freight charges, etc. "Most publishing houses in India have been set up or are owned by entrepreneurs. While well-meaning and genuinely interested in book business, they lack proper understanding of the intricacies of book publishing".[11] Timely distribution of books perhaps constitutes the real Achilles heel of Indian publishing industry. The logical and geographical dimensions are immensely vast in our country that extends over an area of 3,000 kilometres wide both north-south and east-west.

Although there are quite a few importing wholesalers with any interest in Indian books, but retail outlets remain few and far between in urban areas and virtually non-existent in small towns.

(iii) *Shrinking Budgets*: Nowhere in the world, the library budget is keeping pace with rising cost of documents, the growth of literature and ever-increasing demands for it. Moreover, year by year number of publications is increasing manifolds. The realization of importance of information is also increasing. Consequently, there is a heavier demand for the sources of information, but the budget allocation to most of the libraries, remains static or declining year after year. In some cases, the library budgets suffer a cut to save money for other priority items. Even if there is no such cut, the purchasing power with the allocated funds goes on dwindling due to inflation and rising conversion rates. The price of the books and other reading materials, are going up continuously. There is a cycle of conflicting forces like availability of more literature, along with the increasing demand for it, and inadequate money to purchase and meet such ever-growing demands of their users are affecting libraries particularly in India. Although the problem of shirking budget is a universal one, but it is quite serious in India. The rising cost of foreign currency due to devaluation of Indian rupee has further added to financial constraints.

(iv) *Foreign Books and Far Off Markets*: The availability of books in the local markets has always been found helpful in collection development. For higher education and research, the Indian scholars and researchers mostly depend on foreign publications. Since foreign books are quite costly, the Indian representatives of the foreign publishers do not stock them adequately. As a result, most of the foreign publications are procured from abroad against orders. The final supply takes about three to six months due to the distances and the import formalities. Moreover, all the foreign books ordered are not supplied. Distant book markets certainly stand in the way of collection development efforts of the librarians.

(v) *Book Markets in India*: Whereas libraries are spread all over the country, the book markets in India are concentrated in metropolitan cities like Delhi, Mumbai, Chennai, Bangalore and Kolkata. "The libraries situated in these big cities are in an advantageous situation. But the libraries in other towns and cities located, far off from the book-markets, experience difficulties in developing their collections". [12]

(vi) *Regional Language Publications and Lesser Known Publishers*: There is no difficulty in locating and procuring those publications which are brought out by the well-known publishers and are distributed through normal trade channels. But the major problems come regarding the publications which are brought out by upcoming publishers. The percentage of such publications is higher and remains unnoticed as newly emerging publishers or author-publishers in the unorganized sector bring them out. Due to this reason, these publications usually remain unknown and unprocured in spite of their value and usefulness. Similarly, publications which are brought out by regional language publishers are difficult to acquire in the absence of any bibliographical control and far off locations.

(vii) *Poor Coverage in Bibliographical Tools*: The coverage of the Indian books in the bibliographical tools published from abroad is extremely poor. These are, therefore, not perfect tools to use for collection development. As regards the Indian bibliographical tools, there are few sources of national importance but unfortunately they are neither up-to-date, nor comprehensive and also not regular. Indian National Bibliography (INB) covers Books published in various languages but it suffers from several limitations like delayed publications, lack of currency etc. However situation is now improving as INB is being published regularly. Other important national bibliography is Indian Books in Print which does not cover the Indian language books. For acquisition of government publications, theses, technical reports, and non-print materials, etc., hardly any dependable tool is available in India. One is supposed to use a number of other tools to arrive at a respectable coverage. However, the existing Indian bibliographical tools can only be useful if their quality is improved in terms of their coverage, up-to-dateness and regularity, etc.

(ix) *Lack of Knowledge of Each Others' Systems*: Librarians, publishers, and vendors all maintain that they are misunderstood. Librarians and vendors criticize publishers for churning out catalogues and flyers which do not contain the information needed for selection and acquisition. Librarians argue that catalogues should not only contain bibliographic information but should also contain details about editions and date of availability.

(x) *Quotation System*: For acquiring documents, various systems are being followed by the libraries. However, the collection development process in a library suffers where quotation system is followed. Some unreliable booksellers quote the lower rates in order to get the orders. They on appointment, however, never supply most of the books ordered with them. They supply only those books which have remained unsold in their stock. The anxiety of library to purchase the books at the lowest quoted rates deprives it the service of the efficient, established and reputed booksellers who are in position to supply most of the books on order. Therefore, the choice of right and well-established vendor is very important for any library in collection building because it is he, who can execute the orders for maximum books expeditiously.

(xi) *Unstable Price and Exchange Rates*: The booksellers sometimes do not stick on to the price quoted by them because publishers, particularly the foreign ones, frequently revise their price. Some unscrupulous booksellers take undue advantage of this phenomenon. Because of the non-availability of the latest catalogues of the publishers, the library is unable to verify the charged rates as a result, the collection development programme suffers. Similarly the Good Offices Committee (GOC) frequently revises the exchange rates due to devaluation of Indian rupee, upsetting the total procurement programme of the libraries in India. Unfortunately, for last more than five years GOC has got split into two factions due to some differences between ILA and Publishers' Federation. Both the factions are fixing their own conversion rates which vary from each other substantially. The conversion rates fixed by ILA are comparatively low but information about these reaches very late in libraries. Moreover booksellers do not accept these conversion rates due to which libraries have to suffer financially.

(xii) *Sale of Remainder Titles*: Many booksellers in India specialize in acquiring remainder titles (old titles for which new editions are already available). For this purpose they visit foreign book markets and purchase in bulk the easily saleable remainder titles at throw away prices. These remainders though purchased at much lower rates than their normal published price are sold at higher cost. This allows the booksellers a heavy margin of profit. Such traders adopt all sorts of marketing techniques to promote and push their sale. Unsuspecting book-selectors and librarians fall prey to the whole game and become a party in purchasing the out-of-date publications at exorbitant rates. Some unscrupulous librarians also join this racket for petty gains and flood their libraries with the remainder titles. Such uncalled practices affect the development of worthy collection in the libraries.

Conclusion

Library collection development is not an easy task in India. There are many problems. There is always a paucity of funds to purchase even urgently needed publications. The markets for foreign books are far off. Production of Indian books is concentrated in Delhi, Mumbai, Kolkata and Chennai. Moreover, Indian book trade is unorganized, more interested in making easy money and less efficient in service. All the Indian publications are not brought out by the established publishers. Some of them remain unknown because they are published by small scale, new publishers. Publications of the publishers dealing in Indian languages are available in their own regions only. Indian bibliographical tools are suffering with various limitations. Besides these, there are other problems concerning quotation system, advance payment, faulty import policy, ineffective distribution system, unstable price and fluctuating exchange rates, paucity of suppliers of non-print materials, sale of remainders in the name of new and latest publications, etc. Libraries should be well aware of these problems. In spite of all these constraints, librarians should develop the skill and full knowledge of these problems to build-up a need-based, up-to-date, and balanced collection.

Notes

1. Ray, Ron L. (1993). The disintegrating library system: Effects of new technologies in acquisitions. Libr Acquis Prac Th. 17; 127-36.
2. Magrill, Rose M. (1989). Acquisition management and collection development of libraries. American Librarian Association., Chicago. p. 51
3. Singh, S.P. and Krishan Kumar (2005). *Special libraries in the electronic environment.* Bookwell, New Delhi. pp. 81-82.
4. Perkins, P. L., Ed. (1979). *Guidelines for collection development.* Chicago: American Library Association. p. 20.
5. Evans, G. Edward (1987). Developing library and information centre collections.Littleton, Colorado: Libraries Unlimited. p. 146.
6. Barker, Joseph W. and Rebecca, A. Rottman (1998). Acquisitions for effectiveness, efficiency and the future. Libr Acquis Prac Th. 22; 137-63.
7. http://prayatna.typepad.com/satya/2005/05/
8. Aloke, Sitesh (1985). *Study of book industry: Small Publishers.* National Council for Applied Economic Research, New Delhi. p. 88.
9. Boissonnas, Christian M. (1987). The cost is more than that elegant dinner: Your ethics are at work. Libr Acquis Prac Th 11; 154-152.
10. Tejeshwar Singh (1992). Publishing in the third world: learning do's and don'ts from India In Altbach (Philip G), Ed. *Publishing and development in the third world.* Vistar, New Delhi. pp. 243-264.
11. *Ibid.*, p. 266.
12. Malhotra, D.N., Ed. (1998). *50 years of book publishing in India since independence.* Federation of Indian Publishers, New Delhi. p. 323.

30

Explaining the Dawn of Colonial Portuguese Periodicals in Estado da India

LILADHAR R. PENDSE

The importance of print media as a vehicle for the expression of popular culture and associated rise of nationalism is a well studied fact. Often times print culture reinforced the paradigms of national identity as it aided in the standardization of the language.[1] The print culture within a colonial framework evolved differently in different colonies. The rise of the Portuguese press in India can be used to document not only the evolution of popular culture in Goa and other territories of Índia Portuguesa, but it can also be viewed as a valuable tool in understanding various mechanisms that lead to the rise of a complex national identity. In its initial phases, the development of the press in the colonial territories can be examined as a function of the initiatives that the mother country implemented as well as that of the interests of the local elite as permitted by the mother country, and Goa was not an exception.

It is generally assumed that the appearance of Portuguese language periodicals in Índia Portuguesa facilitated the enhanced circulation of ideas from the metropole and the rest of the Europe? We can state that the set of historical conditions that existed in metropole, when transported and implemented in Goa blossomed into a different end-product than in the metropole.

The Portuguese language periodicals could have acted as information-vectors that disseminated not only the information but various ideas to the colonial population. This dissemination of information at times complimented the goals of the Portuguese administrators of the ultramarine territories. Can one assume that in the long run this information dissemination could have led to the internalization of various "Portuguese" ideas by the literate populace of Goa?

The Evolution of the Print Culture in Goa

The print culture in India evolved with arrival of the Portuguese in Goa albeit slowly despite the early introduction of the printing press in Goa. Although there is debate about the exact date of the publication of the first book in Goa (Devi and De Seabra 90-91)[2] , the fact remains that the Portuguese language publications played an important function in the development of national consciousness within India Portuguesa. There is agreement on when and how the art of printing was introduced in Goa (Saldanha 102).[3] C.R. Boxer in his "A tentative check-list of Indo-Portuguese Imprints, 1556-1674" notes the first book printed in Goa was "Conclusões de logica e philosophia, Colegio de São Paulo, Goa, October 1556". There is no known surviving copy of this book. The earliest book with a surviving copy was printed in 1561 in Goa and is entitled, "IESV. COMPENDIO SPIRITVAL DA VIDA Christãa, tirado de muitos autores pello primeiro ARCEBISPO de Goa, e per elle pregado no primeiro anno a seus fregueses, pera Gloria e horra de IESV CHRISTO nosso SALVADOR, e edificaçam de suas OVELHAS..." (Boxer 1-3).[4] Boxer indexed 37 early books with an acknowledgement that the list is not complete.

The initial consumers of these periodicals could have been as Hélder Garmes in his chapter states, citing Vimala Devi & Seabra 1971, were the European administrators, their families and descendents, people of mixed descent and finally and importantly "os bramanes catolicos, cristos oriundos de familias bramanes convertidas, que conciliavam o hinduismo com o cristanismo e que tinham, na maior parte das disputas, o apoio dos chardos (ou chatrias)" (Garmes 22).[5] It is important to note that the last group constituted a majority of the Catholics that were governed. The Goan Catholics and the Hindu elites played undeniably important role of salient cultural resistance to the super-imposed Portuguese dominated governmental structure. This ideological resistance along with the delayed and incomplete ideological amalgamation can be understood as one factor that contributed to the rise of a complex societal identity within the population of India Portuguesa.

What made periodical publications so different than single monographic editions? In the temporal sense each edition of these serials is unique, and we can observe a gradual shift in the ideological norms that are contained within any given periodical publications. This evolution of ideas is evident in Portuguese periodicals of Goa right up to 1961. On the one hand, one may rightfully argue that the books, being monographic publications, can have successive editions. These successive and often enhance editions may end up playing the same role of conveying modified information similar to periodicals. We can say that not all monographs have successive editions. The book as a disseminator of author intended information played an important role earlier on in colonial society provided there was a concerted state policies of literacy dissemination combined with literacy programs.

On the other hand, periodical publications at a fixed interval have unique ability to package information in successive flexible layers. This layered information packaging allows periodical media to be constantly changing and evolving in its context matter. The evolution of a particular community that is served by a serial will demand change in content presentation and organization of information if a particular serial has to survive the socio-economic changes that are unleashed in a community due to perhaps ideological paradigm shifts within the community or due to technological changes. Thus the limited expressivity that was imposed by a monographic book culture seems to have seen overcome by serials publications in India Portuguesa as well as the rest of world.

Gauging the Impact of Portuguese Periodicals Press

By direct impact, I mean the number of readers of the Portuguese periodicals in the region. Although it is difficult to find out how many copies were published of the daily, weekly, bi-weekly and monthly Portuguese periodicals from India and also the circulation statistics for these periodicals, one may still research the direct impact using qualitative methods. One way to analyze this impact is to employ the content analysis methods. The content analysis will allow us to fathom the evolution of the contents and editorials over a specific period of time.

The indirect impact is much harder to gauge. The information vectors for indirect impact do not follow traditional paths from the paper to the reader that periodicals intend to do as information medium. The indirect impact may be caused by the word to mouth information transmittal, i.e. one literate person can convey news that is contained within a information medium using speech to the others, thus creating a kind of ripple effect in information transmission. Thus the periodicals may in turn facilitate dissemination of information in a slightly different manner than monographs. The trajectory of impact of the periodicals is correlated to the number of periodicals, their circulation within a given space. The period of appearance of periodicals thus presents us with an unique opportunity to analyze the impact of the information that might be contained within the periodicals on the milieu within which they circulated.

India Portuguesa or Goa Lusitanizada?

The Portuguese language periodical publications from Goa offer a unique insight into a culture that is effectively termed by some as Indo-Portuguese culture. I specifically used the term Indo-Portuguese culture instead of the term Portuguese Diaspora, because the cultural amalgamation that took place in Goa over the period of five centuries was undoubtedly both Indian and Portuguese.[6] The Portuguese encounter with the Indian subcontinent that began in the early 16th century came to an end with the surrender of Goa, Daman and Diu in 1961. The other term that is used by Pe. Filinto Cristo Dias in his "Esboço da História da Literatura Indo-Portuguesa" is "Goa Lustanizada"[7]. The term "Goa Lusitanizada" alludes to changes that initially took place in Goan culture under the Portuguese rule.

Although, in theory this term "Goa Lusitanizada" can be understood as a rough equivalent to the term "Indo-Portuguese", it is narrower in its scope. The Portuguese empire in 20th century India included, besides Goa, the territories of Daman, Diu, Dadra and Nagar-Haveli. Besides these territories, during the five centuries of Portuguese presence on the subcontinent, there were other territories including Bassein (Baçaim) and its vicinity that were grouped as Províncias do Norte, Chaul and other enclaves. The Portuguese language publications were most extensive in Goa.

The Early Periodicals and the Goan Consciousness

The analysis of the contents and the illustrations of Portuguese periodicals that were published in Goa during this time period will demonstrate only a partial conformity to the dialectics of the socio-political situation in the metropole as well as in the periphery. The view from the periphery that is reflected in these publications must be understood within the context of Índia Portugesa. Although on the periphery, Goa itself was a center for the Portuguese dominions of the orient. This identity that emerged within India Portuguesa was not static, but changing and dynamic.

Besides this conformity, one can get a sense of vision and beliefs of the editors of the respective journals and newsprint. The diversity of the opinions and the diverse types of periodicals that were published during the periods from 1821 to 1962 provide us with a unique evidence that will help enhance our understanding of a gradual formation of the Goan national identity within the context of Portuguese colonialism. The formation of Goan national identity was a gradual evolutionary process that proceeded from "Goa Lusitanizada" to "Indo-Portuguese identity formation" to eventual recognition of the specificities of "Goan Identity". This one significant experience of protracted identity formation is a key that allows us to analyze critically the metropolitan Portuguese attitudes towards their overseas provinces and *vice versa*.

One way to examine these attitudes will be to look at various pivotal events in India Portuguesa's history and compare them to the reporting of these events in the metropole press with the reporting in India Portuguesa periodicals. This comparative approach will allow us to either see the dichotomy of perceptions or similarity of reporting both in the metropole and India Portuguesa presses.

Does the Goan identity that is contained within these editorials reflect a critical view-point of the contemporary situations of the period? Or does this Goan identity instead of criticism place emphasis on the conformity with the metropole? The lack of linearity makes it interesting to analyze popular culture as a cross-section of spaces, i.e., the colonial and the metropolitan. Was Goa really an equivalent appendage of the metropole or was it simply a colonial periphery that was historically relegated a secondary role, which allowed an independent media expressions through out the history of Goa?

Role of Portuguese Language in Goa and Renaissance of Goan Identity

The evolution of a Portuguese press in India Portuguesa cannot be explained simply by using concepts like cultural translation (Ghosh)[8], or vernacular national identity formation, because initially, the goals of the Portuguese press in Goa were subordinated to those of the proselytizing efforts of the church and later to the economic, social and political aspirations of metropole. The fact, however, remains that the rise of the multitude of Portuguese periodicals in Goa in the 19th century opened doors to various ways of expressing popular cultural sentiments.

These cultural sentiments eventually helped in the amalgamation of the complex fabric of Goan national identity without ever replacing the vernacular languages of the region. Did the Portuguese administration in India did not envision creation of Portuguese as the *lingua franca* of the administered territories? Although there were substantial administrative efforts to create Portuguese language based instruction through out history of Goa, all these efforts had only the partial success. Was the policy of Portuguese language as the language of instruction impetus for appearance of the vibrant Portuguese language press in Goa? Can one consider the quantity of the periodicals that were published in Goa to be an accurate indicator of the vibrancy of Portuguese press in India?

In order to answer the above mentioned questions one has to deal with the multiple interpretations about the role that the Portuguese language, the periodicals and the press played in Goa under the Portuguese Rule. These interpretations vary from acceptance of role that Portuguese administration and language played in overall enrichment of the press culture in Goa to partial denial of that role given the frequencies of the revolts that Goa faced under the Portuguese rule.

For example: Lopes in an anthology about the press in Goa states:

> "Um dos aspectos mais salientes da colonização portuguesa é a criação de um ambiente propício para a receptividade cultural, mais ampla e livre, em todas as províncias do Ultramar, principalmene na Índia, onde o fenómeno se revestiu de um carácter psicológico especial.
> Numa terra onde nao havia escolas nem cursos profissionais, o jornalista fez-se por intuição, por auto-educação, pondo ao serviço da sua missão o somatório da suas faculdades e aptidões, aperfeiçoando-se cada vez mais ao contacto da imprensa metropolitana e da vizinha Índia Inglesa, numa irreprímvel conduta de formação e deontologia profissional" (Lopes 8).[9]

Lopes's reflections about the absence of schools in Goa before the arrival of the Portuguese are inaccurate. One can counter-argue that Goa did not have schooling infrastructure as understood in the occidental sense, but schools definitely existed in Goa before the appearance of the Portuguese on the scene.

For example Fr. Dias states,

> " No tocante ao ensino superior sabe-se que, embora não houvesse em Goa centro de alta cultura, como a Universidade de Taxila de tãao larga projecção mental nessa época em toda a Índia, encontravam-se xastris, homens doutos que se votavam ao estudo profundo nao só da religião mas também das ciências e nomeandamente da medicina que marcara na Índia avanço notável.
> O naturalista português Garcia de Orta que em 1542, se achava em Goa e o viajante holandes Linschotten confessam ter achado em Goa médicos indus muito hábeis no tratamento de varías moléstias e cujos serviços eram utilizados pelor próprios reinois." (Dias 2).[10]

Did the Portuguese colonization of Goa created conditions that were proportionate to the cultural sensitivities of Goa? Lopes does not describe to us what this "special character" was? He alludes to the following key fact: that there was self-education of the journalists that evolved within the Goan journalistic milieu after its initial contact with the metropolitan and the press of British India. This self-education became possible because there was a relevant autonomy of the Portuguese periodical press in Goa in the late 19th century. Of course, it is but natural that there was an amalgamation of ideas that eventually gave birth to the Indo-Portuguese identity. The periodical press' audience initially can be understood to be those who were literate and proficient in Portuguese.

Although the first printing press in Goa is dated to the late sixteenth century (Priolkar 2)[11], its religious purposes not only limited its printing efforts, but also impaired its ability to broadly choose materials to be printed in various subject areas. This impairment was defined by the mission of the first printing press, which was brought by the Jesuits to Goa. The first periodical in Goa appears in 1821 under governmental supervision. How can we explain this gap of 265 years between the first book printed in Goa and the appearance of the first periodical named Gazeta de Goa?

The Press in Metropole

The time lag after the appearance of the first books printed using the movable types *versus* periodicals is not necessarily specific only to Goa. On the contrary the first Portuguese language newspaper that appeared was titled "A Gazeta" (Belo).[12] This periodical has been cataloged in the OCLC database as "Gazeta do mes de ianeiro de 1642 [-agosto de 1647]. The publisher is indicated as D. Lopez Rosa, however, the language of the publication is Spanish.

There are different accounts about which newspaper appeared first in Portugal. Tengarrinha in his "História da Imprensa Periodica Portuguesa" states,

> " a primeira das quais, que pode dizer-se inagururar assim o jornalimso em Portugal, tem o título, longo como todos os desse tempo, de Gazeta em Que Se Relatam as Novas Todas Que Houve Nesta Corte e Que Vieram de Várias Partes no Mês de Novembro de 1641 (Lisboa, na Ofic. de Lourenco de Anvers, com privilégio real concedido a Manuel de Galhegos por Alvara de 14 de Novembro de 1641). Ao contrario dar relacoes de Serverim de Faria as gazetas tiveram periodicidade, porque foram, com poucas interrupcoes, viveram desde Novembro de 1641 ate, pelo menos, Setembro de 1647" (Tengarrinha 31-32).[13]

The fact remains that the periodical(s) that disseminated information about the "happenings" appeared in 1641. This perhaps excludes any publications that might have been published using the woodcut types and would have appeared as almanacs etc.

The first printed book in Portugal was "O Pentateuco" in Hebrew that was published by Gacon in 1487(Museu).[14] So the time-lag between the appearance of a monograph and a print serial in the case of Portugal was155 years. The print culture can be considered to be an important paradigm in the evolution of nationalism as proposed by Benedict Anderson in his seminal work "Imagined Communities", where the author proposes the following:

> "It remains only to emphasize that in their origins, the fixing of print-languages and the differentiation of status between them were largely unselfconscious processes resulting from the explosive interaction between capitalism, technology and human linguistic diversity. But as with so much else in history of nationalism, once 'there' they could be formal models to be imitated, and where expedient, consciously exploited in a Machiavellian spirit" (Anderson 45).[15]

There is a common agreement among various authors that the periodicals appeared in significant numbers in the 19th century Portugal (De Sousa, Veloso 31). This resurrgence in Portugal during the period from 1801-1810 has been explained as follows, "Em relação ao desenvolvimento jornalístico além da introdução de novas técnicas no fabrico do papel que passou a utilizar fibras vegetais, é importante assinalar que o jornal surge como uma necessidade de informação corrente. Aparecem os primeiros jornais diários (<<Diário Lisbonense>>, <<Gazeta de Lisboa>> eo <<Mensageiro>>), influência também dos jornais estrangeiros sobretudo <<Le Moniteur> muito lido entre nós. O jornal tinha um carácter utilitário usado pelo governo como forma de controlo da opinião pública, desmentindo boatos e procurando manter estabilidade social" (Motta de Sousa and Veloso 31-32).[16]

One cannot definitively say that all of the populace had an access to these print materials that appeared at the dawn of the printing. The costs of printing these books and levels of literacy of the audience will be other limiting factors that may have played a role in the delaying of the appearance of the periodical news-media. The circulation of the news in-print format depended on the ability to rapidly print the media, thus in turn the technology would have been a limiting factor. All of these factors could have delayed the appearance of the newsprint media. The technological limitations per se can not be simply used to explain this delay satisfactorily. Besides the technological limitations we must look also at the historical conditions that existed in the metropole when it comes to the delayed appearance of periodicals in Goa.

Explaining the Delay

Did the expulsion of Jesuits from Goa in any way delay the further development of printing that they had introduced? Antonio Maria Da Cunha in the essay "A Evolução do Jornalismo" in the anthology called "A Índia Portuguesa" writes,

> "Teriam, acaso, ficado absolutamente silenciosos êsses prelos duranted uǹ seculo, de 1654 a 1754? Não seria natural; mas não se sabe em que se ocuparam durante esse longo periodo de tempo. Investigações mais demoradas, que o curto espaco de dias designado a esta Memória não permite, devem fazer alguma luz sôbre este ponto, que nãoé despido de interêsse" (Cunha 505).[17]

There are several authors who have provided us with some of the answers that explain this delay. José Nicolau da Fonseca in his 1878 book "An Historical and Archaeological Sketch of the City of Goa" states the following:

> "From a document bearing the date of 1754, it appears that the Home Government was averse to the establishment of printing-presses in the territory of Goa, either by the local Government or by private individuals, and that accordingly, instructions were issued to the then viceroy, the Count of Alva, recommending the adoption of stringent measures in the matter. For nearly a century this narrow-minded policy was rigidly followed, regardless of the intellectual and moral advancement of the settlement; and it was only in 1821, the same year in which the constitutional system of government was introduced, that a Government press was established for the first time" (Fonseca 58-59).[18]

There are two components to this observation. First, Fonseca mentions a document that was dated 1754 that shows that the metropole government was against the establishment of printing presses in Goa, but he fails to give us the name of the document. Most probably the document he alludes to is "uma ordem dimandada do marques de Pombal, que reputava porventura a tipografia uma arma perigrosa nas mãos da Companhia de Jesus fez que nao se consentisse establecimento algum de imprensa <<não só particular mas ainda nos conventos, colégios ou qualquer outra comunidade por mais privilegiada que fosse>>.[19]

Second, and more understandably so, he associates the period of the appearance of the printing press in Goa due to the constitutional changes that took place in Portugal in 1821. The observation itself is of interest to us as it points towards the establishment of the Government press and the appearance of the first periodical that is named "Gazeta de Goa". "Gazeta de Goa" was an instrument by which the metropole government asserted its information interests in the community that it ruled.

On the other hand in Brito Aranha's 1898 work, "A Imprensa em Portugal nos Seculos XV E XVI", we find the following statement,

> "Mas, se vimos o desenvolvimento notabilissimo que teve para logo a imprensa na metropole, apregoe-se que os portuguezes levaram ao Oriente com o seu heroismo e com a santa luz da evangelho a nova e nobre luz que derramavam os prelos"(Aranha 6)[20] and he further continues, "Note-se que, ao passo que levavamos os prodigios da nova invenção a muitas das principaes terras do reino e até as possessões ultramarinas, a arte typographica era exercida com esmero."(Aranha 7)[21]

These observations by Fonseca and Aranha on the surface seem to contradict one another. If we look at the contexts in which these statements were written it becomes clear that either way the government played an integral role in the establishment of printing presses in Goa. In the beginning the monographic forms of publications evolved as indicated by Aranha using the term "muitas obras". And the purpose of the press itself in the beginning was to produce works that were needed for proselytizing the population. We also need to correlate the production of the first printed books in Goa with the levels of literacy of the period. While one can ignore the embellishing language that was characteristic of the some of the works of period one can say that there were two differing views on the nature of Portuguese governmental intervention in the realm of the press and printing.[22]

If the lack of the government sponsored printing presses in Goa till 1821 was at the root of the delayed onset of the print serials in the India Portuguesa, then the conditions that supported this late arrival can be complicated by the inadequacy of the Portuguese educational system in Goa. This inadequacy of Portuguese language instruction in the early periods of the creation of Portuguese ruled Goa is mentioned several times in a later anthology named "A Índia Portuguesa."[23] Was this numerical inadequacy of Portuguese language speakers in India a major factor that determined delayed the dawn and protracted dusk of Portuguese language periodicals in India?

To an extent, the number of subscribers to these journals would have been one determinant that ultimately defined the dawn, and dusk of the Portuguese periodicals in India along with the decolonization practices of the Indian government.

Portuguese Language Revisited and the Demographics within Goa

The dynamics that prevented the Portuguese language being a *lingua franca* in Goa was determined in part and parcel by the policies of the Portuguese administration. The number of Portuguese speakers remained relatively small as compared to the number of Konkani speakers. For example, the Census of Goa in 1950 shows us that the total population above the age of 5 who considered their mother-tongue to be Portuguese was approximately 1 per cent of the total population of India Portuguesa as compared to Konkani and Marathi. The total number of people who spoke Konkani and Marathi was 82 per cent and 5 per cent approximately (Recenseamento).[24] This census document does not take into consideration the population who spoke two or more languages at the same time.

If we look at the available statistics on Education in Portugal we find that no data are available about the total number of children and teachers in Portuguese schools until year 1849. In 1849 Portugal had 42000 primary school children and 1169 teachers, then from year 1850 to 1871, there are no data available for Portugal according to "International Historical Statistics: Europe 1750-2000". In 1872, there is a record of 125,000 pupils in primary schools, but the data for the number of teachers is unavailable. The data set available for primary schools becomes consistent from 1883 to 1888. The data then resumes once again in the year 1920. These holes in the statistics create a large number of questions regarding actual levels of literacy in metropole ["Children and teachers in schools (in thousands, except as otherwise indicated)" 870-893].[25] The data for year 1849 for Portugal shows the university enrollment was 1,008 students (Number of Students in Universities, 894).[26] This data when examined with respect to the total population of Portugal for the thirteen years from 1841 to 1854 (which did not include the population of India Portuguesa), we find that the total number of students who were in the universities would have been approximately 0.02 per cent of the total population. We see the percentage of students that were in school is 1.09 per cent of the total population.[27] I was unable to locate official literacy rates for the period.

The earliest official literacy rates in Portugal that I was able to locate using the virtual library of the "Instituto Nacional de Estatística of Portugual" begin from 1890. During 1890, the percentage of the illiterate population was 76.6 per cent in the metropole. In 1900 the literacy rate in the metropole was 24.30 per cent.[28] This data does not offer a concrete explanation for the delayed appearance of periodicals either in Portugal or in India Portuguesa.

The literacy rates from India Portuguesa that I used for the purpose of this work were derived from the "Censo da populaçao do estado da Índia em 26 Fevereiro 1931: Volume II, Conselho das Ilhas" or hitherto referred to as 1931 census. Besides this I have included the data from 1940 and 1959 censuses. The data that is contained within the 1931 census is extremely important to us for it contains a table # 5 that is titled "Populacao de facto Segundo a instrucçao nos rencenseamento de 1900, 1910, 1921 e 1931" and sub-titled "Sabem ler e escrever" that provides us with the literacy rates of Índia Portuguesa. There are three limitations to this data-set in my opinion. First, the data set starts in 1900. I was unable to find literacy rate before 1900 for India Portuguesa. Second, this particular data set does not provide us with language specific information. Thus one cannot derive language specific literacy rates for India Portuguesa. The third limitation is that this data is not arranged by age groups except in the case of 1959 census. This makes it difficult to assess the relationship between the age, literacy and the circulation data of Portuguese periodicals. It is interesting to look at the quantitative levels of overall literacy as this information may help us understand the relativity of direct and indirect social impacts of the Portuguese language periodicals.

The literacy rates in Goa shows increase in overall literacy from 1900 to 1959.[29] However when we examine the data from 1881 India Portuguesa census we find following interesting facts. In Table 5, we find that the district of Ilhas (Panaji and its surrounding was one of populous districts in Goa). The population of this district was 48847, and the total number of Europeans in the district was 512 individuals. Out of these Europeans 410 individuals were males and 102 were females. The Europeans constituted roughly 1 per cent of the population. The census failed to record the mixed population. The literacy rate for the district is 20 per cent which is higher than the rest of the districts of Goa. There were 4 booksellers and 1 lithographer according to the 1881 count. The later censuses of Goa fail to record population by the professions. Although the correlation between the literacy rates and appearance of the periodicals is not a well studied fact, one might state the following hypothesis: The appearance of periodicals within India Portuguesa is related to the historical realities of changes that took place deep within the metropole and Goa. The literacy rates of Goa could have influenced on a longer run rise, growth and demise of various periodicals.

The Dawn of the First Periodical in Goa

As mentioned earlier we do not see an appearance of Portuguese language periodical in India Portuguesa during the periods of 1801-1810, but instead with the second flowering of Portuguese periodicals during the period1821-1830.[30] The appearance of the first government sponsored periodical in Goa in 1821 allows us to draw the following conclusion. The "Gazeta de Goa" arose in Goa with the advent of liberalism in Portugal after the revolution of 1820. If the liberalism unleashed an array of periodical publishing activity in Portugal then in Goa this activity translated into the first periodical on 22 December 1821. It's main contents are described in Lopes' "Imprensa de Goa" as follows, "as deliberações do Governo, o cadastro mensal da receita e despesa do tesouro público, do Senado da Câmera, da Santa Casa de Misericórdia e oturas notícias nacionais e estrangeiras".[31] The Gazeta continued to be published till 1826. Jaime Rangel and António dos Mártires Lopes in their respective works "A Imprensa em Goa" and "Imprensa de Goa" are silent about why the "Gazeta" ceased publication.

Rangel simply states, "A síncope não foi longa e a Gazeta breve recuperava a vida para em 1835 passar ser Chronica Constitucional de Goa, daí em 1837 Boletim do Governo do Estado da India e em 1869 Boletim Oficial, de edição trisemanal, para passar a ser diária de 1882 a 1887, deixando de ter a secção noticiosa e histórica em 1889, para se tornar bissemanal desde o ano anterior até 1939 e seamanal daí em diante"(Rangel 47).[32]

Lopes goes into the details about the history of the "Gazeta de Goa" without giving the details about the political conditions in Goa under which the first periodical appeared (Lopes 13).[33] Although the editor Lúis Prates and his actions are mentioned in great detail, Lopes fails to mention that "a series of disorders and revolts broke out in Portuguese India following the revolution that occurred in Portugal and Brazil in 1820.

The Goans took a leading part in them. The leaders of the disturbances seized the Viceroy Conde do Rio Pardo and having deposed him, appointed on the 16th of September 1821, a provisional junta composed of five members. The acknowledged leader of the Goans, Bernardo Peres da Silva took an active part in the revolt. A new constitution, the "Carta Organica" granting constitutional powers to the colonies was promulgated in Portugal" (Gune 19).[34]

This new constitution included a guarantor of the freedom of the press in the Portuguese territories as stated in article no. 8 states, "A livre comunicação dos pensamentos é um dos mais preciosos direitos do homem. Todo o cidadão pode, consequentemente, sem dependência de censura prévia, manifestar suas opiniões em qualquer matéria, contanto que haja de responder pelo abuso desta liberdade, nos casos e na forma que a lei determinar"(Amaral).[35]

Thus the milieu of liberalism and local aspirations of self-determination can be considered some of the few factors that led to a slightly belated arrival of Goa's first periodical.

Conclusion

Once, the first periodical was published in Goa, it was followed by hundreds of other Portuguese language periodicals with varying goals, aspirations, subject matters and trajectories. Henry Scholberg lists about 190+ Journal and newspapers besides the government serials that were published in Goa under the Portuguese rule (Scholberg, Kakodker, Azevedo).[36] Although the many of these Portuguese language publications were published in Goa, there were some that were published in Bombay by the Goan diaspora. The life-span of some of these periodicals was relatively short, nevertheless the impetus these periodicals might have given to the circulation of ideas and information in India Portuguesa is immeasurable. After all it was this circulation of ideas led to an ever increasing formation of national consciousness within the framework of Índia Portuguesa.

Notes

1. Anderson, Benedict (1991). Imagined Communities. Revised. New York: Verso.
2. Devi, Vimala, and Manuel De Seabra. A Literatura Indo-Portuguesa. 1st. Lisbon: Junta de Investigações do Ultramar, (1971). Here the authors state, "Não há dúvidas de que a primeira tipografia instalada no Oriente foi portuguesa. Parece que tal acontecimento se deu em 1556, havendo, porém, dúvidas sobre a primeira obra impressa em Goa" (Devi and De Seabra 90).
3. Saldanha, Padre M.J.Gabriel de. História de Goa (Politicia e Arqueológica). Reprint. New Delhi: Asian Educational Services, 1990. Saldanha states, "A infatigavel e bene merita Companhia de Jesus introduziu a arte tipografica em Goa" (Saldanha 102).
4. Boxer, C.R. (1956). A tentative check-list of Indo-Portuguese Imprints, 1556-1674. Bastora, Goa: Tipografia Rangel.

5. Garmes, Hélder. (2004). "Origem e estabelecimento da imprensa e da literatura em Goa." Oriente, engenho e arte: Imprensa e literatura de lingua portuguesa em Goa, Macau e Timor Leste. Compiled. Helder Garmes. Sao Paulo: Alameda Casa Editorial.
6. The term Indo-Portuguese has been used in variety of contexts. There are multiple interpretations of the term "Indo-Portuguese". If search the World Cat database using a simple keyword search for the term "Indo-Portuguese" we find various results. One particular monograph by Da Cunha, Joseph Gerson that was published in 1880(3) named "Contributions to the study of Indo-Portuguese Numismatics" denotes the use of term Indo-Portuguese as early as 1880s. Of course WorldCat is by no means a complete database that indexes all of the Indo-Portuguese publications. For example a weekly journal named "A India Portuguesa" whose editor was José Ignacio de Loyola appeared in 1861 in Orlim, Goa and continued to publish till 1898 The founder of this journal was M.L. De Miranda Franco (Lopes, Antonio dos Martires (editor). Imprensa De Goa. Lisboa: Edição do Comissaridado do Governo para os Assuntos do Estado da Índia, 1974.)
7. Dias, Pe. Filinto Cristo (1963). Esboço da História da Literatura Indo-Portuguesa. Bastora-Goa: Tipografia Rangel.
8. Ghosh, Anindita. "An Uncertain 'Coming of the Book': Early Print Cultures in Colonial India." Book History 62003 23-55. 15 Aug 2006 <http://muse.jhu.edu/journals/book_history/v006/6.1ghosh.html#FOOT9>.
9. Lopes, Antonio dos Martires (editor) (1974). Imprensa De Goa. Lisboa: Edição do Comissaridado do Governo para os Assuntos do Estado da Índia.
10. See footnote #7.
11. Priolkar, Anant (1958). The printing press in India, its beginnings and early development, being a quatercentenary commemoration study of the advent of printing in India in 1556. 1st Edition. Bombay: Marathi Samshodhana Mandala.
12. Belo, Andre (7 August, 2006). "Between History and Periodicity: Printed and Hand-Written News in 18th-Century Portugal." e-journal of Portuguese History. Brown University. <http://www.brown.edu/Departments/Portuguese_Brazilian_Studies/ejph/html/issue4/html/belo_main.html>.
13. Tengarrinha, Joseì (1965). Historìria da imprensa perioìdica portuguesa. Lisboa: Portugaìlia.
14. "Museu Virtual da Imprensa, Porto Portugal." (7 August, 2006). Museu Virtual da Imprensa. N/A. <http://www.imultimedia.pt/museuvirtpress/port/frame3.html>.
15. Anderson, Benedict (1991). Imagined Communities. Revised. New York: Verso.
16. Motta de Sousa, Joseì Manuel, and Veloso, Luìcia Maria Mariano (1987). Historìria da imprensa perioìdica portuguesa: subsìdios para uma bibliografia. 1st ed. Coimbra: Biblioteca Geral da Universidade.
17. Da Cunha, Antonio Maria (1923). "A Evolução do Jornalismo." India Portuguesa. ED. Nova Goa: Imprensa Nacional.
18. Fonseca, Jose Nicolau (1986). *An Historical and Archaeological Sketch of the City of Goa.* Reprint. New Delhi: Asian Education Services.
19. Lopes, Antonio dos Martires (editor) (1974). Imprensa De Goa. Lisboa: Edição do Comissaridado do Governo para os Assuntos do Estado da Índia, p. 12.
20. Aranha, Brito (1898). *A Imprensa em Portugal.* Lisbon: Impresna Nacional.
21. *Ibid.* Aranha 7.
22. Aranha, Brito. Subsidios para a Historia do Jornalismo nas provincias ultramarinas

portuguezas. Lisboa: Imprensa Nacional, 1885. The language that seems embellishing today would have been considered to be within the parameters of normal language usage during the late 19th century. I am quoting here few lines of Aranha's introduction in French, "Il a eu une époque de renaissance dans la période homérique de l'établissmente définitf du gouverenment constitutionnnel en 1834. Après, il continua avec quelques intermittences en se faisant remarquer surtout dans l'Inde portugaise, à Macau et à Angola, les vastes contrees ou le pouvoir et le prestige des portugais doivent se maintenir dans toute leur energie et dans tout leur eclat."(Aranha).

23. A India Portuguesa. 1st. Nova Goa: Imprensa Nacional, 1923. On page 17 we find the following, " É de crer que as primeiras escolas de Albuqureque se não foram desenvolvendo expandido. Foi pena que assim fôsse. A verdade é que, trinta anos depois da conquista de Goa, o ensino publico nesta India era um monopólio eclesiàstico, para, daí a nada, ser congreganista ou monacal". Another observation pertains to year 1840 as follows, "Fôra á vista desta insuficiência que, em 1840, o governador Barão de Candal, firmado nas instruções dadas por D. Manuel de Portugal e Castro, e que regulavam o ensino das pouquissimas escolas de português então existentes, determinara: "Que os mestres de canto das paroquias se absenham de ensinar a ler e escrver (portugues), para o que nao sao idoneos por falta de exame...", p. 19.

24. India Portuguesa. Repartição Central de Estatística E Informação.8 Recenseamento Geral da População: Realizado em 15 de Dezembro de 1950. População, presente de 5 ou mais anos de idade, segundo a lingua materna e o sexo, por religões. Goa: Araujo, 1956Table 6. Total number of male and female population above 5 years of age was 599924, Concanim was mother tongue according to this census was 468761, Marathi speakers were 28060, and Portuguese speakers according to the table was 6723. It is unclear, if this census included population of Portuguese speaking soldiers that were serving in Goa at the time, pp. 28-29.

25. Table: "Children and teachers in schools (in thousands, except as otherwise indicated)."International Historical Statistics: Europe 1750-2000. 5th ed. 2003.

26. *Ibid.* p. 894.

27. The population of Portugal according to "International Historical Statistics: Europe 1750-2000" by B.R. Mitchell, Palgrave 2003 indicates the population of Portugal according to census in 1841 was 3,397000 and in 1854 it was 3844000. The 1841 population census did not include Azores and Madeira.

28. One can use the virtual library of the Statistical institute of Portugal to download the tiff files that relate to the social conditions in the Metropole. http://www.ine.pt:8080/biblioteca/sort.do?layoutCollection=0&layoutCollectionProperty=descricao&layoutCollectionState=0.

29. Please attached Excel Sheet that I created using the data from the Goa Censuses.

30. *Ibid.* Please see note 25. The chart on page 23 on Motta de Souza and Veloso book titled Movimento da Imprensa Periodica Portuguesa (Por décadas) tracks appearance of periodical titles from 1641 through 1980. The chart shows the first flowering around 1801/1810 when there were total of 62 periodicals. This trend continued in 1811/1820 with 62 periodicals. However from 1821 there is a second flowering. There were 221 total periodicals in the interval form 1821 to 1830. The data is provided by Veloso. p. 33 (Movimento da Imprensa Periodica Portuguesa-1987).

31. Lopes, Antonio dos Martires (editor) (1974). Imprensa De Goa. Lisboa: Edição do Comissaridado do Governo para os Assuntos do Estado da Índia, p. 13.
32. Rangel, Jaime (1956). A Imprensa em Goa. Bastora, Goa: Tipografia Rangel, p. 47.
33. See note # 8. Lopes documents the names of the editors of Gazeta. This includes a paragraph about editor Lúis Prates who was deported to Brasil in 1819 because of his "extreme-liberal" ideas. Apparently he was back in Goa by 1821. Lopes goes on stating that "Lúis Prates, barbaramente assassinado a baionetadas, o qual "advogava no jornal princípios sãos fulminando as diferenças de nascimento e outros prejuízos da aristrocracia, não duvidando mesmo criticar dessaombradamente os actos governativos e com tudo a junta o nomeou oficial maior interino da seceretaria geral em substituição do que fora suspenso por exigencia da tropa, certamente porque reconhecia nele habilidade para bem se desempenhar desta comissão" (Lopes 13).
34. Gune V.T., Gune (1986). "A brief outline of freedom struggle in Goa, Daman and Diu." Goa Wins Freedom. B.Sheik Ali. B. Sheik Ali. Bambolim, Goa: Goa University.
35. Amaral, Manuel (24 August, 2006). "DOCUMENTOS POLÍTICOS DA." O Portal da Historia. 2005. O Portal da Historia-ANAIS. <http://www.arqnet.pt/portal/portugal/liberalismo/bases82.html>. Article 8.
36. Scholberg, Henry, Archana Ashok Kakodker, and Carmo Azevedo (1982). Bibliography of Goa and the Portuguese India. New Delhi: Promila & Co.

Bibliography

A India Portuguesa. 1st. Nova Goa: Imprensa Nacional, 1923. On page 17 we find the following, " É de crer que as primeiras escolas de Albuqureque se não foram desenvolvendo expandido. Foi pena que assim fôsse. A verdade é que, trinta anos depois da conquista de Goa, o ensino publico nesta India era um monopólio eclesiàstico, para, daí a nada, ser congreganista ou monacal". Another observation pertains to year 1840 as follows, "Fôra á vista desta insuficiência que, em 1840, o governador Barão de Candal, firmado nas instruções dadas por D. Manuel de Portugal e Castro, e que regulavam o ensino das pouquissimas escolas de português então existentes, determinara: "Que os mestres de canto das paroquias se absenham de ensinar a ler e escrver (portugues), para o que nao sao idoneos por falta de exame."(Page 19)

Amaral, Manuel. "DOCUMENTOS POLÍTICOS DA." O Portal da Historia. 2005. O Portal da Historia-ANAIS. 24 Aug 2006 <http://www.arqnet.pt/portal/portugal/liberalismo/bases821.html>. Article 8

Amaral, Manuel. "DOCUMENTOS POLÍTICOS DA." *O Portal da Historia.* 2005. O Portal da Historia-ANAIS. 24 Aug 2006 <http://www.arqnet.pt/portal/portugal/liberalismo/bases821.html>. Article 8

Anderson, Benedict. *Imagined Communities.* Revised. New York: Verso, 1991.

Anderson, Benedict. *Imagined Communities.* Revised. New York: Verso, 1991.

Anderson, Benedict. *Imagined Communities.* Revised. New York: Verso, 1991.

Anderson, Benedict. *Imagined Communities.* Revised. New York: Verso, 1991.

Aranha, Brito. *A Imprensa em Portugal.* Lisbon: Impresna Nacional, 1898.

Aranha, Brito. *A Imprensa em Portugal.* Lisbon: Impresna Nacional, 1898.

Aranha, Brito. Subsidios para a Historia do Jornalismo nas provincias ultramarinas portuguezas. Lisboa: Imprensa Nacional, 1885.

Aranha, Brito. *Subsidios para a Historia do Jornalismo nas provincias ultramarinas portuguezas.* Lisboa: Imprensa Nacional, 1885. The language that seems embellishing today would have been considered to be within the parameters of normal language usage during the late 19th century. I am quoting here few lines of Aranha's introduction in French, "Il a eu une époque de renaissance dans la période homérique de l'établissmente définitf du gouverenment constitutionnnel en 1834. Après, il continua avec quelques intermittences en se faisant remarquer surtout dans l'Inde portugaise, à Macau et à Angola, les vastes contrees ou le pouvoir et le prestige des portugais doivent se maintenir dans toute leur energie et dans tout leur eclat."(Aranha)

Belo, Andre. "Between History and Periodicity: Printed and Hand-Written News in 18th-Century Portugal."

Belo, Andre. "Between History and Periodicity: Printed and Hand-Written News in 18th-Century Portugal." e-journal of Portuguese History. Brown University. 7 Aug 2006 <http:/ /www.brown.edu/Departments/Portuguese_Brazilian_Studies/ejph/html/issue4/html/ belo_main.html>.

Boxer, C.R. *A tentative check-list of Indo-Portuguese Imprints, 1556-1674.* Bastora, Goa: Tipografia Rangel, 1956.

Boxer, C.R. *A tentative check-list of Indo-Portuguese Imprints, 1556-1674.* Bastora, Goa: Tipografia Rangel, 1956.

Boxer, C.R. *A tentative check-list of Indo-Portuguese Imprints, 1556-1674.* Bastora, Goa: Tipografia Rangel, 1956.

Da Cunha; Antonio Maria. "A Evolução do Jornalismo." India Portuguesa. ED. Nova Goa: Imprensa Nacional, 1923.

Da Cunha, Antonio Maria. "A Evolução do Jornalismo." India Portuguesa. ED. Nova Goa: Imprensa Nacional, 1923.

De Miranda Franço (Lopes, Antonio dos Martires (editor). Imprensa De Goa. Lisboa: Edição do Comissaridado do Governo para os Assuntos do Estado da Índia, 1974.)

Devi, Vimala, and Manuel De Seabra. *A Literatura Indo-Portuguesa.* 1st. Lisbon: Junta de Investigações do Ultramar, 1971.

Devi, Vimala, and Manuel De Seabra. *A Literatura Indo-Portuguesa.* 1st. Lisbon: Junta de Investigações do Ultramar, 1971. Here the authors state, "Não há dúvidas de que a primeira tipografia instalada no Oriente foi portuguesa. Parece que tal acontecimento se deu em 1556, havendo, porém, dúvidas sobre a primeira obra impressa em Goa" (Devi and De Seabra 90).

Devi, Vimala, and Manuel De Seabra. *A Literatura Indo-Portuguesa.* 1st. Lisbon: Junta de Investigações do Ultramar, 1971. Here the authors state, "Não há dúvidas de que a primeira tipografia instalada no Oriente foi portuguesa. Parece que tal acontecimento se deu em 1556, havendo, porém, dúvidas sobre a primeira obra impressa em Goa" (Devi and De Seabra 90).

Dias, Pe. Filinto Cristo. Esboço da História da Literatura Indo-Portuguesa. Bastora-Goa: Tipografia Rangel, 1963.

Dias, Pe. Filinto Cristo. Esboço da História da Literatura Indo-Portuguesa. Bastora-Goa: Tipografia Rangel, 1963.

e-journal of Portuguese History. Brown University. 7 Aug 2006 <http://www.brown.edu/Departments/Portuguese_Brazilian_Studies/ejph/html/issue4/html/belo_main.html>.

Fonseca, Jose Nicolau. *An Historical and Archaeological Sketch of the City of Goa.* Reprint. New Delhi: Asian Education Services, 1986.

Fonseca, Jose Nicolau. *An Historical and Archaeological Sketch of the City of Goa.* Reprint. New Delhi: Asian Education Services, 1986.

Garmes, Hélder. "Origem e estabelecimento da imprensa e da literatura em Goa." Oriente, engenho e arte: Imprensa e literatura de lingua portuguesa em Goa, Macau e Timor Leste. Ed. Helder Garmes. Sao Paulo: Alameda Casa Editorial, 2004.

Garmes, Hélder. "Origem e estabelecimento da imprensa e da literatura em Goa." Oriente, engenho e arte: Imprensa e literatura de lingua portuguesa em Goa, Macau e Timor Leste. Compiled. Helder Garmes. Sao Paulo: Alameda Casa Editorial, 2004.

Garmes, Hélder. "Origem e estabelecimento da imprensa e da literatura em Goa." Oriente, engenho e arte: Imprensa e literatura de lingua portuguesa em Goa, Macau e Timor Leste. Compiled. Helder Garmes. Sao Paulo: Alameda Casa Editorial, 2004.

Ghosh, Anindita. "An Uncertain "Coming of the Book": Early Print Cultures in Colonial India." Book History 62003 23-55. 15 Aug 2006 <http://muse.jhu.edu/journals/book_history/v006/6.1ghosh.html#FOOT9>.

Ghosh, Anindita. "An Uncertain "Coming of the Book": Early Print Cultures in Colonial India." Book History 62003 23-55. 15 Aug 2006 <http://muse.jhu.edu/journals/book_history/v006/6.1ghosh.html#FOOT9>.

Gune V.T., Gune. "A brief outline of freedom struggle in Goa, Daman and Diu." *Goa Wins Freedom.* B.Sheik Ali. B. Sheik Ali. Bambolim, Goa: Goa University, 1986.

Gune V.T., Gune. "A brief outline of freedom struggle in Goa, Daman and Diu." *Goa Wins Freedom.* B.Sheik Ali. B. Sheik Ali. Bambolim, Goa: Goa University, 1986.

http://www.ine.pt:8080/biblioteca sort.do?layoutCollection=0&layoutCollectionProperty=descricao&layoutCollectionState=0

Ibid. Please see note 25. The chart on page 23 on Motta de Souza and Veloso book titled Movimento da Imprensa Periodica Portuguesa (Por décadas) tracks appearance of periodical titles from 1641 through 1980. The chart shows the first flowering around 1801/1810 when there were total of 62 periodicals. This trend continued in 1811/1820 with 62 periodicals. However from 1821 there is a second flowering. There were 221 total periodicals in the interval from 1821 to 1830. The data is provided by Veloso. p. 33 (Movimento da Imprensa Periodica Portuguesa-1987)

India Portuguesa (A). 1st. Nova Goa: Imprensa Nacional, 1923.

India Portuguesa. Repartição Central de Estatística E Informação.8 Recenseamento Geral da População: Realizado em 15 de Dezembro de 1950.População, presente de 5 ou mais anos de idade, segundo a lingua materna e o sexo, por religões. Goa: Araujo, 195637

India Portuguesa. Repartição Central de Estatística E Informação.8 Recenseamento Geral da População: Realizado em 15 de Dezembro de 1950. *População, presente de 5 ou mais anos de idade, segundo a lingua materna e o sexo, por religões.* Goa: Araujo, 1956. Table 6. Total number of male and female population above 5 years of age was 599924, Concanim was mother tongue according to this census was 468761, Marathi speakers were 28060, and Portuguese speakers according to the table was 6723. It is unclear, if this census included population of Portuguese speaking soldiers that were serving in Goa at the time. (Page 28-29).

Lopes, Antonio dos Martires (editor). *Imprensa De Goa.* Lisboa: Edição do Comissaridado do Governo para os Assuntos do Estado da Índia, 1974.

Lopes, Antonio dos Martires (editor). *Imprensa De Goa.* Lisboa: Edição do Comissaridado do Governo para os Assuntos do Estado da Índia, 1974.

Lopes, Antonio dos Martires (editor). *Imprensa De Goa.* Lisboa: Edição do Comissaridado do Governo para os Assuntos do Estado da Índia, 1974. p. 12

Lopes, Antonio dos Martires (editor). *Imprensa De Goa.* Lisboa: Edição do Comissaridado do Governo para os Assuntos do Estado da Índia, 1974. p. 13.

Motta de Sousa, Joseì Manuel, and Veloso, Luìcia Maria Mariano. Història da imprensa periòdica portuguesa: subsìdios para uma bibliografia. 1st ed. Coimbra: Biblioteca Geral da Universidade, 1987.

Motta de Sousa, Joseì Manuel, and Veloso, Luìcia Maria Mariano. Història da imprensa periòdica portuguesa: subsìdios para uma bibliografia. 1st ed. Coimbra: Biblioteca Geral da Universidade, 1987.

"Museu Virtual da Imprensa, Porto Portugal." Museu Virtual da Imprensa. N/A. 7 Aug 2006 <http://www.imultimedia.pt/museuvirtpress/port/frame3.html>.

"Museu Virtual da Imprensa, Porto Portugal." Museu Virtual da Imprensa. N/A. 7 Aug 2006 <http://www.imultimedia.pt/museuvirtpress/port/frame3.html>.

National Institute of Statistics, Portugal http://www.ine.pt:8080/biblioteca/sort.do?layoutCollection=0&layoutCollectionProperty=descricao&layoutCollectionState=0

One can use the virtual library of the Statistical Institute of Portugal to download the tiff files that relate to the social conditions in the Metropole.

Pendse, Liladher R., *Explaining the Dawn of Colonial Portuguese Periodicals in Estado da India.*

Please attached Excel Sheet that I created using the data from the Goa Censuses.

Priolkar, Anant. The printing press in India, its beginnings and early development, being a quatercentenary commemoration study of the advent of printing in India in 1556. 1st Edition. Bombay: Marathi Samshodhana Mandala, 1958.

Priolkar, Anant. *The printing press in India, its beginnings and early development, being a quatercentenary commemoration study of the advent of printing in India in 1556.* 1st Edition. Bombay: Marathi Samshodhana Mandala, 1958.

Rangel, Jaime. *A Imprensa em Goa.* Bastora, Goa: Tipografia Rangel, 1956.

Rangel, Jaime. *A Imprensa em Goa.* Bastora, Goa: Tipografia Rangel, 1956. p. 47

Saldanha, Padre M.J.Gabriel de. História de Goa (Politicia e Arqueológica). Reprint. New Delhi: Asian Educational Services, 1990.

Saldanha, Padre M.J.Gabriel de. História de Goa (Politicia e Arqueológica). Reprint. New Delhi: Asian Educational Services, 1990. Saldanha states, " A infatigavel e bene merita Companhia de Jesus introduziu a arte tipografica em Goa'(Saldanha 102).

Saldanha, Padre M.J.Gabriel de. História de Goa (Politicia e Arqueológica). Reprint. New Delhi: Asian Educational Services, 1990. Saldanha states, " A infatigavel e bene merita Companhia de Jesus introduziu a arte tipografica em Goa'(Saldanha 102).

Scholberg, Henry, Archana Ashok Kakodker, and Carmo Azevedo. Bibliography of Goa and the Portuguese India. New Delhi: Promila & Co.

Scholberg, Henry, Archana Ashok Kakodker, and Carmo Azevedo. Bibliography of Goa and the Portuguese India. New Delhi: Promila & Co., 1982.

See note # 8. Lopes documents the names of the editors of Gazeta. This includes a paragraph about editor Lúis Prates who was deported to Brasil in 1819 because of his "extreme-liberal" ideas. Apparently he was back in Goa by 1821. Lopes goes on stating that "Lúis Prates, barbaramente assassinado a baionetadas, o qual "advogava no jornal princípios sãos fulminando as diferenças de nascimento e outros prejuízos da aristrocracia, não duvidando mesmo criticar dessaombradamente os actos governativos e com tudo a junta o nomeou oficial maior interino da seceretaria geral em substituição do que fora suspenso por exigencia da tropa, certamente porque reconhecia nele habilidade para bem se desempenhar desta comissão"(Lopes 13)

Table: "Children and teachers in schools (in thousands, except as otherwise indicated)."International Historical Statistics: Europe 1750-2000. 5th ed. 2003.

Tengarrinha, Joseì. *Història da imprensa perioìdica portuguesa.* Lisboa: Portugaìlia, 1965.

Tengarrinha, Joseì. *Història da imprensa perioìdica portuguesa.* Lisboa: Portugaìlia, 1965.

The population of Portugal according to "International Historical Statistics: Europe 1750-2000" by B.R. Mitchell, Palgrave 2003 indicates the population of Portugal according to census in 1841 was 3,397000 and in 1854 it was 3844000. The 1841 population census did not include Azores and Madeira.

The term Indo-Portuguese has been used in variety of contexts. There are multiple interpretations of the term "Indo-Portuguese". If search the World Cat database using a simple keyword search for the term "Indo-Portuguese" we find various results. One particular monograph by Da Cunha, Joseph Gerson that was published in 1880(3) named "Contributions to the study of Indo-Portuguese Numismatics" denotes the use of term Indo-Portuguese as early as 1880s. Of course WorldCat is by no means a complete database that indexes all of the Indo-Portuguese publications. For example a weekly journal named "A India Portuguesa" whose editor was José Ignacio de Loyola appeared in 1861 in Orlim, Goa and continued to publish till 1898. The founder of this journal was M.L. De Miranda Franco (Lopes, Antonio dos Martires (editor). Imprensa De Goa. Lisboa: Edição do Comissaridado do Governo para os Assuntos do Estado da Índia, 1974.)

The term Indo-Portuguese has been used in variety of contexts. There are multiple interpretations of the term "Indo-Portuguese". If search the WorldCat database using a simple keyword search for the term "Indo-Portuguese" we find various results. One particular monograph by Da Cunha, Joseph Gerson that was published in 1880(3) named "Contributions to the study of Indo-Portuguese Numismatics" denotes the use of term Indo-Portuguese as early as 1880s. Of course WorldCat is by no means a complete database that indexes all of the Indo-Portuguese publications. For example a weekly journal named "A India Portuguesa" whose editor was José Ignacio de Loyola appeared in 1861 in Orlim, Goa and continued to publish till 1898 The founder of this journal was M.L. De Miranda Franco (Lopes, Antonio dos Martires (editor). Imprensa De Goa. Lisboa: Edição do Comissaridado do Governo para os Assuntos do Estado da Índia, 1974.)

31

South Asia Publishing and American Academic Libraries: A Personal Account, 1965-2006

N. GERALD BARRIER

Numerous books and articles have surveyed the South Asian book trade, often basing comments and analysis upon statistical compilations and material available in association newsletters. This essay is a more personal account based on four decades of interaction with American librarian programs and Indian publishers. In that period, I worked with the South Asia Microform Project and the Committee on South Asian Libraries and Documentation, and also helped organize seminars and international conferences. In addition to my own research on the Punjab and Sikhs, I worked closely with several libraries and consulted with Duke in evaluating its collection and accession options. Equally as important was my role as a book dealer. In 1969, I founded South Asia Books which grew over time to become a major conduit for bringing books from the subcontinent to America. Between then and now, the book trade has changed dramatically, as have US library programs, and widening access to India through new programs and especially the internet.

The basic infrastructure of South Asian Studies in America had begun to evolve before I entered the Duke graduate program in 1962. The National Defense Education Act facilitated new programs, scholarship, and enhanced library development. The need for enhanced library holdings and access accompanied the institutionalization of area training. After intense lobbying, the Wheat Loan Act (Public Law 480) was amended in 1958 so that Indian printed books and journals could be purchased from the accumulating rupee account in India. The approval of appropriations in 1961 led to the creation of a Library of Congress office in Delhi and the systematic collection of documents. The LC Accessions List quickly became a major bibliographic guide to publications, both for Indians and Americans, and the monthly shipments of books to a widening group of American libraries meant that immensely rich collections became readily available.[1]

The South Asia Book World I encountered initially in 1965 was disorganized, with generally poor production quality and only primitive networks for distributing books to local academic institutions. Print runs were short, paper quality dismal, and binding mediocre. The one golden feature of the trade was the used book market, where lodes of rich classics and official publications could be found in the major cities as well as in scattered state book depots. In fact, I got into book selling as a used book specialist dealing primarily with official publications that could be purchased often for the original rupee prices. My first major purchase was in Lahore, where I picked up sets of Punjab Censuses (back to 1891) at approximately Rs. 25 a set. Similar values could be found throughout India. My used book interest gave way to circulating new publications among academics and libraries not in the LC system. I also discovered *Choice*, the American Library Association review journal, and managed to have several books a year reviewed there for approximately 25 years. Eventually the journal moved away from books published in India, partially because of quality problems but probably more for the reason that increasingly University presses and some trade publishers began to publish good books on a regular basis, and understandably received priority.

Three cities accounted for most of the academic production in the 1960s. In Bombay, Asia Publishers, Popular Prakashan, and Somiya published monographs. In Calcutta, in addition to academic enterprises such as the various University presses and the Institute of Historical Research, Firma KL Mukhopadhyay was dominant, joined by Minerva and other smaller firms. Delhi then and now served as the center of the book trade. Oxford University Press was the major academic publisher in history and the social sciences, while Motilal Banarsidass and Munshiram Manoharlal provided the bulk of Indological works. By 1969, several book dealers began a transition to publishers. The most notable was Manohar Book Service, among whose initial publication was my *Sikhs and Their Literature* (Manohar, 1969). Within 35 years, Manohar has grown to a major publisher of very good social science works, as well as numerous series and monographs associated with the publication program of the American Institute of Indian Studies. Allied Publishers also appeared on the scene, eventually joined by DK Publications and other firms owned by the same family, joined shortly thereafter by Macmillan India and the most formidable firm publishing excellent reprints, Asian Educational Services.

The primary market for academic books was local or national, not international. Jobbers picked up quantities of titles and work with individual libraries, selling individually or in bulk. The availability of funds from the University Grants Commission helped support the market, which rose and fell depending on funding and distribution access. Since India had an expanding universe of higher education institutions, the India trade did fairly well. Neighbouring countries tended to be smaller with fewer investments in academic and library facilities so that except for a handful of publishers (in Lahore, Ferozsons, in Sri Lanka, Lake Book House, and in Bangladesh, eventually the University Press in Dhaka) sales tended to be erratic and underdeveloped.

The export trade, limited as it was, tended to be a buyer's market. Until approximately 1990, the quality of production and the paucity of competing companies dedicated to creating networks between India and western markets led to minimal sales abroad except for a growing market in school books and reprints. In the last two decades, that has changed dramatically.

First, despite persistent problems with paper quality, Indian publications frequently compete well in an international market. Delhi remains the center of the publishing and printing trade, with first-class firms and high quality production, but Mumbai and Kolkata have excellent printers that turn out excellent books. At the same time, the editorial quality of many publishers has improved. Availability of seasoned editors who work in house or on a contract basis insures reasonable proof reading. The use of external readers in evaluating manuscripts also has become common. Numerous western scholars now publish regularly in a variety of publishing networks generally located in the Delhi area.

Quality monographs also have resulted from joint publishing arrangements that link western publishers with specific Indian firms. At one time or another, Indiana, SUNY, Chicago, and other US University presses worked closely with Indian collaborators.

Two more permanent arrangements are especially noteworthy. Sage India produces dozens of excellent volumes in the social sciences that immediately move into the U.S. Sage network, as well as distributing American volumes in India. Foundation Books in New Delhi handles reprints and other material from Cambridge University Press, and makes those available to Indian institutions with substantially lower prices.

Similarly, institutes or programs outside or inside India have generated collaborative projects and enhanced quality. For example, Motilal has several series based upon funding and academic input from specific groups or associations. The *Encyclopaedia of Indian Philosophies,* edited by Karl Potter and other specialists, is an ongoing and successful guide to sources and issues with collaboration from many sources. The American Institute of Indian Studies and other funding agencies have contributed to the Encyclopaedia. Approximately ten volumes have been produced in another series on Indian medical traditions, with subsidies and ongoing contributions from scholars associated with the Wellcome Trust Centre in London and the European Ayurvedic Society. The Indira Gandhi Centre has provided funding and editorial support for many collections of documents on art, dance, music, and cultural traditions. Their monographs have been spread among several publishers, with Motilal publishing the most extensive group in its Kalamulasastra series. Similarly, Manohar has worked with Heidenburg University and academic groups and networks in France and Japan. Titles in the most notable two new series, the People of India Series (sponsored by the Anthropological Society of India with extensive grants) and the History of Science, Philosophy and Culture in Indian Civilization (general editor, D.P. Chattopadhyay, organized by the Centre for Study of Civilizations) have been published by Concept, Popular Prakashan, Manohar, Motilal, Munshiram, and OUP among others.

There presently are three tiers of publishers, some at the highest level of academic and production excellence, and a secondary group that turn out reasonable publications with mixed quality. The lowest and often largest group of publishers churns out poorly edited volumes and frequently engages in generating substantial projects loosely labelled as "Encyclopaedias" that in fact are hodge-podge collections of essays, reprints, and documents that may have some interest but are often unusable for academic purposes.

Older firms such as Orient Longman, DK Printworld, and Rawat now have joined the group recognized as sources for premier works such as OUP, Motilal, Munshiram, and Manohar. Seagull in Calcutta and also now in Delhi has an extensive line in cinema and drama, as well as publishing many play and film scripts. Marg continues to produce some of the most beautiful and scholarly works on art, architecture, religion, and dance available anywhere. Other publishers noted for a particular genre or a lower quality mass production have improved quality and expanded their academic list. Lotus/Lustre Press has an ongoing program involving literature and art, often using art paper and excellent printers. The most notable change in that category, however, is Rupa Publications. Once known for novels and reprints, the firm has expanded its literature selection, and now has an academic program with quality editing and production.

New smaller but excellent publishers appear almost every few months, developing a niche or specialty that insures a place in the market. The evolution of Permanent Black illustrates how and why new publishers operate. The owner and staff associated with the firm originally had provided leadership for Oxford University Press, and then decided to use their expertise in creating another conduit for notable authors in history and the social sciences. Within a few years, Permanent Black has an international reputation and regularly publishes work by some of the best scholars in India and throughout the world. Many of the titles are joint publications with western firms, usually with Permanent Black performing the editorial and production effort and then selling sheets or plates to their partners. Oxford employees also have set up several other small but very good firms. A similar pattern can be found with the premier publisher in feminist literature, Kali for Women. Associates from that firm now have set up two publishing houses, Zubaan and Women Unlimited, both of which produce high quality books often in collaboration with foreign presses.

The book trade in neighbouring countries has not kept up with changes in Indian publishing. Nepal has several reputable publishers, but most of the titles do not reach a broader audience except those available through Indian sellers or direct sale by mail. Bangladesh also has a variety of institutional publishers along with University Press, but again, access is limited and supply through India often hit and miss. The premier English language publisher in Pakistan remains Oxford University Press, Karachi, which produces a stream of new editions and reprints with quality similar to those of its sister organization in Delhi. The Karachi books often go through the Delhi network or occasionally into the US or UK inventories. Sri Lanka has undergone some of the most significant changes recently, with several efforts to coordinate distribution and sales both within country as well as exports. Many academic libraries tied to the LC system acquire books from all these countries on a regular basis, although the LC staff in Delhi often faces major hurdles in ensuring a steady supply of good books from outside India.

Since the mid-1990s, Indian publishers have been able to publish on the average over two thousand quality monographs and series per year. This sustained growth has coincided with significant changes in the US and international market that have opened new opportunities for selling Indian books abroad. In Europe, expansion of South Asia studies has led to more acquisition demands for new and established libraries. Japan, China, and especially Australia have been more interested in books from India.[2]

The expansion of the American market has been facilitated by at least four interconnected developments. First, academic and teaching interest in South Asia has grown at a rate almost unimaginable a couple of decades ago. Literally hundreds of colleges and universities now have courses relating to the region, either free-standing offerings in history, social sciences, women's studies, literature, language, and religion, or more frequently inclusion of South Asia topics in comparative courses. Discussion with faculty at major conferences suggests that new programs are sprouting up all over the country. Increases in job opportunities also points to steady growth. For example, there often are several positions open annually for instruction in Hindi, Sanskrit, and other Indian languages, as well as regular permanent and temporary posts in religion and other fields. Last year over a dozen schools had openings for history professors, and this year, the number exceeds twenty. The combination of library acquisition and textbook requirements resulting from this expansion offers new opportunities for purchase and use of the best books from the Indian market.

The changes in the LC acquisition system combined with the strengthening of regular distribution systems from India have enhanced the American market. With the end of Rupee funding for the LC program, the Delhi operation moved to a dollar-based acquisition program. Acquisitions became streamlined in light of individual library and consortia criteria and profiles, but with some notable exceptions, a stream of scholarly books from first-line publishers has continued to reach libraries in the LC system. In fact, the accession program has expanded to include numerous new programs, so that approximately forty libraries in North America and other countries receive books regularly from the Delhi office. Similar expansion of the Shastri Library Program in Canada also has led to more regularized sales.

At the same time several Indian distributors have strengthened networks into the U.S. market. The oldest, DK Agencies, continues to offer timely and accurate information on recent books and serials. Its mailers and internet offerings reach literally hundreds of academics and libraries. UBSPD in Delhi has a similar program, distributing literature as well as sending sales representatives on regular trips throughout the world. Other publishers have attempted to set up their own branches, usually a failure because of competition and the high administrative costs. Motilal, however, has managed to develop an effective branch operation in the UK which provides its publications along with other titles throughout Europe. Most publishers work with established US vendors, most notably, my firm South Asia Books. We have distribution arrangements for sixty publishers and regularly register their titles in Bowker's Books in Print. Presently over 20,000 titles are available in that network. We warehouse many, and special order others as needed.

In a real sense, all the old marketing networks and strategies now are being made obsolete by the rapid rise of e-commerce. Virtually every major Indian publisher now has a website and sells directly to customers world-wide. Joining them is a growing number of dealers who supply titles on demand from the Indian market. Reasonable airmail charges from India help facilitate rapid supply. Most other countries continue to be far behind in this area except that now Yapa Publishers has a major website and regularly supplies Sri Lankan books.

As in the case of the American book trade, Amazon.Com is the major source for Indian books in North America and to some extent, throughout the world. BN.Com has a parallel network, but Amazon remains dominant in the supply of academic and popular books. Amazon has two programs that account for very significant sales. First, its Advantage program offers Indian books from regular stock. Since Amazon requires books either to be published in North America or have recognized distribution, South Asia Books is the primary supplier with over

5,000 titles in the system. Advantage is consignment only, with monthly payments and restocking based on actual or projected sales.

The second Amazon venue, Marketplace, could be summarized as the "wild west of Indian book sales" where few rules hamper sales and offerings. Anyone can sell virtually any book, despite publication or distribution rights, through the system. Amazon receives the payment, receives a nominal commission, and then the vendor supplies the book directly and receives payment on a regular basis from Amazon. At present there are approximately ten major sellers offering books through the program. Most operate more or less from the US although since several claims to have over 100,000 titles in active stock, they obviously buy on demand and then airfreight in stock as needed. At least one supplier claims to be in the US but ships from outside Delhi, a model that probably will become more prominent. Amazon provides only minimal supervision and intervention in Marketplace sales. Sellers compete with each other, often reducing prices by a penny or two to undercut others, with the result that often book prices drop drastically. Apparently the mass sellers make their profits through quantity rather than margins on individual prices.

Amazon, new websites, and in general e-commerce have globalized the Indian book trade and opened new markets. Literally hundreds of individuals and libraries make purchases everyday.[3] The new availability of good books and market changes, however, has been accompanied by new problems and challenges. Some are obvious and will be addressed by market demands. For example, quality control by new sellers unaccustomed to expectations of sophisticated buyers has and will continue to be problematic. Poor service and inability to supply books not readily available from the market creates problems and probably sours the interest and trust of unsophisticated customers. The lack of rules and supervision of what can and cannot be sold remains a persistent problem for US publishers who are involved in reprint or joint publication arrangements with Indian firms. The Indian publishers usually do not sell books marked "for the South Asia market only" directly into the US, but distributors and individual sellers have no such qualms.

Thus several US firms have withdrawn from these experiments, cutting off the availability of some US scholarship from access to the Indian market.

In terms of sellers such as South Asia Books, which had a model of warehousing substantial stock of thousands of books, the new challenges have forced strategic changes. Several bookstores that used to carry an extensive range of titles from India now are out of business. Others try to buy directly from publishers, or in most cases, reduce active inventories because of e-commerce competition. They also set up websites and adapt with changing business models.

For example, South Asia Books now purchases only a few copies of major publications and then restock through airfreight (expensive) or seacargo (inexpensive) as needed. We compete regularly in Marketplace where possible, but frankly, many of the prices get so low that even with books in stock, we would lose money to sell at that level. Advertising at conferences also has become less attractive. Given the rising costs for exhibiting and declining sales dues to customers often buying directly from publishers or through e-commerce, South Asia Books is reducing its exhibit presence at the Madison South Asia Conference and the Association of Asian Studies, and trimming back on the American Academy of Religion annual meetings. On the other hand, our new website has over 5,000 titles at attractive prices and draws more and more customers. We also have developed new library programs that build upon our ability to supply from stock and forty years of expertise in academics and the Indian market.

Librarians and faculty also are trying to unsort options and develop a successful acquisition strategy. Problems for major libraries in the LC acquisition system are three-fold. Scholarly Indian books are increasingly in number and cost, thus putting pressure on individual institutions with limited dollar funds or shifting priorities. Many of the programs also have a commitment to maintaining collections in various Indian languages. This in turn consumes time and also resources available for English-language acquisitions.

At the same time, some worthwhile books do not enter the accessions system with consequent gaps in core collections. Although constrictions caused by inadequate dollars contribute to the problem, probably most of the omissions result from the collection system itself. Distributors compete to supply books to the LC staff, and as a result of the financial squeeze, more specialized or lower discount publications sometimes get lost in the process.[4]

Finally, South Asia bibliographers now play additional roles in their respective libraries and have little time to locate lacunae and fill them systematically. Some of the pioneers in South Asia libraries have retired, sometimes being replaced or responsibilities being transferred to librarians with multiple responsibilities.

Libraries not in the LC system or without area specialists confront an even more daunting task. Some have approval programs that incorporate a few books from India, usually Sage and Oxford University Press, but Baker and Taylor, Midwest, Yankee Book Peddler, Blackwell North America, and other distributors offering approvals generally do not purchase Indian books except on special order. When faculty send over checked lists or individual requests, problems of evaluating the new titles and ranking them in light of existing discipline or area priorities come into play. The flood of email lists and the availability to titles on Amazon and other venues compound the problem. There are too many good books, and too few funds. Sometimes one-time boosts to collection development or year-end funds permits strengthening holdings, but the struggle to maintain a combined teaching and research collection continues to plague most libraries including those with expanding South Asia programs.

Several solutions appear prominent, most notably the formation of consortia by region or groups of local institutions, or the emergence of approval programs or relations with one or more vendors that helps insure steady supply. Whatever the problems and solutions, however, individual buyers and libraries in America increasingly need reliable information and regularized systems for tapping the dynamic Indian market. Although the transitions and options may be troublesome, the network that links Indian publishers and the US market has never been more healthy. Globalization has brought India to the doorstep of many Americans and especially into the acquisition systems of US academic libraries.

Notes

1. Evolution of the library program and area studies reviewed in Louis A. Jacob, ed. *American Understanding of India* (Manohar, 2001). My book prepared for the 1985 Festival India, sponsored by the Ford Foundation, covers the evolution of American-Indian intellectual exchange and the resulting publications and printed record: *India and America: American Publishing on India 1930-1985* (American Institute of Indian Studies, 1986).
2. Based upon my systematic monitoring of publication lists, and accumulation of regular new book catalogs from several highly organized distributors such as UBSPD and DK Agencies. Although there is no scholarly literature available on networks and sales in these countries, anecdotal evidence from discussions with individual publishers and distributors suggests a rapid strengthening of sales into the world market. My observations on trends in the US are based on regular discussions with librarians and faculty at conferences and through extensive internet communications.
3. Based on study of sales and customer comments for eight major Amazon Marketplace sellers. A couple probably sell between fifty and a hundred books a day. We average around 20 a day, and in the Advantage program, approximately 600 books a month.
4. I have been working through our large inventory and checking holdings against online catalogs of major publishers. Some publishers have been under-represented, while others such as Sage and Oxford University Press (which have US outlets) apparently sometimes are not included in the bulk purchases. Novels and literature also tends to have gaps, especially Penguin India. I appreciate Merry Burlingham commenting on the paper. As she notes, the individual profiles vary so that any detailed assessment of the system must take into consideration many variables. My generalizations are based primarily on my research in online catalogs and also almost four decades of experience in the book trade and not an exhaustive assessment of the profiles and purchase patterns that keep changing with program demands and shifts in funding.

Part VII
Technical Services

32

Authority Control of Romanised Arabic Names in OPAC

VEERANKUTTY CHELATAYAKKOT and V. JALAJA,

Introduction

The selection of one form of heading as entry heading and creating cross-references from other headings was the usual practice of the cataloguer. For consistency, an authority file is created to record the selection of heading. The authority control helped the cataloguer to prepare entries of all the works of an author under one standard form of name and provide references to this form of name from variant forms. Authority work consists of "the creation of authority records, the formation of such records into an authority file, the linking of that file to the bibliographic file to form a system, the maintenance of the authority file and system, and the evaluation of the file and system"[1]. On the cataloguer's perspective authority control has following functions: (a) authority functions,(b) finding functions, (c) information functions, and (d) maintenance functions.

The name authority file links variant forms of heading to the preferred form of heading to help preparation of cross-references. An author may use different names/pseudonyms or variant spellings may be occurred due to the transliteration process. In both situations, the cataloguer should create cross-references from variant names/pseudonyms or variant spelling of a unique name to the preferred heading.

In the automated environment, MARC records are created for authorities and serve the same function as in the card environment. 1xxs are used to denote established headings and 4xxs for See References. The Web environment opens up new uses for authority records and adds new objectives to augment the traditional objectives. Authority record in web environment enabled users to access information in any language, script and form they prefer and it work as a link to digital resources such as biographical dictionaries, abstracting and indexing services, telephone directory and other reference sources in the web. In an automated/ online environment, when a user keyed in known form of a heading, the system would automatically link variant form of headings to the preferred form of headings. Here, the authority control mechanism works as invisible so far as a user is concerned.

Transliteration Schemes and Unicode

The aim of transliteration is to represent the script of a source language by using the letters or symbols of another script, usually in accordance with the orthographical conventions of the target language. By the result, a unique name in one language or culture may have variant spelling in another language. For consistency in transliteration process, the ideal solution would be to have a standard, internationally agreed, transliteration system. Event though the usage of standardized transliteration tables, which may helps for consistency in transliteration process, were founded as inconvenient in naming process. A person born in Muslim family in Kerala, possessing an Arabic name, at first, use Malayalam to write his name, and later, transliterate into English for any official purpose causes for variant spellings of a unique name.

Since the advent of Unicode as a universal character code, electronic representation of non-Roman character is not an issue. Unicode provides a unique number to every character used in modern script.[2] However, in a database having Arabic names entered in Arabic using Unicode cannot be of use to such people who does not know that language. So transliteration is inevitable to meet the need of international users.

Authority Control *versus* Access Control

The access control record is the next generation of the authority record. It may be called as "super authority record" because of the potential it contains for enriched information for indexing. Access control records can be linked both to bibliographic records, to collocate all manifestations of a work, and to other related access control records, to collocate related works. The basic concept behind the access control record is removing both the label and notion of "authority". While authority control record declare a heading as "authorized" form, access control record links all variations without declaring one heading as authorized form. Access control records allow users to choose their preferred form or name, or to have displayed a default heading. It allows for more flexibility in display.[3] The concept of access control is entirely contradicts the whole second part of AACR-2, which is devoted to painstaking rules for how to construct authorized forms of names and titles.

Name Searching and Information Retrieval

Information scientist had developed a number of methods to solve the problem of variant spelling in Information Retrieval process. In most commercial information retrieval systems, the user only has the possibility to mark his query with elaborated wildcards to find derived or similar words. Stemming algorithms is another technique used in many systems. But this technique is not appropriate in the case of non-regular (Out of Vocabulary) words. Out of Vocabulary (OOV) words are a common source of errors in Cross Lingual Information Retrieval (CLIR). Bilingual dictionaries are often limited in their coverage of named-entities, numbers, technical terms and acronyms. A significant proportion of OOV words are named entities and technical terms. Typical analysis finds around 50 per cent of OOV words to be named entities. Variations in the English spelling of words of foreign origin may contribute to OOV errors.

Similarity measures are widely used to solve the problem of variant spellings. Most of non-linguistic similarity measures can be subdivided into three categories: (a) String similarity measures. which includes n-gram matching, (b) similarity with respect to typing errors, which counts the insertion, deletion, substitution, permutation and transposition needed to transform one string into another (Edit Distance Measure), and (c) phonetic similarity, which compare the similarity of sounds. A simple form of string similarity measure is an Edit-Distance measure. This method measures the number of single characters needed to be inserted and deleted to transform one string to another.[4]

The quality of online databases is very much related to the quality of data in the database. There will be variant spelling, omission, deletion or typing errors for a unique entity. By the acceleration of electronic publishing, there is increase in number of online databases. The challenge is to acquire correct information from the databases. One aspect of improving data quality is detection of variant names for a unique entity and linking them to improve searching. This is similar to authority work. The technique of authority work has wide implication in the effectiveness of Information Retrieval in online databases.

When a user keyed in a known form of a heading, the system would follows internal linkage and displays the requested item even though the preferred form of heading might be quite different from the form entered. There should be direct linkage between the form of heading entered and record displayed. The authority control mechanism works as invisible mechanism so far as a user is concerned.

Authority Files of Romanized Arabic Names

A study on authority files of transliterated Arabic names in Library of Congress Name Authority File reveals many interesting findings. Most of 4xx entries (cross-references) are variant spellings of unique Arabic names. For example,

	Heading (1xx)	Cross-reference (4xx)
1.	Bashier, Zakaria	Bashir Zakaria
2.	Bas¯ir Totiyil	Basheer Todiyil
3.	Basheer, Vaikom Muhammad	Basir, Vaikkam Muhammada
4.	Bash¯ir Husain, Em	Basheer Hussain M
5.	Basheer, Tahseen	Bashir Tahseen

A close analysis of headings (1xx) and Cross-reference (4xx) show that some possible spellings are due to permutation of each other i.e. ‘ie’ as ‘i’, ‘i’ as ‘ee’ ‘sh’as ‘s’. It is also seen that the heading (1xx) used in one authority file is the cross-reference (4xx) in another authority file and *vice versa*. This implication has vided importance in the automation of authority file of transliterated Arabic names.

Arabic names include four elements, i.e., Ism, Laqab, Kunya and Nisbah.[5] Among these, Ism is most prominent and it is an essential element of Arabic name, even though there are exceptions. The inclusion of other elements in Muslim names is differing from region to region. It would be place name as in Basheer, Vaikom Muhammad or initial as in Bash¯ir Husain, Em. or expansion of initial as in Bas¯ir Totiyil. But the Ism, the central elements, would be there in almost all Muslim names throughout the world. So the variant spellings or usage of other elements have less importance in authority file.

As stated earlier, the permutations of spelling in headings/cross-references have vide implication in the automation of name authority files. If we apply the techniques of access control in this context, it would give a better solution to the automation of transliterated Arabic names' authority file. In access control, instead of selecting one heading as preferred heading, all headings are linked to each other. Then while the user searching on a heading would automatically be linked to the other headings. If we can create the variant spellings of an Arabic name through permutation, we can link the non-preferred headings very easily. While the user searching for one heading, the system automatically creates the possible variant spellings of the input heading and links them together. The burden of selecting one heading as preferred heading by showing the reference sources in the field of 670 in MARC records would be saved for the cataloguer. This can be diagrammatically represented as follows:

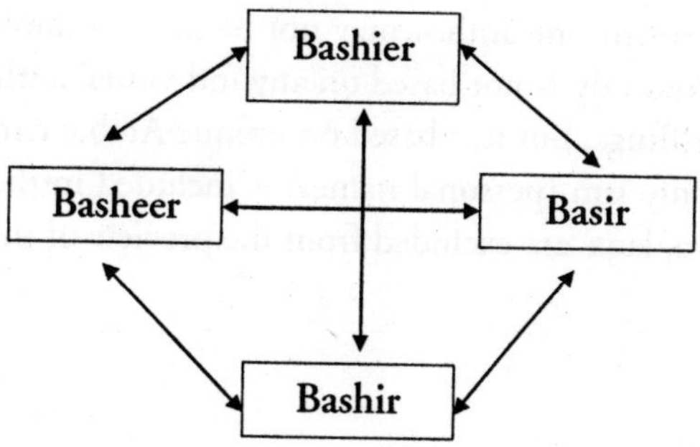

Fig. 33.1 Diagrammatic Representation of Access Control

Methodology

The study is intended to understand the spelling variation in usage of Arabic name. This study can be done in two methods. One is listing all unique Arabic names and its spelling variations, i.e. name approach. The second method is to compare Arabic alphabet with corresponding/similar Roman letters and find out the variations with the help of standardized Romanization table, i.e. spelling approach. The researcher selected the second method.

There are 28 alphabets in Arabic and 26 alphabets in English. Among these, B(ب), H(ح), D(د), R(ر), K(ك), L(ل), M(م), N(ن) are the correct pronunciation/transliterations of corresponding Arabic alphabets. The other alphabets are slight difference in pronunciations. Even though the alphabets like F(ف), S(س), SH(ش), Z(ز), W(و) are the correct pronunciation of corresponding Arabic alphabets, they are also used to represent the other Arabic letters. The plan of the study can be diagrammatically represent as below:

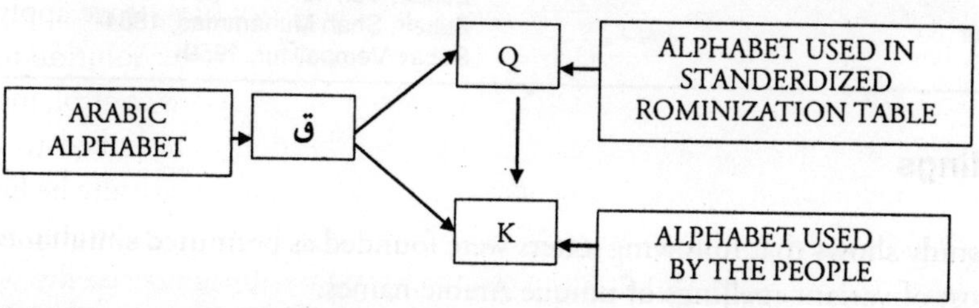

Fig. 33.2 Diagrammatic Representation of Analysis

The alphabets are grouped as consonants and vowels. The Library of Congress Romanization Table has taken standardized Romanization table. All the personal names (name of authors) selected as example were lived/living personalities, which are used as headings in Library of Congress Name Authority File (LCNAF).

Generally, authority file is created for individual authors. It means that an authority file created for one author may not be same as another author having the same name. The study is not based on any individual authors who are using different names/spellings, but it is based on unique Arabic names and its variant spellings in use. Only ism (personal names) is included in the study. The other elements like kunya, laqa' are excluded from the preview of the study.

Analysis

A sample from analysis:

S and Z

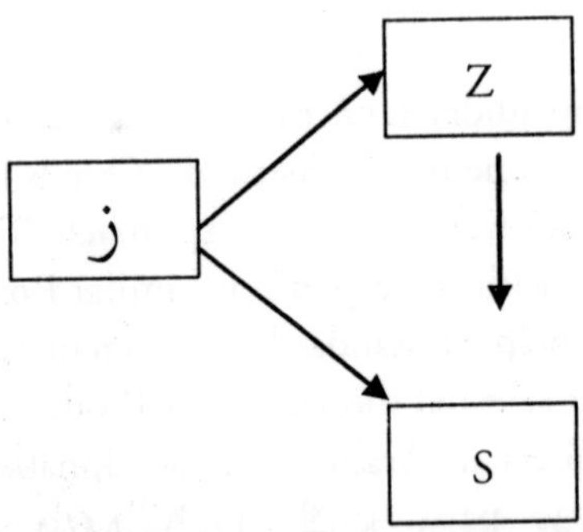

Name	Name in Arabic	Name as Headings in LCNAF
Zuhra	هرهز	Suha_ra, Bi. Em Nur Nina Zuhra
Zaid	ديز	Zaid, Abdulla S., 1945- Said, A. Fuad, 1924-
Zuhair	ريهز	Suhair Cunkatta_ra Zuhair, Vah¯id
Zubair	ريبز	Zubair, Shah Muhammad, 1884- Subair Vempall¯ur, 1959-

Findings

The study shows that following letters were founded as permuted simultaneously in most of variant spellings of unique Arabic names.

Table 32.1 Pairs of Letters Simultaneously Used in Transliterated Arabic Names

Arabic Alphabet	Transliteration by LC	Transliteration in Usage	Arabic Alphabet	Transliteration by LC	Transliteration in Usage
ق	Q	K	ي	Y	YY
ز	Z	S	!	i	e
ش	SH	S	!	i	a
ط	T	TH	ع	u	o
ج	J	G	ي	i	ee
ف	F	PH	ي	i	ie
ق	Q	KH	أ	u	o
خ	KH	K	ي	i	y
غ	GH	G	أ	a	e
و	W	V	وا	u	ou
س	S	SS	أ	a	u/e
م	M	MM	وا	oo	u

Conclusion: Automated Authority Control System

In the proposed system, the input is transliterated Arabic name. The system would automatically create major variant spellings by permuting the alphabets, which are found from the analysis of transliterated Arabic names. But the pairs of letter shown above may not be occurs in all names having the same letter. For example: when i is permuted as ee, then Bashir is permuted as Basheer which is correct, but when Zainaba is permuted as Zaeenaba, it is wrong.

So, while manipulating the common variant alphabet, the system will retrieve false hints. In order to overcome this task, a filter program has to be incorporated in the system. The researcher developed a program to perform this function.

Methodology of Performance Evaluation

Each name's possible (not rare) spelling variations were searched in Google search engine and total hits were summed. This sum was taken as 100. Then, the percentage of each spelling variations were calculated. By using this percentage for each spelling variations, the performance of the output were calculated. The performance evaluation was done on March 2005. Since Google search engine indexes thousands of new web pages daily, the figure may be changed. A sample of performance evaluation shown in Table 32.2.

The performance of the program was evaluated by comparing common variant spellings of Arabic names in use and output of the program. Each name's variant spellings and output were searched in Google search engine and total hits were counted and analyzed. The program shows 83.2 per cent performance.

Table 32.2 Performance Evaluation of the Automated Authority Control System

Name/ Input	Permu- tation	Commonly Found Variant Spellings	Hits in Google	Per Cent (Total of (4) as 100)	Output	Per cent	Total of (7)
(1)	(2)	(3)	(4)	(5)	(6)	(7)	(8)
Ahmad	a/e	Ahmad	2,570,000	37.00	Ahmad	37.00	99.92
		Ahmed	4,370,000	62.92	Ahmed	62.92	
		Ahammad	4,340	0.06			
		Ahammed	781	0.02			
Ahmed	e/a	—do—	—do—	—do—	—do—	—do—	99.92
Raheem	ee/i	Raheem	191,000	22.87	Raheem	22.87	98.48
	ee/ie	Rahim	615,000	73.67	Rahim	73.67	
		Rahiem	9,070	1.09	Rahiem	1.09	
		Rahem	7,090	0.85	Rahem	0.85	
		Rehim	12,700	1.52			
Rehim	a/a	—do—	—do—	—do—	Raheem	22.87	100
					Rahim	73.67	
					Rahiem	1.09	
					Rahem	0.85	
					Rehim	1.52	
Rahim	i/ee	—do-	—do—	—do—	Raheem	22.87	98.48
	i/ie				Rahim	73.67	
					Rahiem	1.09	
					Rahem	0.85	

Application of Automated Name Authority Control System

This automation program has wider applications in Information Retrieval.

In OPAC, it helps to replace the current practice of authority control. It supports access control, the "super authority record". While authority control record declare a heading as "authorized" form, access control record links all variations without declaring one heading as authorized form. The painstaking cataloguing rules for how to construct authorized forms can be put off. The cost of authority work can be minimized.

This program can be used as an interface in database name searching. When a searcher key in a known form (spelling) of a name, the system automatically creates spelling variations and displays the requested item even though the preferred spelling might be quite different from what is entered. The researcher has developed a prototype interface for this purpose.

This program can be used as a tool in free text name searching in corpora like newspaper articles, press cuttings etc.

This program helps to detect Arabic proper names and their spelling variations in automatic speech recognition output, where, the pronunciation difference, in speech recognition system, creates spelling variations.

This program will be helpful in detecting spelling errors, omissions, and deletions of Arabic names in databases.

This program can be used as a tool to increase recall in Information Retrieval.

Notes

1. Barnhart, Linda. 1996. Access Control Records: Precepts and Challenges Authority Control in 21st Century: An invitational Conference 10 March 2005 http://digitalarchive.oclc.org/
2. Burger, Robert H. (1985). Authority Work: the Creation, Use, Maintenance and Evaluation of Authority Records and Files. Littleton, Colo.: Libraries Unlimited.
3. Encyclopedia of Islam Ed. Evan Donzel et al. New ed. Vol. 4. Leiden: E.J.Brill, (1978). 179-181.
4. Pfeifer, Olrich, Poersch, (1996). Thomas and Fuhr, Norbert "Retrieval Effectiveness of Proper Name Search Methods" Information Processing and Management 32.6, pp. 667-679.
5. Unicode Home Page. (2004). 26 November 2004 <http://www.unicode.org>

33

Classification and Cataloguing Services: Skill Requirements of a Large Academic Library in Digital Environment—Study of JRD Tata Memorial Library, Bangalore

K.S. CHUDAMANI and H.C. NAGARATHNA

Introduction

Classification and cataloguing activities have developed for more than a hundred years. When theoretical developments in these areas had reached a dead end, Library automation was inducted, it opened a plethora of new areas of research and practical system development like automated classification and cataloguing. This also required new skills to be acquired by the Library and information science professionals. This paper explores these developments in the context of JRD Tata Memorial Library an academic library catering to the research and teaching requirements of the faculty and students.

Academic Libraries

Large academic libraries were established as part of large universities carrying out research and teaching activities. The universities have many departments devoted to research and development in the areas of work assigned to them. As and when research turned interdisciplinary, the existing departments collaborated not only with other departments within the Institution to carry on research but also sought outside collaboration beyond their countries. As such research has turned global. Now, the research world has reached a stage wherein the world has become a global village. Large number of open access information repositories have come into existence to compete with published journals.

The information professionals now require skills that enable them to search and retrieve and record valuable research from the repositories to serve their clientele. The information skills dominating the digital environment will be described in the following section.

Information skills

Information literacy is not only recognized more widely but also seen as a key to social inclusion. Information literacy implies the knowledge of using Information technology. Which technology and to what extent depends on the need. It implies the finding of information at the right time to the right user. It is a chaining process which leads from one type of skill to another. It controls the delivery of information. It also leads to building up personal knowledge base. It enhances individual knowledge and enables novel insights. It is also a skill which can benefit others.

Information literacy is basic to information skills. In this context, it connotes "the set of skills needed to find, retrieve, analyze, and use information" (ALA, 2003). Further, according to SCONUL (1999) there are seven pillars. From the point of view of the current approach, they are the capability to identify a need, the mode of addressing the problem which may lead to a solution, knowledge about available resources or identification of the need for a new resource, selection of the most appropriate resources, capability to handle the resource, the ability to modify and reuse the resource, to device a systematic approach to apply or use the resource and lastly, a knowledge of the principles involved in the creation and generation of new tools, if necessary. The next section looks at the digital library era as delineated by Wikipedia.

Digital Library

According to Wikipedia (http://en.wikipedia.org/wiki/Digital_library), A digital library is a library in which a significant proportion of the resources are available in machine-readable format (as opposed to print or microform), accessible by means of computers.[1] The digital content may be locally held or accessed remotely *via* computer networks. In libraries, the process of digitization began with the catalog, moved to periodical indexes and abstracting services, then to periodicals and large reference works, and finally, to book publishing. Some of the largest digital libraries are purely digital having few if any physical holdings. According to Murugesan and Babu, Digital library offers the creation of open, distributed and publicly accessible resource, establish a collaborative structure that defines the accessibility, develops criteria and standards to guide the selection of materials and adds value to digital resources.[2]

In the digital context, the library catalogue is also a digital resource. It enables remote access to information about its records and ' or full text access to its holdings.

The next section presents a description of the classification and cataloguing section and its information skill requirement.

Information skills for Classification and cataloguing section, JRDTML

The JRD Tata Memorial Library is popularly known as the Indian Institute of Science Library (IISc). It being one of the best Science and Technology Libraries in India, was started in 1911, as one of the first three departments in the Institute. It has become a precious national resource center in the field of Science and Technology.

IISc Library's role is to develop and maintain a special collection of materials and to make this material available to all research students and scholars mainly from the Institute. In this aspect this has meant collecting and preserving print and other physical objects supplemented with the provision of access to the electronic collection. Print and electronic sources of information now need to be integrated to provide our users with continuous access to information.

The library is recognized as a Special Library for Researchers who increasingly expect direct access to information resources in their department through network system at location and time of their choice. IISc has also recognized the importance of the network as a mechanism to deliver services to all students and faculties. While digital access to parts of the collection has been provided for some time, the network provides a framework through which future digitization activities will be undertaken.

The JRD Tata Memorial Library was established in 1909 (earlier called IISc library) as soon as the Indian Institute of Science was started. But, it was formally inaugurated in 1911. It initially organized its collection by arranging the books in broad discipline based categories like physics, chemistry, etc. With the advent of Colon classification and its widespread use in India, it classified its collection using CC. After facing some problems relating to enumeration of new subjects, it changed its classification scheme to DDC 18th edition in 1979. Later DDC 20th edition was introduced after a detailed comparative study of 20th edition and 18th addition without any reclassification. But with the emergence of DDC 22nd edition[3] it faced difficulties in changing over to 22nd edition. A reclassification of the revision in biology has been ventured into though it is difficult to transcend. Thus, with the advent of later editions sectional reclassification will have to be considered to cope with emerging knowledge development. In addition, DDC 22nd edition is built on sound principles that make it deal as a general knowledge organization tool: Meaningful notation in universally recognized Arabic numerals, well-defined categories. Well-developed hierarchies, and a rich network of relationships among topics. It has more faceted features like tables, schedule mnemonics divide like, add to mnemonic features compared to the earlier editions which is helpful in fulfilling classification needs. Webdewey is another development that has not been utilized. In future, the library may switchover for the web version, if warranted.

Classification skills: This development requires the knowledge of comparing schedules recaptulating the differences and enhancements in the schedule development. Also, enumeration of new terms to fit into already enumerated classes. Also, allocation and collocation prospects of the schedules. Retrieval problems. Organization of the reclassified items and avoiding homonyms. Also design and development of depth classification schedules, expansion of schedules as and when needed, etc.[4]

Cataloguing: The library started with the minimum information requirements of 5*3 cards as in CCC. Later with the change to DDC, 18th edition in 1979, it moved to AACR2. But the old cards were not replaced. Only class numbers were changed without changing the description. Thus, it continued to have CCC cards with DDC (18th edition) numbers. When automation was started in 1987-88 using Dbase, unit cards were generated for the new books. This worked quite well as the user's needs were met out of the card catalogue. However when full automation was taken up in 1996 records were input from the accession register, the records remained incomplete. The records were edited in two projects and upgraded to some level of satisfaction. This requires a thorough knowledge of AACR2 and its rules, rendering of names, and other fields, etc.

E-books: Classification and Cataloguing

The JRD Tata Memorial library acquired 10000 e-books in 2004. As it is well known, an e-book is an electronic resource which can be read on a computer screen. Access to these were initially provided via a website. In 2005, it was decided to include them in the weekly list of additions alphabetically by title. The first set procured from e-brary had almost the essential bibliographic information required for processing these items and were easily included in the weekly list. They were then transferred to an excel file. As a next step, when engbase e-books were selected,

Marc records were available for them. The whole text file was downloaded and initially the bibliographic data was manually captured and added to our collection. It was noticed that the e-books were classified in locations not suitable for our library. They were reclassified. But, physical separation of bibliographic details was an arduous task; taxing the brain and physical well-being. So, when marcedit program was found, it was installed and converted all the records to Dublin core format. This appeared to be easy for handling. But, this program turned out to be a half baked one because it did not retrieve all the information that was needed to gather. The addition process continues without omitting the fields that are not available for the time being.

This shows that there is a need for finding suitable data conversion programs, classification knowledge, knowledge of AACR2 for converting the data and associated knowledge.

Conclusion

From the above presentation, it can be noted that the fundamental knowledge that is gained from an library and information science course like classification, cataloguing etc. need to be strengthened and information about availability of suitable software from a reliable source are essential for the work in an academic library.

Notes

1. WIKIPedia
2. Murugesan, M. and Babu, R. Jawahar (2006). Role of digital libraries in engineering colleges in *Digital libraries: from technology to culture*, ed. by C. Anandan and M. Gangatharan, New Delhi, Kanishka Publishers.
3. DDC 22nd edition
4. Webb, Jo and Powis, Chris (2004). *Teaching information skills: theory and practice*, London, Facet publishing.

Part VIII
Miscellaneous Issues

34

Future of Reference Service and Reference Librarians

B. MINI DEVI

Introduction

The concept about reference librarian has changed over the last twenty years. With the explosive development of electronic resources, especially Internet, is revolutionising the concept of reference librarian. The increase in the number of students engaged in distance-education, full text electronic e-journals add new challenges to the profession. The digital and virtual reference sources are dragging reference librarian out of the reference desk and encouraging to think globally. To Martell "librarians must begin to design an imaginative, easily identifiable space in cyberspace as the centrality of the library as a physical phenomenon slowly fades. This does not mean that librarians will be irrelevant or obsolete. It does mean that the services of librarians will be provided most effectively in a virtual environment." Today the face to face interaction between the user and the librarian became atypical. The figure of reference librarian has changed to an "instruction librarian" in South Asia. Library instruction and more and more resources available through the Web, online research services such as Questia and Ebrary add more complexity of the problem. Reference librarian should be able to demonstrate proficiency in information literacy instruction. The definition of information literacy by ALA Presidential Committee on Information Literacy, "To be information literate, a person must be able to recognize when information is needed and have the ability to locate, evaluate and use effectively the needed information, is best suit for reference librarian."

Qualities of Reference Librarian

An enthusiastic service oriented high-qualified reference librarian should possess the following qualities:

(1) *Flexible and creative*: Beyond cultural limitations librarians should be flexible to meet the diverse information needs of the users. They should be always alert about the recent developments in and around the country, international issue, scientific and technologic news. In a nutshell knowledge without walls. As push technology dominates the todays information age, reference librarians should be more creative in constructing new information products with the elements available through Internet, online databases, e-journal etc. Hence the physical access and delivery of methods expand the flow of information to independent users in and out of the campus. The problem solving skills, creative and critical responses of reference librarian will increase with the digital reference services and collaborative 24/7 reference services.

(2) *Ability to market library information products and services*: The 21st century is regarded as an era of marketing information and knowledge. To survive in the competitive information age, reference librarians should have in depth knowledge in public relation and marketing of library services.

(3) *Team spirit*: No library is self-sufficient for its resources. The reference librarian should have a capability to collaborate persons from different spheres of the society. The knowledge and skill of fellow workers can be used for analysing strategic goals and to start new ventures. Reference librarian can share knowledge in preparing bibliographies, indexes, abstracts, project reports, conference paper to faculty members. With information technology expert librarians can plan methods to access electronic resources, web application etc. Hence, a reference librarian can influence the campus, as the library is still a growing organism within the constrained growth of electronic resources.

(4) *Communication skill*: Reference librarians should be energetic, persuasive and friendly in querying customers to determine information needs. Active listening enables the reference librarian to reflect on another person's message while soliciting feedback to better understand the speaker's frame of reference.

Reference librarians are becoming information generators rather than information conservators.

The development in the IT Sector and ICTs (Information and Communication Technologies) are creating a new role to libraries and reference librarians. For example UGC's INFONET, SPARC, Infomine and Librarian's Index to the Internet are the enormous efforts by librarians to take greater control of information production and information dissemination. With the great pressure of information flood the users are immersed in it. They are not aware of different databases, website, indexes to extract a particular information. The one and only one person who can do these types of works technically is the reference librarian. Hence reference librarian have a great role in selecting, organizing, servicing and creating information. For the success of reference service, the reference librarian should be enthusiastic, patience, humorist innovative and having a teamwork spirit. Along with these qualities, he should be able for organization, critical thinking and service minded. He should be curious and having the skill to explore knowledge to get up-to-date information. Today the field of librarianship is influenced more by the techniques and technologies of IT. As a result of this, activities which need active intelligence and creativity are ignoring now-a-days. To create a fruitful result librarian should apply modern techniques of IT to these creative activities. A user needs the help of the librarian in finding out a traditional print source or for surfing the Internet.

Librarians are faced with a much more difficult task than the profit sector because library services are only indirectly tied to revenues. To nature of funding and customers makes it very difficult for the society to transform the role of reference librarians and their services. But with the drastic changes of 21st century many organizations are in new paths for restricting reference service with user community as target group. To make a rumbling revolution to change the professional culture and allow libraries to play a leadership role in designing future reference services, each organisation should satisfy the following responsibilities:

- To maximise the quality of reference service, libraries must invest substantially more fiscal resources in staff training.
- To develop efficient and effective continuous feed back methods from users about the quality of services provided.

Schools of Library and Information Sciences offering masters degrees in library science should frame core courses that cover the significant portions of the curriculum devoted in developing marketing values and skills in young professionals.

Conclusion

The future of reference services in librarians is in a dilemma. With the explosive growth of ICTs, reference librarians from many libraries report the drop in the quantity of reference questions and questions have become more complex. Now-a-days, answering questions requires more faces on instruction in search strategies and other elements related to the basic information competencies of identifying the type of information needed, finding, evaluating and communicating the information successfully. The old concept about the nature of reference service from answering the quick, routine, less than five-minute question changed to a more elaborated counselling or coaching are moving towards the direction of a knowledge counselling role, directing users in locating and utilizing effectively resources related to recorded knowledge. Because these type of interactions take a long time in future we must become more customer oriented in our service strategies.

Today in academic librarians, the part played by a reference librarian is diminishing. The face to face "beautiful reference moments" are replacing by the online reference tools. Here the reference librarian should recognize the need of 'content service'. From the Internet, online databases, there is information overload. But librarian has the technical skill to evaluate the needed information, just like to separate rice from chaff. He should have control over the virtual environments. For the subscription of e-books, e-journals and online indexes develop consortia among libraries.

Technology has created great threats and opportunities for the future of reference librarians. The reference librarians and managers of reference services may be able to influence the structure and shape of future reference services. A surfeit of information is not enough. More skills are needed to evaluate the information just as to separate wheat from the chaff. Hence the librarian's skills transcend the limits of technology.

Reference librarian can develop interactions with teaching faculty and can incorporate information literacy skills in classroom, which will reinforce the importance of the library.

Like in other fields, in the case of librarians personal computer has proved a revolutionary force in the working place. With these computers and the help of ICTs, reference librarian can provide access to reference and research materials to clients, peers located far away and even librarians and students in different countries. Now-a-days reading materials are available to users through online bookstores. If reference librarians fail to provide both convenience and speed in their service, private businesses will step up and fill the vacuum.

35

Research Methodology and Problems in South Asian Studies

SUNITA VAZE

This article is based on the needs of a general researcher. The ideas and information of this article are based on the necessity of the work performed by the reader in the research library's atmosphere.

The Academic library in many senses is restricted to its course work, the goals of the institutions and the aims of the faculty as well as the interest of the students. It does have wide perspective of the area studies, but still it is within the range of the subject areas being taught in the school curriculum.

The coverage of this paper is limited to Humanities. Humanities encompass philosophy, religion, languages, literature and art. Any research is challenging and intriguing. Research in South Asian subjects is more challenging and complex in nature because of the structure and the nature of South Asia. South Asia has a history of thousands of years with no written documentation other than the work on religion, rituals or poetry from ancient times. The literature is handed down for centuries by oral tradition, and still being preserved to the letter in its original form. India is a multi-cultural, multi-lingual country.

Ancient literature in India shows the trends of research methodology. Vedic Anukramanika is the first word index of Vedas. Six branches of Vedic studies have methodological study of words, grammar, ritualistic procedures, accents and accentuation and the science of all of these subjects. Unfortunately, over the centuries Indian people lost all the proper knowledge of it because of more emphasis on knowing the text only by heart, but not knowing the actual logic behind it and keeping it from using scientific methods to interpret it.

Various languages and scripts are derived, in current India, from ancient languages like Sanskrit and Tamil. India has 21 official languages and over 5000 dialects. This itself poses a difficulty for a reader, researcher and a librarian.

General Reader

When a librarian works with a general reader, who just wants to get quick information about India, it can be anything from travel information to politics to religion. Now-a-days, most readers rely on Internet. Sometimes, the changes in spelling or wrong subject don't give the reader the information he/she wants. When the information is not found, then the reader resolved to a printed source. This is a real challenge for a librarian, since the question of the reader could be anything and everything under the sun. For example, here is the question a librarian received. The question was "a total word count in *Mahabharata* and *Ramayana*". The reader just had heard that these two epics were much larger than the Greek epics *Eliad* and *Odyssey* combined. The problem for the librarian in this case is to find a word indexes for both of those epic poems, which don't exist. There are name indexes for *Mahabharata* and the verse index for both epics but there is no word index. To make matter worse, the reader didn't know and wasn't aware of what recension the reader wanted. In this case, the best solution is to rely on Internet source, which may not be accurate but gives the closest information in general. Somewhat satisfactory answer was found in Wikipedia, which reader didn't even searched to begin with. Since the reader is not a serious scholar and just wanted general information it worked in this situation.

Unfortunately this brings us to the other problem in this area, which is the age of the reader. If the reader is young, first thing he does is to refer to Internet, but not aware of the printed source, and if the reader is not computer friendly or old, he prefers the book source. Most general readers think that it is a librarian's job to find them an answer.

Common reader generally comes with simple questions like "how to find certain book, or the year of the publication of certain title, or the edition they have read some time ago" etc. Many of them want the names of the book dealers in the USA where they can buy the Indian books. Librarian can work with them guiding to the online databases like OCLC first search etc. or the Institution's catalogs and if they are more serious about their work, librarian can show them the search strategies like key word searches, Boolean logic for finer searches, dictionaries, encyclopedias or bibliographies. Sometimes some beginners don't even know what are the primary and secondary sources. A librarian has to guide them about it. These are the problems with any library environment, but it happens more in South Asian areas because of the lack of the basic knowledge on the part of the reader. A librarian has to figure out what the reader wants. The librarian has to identify actual needs of the reader with variety of questions. It becomes more difficult in South Asian area because of different ethnic groups, scripts, and even pronunciation. The spelling of the names as well as cities vary with different provinces and the ethnicity of the reader can create problem understanding the exact nature of the question, and when the reader is from foreign country, it makes it even more difficult. Only solutions in this matter are to do some manipulation of the spellings. It is easy to find simple answers with the help of some encyclopedia, or dictionaries. For example, there was one question about the word "*Mesh/Mash*" which was used to measure gold in ancient times, which was resolved with the dictionary meaning of the word "*mash*" in Sanskrit.

Now-a-days, Internet is also a great help for general questions. One question "the word Cochin and Cochinchina" was answered with the help of Internet and with a specialist who knew the history of Cochin.

Once a reader wanted the list of books written by her grandfather. The name given was not in the authority files, but with some changes in the name a librarian could find the list of six books written by her grandfather. All that reader wanted was to get the list of the books of her grandfather and which libraries have those books. She didn't even know the titles. Basically one of the problems South Asian Librarian faces is the different spelling of names. Unless, one is not familiar with the Indian names and the British formations of those names, it becomes difficult to get the answers and this is the biggest problem in solving the questions of the general reader. A librarian is not concerned with actual research tools or methodology or the application of it. Just the general knowledge of the librarian is sufficient in these matters. For a general reader it may be a great problem or challenge but for a librarian, it is a simple question resolved with some effort and basic search strategies.

Researcher

Most of the researchers are familiar with the system of the library, and know how to prepare a search for their need. They know how to identify the resources and how to check bibliographies and indexes, the material in print as well as online. They know how to search keywords, use the Boolean logic, use identifiers, dictionaries, to narrow their search.

A good researcher follows the guidelines to do the research as well as look for the sources which have a good research criteria, which is clear statements, appropriate use of the language, easy layouts and structure, properly expressed scholarship, neatness of thought process, annotated or properly cited bibliography and up-to-date books and research papers. This is an ideal situation for research.

When one has to look into these criteria, the problem starts right there. There are few obstacles from the researcher's point of view.

Considering the clear statements, many scholars who may not have a mastery over English language, can find the work of great scholars ambiguous and hard to follow. The structure of the book may be ideal, but the points made may not very clear. It happens with the works of most famous scholars. There is no need to have a list of the viewpoints, but there were some questions about the ambiguity of the work and losing the real point during discussion and the scholar has to go over and over again to get the point which can be time consuming and still not getting the right point through or the point can be misinterpreted because of the ambiguity of the style.

Another point is appropriate language. In many translations, the structure of language can be of old style and can be interpreted differently. In process, the scholar can misinterpret the meaning of the words. A very old (in late 1950s) example is about Vedic rituals where it is said that "the priest takes a clay pot with 16 portions", but the translator translated it as "the priest takes a clay pot with 16 year old (girl) because of the Sanskrit word "*shodasin*" was translated as "16 year old girl". It became kind of a joke between Sanskritist, but it is a classic example of how the wrong language and wrong knowledge of language can create wrong impression. This is also a classic example of improper scholarship. At the same time, many meanings of the same word can also pose a problem, and if the scholar is not familiar with the context, the translation can be totally wrong.

Unfortunately many books published in India have no word indexes. In a scholarly work, word index plays a very important role. If one just wants to get the important word, it is easy to go through word index. Luckily, the things are changing now, but still, many books come with no word index, which is a big set back for a researcher.

Another problem with the books published in India, there is improper bibliographic citation. As a researcher comes to the library with the citation to see the citation from the book, and a librarian searches for it, it is not found. It has occurred too many times. Once there was a citation about one rare Upanishad, which was not found as it was cited. Luckily one of the newly published Upanishads had it, but that was not found from the table of contents or the index, but by browsing the two volumes set of the work. This problem occurs more in books approximately printed between 1945-1960, because there was no set guideline for the bibliographic citations. Only requirement during that time period was to give the title of the source.

Many research works just give the lists of the works with the translations, instead of making a valid point or giving the writer's viewpoint, but if one wants to find the valid point or the neatness of thought process, the work is lacking it.

This happens more with the epic literature, like *Mahabharata* and *Ramayana* where one finds the order and description of the episodes as references for proving the point than actually making a point, because many scholars think that a general reader is familiar with the contents of the epics. The researcher does not have a clear idea what he or she is emphasizing on. The researcher in many cases doesn't give the edition of the text he or she is using for the research.

The biggest problem in Indian languages is the transliteration. It is not adequate. Many scholars now a days, are giving a table of the transliteration in the preface but there is no uniformity. In USA most of the scholars follow LC transliteration, which is giving some form of unification, still many scholars follow the old style transliteration. It is a heated issue of discussion among many librarians. The databases are exploring scripts now. May be in future, it will be very helpful, assuming the scholar knows the script of vernacular language, which brings the next issue.

Various dictionaries are the best tools for researchers, but most of them are not with transliterations. Even the heavily used Sanskrit-English dictionary of Monier Williams doesn't have all of his words transliterated. Besides, the order of the dictionary is the order of Indian alphabets and not the Roman alphabets. This poses more problem for a common reader than a scholar, still there are some scholars who are familiar with the Indian literature, but not with the order of alphabets. There is a very nice and informative guide at the beginning of the dictionary of Monier Williams, but not all dictionaries give the guide to the structure of the dictionary.

Geographical areas are another hard issue. If one wants the information of the city of "Wai" in the state of Maharashtra, one has to go through the map, the gazette, a provincial document etc. Spellings of the geographical name are another complicated issue. Whether to call the city Mumbai or Bombay, Madras or Chennai, Calcutta or Kolkata and to find out what was the name used in the literature, and what was used in older document, and which one is appropriate to use in one's research paper is another dilemma.

Librarian

Librarians face the same problems found by most of the researchers. But the function of the librarian is to solve these issues and help the researcher deal with his or her problem so his/her research will be easier and smooth. The tools for the librarian are bibliographies, encyclopedias, and dictionaries, book reviews. Librarian has to keep himself up to date with the publications as well as be familiar with the older sources. Bibliographic control is the key part in a librarian's daily routine. Bibliographic control means a system of adequate recording of forms of information/knowledge material, which add to sum total of human knowledge. Librarian needs a mastery over written or published records. This does not mean that a librarian has to read each and every book. It is humanly impossible, but the librarian must have a know how of what is happening in the world of publishing. Librarian is not a guardian of the books, but a guide to the proper resources for the reader. Every year about 60,000 books are published in India in Indian and English languages. For the librarian, keeping touch with book reviews, gives a general idea of the contents of the printed sources so a librarian can have a bibliographic control over the printed material and offer a critical evaluation of the merit of the book. This way a librarian can guide the reader.

National bibliography printed in Kolkata is a powerful tool, but the flaw of it is it is neither comprehensive not prompt in publication. It still can be a good guideline to find the resource.

Indexes are very good sources for the librarian. As earlier mentioned, indexing goes way back to Vedic period. *Times of India* have book reviews up to 1990. There is no good Newspaper index is available. There are gaps in indexing and non-roman work is not indexed. Few good references sources are Bibliography of Indian philosophies (by Karl Potter in 1970) or Vedic Bibliography by Dr. R.N. Dandekar, which is a scholarly resource. Tulip is another source to find periodicals in Indian literature, but the structure of the work is kind of ambiguous. The large volumes of history of *Dhrmasastra* by P.V. Kane, or the current dictionary program by Deccan College are worth mentioning as good resources. *Bibliography of Art* by Jagdish Chandra is also worth mentioning.

Unfortunately, there are not any comprehensive bibliographies about Jainism, and Sikhism. Islam has many encyclopaedias, which can be used for the information needed, basically can be used as the resources to start the research. Then one has to rely on the databases like OCLC. In India, one cannot find such database. Libraries in India are working on it. One still has to rely on old style card catalogs. Luckily, due to British influence, there is uniform official policy for Gazettes and Census. A lot of revolutionary literature is also published in various Indian languages, which we have very little control in acquiring.

Indian archival material is really very difficult to find. It has very inadequate coverage. Complexity of the arrangement of loose papers makes finding the material next to impossible. Another area is the doctoral dissertations. Most of the universities publish their thesis at their annual report. To acquire that work is the pivotal task.

Online data is a very current and a very powerful tool. With the proliferation of the websites, it is always advised to check the authenticity of the webpage and the work on it and references quoted there. These websites may be promoting their own agenda. Various Universities like University of Columbia, University of

Michigan are having their own databases, set and updated time to time. Columbia has South Asian Bibliography online which is a very powerful tool. Various dictionaries are also available online. Bibliographies and e-journals have up-to-date information and very useful. Full text journals and valid bibliographic sources are available on online databases. The problem with this is that those can be fee based and cannot be accessed easily. A librarian has to identify valid online databases and articles. Many digitized images are also online now-a-days. Google has a big digitizing online book project, as well as microsoft is also getting into it. They are very good to find images; still, one has to be very careful about them because the edition stated on the webpage may be different from actual printed material. With online proliferation, it is librarian's responsibility to verify, identify, interpret and analyze the published and electronic data. To do this, it is librarian's responsibility to keep up with the new technology, and know the tools of trade. It makes librarians job even harder. It is very hard to keep up with online databases and to check the authenticity of those. A librarian must really know his/her subject area to validate these databases. Though, they are very good for general information.

There are co-operative services like ILL, copy services, borrow from other resources. Collection development is becoming more of a challenge. With electronic resources as well as publishing proliferation, one really has to select. Cooperative effort is the way. Bodies like CONSALD or SAMP can provide these services and more and more librarians should get involved in their processes. Library of Congress has a serials list, but the difficult part for the librarian is to keep up with that. International serials data system or ISDS is available online, but Asian and Aftican language periodicals hardly find any place in the printed and digital reference tools of periodicals due to the lack of proper information. Changes in periodicals schedules are usually not made known to the institutes. Another issues for the periodicals coming from India are the postal issue. The death and birth of periodicals is very high in Indian subcontinent and it is really very hard to keep the record up-to-date especially with irregular postal deliveries. By the time the serial is in hand, it may have already died down. It is actually very difficult in India, to get the resources handy. There is not much cooperative program except from very famous universities and the relation and communication of the faculty of various universities.

Few Suggestions to Get More Control Over the Problems

Most important part is that a librarian must have a better bibliographic control. One of the suggestions was to include table of contents of the book if it is an anthology or articles about varied subjects in bibliographic record. It actually makes a sense. Especially, since many libraries are sending the materials at their offsite storage, it is a great tool to get the information without actually getting the material in hand. More work should be done on creating more indexes to get the grasp of the subject, which makes identify the research work easily. There should be more research literature reviews so it will help more researchers. A librarian should know the tools of the trade like indexes, bibliographies and Internet resources. Most librarians now-a-days are up-to-date with these areas. Especially, South Asian librarians must keep up with the history of South Asia, the politics, the languages, the development of these languages, the knowledge of ancient literature as well as the current trends in the areas of different studies. For example, the World Sanksrit Conference in Turin had emphasis on the study of Puranas, but the Conference in Edinburgh, Scotland had papers more related to comparative studies between two types of literature.

In geographical areas, an attempt must be made to unify the names and records. Unfortunately the political situation is something beyond one's control, still the efforts of the Library of Congress as well as some private publishers must be noticed to get more bibliographic control. Many publishing companies in India are creating their own websites like D.K. Agencies, Motilal Banarasidass, Munshiram Manoharlal, etc. More information will be available on "National Bibliographical Control: Problems and Perspectives".

First book was published in India was in Portuguese in Goa in 1557. Since then India has come a long way.

For the librarian who is specialized in Medical or Economic field, its a totally different world out there. That field involves case studies, various reports etc. which this article hasn't touched at all.

In all, a new librarian should be a guide, a helper and not just a book-patrol with a knowledge of identifying subject areas, varied interests of the reader and researcher and acquire a level of expertise to provide material for the interest of the reader or researcher. A librarian in true sense must be an information scientist of new era, to face new challenges, to acquire new knowledge and welcome the new era of computer without losing the touch with our good old trusting printed material.

Bibliography

Gidwani, N.N. (ed.) (1973). "Comparative librarianship: essays in honour of Professor D.N. Marshall". Delhi: Vikas Publ.

"Index India, a quarterly documentation list of selected articles...all over the world." Jaipur: Rajasthan University Library.

Jagdish S. Sharma (1974). "India's contribution in the field of bibliography", Delhi: Delhi Library Association.

Lawrence F. Locke, Stephen J. Silvereman, Waneen Wyrick Spirduso. *Reading and understanding research*, Thousand Oaks, Calif.; London: Sage Publication, c2004. (2nd ed.)

Nick Moore (2006). *How to do research*, London: Facet, (3rd ed.).

Raju, A.A.N. and L.S. Ramaiah (editors) (2003). *National bibliographical control: problems and perspectives: essays for A.K. Dasgupta*. New Delhi: Allied Publication.

Ranjit Kumar (2005). *Research methodology: a step by step guide for beginners*, London: Sage.

Reference sources on South Asia compiled by Kanta Bhatia, with the assistance of Michael D. Rosse. Philadelphia: South Asia Regional Studies, University of Philadelphia, c1978.

Steve McCurry (2006). *Looking East: Portraits*, London; New York: Phaidon Press.

Contributors Profile

Dr. Kanwal Ameen is an Assistant Professor at the Department of Library and Information Science, University of the Punjab, Lahore, Pakistan. Currently she is Editor of the Pakistan *Journal of Library and Information Science,* and has been Secretary, IFLA Discussion Group on Library & Information Science Education in Developing Countries, as well as member of national and international library associations (ALA, CILIP, and IFLA). She holds MLS and PhD from the University of the Punjab, Lahore (Pakistan). She actively participates in various international conferences, and got her research papers published in national and international journals. Dr. Ameen was a Fulbright fellow (2000-2001) at the University of Texas at Austin. E-mail: kanwalameen@yahoo.com

Dr. A. Amudhavalli is Professor and Head of the Department of Library and Information Science, University of Madras, Chennai (India), and is the Chairperson of the School of Information & Communication Studies. She holds MA, MLS, MPhil, and PhD degrees. She has many publications to her credit and is on the several editorial boards and is referee for certain reputed journals. Professor Amudhavalli takes active part in the professional associations, and presently she is President of Madras Library Association (MALA). E-mail: amudha75@yahoo.com

Dr. Tariq Ashraf is a Deputy Librarian at the University of Delhi, Delhi, India. Prior to that he had worked as Librarian at the Centre for Policy Research, New Delhi as well as at the Indian Institute of Management, Lucknow. Dr. Ashraf is a prolific writer and has authored four books, and many research papers. He is a winner of International Paper contest held by ASIST and visited United States on Eugene Garfield Travel Grant in year 2003. Dr. Ashraf is on the Editorial Board of *ILA Bulletin*, a quarterly journal published by Indian Library Association, and is also Editor of *MANLIBNET Review, a quarterly newsletter of Management Libraries Network,* New Delhi. E-mail: tariq22@gmail.com

Dr. Deepa Banerjee is a South Asian Studies Librarian at the University of Washington, Seattle since April 2006. Prior to this position, she has worked as a Reference and Research, as well as Children's librarian in public libraries of Sydney (Australia), Vancouver (Canada) and King County, Seattle. Dr. Banerjee has a PhD in American Literature from India and an MLIS from Australia. E-mail: dbaner@u.washington.edu

Dr. N. Gerald Barrier has MA and PhD degree from Duke University, and has been a Professor and researcher in South Asian studies at the University of Missouri, Columbia for the last three decades. Besides writing intensive courses in nonviolence in modern world history and communalism in modern India, his teaching has included a revised course on Gandhi and his times and two new courses: The partition of India and women in Indian history. Professor Barrier's research continues to focus on recent Sikh history. He has published several books and research papers on various aspects of South Asia. E-mail: barriern@missouri.edu

Dr. Rakesh Kumar Bhatt is an Associate Professor (Reader) at the Department of Library and Information Science, University of Delhi, Delhi, India. He holds MA and PhD (History), MLS and PhD in Library and Information Science. Dr. Bhatt has also worked as Librarian at the Indian Institute of Technology, New Delhi, and has published many research papers in national and international journals. Currently he is managing editor of *Libraries, Information, and Knowledge: An International Journal.* E-mail: rakeshkumarbhatt@yahoo.co.in

Dr. Veerankutty Chelatayakkot received his MLISc in 1997 and PhD in 2006 from University of Calicut, Kerala. Currently he is working as a Librarian in Cochin University of Science and Technology, Kochi, India. E-mail: veerankutty@cusat.ac.in

Mr. Ron Chepesiuk is a freelance journalist and writer based in Rock Hill and Surfside Beach, South Carolina. He has been reporting on international drug trafficking since 1987, and is the author of *Hard Target; the U.S.'s War on International Drug Trafficking,* 1992-1997 (McFarland, 1998) and *The War on Drugs: an International Encyclopedia* (ABC—CLIO, 1999). He holds Master's degree in library science from Atlanta Clark University and a post graduate diploma in archival science from the National University of Ireland, University College Dublin. Prior to becoming a full-time freelance writer, he was a professor of library science at Winthrop University in Rock Hill. Mr. Chepesiuk has authored 18 books and more than 2,700 articles that have appeared in such publications as *USA Today, The National Review, New York Times, Syndicate* and *Woman World.* In 2003, Chepesiuk was a Fulbright Scholar and visiting professor at Chittagong University in Chittagong, Bangladesh. E-mail: dmonitor1@yahoo.com

Dr. H.S. Chopra is university librarian at the Guru Nanak Dev University Library, Amritsar, India. He has a rare distinction of holding two doctoral degrees, one in History and the other in Library and Information Science. Dr. Chopra has contributed many research papers to national and international journals including *Encyclopedia of Library and Information Science* ed. by Allen Kent (USA). He has eight books published to his credit. E-mail: chopra_gndu@yahoo.com

Dr. K.S. Chudamani is a Librarian at the JRD Tata Memorial Library, Indian Institute of Science, Bangalore, India. He holds MSc (Physics) & MLS from Mysore University, PhD from Bangalore University, and MSc (Information Science) from University of Sheffield. Dr. Chudamani visited USA on Fulbright fellowship in 1989. He has published more than 70 papers on infometrics, bibliometrics, citation analysis, classification, cataloguing, library management, reference service, and knowledge based systems. E-mail: ksc@library.iisc.ernet.in

Dr. B. Mini Devi is a Librarian at the University of Kerala, Trivandrum, India. She obtained her MSc degree in Botany, MLISc from University of Kerala, and PhD Degree in Library and Information Science from the Cochin University of Science and Technology. She has also worked as librarian in the British Library, Trivandrum and Government

Model Engineering College, Eranakulam, and has participated in many national and international conferences and presented scholarly papers on various issues in Library Science. She has published over a dozen articles and research papers in reputed journals and edited books. E-mail: minidevi_b@yahoo.co.in

Dr. Y. Ganesh received his Master degree in library & information science from Annamalai University, Tamil Nadu, and PhD in library & information science from G.G. University, Bilaspur, India. He has a professional experience of more than 15 years, and is presently working as the Librarian of State Library, Port Blair of Andaman & Nicobar Islands, India.

Dr. Ramesh C. Gaur is Librarian & Head, Kalanidhi Division at Indira Gandhi National Centre for the Arts (IGNCA), New Delhi. He is a Science graduate with PhD in Library and Information Science, and has published several books and research papers. Earlier Dr. Gaur served as librarian at the Tata Institute of Fundamental Research, Mumbai and also at Management Development Institute (MDI), Gurgaon, India. In his professional career of 16 years, he has published over 30 papers, authored/edited three important books in his chosen field, and sponsored/supported organizations and causes related to Library Science. E-mail: gaur@ignca.org; rcgaur@bol.net.in

Dr. M.A. Gopinath is a visiting Professor at School of Library and Information Sciences, North Carolina Central University, Durham, NC. Earlier he served as Professor and Head at the Documentation Research & Training Center, Bangalore, India. He has authored five books and over hundred research papers in library and information journals. Dr. Gopinath has been Chairman, Convener and member of several commissions, conferences and governmental organizations. He has been Consulting Editor, *Journal of Librarianship and Information Science* (Bauker-Saur London), 1984-1995, Member, Editorial Board, *Knowledge Organization* (Indeks Verlag, Frankfurt), Joint Editor, *Library Science with a slant to Documentation and Information Studies,* 1985-1994 and Editor since 1995- (titled changed to *SRELS Journal of Information Management* since 2000. E-mail: yadugirig@yahoo.com, gopi17nath@gmail.com

Dr. P.R. Goswami is Director of the National Social Science Documentation Centre, Indian Council of Social Science Research, New Delhi, India. He held the position of Chief-Librarian-cum-Documentation Officer in Planning Commission (2001-2002), and was Librarian of the Faculty of Management Studies, University of Delhi (1986-2001) and Central Statistical Organization, Government of India (1982-1986). He has MA (History), MLS and PhD from the University of Delhi. Dr. Goswami was General Secretary of the Indian Library Association (2000-2002), and has published many papers in professional journals. He held the Membership of the ASIST for four years, from 2001 to 2005. E-mail: prgoswami@hotmail.com

Dr. B.M. Gupta is a Senior Scientist at the National Institute of Science, Technology and Development Studies, New Delhi, India. He holds MLS and PhD degrees. Dr. Gupta has authored and edited many books, and has published several research papers in the field of scientometrics. He is editor of the popular 16 volume set "*Handbook of Libraries, Archives and Information Centers in India*", and nine volume set "*South Asia bibliography and documentation*". Dr. Gupta is involved in various committees and professional associations. E-mail: bmgupta1@yahoo.com

Dr. V. Jalaja is presently working as Reader, Department of Library and Information Science, University of Calicut, India. She has 15 years of experience in teaching and research, and published more than 30 papers in national and international conferences/journals.

Dr. Abulfazal M. Fazle Kabir worked as an Associate Professor in the School of Library and Information Studies at Clark Atlanta University in Atlanta, Georgia. He holds PhD in Library and Information Sciences, and has authored two books, and several research papers. He is also Global Scene Editor of *The Library Times International*, where he has published several articles and is a regular contributor of book reviews. Dr. Kabir is an active member of American Library Association, and Association for Library and Information Science Education (ALISE), and has also served as Secretary and President of the Asian Pacific Librarians.E-mail: kabir@cau.edu

Dr. M. Kanakachary is a Deputy Librarian at the Central Institute of English and Foreign Languages, (Deemed University) Hyderabad, India.

Dr. Neena Talwar-Kanungo is a Reader (Associate Professor) in the Faculty of Library and Information Science, Indira Gandhi National Open University, New Delhi, India. She holds Master degree in Political Science, MLS and PhD in Library and Information Science from Delhi University. Her area of research includes user studies in social sciences, library classification, library and information science education through distance mode. E-mail: neenakanungo@gmail.com

Dr. H.K. Kaul is Director of the Developing Library Network (DELNET), New Delhi, India, and has also served as Chief Librarian of the India International Center, New Delhi. He holds Masters in Library Science from the University of Bombay, and PhD in Library and Information Science from the University of Pune. Dr. Kaul has authored and edited more than 30 books and has contributed many research papers. He has been a member of various important national Committees and Commissions appointed by the Government of India including Indian National Commission for UNESCO. E-mail: hkkaul@delnet.ren.nic.in

Prof Krishan Kumar received library science education at—University of Delhi and University of Chicago. He retired as Professor and Head, Department of Library and Information Science, University of Delhi in 1998, and has also been Dean, Faculty of Arts at the same university. He is Past-President, Indian Library Association, 1988-90, President, Indian Association of Teachers of Library and Information Science, 1985-89, Past-Vice-President, Delhi Library Association, former Director of its School of Library Science, Editor, *Library Herald*, 1981-2002; Ex-Chairman, Editorial Board, *Journal of Library and Information Science*; Ex-Consulting Editor, *Knowledge Organization* (organ of International Society for Knowledge Organization); Ex-chairman, Editorial Board, *ILA Bulletin*. E-mail: krishan14@hotmail.com

Dr. Ramesh Kundra is working as senior scientist at the National Institute of Science and Technology Development Studies, New Delhi, India. He holds MSc (Analytical Chemistry), Associateship in Information Science, and PhD. He has published many papers in the field of Scientometrics. Dr. Kundra has been Secretary of the Society for Information Science (India) since 2002. E-mail: r_kundra@yahoo.com

Mr. Binh P. Le is an Associate Librarian at the Pennsylvania State University, Abington, and has been Chair of the Asian, African, and Middle Eastern Section of the Association of College and Research Libraries/American Library Association. Earlier he served as an assistant librarian at the Purdue University. He holds an MLS from the Indian a University, Bloomington, and is a PhD candidate at the Pennsylvania State University. Mr. Lee has edited a book and published many papers. E-mail: bpl1@psu.edu

Dr. Inder Vir Malhan is Professor and Head at the Department of Library and Information Science, University of Jammu, India. He also worked as University Librarian for more than six years, and has authored five books, and contributed more than seventy papers in national and international journals. Dr. Malhan has participated in several conferences in Asia, Europe and the United States. He was awarded Fulbright Fellowship in 1996 to visit the USA to study the Impact of Information Technology on Library and Information Science Education. E-mail: imalhan_47@rediffmail.com

Professor P.B. Mangla is a former Dean, Faculty of Arts and Head of the Department of Library and Information Science, University of Delhi, India. He was President of Indian Library Association (ILA) from 1981-1983. He has a long association with IFLA also, as Member of the Executive Board during 1985 to 1991, and later as Vice President. Professor Mangla has been editor of the *ILA Bulletin* of Indian Library Association, and is also on the editorial board of a number of LIS journals. He was awarded Rockefeller Foundation Scholarship for higher education. Professor Mangla has been awarded IFLA Gold Medal and Certificate for his innovative and outstanding contribution to the furtherance of National and International Librarianship. He has edited books and contributed many papers in professional journals. E-mail: manglapb@yahoo.co.in

P.K. Mishra is a Librarian at the Indian National Science Academy, New Delhi, India. E-mail: pkmishra@insa.nic.in

Irangani Mudannayake is a Senior Librarian at the Agricultural Institute, University of Paradeniya, Sri Lanka. She holds an MLS degree from the University of Philippines, and has published many papers. She is Chairperson of the AGRINET Advisory Committee since 2002. E-mail: iram@pdn.ac.lk

Dr. Usha Mujoo-Munshi is Chief Librarian of the Indian Statistical Institute, Calcutta, and also served as Librarian at the Indian National Science Academy, New Delhi, India. She earned MLISc from Delhi University, Masters in Public Administration from University of Rajasthan, and PhD from Jiwaji University, Gwalior. Her special interests include science popularization, science and society, and produces a quarterly publication—*Science Information Notes (SIN)*. E-mail: umunshi@insa.nic.in

Dr. T. A.V. Murthy is the University Librarian of Central Institute of English and Foreign Languages, Hyderabad, India. He holds BSc, MS and PhD in Library and Information from India along with another MSLS from Catholic University, USA. He is the first Library Science professional to become the Director of Information and Library Network Centre (INFLIBNET). Dr. Murthy is also the President and Fellow of Society for Information Science (SIS), India, Member Secretary of Ahmedabad Library Network (ADINET) and Council Member of Indian Association for Special Libraries (IASLIC). He is the recipient of STAKAL Librarian Award, SIS Fellowships, and SALIS Harish

Chandra—Sushila Chandra Best Librarian Award. Dr. Murthy has published several books and many papers. He has visited many countries and organized several national and international conferences and seminars. E-mail: adivaraham@yahoo.com

H.C. Nagarathna is working as Librarian at the JRD Tata Memorial Library, Indian Institute of Science, Bangalore-560012, India. E-mail: puna_05@yahoo.co.in

Dr. Liladhar R. Pendse is European & South Asian Studies Librarian at the, Young Research Library, UCLA, Los Angeles, California. He completed his MA in Latin American Studies, and MS in Library and Information Science from the University of California, Los Angeles. Earlier he received his MD in Internal Medicine from the Minsk State Medical Institute, Belarus. Dr. Pendse is recipient of many awards and fellowships. E-mail: Lpendse@library.ucla.edu

Dr. Kshema Prakash is a Faculty Librarian at Dayalbagh Educational Institute (Deemed University), Dayalbagh, Agra, India. She holds MLS and PhD degrees, and has published many papers in professional journals. Dr. Prakash has participated in various seminars, conferences and workshops. E-mail: kshemaprakash@gmail.com

Dr. Tella Ramadevi is a Senior Documentation Officer at the Centre for Media and Rural Documentation, National Institute of Rural Development, Hyderabad, India. She possesses MA, MLS and PhD degrees, and was a Fulbright Scholar at the University of Illinois, 2003-2004. She has contributed several research papers in professional journals and conferences. Dr. Ramadevi has actively participated in many national and international conferences and seminars. E-mail: trd@nird.gov.in

Dr. Sunil Kumar Satpathy is a Senior Librarian of C.V. Raman College of Engineering, Bhuabaneswar, India. He received his Master Degree & PhD in Library & Information Science from Sambalpur University, India. He has professional experience as Librarian and Senior Librarian for more than 12 years, and has co-authored one book on Library Classification and has contributed more than 20 papers in different journals/Seminar publications. He has also attended many International/National workshops and Seminars. E-mail: drsksatpathy@gmail.com

Dr. Jaideep Sharma is an Associate Professor (Reader) in the Faculty of Library and Information Science at the Indira Gandhi National Open University, New Delhi, India since 2003. Earlier he worked as Faculty for 14 years in Kurukshetra University, Kurukshetra. Dr. Sharma holds MSc (Chemistry), MLIS from University of Delhi, and PhD from Sambalpur University. He has published two books and contributed many papers in Indian and International journals. E-mail: jaydeepsharma@gmail.com

Dr. Lokesh Sharma is currently working as Deputy University Librarian at the Delhi University Library system, and also served as College Librarian for ten years. He holds BSc, MA, MLS and PhD degrees. Dr. Sharma has authored five books and over ten papers, and is actively involved in the professional association and Indian Red Cross Society. E-mail: drlokesh@hotmail.com

Dr. Prabha Sharma is a Deputy Librarian at the Rajasthan University Library, Jaipur, India. She was conferred PhD degree on the topic "Information and universal accessibility to information—Role of national and subject libraries with special reference to India" by the University of Rajasthan. Dr. Sharma has published many research papers and is actively involved in professional associations. E-mail: prabha106_sharma@yahoo.com

Dr. R.K. Sharma is presently the Librarian at the United Nations Information Centre, New Delhi, India. He has also been the Librarian of National Institute of Public Finance Policy, New Delhi. He holds PhD degree in Library and Information Science, and has been a Fulbright scholar at the Graduate School of Library and Information Science, Simmons College, Boston, USA. He has visited a number of world famous library and information systems in the USA, UK and Thailand. Dr. Sharma has also contributed papers in the professional journals, and participated in many conferences and seminars. E-mail: sharma@unicindia.org

Mr. Rajesh Singh is a Professional Senior (Deputy University Librarian) at the University of Delhi Library, India, and is responsible for managing electronic resources. He is a graduate and Gold Medalist from the Banaras Hindu University, Varanasi. Mr. Singh has served various organizations in different professional capacities. He has served as a Librarian at the Indian School of Mines, Dhanbad, as well as at the Rohilkhand University, Bareilly, and Dr. RML Avadh University, Faizabad. Mr. Singh has around two dozens of research papers published to his credit. E-mail: rsingh@duls.du.ac.in

Dr. S.P. Singh holds MSc (Zoology) from Meerut University, MLISc and PhD from the University of Delhi, and is Professor and Head of the Department of Library and Information Science at the University of Delhi, India. Earlier she worked as an Associate Professor and Assistant University Librarian at the same university. Dr. Singh has published two books and several research papers, reports and book reviews, and is actively involved in various national and international professional organizations/institutions. E-mail: singh_34@yahoo.com

Dr. Divya Srivastava is an Assistant Director General in Scientometric Unit at Indian Council of Medical Research. She holds MSc (Botany), PhD, and Associateship in Information Science from Indian National Scientific Documentation Center, INSDOC, New Delhi, India. Dr. Srivastava is actively involved in research and publication in applied bibliometrics, infometrics, scientometrics, information retrieval and information management particularly in the field of biomedical sciences. E-mail: drdivya.srivastava@gmail.com

Dr. K. Santi Swarup is a Senior Lecturer in the Department of Management, Faculty of Social Sciences, Dayalbagh Educational Institute (Deemed University), Agra, India. Basically an Engineering graduate, he holds MBA and PhD in Management. His area of specialization is Financial Management, and has supervised 2 PhD students. He has 24 national and international publications to his credit. Dr. Swarup has attended several national and international seminars and conferences and delivered key note addresses too.

Dr. Sunita Vaze is currently Head of the South Asia Section, Asian and Middle Eastern Division of the New York Public Library, New York. She holds MLS and PhD, and has published some papers. Dr. Sunita has good knowledge of many languages including Sanskrit, Pali, Prakrit, Tibetan and other North Indian languages. Email: svaze@nypl.org

Dr. Paramjeet Kaur Walia is working as an Associate Professor (Reader) at the Department of Library & Information Science, University of Delhi, Delhi, India. Earlier she taught for several years at the Panjab University, Chandigarh. She holds MA, MLS, MPhil and PhD degrees from the University of Delhi, and has published many research papers. E-mail: PKWalia2002@yahoo.co.in

Dr. S.D. Vyas is University Librarian of the Banasthali Vidyapith (Deemed University), Rajasthan, India, for the last seventeen years. Formerly he served as Deputy Librarian of American Studies Research Centre, and Librarian of Hindu College, Delhi University. He is an author of thirteen books and fifty-five articles. He is on the editorial boards of the *Advances in Library and Information Science*, and *Indian Journal of Information, Library and Society.* E-mail: sdvyas15@yahoo.com

Mrs. Parul Zaveri has been a Senior Lecturer at the Department of Library & Information Science, SNDT Women's University, Mumbai, India for the last fifteen years. She was a Fulbright Scholar in Information Science and Technology for six months (September 2005—March 2006) at the University of Illinois, Urbana-Champaign, USA. She holds BSc and MLS degrees, and has published over five papers. Parul is life member of the Indian Library Association and Indian Association of Special Libraries & Information Centers. E-mail: parulzaveri2004@yahoo.co.in

Index